PIONEER

BEING AN ACCOUNT OF THE FIRST EXAMINATIONS OF THE

OHIO VALLEY,

AND THE EARLY SETTLEMENT OF

THE NORTHWEST TERRITORY.

CHIEFLY FROM ORIGINAL MANUSCRIPTS; CONTAINING THE PAPERS OF
COL. GEORGE MORGAN; THOSE OF JUDGE BARKER; THE DIARIES
OF JOSEPH BUELL AND JOHN MATHEWS; THE RECORDS
OF THE OHIO COMPANY, &c., &c., &c.

BY S. P. HILDRETH.

CINCINNATI:
H. W. DERBY & CO., PUBLISHERS.
NEW YORK:
A. S. BARNES & CO.
1848.

Badgley Publishing Company

2011

Pioneer landing at Marietta
From a re-enactment in 1938

Rufus Putnam

House of Rufus Putnam
On Campus Martius ,Marietta, Ohio

INTRODUCTION

There having been no historical account published of the first settlement of the Ohio Company at Marietta, but the brief one by the Rev. Thaddeus M. Harris, and the materials on which it was to be founded becoming annually more and more scarce, from the death of the early inhabitants, the author, in the year 1841, was led to commence this difficult, but, to him, pleasant labor. Having himself lived in the county more than forty years, he was personally acquainted with a large number of the first pioneers, and heard them relate many of the scenes described in these pages. No regular journal, or diary, of the progress of the settlements having been kept, to which he could have access, it has been a tedious work to collect all the dates of events with the accuracy desired. Many were ascertained from old letters; some by a journal kept by Simeon Wright, which was lost soon after his death; but an abstract of the most important things in which, was obtained several years previous. General Rufus Putnam's journal furnished the dates for many facts, but more were obtained from his letters. The files of old newspapers in the Antiquarian Library at Worcester, Massachusetts, supplied numerous authentic documents, from the letters of the pioneers to their friends, and to Isaiah Thomas, the editor of the "Massachusetts Spy." The diaries of John Mathews, Esq., and General Joseph Buell, of events on the Ohio River, before the settlement of the Ohio Company, afford many valuable facts in the early history of the country, deemed worthy of preservation, and are inserted previous to the account of that event. The journal of the transactions of the Ohio Company has been very freely quoted, and goes hand in hand with the historical events that transpired among the colonists. One mode of collecting materials for the history, was to employ some of the few that remained of the first settlers to write down their recollections of the events as they occurred in the settlement to which they belonged, in Marietta, Waterford or Belpre; and by collating these several sketches, the truth could be very nearly ascertained. The larger portion of these men are now dead, and many of the events would have perished with them, had they not been preserved in this manner.

The late Judge Barker furnished the most copious notes, sufficient for quite a good sized volume, on which is founded a large portion of this history. He was a man of a clear, sound mind, retentive memory, and correct observation. His character will be found in the volume of biographical sketches of the Ohio Company settlers. Colonel Ichabod Nye, and Mr. Horace Nye, of Putnam, and the late Charles Devoll, Esq., also supplied valuable materials for Marietta and Belpre. Many events are detailed with a minuteness not usual in ordinary history, but will be interesting to the descendants of the early settlers, and afford matter for the future historian. The period embraced extends only to the termination of the territorial government under Governor St. Clair, A preliminary account of the discoveries by La Salle, with the occupancy of the country on the Ohio River by the French, and the events about Pittsburgh, especially the campaign of Colonel Bouquet in 1764, are matters of history but little known to the community, and very properly precede the account of the settlements of the Ohio Company. The closing chapter, on the early and present climate of Ohio, with the natural productions of the country, will be interesting to the student of natural history. In the Appendix will be found the address of Governor St. Clair, on taking possession of the territory under his charge; the 4th of July oration of General Varnum, 1788, delivered at Marietta; the yet unpublished eulogy of Dr. Drown, on his death, in January, 1789; and an oration on the settlement of Marietta, April 7th, 1789; documents long out of print and now rarely found. For these, the author is indebted to the Honorable Wilkins Updike, of Rhode Island, who has preserved them with great care, and had them transcribed for this history. The labor bestowed on the work now offered to the public, through the Historical Society of Cincinnati, has been accomplished in such periods of time as could be found in the intervals of the regular practice of medicine, which must apologize for its many imperfections.

Marietta, January 1, 1848.

TABLE OF CONTENTS.

CHAPTER V.

CHAPTER VI.

CHAPTER VII.

CHAPTER VIII.

CHAPTER IX.

CHAPTER X.

corn. — Description of Campus Martius, with a plate. — Public dinner to Governor St. Clair.—Rev. M. Cutler preaches in Campus Martius. — Character. — First court held in the territory. — Names of the Judges.— Second court of quarter sessions held. — Judges. — Names of grand jurors. — Griffin Green, Jos. Gilman and R. Oliver, judges. — First death. — Number of settlers in 1788. — Progress of the Indian treaty. — Good feeling of the colonists. — Articles of the treaty. — Indians invited to a feast. — Transactions of the Ohio Company. — Section twenty-nine. — Donation lands. — Regulations concerning them.—Early winter.—Inhabitants suffer for provisions.—New road from Alexandria in Virginia, to the mouth of Muskingum River.....Page 211

CHAPTER XI.
Death of General Varnum. — Oration of Dr. Drown. — Police laws passed at Marietta. — Address of the inhabitants to Governor St. Clair. — First marriage at Marietta. — Doings of the Ohio Company. — The 7th of April, directed to be perpetually kept as a public festival. — Encouragement to build mills. — Hostility of the Indians. — Attack on John Mathews, when surveying the sixteenth Range.—Seven men killed. — Mathews escapes to the river. — Colonel Meigs builds a blockhouse.—Returns to Marietta. — Arrival of Rev. D. Story. — Early frost.—Destroys the corn. — Sickness among the settlers.—Number of inhabitants. — Death of General Parsons by drowning.....Page 233

CHAPTER XII.
Doings of the Ohio Company. — A mill built. — Rev. D. Story to preach at Marietta, Belpre and Waterford.—Company lands explored. — Salt springs. — Funds for schools. — Money loaned to the settlers. — Prospect of Indian war.—Guards of soldiers raised by the directors.—Spies or rangers.— Family of Governor St. Clair described.—Small-pox breaks out at Marietta. — Famine of 1790.—Sufferings of the settlers. — Relief afforded by the directors. — Indian hostilities.—Letter of Governor St. Clair.—Colonel Vigo. — R. J. Meigs, Jr., sent on a mission to Detroit.—French emigrants arrive. —Settle Gallipolis.—Grant of land to them by Congress.—First townships organized.....Page 245

CHAPTER XIII.
Indian war begins. — Massacre at Big Bottom.—Action of the court of quarter session on the news. — Spirited resolutions of directors for the

defense of the colony. — Letter to Governor St. Clair, who is absent.—Soldiers raised.—Garrisons built. — Eleven thousand dollars expended by Ohio Company. —Improvement of the public squares.—To be ornamented with trees. — Trustees appointed to take charge of them. — Letter of General Putnam to General Washington on the state of the colony.—Remarks on the war.—Company of United States rangers. — Dress of these men.—Captain Rogers killed.—Escape of Henderson, — Alarm of the inhabitants at the event.—: Mathew Kerr killed.—Discipline at Campus Martins.—Cattle shot by the Indians.—Attack on a party of Indians. — Alarm at the news. — Indians killed at Little Muskingum. — Incidents attending that event.—Ohio Company raise more troops.—Wisdom of their transactions.—Funds for religious instruction. — Surgeons appointed.—News of the defeat of the army under Governor St. Clair. — Emigrants from Nova Scotia Providential escape of W. R. Putnam. — Nicholas Carpenter and four others killed....Page 257

CHAPTER XIV.
The Ohio Company fails to pay for their lands. — Amount of acres reduced.—Petition to Congress for one hundred thousand acres as donation lands. — Trustees of the land General R. Putnam treats with the Wabash tribes.—Cedar barge. —Dinner given to the Indian chiefs at Marietta Strength of the colony. — Rangers. — R.J. Meigs, Jr., attacked by Indians. — Names of the heads of families in Campus Martius. — Fort Harmer.—Names of families there.—Anecdotes of the French emigrants. .... Page 283

CHAPTER XV.
Plate and description of the Marietta garrison at "the Point." —Night adventure. — Names of families and persons, with the houses in which they lived. —Anecdotes. — Schools. — Ohio Company in 1793 Donation lands. — Scarlet fever. — Small Pox. — Indian adventure. — Bird Lockhart. — Crops of corn.—1794. — R. Warth killed. — Packet mail boats established on the Ohio. —Adventure with the Indians. —1795. — Ohio Company acts.—College lands surveyed.—Fund for support of gospel—Colonists goon to their farms after the peace. — Rapid improvements. — First legislature under the territory.— Difficulties of traveling. — Delegate to Congress.—Constitution adopted and the state of Ohio formed. ..... Page 301

CHAPTER XVI.
Settlement of Belpre.—Topography and description of the settlement.—

11

CHAPTER I.

For many years before the white man had any knowledge of that beautiful region of country which borders the Ohio River from Pittsburgh to the mouth of the Big Miami, and perhaps still lower down, it was destitute of any fixed inhabitants — a belt of country from forty to sixty miles in width, on both the north and south banks of the river, seems to have been appropriated by the tribes who laid claim to the territory, almost exclusively, as hunting grounds. Few villages were built near its shores,* nor were many of its rich alluvions planted with cornfields; although a country affording more bountifully all the articles needed for the well being of savage life, could not be found. The rivers teemed with fish, and the valleys and hill sides abounded in animals of the chase. A soil more productive of corn, beans and squashes, could hardly be imagined; and yet no fire was kindled along its borders, save that of the warrior or the hunter. The mirth and revelry of "the feast of new corn" echoed not through its groves; and the silence of the forest was only broken by the moaning of the wintry winds or the howling of wild beasts.

* Logstown and the Shawnee village near the mouth of Scioto were exceptions.

This having been the condition of the country, we are led to inquire, why was it so? And what could have produced this abandonment of so desirable a region? There doubtless was a period, soon after the removal or destruction of that half-civilized race who filled the country with mounds and fortified cities, when their conquerors occupied the land, and lined the shores of the Ohio with their wigwams and villages, and nothing but some potent and irresistible cause could have led them to abandon it. From the traditions of the Indians themselves we find that cause to have been, the repeated and sanguinary invasions of a merciless enemy. Year after year the savage and warlike inhabitants of the north invaded the country of the more peaceable and quiet tribes of the south. Fleets of canoes, built on the head waters of the Ohio, and manned with the fierce warriors of the Iroquois, or Five Nations, annually floated down this quiet stream, carrying death and destruction to the inhabitants who lived along its borders. All the fatigue and trouble of marching long distances by land was thus avoided; while the river afforded them a constant magazine of food in the multitude of fishes which filled its waters. The canoe supplied to the Indian the place of the horse and wagon to the white man, in transporting the munitions of war. These they could moor to the shore, and leave under a guard, while the main body made excursions against tribes and villages, living at one or more day's march in the interior. If defeated their canoes afforded a safe and ready mode of securing a retreat, far more certain than it could be by land. When invading a country, they could travel by night as well as by day, and thus fall upon the inhabitants very unexpectedly; while in approaching by land, they could hardly fail of being discovered by some of the young hunters in time to give at least some notice of their approach. The battles thus fought along the shores of the Ohio, could they have been recorded, would fill many volumes. That much of the ancient warfare carried on by that race of men, who occupied the country prior to the modern Indians, was done on and by means of the Ohio River, is rendered probable from the mounds, or watch towers, built on the tops of the highest hills near the shores. They almost invariably occupy points commanding an extensive view of the river, both up and down the stream. Prom these elevations the watchman could often give notice of the approach of a fleet, for some time before its arrival, merely by his eye; and if signal fires by night, and smoke by day, were used, the notice could be extended to many hours, or even days. That many of the river hill mounds were built for this purpose, there can be but little doubt.

These repeated invasions of the Iroquois discouraged the inhabitants of the valley of the Ohio from occupying its borders; and for many years before it was visited by any white man, they had retired to the distance of forty or sixty miles from its banks. Nearly all their villages and permanent places of abode were located at least thus far from the Ohio. This abandoned region was, however, still of use to them as hunting grounds, and probably more abounded in game from this circumstance.

The country bordering the Ohio River was in this condition, when the almost unknown regions of the West were visited by La Salle, the first traveler who has given us any valuable account of the climate, soil, and productions of the great valley of the Mississippi. As early as the year 1668, fathers Marquette, and Allouez, Jesuit Missionaries, prepared a map of Lake Tracy, or Superior, and parts of Huron and Michigan, or "Lake of the Illinois." In 1673, Marquette and Monsignor Joliet, a merchant of Quebec, passed through the lakes, up Green Bay and Fox Rivers, and down the Wisconsin to the river Mississippi, which they descended as low as the mouth of the Arkansas. But it was many years after this time, before any white man visited the shores of the Ohio River, above its junction with the Wabash— indeed the whole river was, for a long period after, known by the name of Ouabache.

Rene Robert De La Salle

Too little credit has been given to La Salle, by us Americans, for his discoveries; travels which occupied several years, and in which he finally sacrificed his life. Many of the cotemporary statements have been treated as apocryphal, and doubtless some of them are so, while others, relating to the productions of the country and the intercourse with the inhabitants, may be considered as inclining to the marvelous; but the descriptions of the rivers, headlands, and general geography of the country, are as correct as could have been expected from the hurried manner in which the region was passed over. Besides, we have no account of these discoveries from La Salle himself, and only from some of his companions. He doubtless had made notes of his travels and discoveries, which were in his possession at the time of his death, and had he lived, would have been published; but dying as he did by the hands of traitors and assassins, his papers were all lost. Louis Hennepin, one of his subalterns, a monk of the order of Franciscans, who accompanied him in his expedition, attempted, sometime after his death, to rob him of his right to the discovery of the country on the lower Mississippi, and appropriate the honor to himself. He wrote first a history of the discoveries on the upper

Mississippi, which he really made. This work he afterwards enlarged, by adding a fictitious account of a voyage to the mouth of the Great River.

In the actual voyage, the discoverers took with them arms and ammunition, and some merchandise to trade with the nations. This expedition started from the Illinois River, a little below Peoria, the 28th February, 1680. Hennepin's account of their voyage is said to contain many inaccuracies. "Monsieur Cavalier de la Salle, a native of Rouen in Normandy, the chief undertaker of the discoveries in Northern America, which make the subject matter of this book, was a man of extraordinary parts and undaunted courage. He was the first that formed the design of traveling from the Lake of Frontenac, or Ontario, in Canada, to the Gulf of Mexico, through a vast unknown country, in order to bring the inhabitants to the knowledge of the Christian religion, and extend the dominions of the king of France." He was patronized by the king; and Tonti, who had been an old soldier, happening then to be at court, was appointed his lieutenant. They left Rochelle, July 14th, 1678, accompanied by thirty men, and reached Quebec the 15th September. Count Frontenac was then Governor General of Canada. The following autumn was spent in visiting Fort Frontenac, near the outlet of the lake, one hundred and twenty leagues above Quebec, built by La Salle. The 18th November, they embarked on Lake Frontenac in a vessel of forty tons, which was the first ship that ever sailed upon this fresh water sea. From contrary winds they were a month in reaching Niagara. Niagara was the name of an Iroquois village, situated at the lower end of Lake Conti, or Erie, above the falls."

Three leagues further up the lake, La Salle laid the foundation of a fort, but the Iroquois expressing their dislike to it, he refrained, and secured his goods and merchandise by strong palisades. While lying here through the winter, he set his men to work to build a new ship, or great barque, but the winter was so severe, freezing the lakes all over, that the work progressed slowly. He also sent forward fifteen men to find out the Illinois Indians, while he himself returned by land to Fort Frontenac, to bring up more merchandise, their present stock being reduced in trading with the Indians for furs.

"Our barque of sixty tons burthen, and named the Griffin, being finished, and everything ready for our departure, we sailed towards the middle of August, 1679, and having happily crossed the Lake Herie, got into

that of the Hurons, which is much larger than the other two. We met here with a dreadful storm, as great as any I ever heard of upon the ocean, or any other sea; but we had the good fortune to find a good road called Missilimachinac. It is an isthmus or neck of land about twenty leagues broad, and one hundred and twenty long, between the lake of the Hurons and that of the Illinois."

This writer speaks in great praise of the fertility of the soil, and the abundance of game and fish to be found here. La Salle took a survey of the country, and laid the foundations of a fort for the security of his men. From this point Tonti was sent out to explore the country, and was absent eight days. On an elevated plain or headland, between the northern extremities of Lakes Huron and Illinois, he discovered a fine settlement belonging to the Jesuits, who, in 1671, had established a mission among the northern savages. Towards the end of September, La Salle sailed from Michillimackinac for the Bay of Puans, or Green Bay, where he arrived the 8th of October.

"This bay of the Puans is formed by an overflowing of the lake of the Illinois, occasioned by a great river which falls into this lake. This river, called Ouisconcing, comes from another lake about one hundred leagues distant, from which arises another river which falls into the Mississippi, and therefore this lake may be looked upon as a communication between Canada and the Gulf of Mexico, as one may see by the map."

From the bay of Puans, M. La Salle sent back his barque laden with furs to Niagara, while himself, with seventeen men and a Recollect, or Franciscan monk, embarked in canoes, and landed at the mouth of the river of the Miamis, the 1st of November, 1679. This river is now called St. Joseph's, and by its means the early discoverers and traders passed into the river of the Illinois, through a swamp or lake which united these two streams during the winter and spring months. At the mouth of this river he built a trading fort, called Fort Miamis. The beginning of December, La Salle commenced his journey for making discoveries on the river of the Illinois, carrying his canoes and equipage four days journey over land to the branch of the Illinois, now called the Kankakee, down which they proceeded to the Illinois. In six days of easy journeys, the better to observe the country, which he describes as very fertile and abounding in game, they reached an Indian village of several hundred cabins, but destitute of inhabitants, probably yet out on their fall hunt. Their cottages are described as made with great pieces of timber, interlaced with branches and covered with bark. The insides and floors covered with mats. Every cottage had two apartments, and under them a cave or cellar wherein they preserved their Indian corn. Of this they took a sufficient quantity, because they wanted provisions. About thirty leagues lower down, La Salle came into a lake, or pond, seven leagues long, where they caught plenty of excellent fish, and following the stream, fell again into the channel of the river. This lake or expansion of the Illinois was what is now called "Peoria Lake."

Just below Peoria they met with the first Illinois Indians. Like all other savages, they received them with demonstrations of hostility; but, by the aid of their interpreter, they soon came to a friendly understanding, and passed several days in feasting. He describes them as far more friendly, and civil, than the Iroquois, with whom they are often engaged in war. Near their largest village he built a trading fort for the security of his goods and men. It was from this place that M. La Salle fitted out the expedition to make discoveries on the upper Mississippi, under Hennepin, previously noticed; while he reserved for himself the right of discovering the mouth of that river, and the country along its borders. While Hennepin was carrying on his discoveries in the district assigned to him, La Salle returned by land to Fort Frontenac, *"to procure a new supply of men and ammunition, and likewise to view in what condition were his forts, magazines, &c."* Tonti was left in command of the fort, during his absence, with directions to build another. The place La Salle had pitched upon was a rock, very high, the top of which was even and of a convenient space, so that it commanded the river and the country round about." He had hardly commenced, however, before a mutiny among the men left at the first fort caused him to abandon it. La Salle's men appear to have been made up of the most base and vile individuals, and had a short time before nearly killed him by poisoning his food. During the residence of Tonti on the Illinois, the Iroquois invaded the country, with an army of five hundred men. The Illinois Indians were in great dread of them, from the circumstance of many of them having fire arms, which they had procured from the English Traders from about Albany. The French were always cautious in the early settlement of Canada in selling fire arms to any of the tribes, as by that weapon they could only hope to maintain their superiority. By the interference of Tonti, after a little skirmishing, a peace was established between them. From the manner in which the Iroquois are mentioned as the ancient and implacable enemies of the Illinois, there can be no rational doubt of their having been in the practice of invading and warring with all the western tribes to the shores of the Mississippi, for many years before this time. Eighteen months more were spent by La Salle in passing back and forth between Michillimackinac and Fort Frontenac, trading and procuring merchandise and men, before he commenced his grand voyage for discovering the mouth of the Mississippi. At length, in November, 1681, La Salle and Tonti joined each other, and upon the 5th or 6th of January, 1682, left the shores of Lake Michigan, and by the way of the Chicago River, passed to the Illinois,— carrying their baggage on sledges. On the 6th of February, they were upon the banks of the Mississippi.

The events that next followed we relate, in the words of the notarial act prepared at the time, and first published by Mr. Sparks, in the appendix to his life of La Salle:

"On the 13th of February, all having assembled, we renewed our voyage, being twenty-two French, carrying arms, accompanied by the Reverend Father Zenobe Membra, one of the Recollect Missionaries, and followed by eighteen New England savages, and several women, Ugonquines, Otchipoises, and Huronnes.

"On the 14th, we arrived at the village of Maroa, consisting of a hundred cabins, without inhabitants. Proceeding about a hundred leagues down the river Colbert, we went ashore to hunt on the 26th of February. A Frenchman was lost in the woods, and it was reported to M. de la Salle, that a large number of savages had been seen in the vicinity. Thinking that they might have seized the Frenchman, and in order to observe these savages, he marched through the woods during two days, but without finding them, because they had all been frightened by the guns which they had heard, and had fled.

"Returning to camp, he sent in every direction French and savages on the search, with orders, if they fell in with savages, to take them alive without injury, that he might gain from them intelligence of this Frenchman. Gabriel Barbie, with two savages, having met five of the Chikacha Nation, captured two of them. They were received with all possible kindness, and, after he had explained to them that he was anxious about a Frenchman who had been lost, and that he only detained them that he might rescue him from their hands, if he was really among them, and afterward make with them an advantageous peace, (the French doing good to everybody,) they assured him that they had

21

not seen the man whom we sought, but that peace would be received with the greatest satisfaction. Presents were then given to them, and, as they had signified that one of their villages was not more than half a day's journey distant, M. de la Salle set out the next day to go thither; but, after traveling until night, and having remarked that they often contradicted themselves in their discourse, he declined going further, without more provisions. Having pressed them to tell the truth, they confessed that it was yet four days' journey to their villages; and, perceiving that M. de la Salle was angry at having been deceived, they proposed that one of them should remain with him, while the other carried the news to the village, whence the elders would come and join them four days' journey below that place. The said Sieur de la Salle returned to the camp with one of these Chikachas; and the Frenchman whom we sought having been found, he continued his voyage, and passed the river of the Chepontias, and the village of the Metsigameas. The fog, which was very thick, prevented his finding the passage which led to the rendezvous proposed by the Chikachas.

"On the 12th of March, we arrived at the Kapaha village of Akansa. Having established a peace there, and taken possession, we passed on the 15th, another of their villages, situate on the border of their river, and also two others, further off in the depth of the forest, and arrived at that of Imaha, the largest village in this nation, where peace was confirmed, and where the chief acknowledged that the village belonged to his majesty. Two Akansas embarked with M. de la Salle to conduct him to the Talusas, their allies, about fifty leagues distant, who inhabit eight villages upon the borders of a little lake. On the 19th, we passed the villages of Tourika, Jason, and Kouera, but, as they did not border on the river, and were hostile to the Akansas and Taensas, we did not stop there.

"On the 20th, we arrived at the Taensas, by whom we were exceedingly well received, and supplied with a large quantity of provisions. M. de Tonty passed a night at one of their villages, where there were about seven hundred men carrying arms, assembled in the place. Here again a peace was concluded. A peace was also made with the Koroas, whose chief came there from the principal village of the Koroas, two leagues distant from that of the Natches. The two chiefs accompanied M. de la Salle to the banks of the river. Here the Koroa chief embarked with him, to conduct him to his village, where peace was again concluded with this nation, which, beside the five other villages of which it is composed, is allied to nearly forty others. On the

31st, we passed the village of the Oumas without knowing it, on account of the fog, and its distance from the river.

"On the 3d of April, at about ten o'clock in the morning, we saw among the canes thirteen or fourteen canoes. M. de la Salle landed, with several of his people. Footprints were seen, and also savages, a little lower down, who were fishing, and who fled precipitately as soon as they discovered us. Others of our party then went ashore on the borders of a marsh formed by the inundation of the river. M. de la Salle sent two Frenchmen, and then two savages, to reconnoiter, who reported that there was a village not far off, but that the whole of this marsh, covered with canes, must be crossed to reach it; that they had been assailed with a shower of arrows by the inhabitants of the town, who had not dared to engage with them in the marsh, but who had then withdrawn, although neither the French nor the savages with them had fired, on account of the orders they had received not to act unless in pressing danger. Presently we heard a drum beat in the village, and the cries and howlings with which these barbarians are accustomed to make attacks. We waited three or four hours, and, as we could not encamp in this marsh, and seeing no one, and no longer hearing anything, we embarked.

"An hour afterward, we came to the village of Maheouala, lately destroyed, and containing dead bodies and marks of blood. Two leagues below this place we encamped. We continued our voyage until the 6th, when we discovered three channels by which the river Colbert discharges itself into the sea. We landed on the bank of the most western channel, about three leagues from its mouth. On the 7th, M. de la Salle went to reconnoiter the shores of the neighboring sea, and M. de Tonti likewise examined the great middle channel. They found these two outlets beautiful, large, and deep. On the 8th, we re-ascended the river, a little above its confluence with the sea, to find a dry place, beyond the reach of inundations. The elevation of the North Pole was here about twenty-seven degrees. Here we prepared a column and a cross, and to the said column were affixed the arms of France, with this inscription:

LOUIS LE GRAND, ROI DE FRANCE ET DE NAVARRE, REGNE; LE NEUVIEME AVRIL, 1682.

The whole party, under arms, chanted the *Te Deum,* the *Exaudiat,* the *Domine salvum fac Regem;* and then, after a salute of firearms and cries of

Vive le Roi, the column was erected by M. de la Salle, who, standing near it, said, with a loud voice, in French:—

"In the name of the most high, mighty, invincible, and victorious Prince, Louis the Great, by the Grace of God King of France and of Navarre, fourteenth of that name, this ninth day of April, one thousand six hundred and eighty-two, I, in virtue of the commission of his Majesty which I hold in my hand, and which may be seen by all whom it may concern, have taken, and do now take, in the name of his Majesty and of his successors to the crown, possession of this country of Louisiana, the seas, harbors, ports, bays, adjacent straits; and all the nations, people, provinces, cities, towns, villages, mines, minerals, fisheries, streams, and rivers, comprised in the extent of the said Louisiana, from the mouth of the great river St. Louis, on the eastern side, otherwise called Ohio, Alighin, Sipore, or Chukagona, and this with the consent of the Chaouanons, Chikachas, and other people dwelling therein, with whom we have made alliance; as also along the river Colbert, or Mississippi, and rivers which discharge themselves therein, from its source beyond the country of the Kious or Nadouessious, and this with their consent, and with the consent of the Motantees, Illinois, Mesigameas, Natches, Koroas, which are the most considerable nations dwelling therein, with whom also we have made alliance either by ourselves, or by others in our behalf;* as far as its mouth at the sea, or Gulf of Mexico, about the twenty-seventh degree of the elevation of the North Pole, and also to the mouth of the river of Palms; upon the assurance, which we have received from all these nations, that we are the first Europeans who have descended or ascended the said river Colbert; hereby protesting against all those, who may in future undertake to invade any or all of these countries, people, or lands, above described, to the prejudice of the right of his Majesty, acquired by the consent of the nations herein named. Of which, and of all that can be needed, I hereby take to witness those who hear me, and demand an act of the Notary, as required by law."

*There is an obscurity in this enumeration of places and Indian nations which may be ascribed to an ignorance of the geography of the country; but it seems to be the design of the Sieur de la Salle to take possession of the whole territory watered by the Mississippi from its mouth to its source, and by the streams flowing into it on both sides.

To which the whole assembly responded with shouts of *Vive le Roi,* and with salutes of firearms. Moreover, the said Sieur de la Salle caused to be buried at the foot of the tree, to which the cross was attached, a leaden plate, on one side of which were engraved the arms of France, and the following Latin inscription:

LVDOVCIVS MAGNVS REGNAT.
NONO APRILIS Ciq Iqc LXXXII.
ROBETVS CAVALIER, CVM DOMINO DE TONTY,
LEGATO, R. P. ZENOBIO MEMBRE, RECOLLECTO,
ET VIGINTI GALLIS, PRIMVS HOC FLVMEN, 1NDE
AB 1LINEORVM PAGO, ENAVIGAVIT, EJVSQVE
OSTIVM FECIT PERVIVM, NONO APRILIS ANNI
Ciq Iqc LXXXII.

"After which the Sieur de la Salle said, that his Majesty, as eldest son of the Church, would annex no country to his crown, without making it his chief care to establish the Christian religion therein, and that its symbol must now be planted; which was accordingly done at once by erecting a cross, before which the *Vexilla,* and the *Doming salvum fac Regum,* were sung. Whereupon the ceremony was concluded with cries of *Vive le Roi.*

"Of all and every of the above, the said Sieur de la Salle having required of us an instrument, we have delivered to him the same, signed by us, and by the undersigned witnesses, this 9th day of April, 1682.

"le Mataire, *Notary. "* De La Salle.
P. Zenobe, *Recollect Missionary.*
Henry De Tonty.
Francois De Boisrondet.
Jean Bourdon.
Sieur D'autray.
Jaques Cauchois.
Pierre You.
Gilles Meucret.
Jean Michel, *Surgeon.*
Jean Mas.
Jean Dulignon.
Nicolas De La Salle."

The return voyage of the discoverers, against the powerful current of the Mississippi, was slow and laborious. They reached Fort Prudhomme, built in their descent, the 10th of May. Here La Salle fell sick, and was left in charge of Father Gabriel and a part of the men; while Tonti was ordered on with the rest to Michillimackinac, where he arrived in the beginning of July following.

M. La Salle joined Tonti at Michillimackinac, in September following, where he stayed only three days, and then pursued his journey to Quebec to make a report of his discoveries to Count de Frontenac, who much to his regret and disappointment had been recalled to France during his absence. M. De la Barre was sent out to supply his place.

The news of La Salle's discoveries was received with great joy in Quebec, and the "Te Deum" was sung in the churches. Early in October he sailed for France for the purpose of reporting his discoveries to the king, who received him very graciously, and in the spring of 1684, fitted out an expedition under his command to take possession of the mouth of the Mississippi, and make settlements along the coast. This expedition consisted of four ships. In the meantime Tonti, who had been placed in the command of Fort St. Lewis, became uneasy at not hearing anything from La Salle, to whom he appears to have been greatly attached, and learning, by way of Fort Michillimackinac, of his sailing from France for the Gulf of Mexico, immediately set out with a party of forty men, by water, to join him at the mouth of the river. He left his station on the Illinois, sometime in 1686; but he could find nothing of La Salle, and returned to his post again.

On his return, after reaching the territory of the Akanceas, a very friendly tribe, his men were so delighted with the country, that at their request he left a colony to form a settlement in that country. This was probably the first settlement, for cultivating the earth, ever made on the Mississippi by white men.

As for Mons. La Salle, being unable to find the mouth of the Mississippi with his ships, he landed in the Bay of St. Bernard, within the present territory of Texas, in February, 1685, and took possession of the country, and erected a fort. From this spot he made excursions by land into the adjacent territories. In one of these excursions he was murdered by two of his own men, March 17, 1687. Thus perished this enterprising man in the midst of his discoveries. How his noble heart would exult, were he now living and could see the millions of white men who people the Illinois and the shores of the

Mississippi, with the hundreds of vessels and steamships that navigate the lakes first traversed by his little barque, "The Griffin."

CHAPTER II.

From the death of La Salle, to near the period of the old colonial Ohio Company's formation, we have but little authentic history, of the discoveries on the Ohio River, except what is furnished by the French missionaries, who traversed the country on the Wabash and Illinois, establishing several missions among the Indians. Proofs of their intercourse with the western tribes are seen in the small silver crosses often found near the Ohio, several of which, have been seen by the writer. Their imposing ritual, and showy forms of worship, attracted the attention of the savages, while their unwearied labors to conciliate them, strongly attached them to the interest of the French, whose king they were taught to consider their great father. No traveler ventured from the Atlantic settlements to visit the country west of the Allegheny Mountains. It is stated, in Gordon's History of Pennsylvania, that as early as the year 1740, traders from that colony and Virginia, "went among the Indians on the Ohio and tributary streams, to deal for peltries," and in 1745, Peter Chartier, an influential Indian interpreter, went and joined the French Indians on the Ohio, to the injury of Pennsylvania. This same Peter, at the head of four hundred Shawnee Indians, attacked James Dinnew and Peter Teete, and robbed them of their goods. They were considered respectable Indian traders, and much excitement prevailed in consequence of their robbery." (Hist. Notes of Pa. in Hazard's Register.) From this record it appears that traders visited the Ohio River as early as 1740; also, that Chartier's Creek, a few miles below Pittsburgh, was named after this same Peter Chartier, probably from his having a station on, or near, the mouth of the creek. In the second volume of Sparks's writings of Washington, note 6, we find an account of the first movement towards a settlement on the Ohio River:

"In the year 1748, Thomas Lee, one of his Majesty's council, in Virginia, formed the design of effecting a settlement on the wild lands west of the Allegheny Mountains, through the association of a number of gentlemen. Before this date there were no English residents in those regions. A few traders wandered from tribe to tribe and dwelt among the Indians; but they

neither cultivated nor occupied the land. Mr. Lee associated with himself Mr. Hanbury, a merchant from London, and twelve persons in Virginia and Maryland, composing the 'Ohio Land Company.' A half million of acres of land was granted them, to be taken principally on the south side of the Ohio River, between the Monongahela and Kanawha Rivers."

In the year 1749, or that following the treaty of Aix la Chapelle, the French began to take formal possession of their discoveries on the Ohio River and its tributary branches. The manner of doing this was by erecting a wooden cross, near the mouth of the stream, and burying a leaden plate at its foot, on which was engraved a legend, setting forth the claim of Louis the Fifteenth to the country by right of prior discovery, and by formal treaties with the European powers. This was done by the order of the Marquis De la Galissoniere, commandant general of New France, and under the immediate direction of Captain Celeron de Bienville, commander of the detachment, who, while engaged in this service, directed a letter to Governor Hamilton, of Pennsylvania, dated, "*Camp sur le Belle Riviere, a une ancienne village des Chouans, 6th August, 1749,*" notifying him to forbid the colonial or English traders, visiting that region, as the English never had any claim to it, and he was surprised to find them there without permission, trespassing on the territory of the French king. This was dispatched by a trader, whom he had taken prisoner, somewhere on the waters of the Allegheny River, and set at liberty with two others, who were charged with similar dispatches, so that there should be little chance of their failing to reach the Governor. The route pursued by Captain Celeron must have been from Presque Isle, over on to the heads of Le Beouf or French Creek, and thence down the Allegheny to the Ohio River. We have proof of this fact in the dates of the leaden plates, since found at several places. The first is dated July 29th, and was doubtless dug up by the Seneca Indians, after the departure of the French, and who might have been present at the ceremony, and carried to Governor Clinton, of New York, at Fort George. He sent a copy of it to the Governor of Pennsylvania, a transcript of which is published in Patterson's History of the Backwoods.

On the 6th of August he wrote the letter above noticed, dated at the ancient village of the Chouans or Shawnee, and might have been at Venango, where there was an old Indian town. On the 16th of August he was at the mouth of the Muskingum, and on the 18th, at Big Kanawha, as will be shown by the dates on the plates buried at these places, a history of which follows:

In the spring of the year 1798, there was a freshet in the Muskingum River, which bore away large masses of earth from the bank at the mouth, leaving it quite perpendicular. In the summer following, some boys, who were bathing, discovered projecting from the face of the bank, three or four feet below the surface of the earth, a square metallic plate. By the aid of a pole, they succeeded in loosening it from its bed. On a more close inspection, it was found to be lead, engraved with letters in a language which they did not understand. Not thinking it of any value, except for the lead, which was then a scarce and dear article, they took it home, and being in want of rifle bullets, a portion of it was cut up and cast into balls. It shortly after came to the knowledge of Paul Fearing, Esq., that a curious old lead plate had been found by the boys, a little below, or nearly opposite to, the site of Fort Harmar. He immediately got possession of it, and ascertained that the inscription was in the French language. The present Hon. William Woodbridge, of Detroit, from whom we have these facts, then quite a youth, was living in Marietta, and had recently returned from Gallipolis, where he had been learning the French language. Mr. Fearing took the plate to him, and ascertained that it had been deposited there by the French as an evidence of their right to the possession of the country. Quite a large portion of the inscription had then been cut away by the boys, so that the whole could not be deciphered, but sufficient to ascertain its object. About the year 1821, it came into the possession of Caleb Atwater, and soon after was sent to Governor De Witt Clinton, who, in October, 1827, sent it to the Antiquarian Society of Massachusetts, in whose cabinet it still remains. The following extract from the letter of Governor Clinton, accompanying the plate, copied from Smith's History of Canada, volume 1, page 209, will throw still more light on the subject.

"Galissoniere, persuaded that peace would soon be concluded, and sensible of the importance of giving certain boundaries both to Canada and Nova Scotia, detached an officer, M. Celeron de Bienville, with three hundred men, with orders to repair to Detroit, and from thence to traverse the country, as far as the Appalachian Mountains, which he admitted to be the bounds of the English plantations in America, and beyond which he denied that they had any pretensions. This officer was directed, not only to use his influence to procure a number of Indians to accompany him, but to exact a promise from them, that they would not in the future admit English traders among them. This officer was furnished with leaden plates, with the arms of France engraved on them, and he was ordered to bury them at particular stations. A process verbal was then drawn up, signed by himself and those officers that accompanied him. With this gentleman Galissoniere sent a letter to Mr. Hamilton, the governor of Pennsylvania, apprizing him of the step he had taken, and requesting that in the future he would give orders to prevent his people from trading beyond the Appalachian Mountains, as he had received commands, from the court of France, to seize the merchants and confiscate the goods of t hose trading in these countries, incontestably belonging to France. De Celeron discharged his commission with punctuality, but not without exiting the apprehensions of the natives, who declared that the object of France, in taking possession of their country, was either to make them subjects or perhaps slaves. The immense load of *process verbaux* that had been drawn up on this expedition, were handed over to Galissoniere and transmitted to the court of France. As a recompense for his trouble, Celeron was, two years after, appointed to the command of Detroit, with the rank of Major. Galissoniere was appointed Governor of Canada on the 25th of September, 1747, and the Treaty of Aix-la-Chapelle, alluded to in the above extract, was concluded in 1748."

Accompanying the description, on another page, is shown an exact copy of the remains of the ancient plate, found at Marietta, as it now appears in the museum of the Antiquarian Society at Worcester, taken from the original for this history, by James Tenny, M. D.

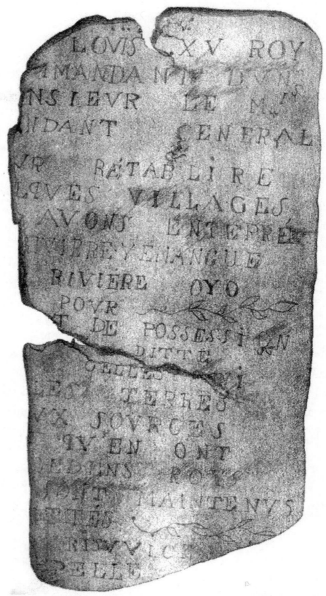

**Leaden Plate found at the Mouth of the Muskingum River
in 1798**

In March, 1846, a similar plate was found at the mouth of the Kanawha, a short distance above its junction with the Ohio River. It was discovered projecting from the face of the bank, like that at Marietta, by a boy, R. P.

Hereford, a few feet below the surface of the soil, which must probably have accumulated considerably from the deposits of earth by freshets, in the course of nearly a hundred years— the period which has elapsed since the time of its burial, August 18th, 1749. The size of this plate is eleven inches and three lines long, by seven inches and six lines broad. The thickness varies, on the different edges, from one fourth to one eighth of an inch. The engraving of the letters is quite distinct and deeply cut, except the name of the river and date, which appear to have been filled in at the time, and are more lightly cut. This was probably the case with all the tablets, as the period and place would depend on circumstances; but all the other matters set forth could have been put on by Paul Le Brosse, the engraver, as his name is on the back of the plate, but whether he lived in Quebec or Paris, does not appear—and as they all contained the same amount of matter, they were probably nearly of the same size. The name of the river " Chi-noda-hich-e-tha," now known by that of Kanawha, is doubtless its original Indian name, as known by the savages, who accompanied Captain Celeron, as well as that of the Muskingum being called by them " Ye-nan-gu-e." It has been surmised that the plate found at Marietta was originally deposited at the mouth of the Venango, and subsequently removed by some person to the mouth of the Muskingum. But this is highly improbable; and there can be no reasonable doubt of its being found in the exact spot where the French commander left it, and intended it should remain. Venango was the name of an old Indian village at the mouth of Le Beouf, or French Creek, and was one hundred and thirty miles by water, and eighty by land, above the site of Fort Du Quesne. It is not probable that the plates were buried at any other points, than at the mouths of the principal rivers that fall into the Ohio; and this was doubtless done from the Allegheny to its junction with the Mississippi, and with the legal forms attending the reading of the *"process verbaux,"* must have occupied the time of several months. The object of the mission was to take possession of the country in a legal form, and in such manner as could be established hereafter by written evidence. To this they were probably urged by the proceedings of the Ohio land company, then forming. No nation ever had a fairer claim to a newly discovered country, than the French had to the valley of the Ohio, but a wise Providence had ordained, that the beautiful region should be possessed by the Anglo Saxon race, and not by the Gallic.

The following is a copy of the inscription on the Kanawha River tablet, and below, a translation made by L. Soyer, Esq., mayor of the city of Marietta, and one well skilled in the French language, being himself a native of France:

"LAN, 1749, DV REGNE DE LOVIS XV ROY DE FRANCE, NOVS CELORON, COMMANDANT DVN DETACHEMENT ENVOIE PAR MONSIEVR LE Ms. DE LA GALISSONIERE, COMMANDANT GENERAL DE LA NOVVELLE FRANCE, POVR RETABLIR LA TRANQVILLITE DANS QVELQVES VILLAGES SAUVAGES DE CES, CANTONS AVONS ENTERRE CETTE PLAQVE A LENTREE DE LA RIVIERE CHINODAHICHETHA, LE 18 AOUST, PRES DE LA RIVIERE OYO, AUTREMENT BELLE RIVIERE, POVR MONVMENT DV RENOVVELLEMENT DE POSSESSION, QVE NOVS AVONS PRIS DE LA DITTE RIVIERE OYO, ET DE TOVTES CELLES QVI Y TOMB'NT.ET DE TOVES LES TERRES DES DEVX COTES JVSQVE AVX SOVRCES DES DITTES RIVIES, AINSI QVEL ONT JOVY OV DV JOVIR LES PRECEDENTS ROYS DE FRANCE, ET QVILS SISONT MAINTENVS PAR LES ARMES, ET PAR LESTRAITTES, SPECIALEMENT PAR CEVX DE RISVVICK DVTRCHT ET DAIX LA CHAPELLE."

Translation:

In the year 1749, of the reign of Louis XV, of France, We, Celeron, commandant of a detachment sent by the Marquis de la Galissoniere, Captain-General of New France, in order to re-establish tranquility among some villages of savages of these parts, have buried this plate at the mouth of the river Chi-no-da-hich-e-tha, the 18th August, near the river Ohio, otherwise beautiful river, as a monument of renewal of possession, which we have taken of the said river Ohio, and of all those which empty themselves into it, and of all the lands of both sides, even to the sources of said rivers; as have enjoyed, or ought to have enjoyed the preceding kings of France, and that they have maintained themselves there, by force of arms and by treaties, especially by those of Riswick, of Utrecht, and of Aix-la-Chapelle.

LAN 1749 DV REGNE DE LOVIS XV ROY DE
FRANCE NOVS CELORON COMMANDANT DVN DE
TACHEMENT ENVOIE PAR MONSIEVR LE Mis DE LA
GALISSONIERE COMMANDANT GENERAL DE LA
NOVVELLE FRANCE POVR RETABLIR LA TRANQVILLITE
DANS QVELQVES VILLAGES SAUVAGES DE CES CANTONS
AVONS ENTERRE CETTE PLAQVE A LENTREE DE LA
RIVIERE CHINODAHICHETHA LE 18 AOUST
PRES DE LA RIVIERE OYO AUTREMENT BELLE
RIVIERE POVR MONVMENT DV RENOVVELLEMENT DE
POSSESSION QVE NOVS AVONS PRIS DE LA DITTE
RIVIERE OYO ET DE TOVTES CELLES QVI Y TOMBENT
ET DE TOVES LES TERRES DES DEVX COTES JVSQVE
AVX SOVRCES DES DITTES RIVIES VINSI QVEN ONT
JOVY OV DV JOVIR LES PRECEDENTS ROYS DE FRANCE
ET QVILS SISONT MAINTENVS PAR LES ARMES ET
PAR LES TRAITTES SPECIALEMENT PAR CEVX DE
RISVVICK DVTRCHT ET DAIX LA CHPELLE

Leaden plate found at the Mouth of the Kanawha River in 1846

In the year 1750, after the return of Captain Celeron from his voyage of reconnaissance, the French proceeded to erect forts, or stockaded garrisons, answering for defense, as well as for trading posts with the Indians, at the most commanding points along the water courses. The first was at Presque Isle, on an inlet or bay, at the easterly end of Lake Erie. The second at Le Beouf, on the head water of that branch of the Allegheny, distant about fifteen miles from the lake, making a carrying place between that stream and Presque Isle. All their intercourse and travel was by water, carried on in canoes and batteaux. At this point was the nearest approach of the waters of the Ohio to Lake Erie. The third post was at the mouth of Le Beouf, called Fort Venango, from an ancient Indian village located at this place. These forts were occupied by the troops which erected them.

Their claim to the Ohio River, and the adjacent territory, was founded on the discoveries of La Salle and his successors, seventy years before, and their present measures for its defense arose from the attempt of the colonial land company to occupy its banks. In the year 1744, a treaty was made with the Iroquois and Delaware Indians at Lancaster, Pennsylvania, by which they ceded to the king of England all the lands within the bounds of Virginia. This was the *first treaty,* supposed to contain a cession of lands on the Ohio; but at a subsequent treaty in 1752, held at Logstown, an Indian village on the north side of the Ohio, seventeen miles below Fort Du Quesne, Colonel Frye and two other commissioners being present on the part of Virginia, and Mr. Gist as agent of the Ohio Company, one of the old chiefs declared that the Indians considered that the treaty at Lancaster did not cede any lands west of the first range of hills on the east side of the Allegany Mountains, *"not thinking that the boundaries of Virginia extended to the Ohio River, or even west of the mountains."* They agreed, however, not to molest any settlements that might be made on the south east side of the Ohio.

At a treaty held at Fort Stanwix in 1768, by Sir William Johnson, with the six nations and many western tribes, the Iroquois accused the Delawares of selling lands to the whites which did not belong to them; they claiming by right of conquest all the lands on the Ohio, as far south as the Tennessee River. Soon after the treaty at Logstown, Gist was appointed surveyor to the Ohio Company, and directed to lay off a town and fort near the mouth of Chartier's Creek. Nothing however, we presume, was done in the matter, as Washington, in his journal of his visit to Le Beouf, uses the following language: *"About two miles from this (the forks) on the south east side of the* *river, at the place where the Ohio Company intended to lay off their fort, lives Shingiss, king of the Delawares."* The place where Shingiss resided was near the river, and a short distance south of Mr. Rees's rocks.*

*Extracted from N. B. Craig, Esq's, writings, published in the Pittsburg Gazette, 1841.

In the autumn of the year 1750, the agents of the Ohio Company employed Christopher Gist, a land surveyor and familiar with the woods, to explore their contemplated possessions on the Ohio River, as well as the adjacent country, the situation of which was only known from the vague reports of Indian traders, as no English traveler had visited that region. He kept a journal of his proceedings, which was published, and is entitled, "*A Journal of Christopher Gist's Journey, Began from Colonel Cresap's, at the old town on the Potomac River, Maryland, October 31, 1750, continued down the Ohio within fifteen miles of the falls thereof; and from thence to Roanoke River in North Carolina, where he arrived in May, 1751."*

Not having the advantage of the whole journal to examine, but only extracts kindly made by Dr. Johnson, member of Congress from Morgan County, Ohio, from Pownal's "*Topographical Description,*" it is difficult to point out the route pursued until he struck the Ohio River. Mr. Craig, in his notes on the early history of Pittsburgh, thinks from what he can ascertain, that he "*ascended the Juniata, after crossing over from the Potomac, and descended the Kiskeminetas to the Allegheny, which stream he crossed about four miles above the present city, and passed on to the Ohio."* As he makes no mention of the Monongahela, it is presumed that he was ignorant of its existence. "*If he passed to the north of Hogback Hill, that river might readily escape his notice."* From the mouth of Beaver Creek he passed over on to the Tuscarawas, or Muskingum River, called by him, and by the Indians, Elk Eye Creek; striking it on the 5th of December, or thirty-five days after leaving the Potomac, at a point about fifty miles above the present town of Coshocton, as near as can be ascertained from the journal. On the 7th, he crossed over the Elk Eye to a small village of Ottawas, who were in the French interest. He speaks of the land as broken, and the bottoms rather narrow, on this stream. On the 14th December he reached an Indian town, a few miles above the mouth of the White Woman Creek, called Muskingum, inhabited by Wyandots, who, he says, are half of them attached to the French, and half to the English, containing about one hundred families:

"When we came in sight of it, we perceived English colors hoisted on the King's house, and at George Croghan's. Upon inquiring the reasons, I was

informed that the French had lately taken several English traders, and that Mr. Croghan had ordered all the white men to come into this town, and had sent expresses to the traders of the lower towns, and among the Piquatinces, and that the Indians had sent to their people to come to council about it."

"Monday, 17th. Two traders belonging to Mr. Croghan, came into town, and informed us that two of his people had been taken by forty Frenchmen and twenty Indians, who had carried them with seven horse loads of skins to a new fort the French were building on one of the branches of Lake Erie," (probably Fort Le Beouf.)

"Tuesday, 18th. I acquainted Mr. Croghan and Mr. Montour with my business with the Indians, and talked much of a regulation of trade, with which they were pleased, and treated me very well."

"Tuesday, 25th. This being Christmas day I intended to read prayers, but after inviting some of the white men, they informed each other of my intentions, and being of several persuasions, and few of them inclined to hear any good, they refused to come; but one Thomas Burney, a blacksmith, who is settled there, went about and talked to them, and then several of the well disposed Indians came freely, being invited by Andrew Montour." Mr. Gist delivered a discourse, which was interpreted to the Indians, and read the English church service. He then says, *"The Indians seem to be well pleased, and came up to me and returned me their thanks, and then invited me to live among them,"* &c. They were desirous of being instructed in the principles of Christianity; that they liked me very well, and wanted me to marry them after the Christian, manner, and baptize their children, and then they said they would never desire to return to the French, or suffer them, or their priests, to come near them more, for they loved the English, but had seen little religion among them."

Wednesday, 26th. "This day a woman that had long been a prisoner and had deserted, being retaken and brought into the town on Christmas Eve, was put to death in the following manner:

They carried her without the town, and let her loose; and when she attempted to run away, the persons appointed for that purpose pursued her and struck her on the ear on the right side of her head, which bent her flat on her face to the ground. They then struck her several times through the back with a dart, to the heart; scalped her, and threw the scalp in the air, and another cut off her head. Thus the dismal spectacle lay until the evening, and then Barney Curran desired leave to bury her, which he and his men and some of the Indians did, just at dark."

"Friday, 4th January, 1751. One Taaf, an Indian trader, came to town from near Lake Erie, and informed us that the Wyandots had advised him to keep clear of the Ottowas, (a nation firmly attached to the French, living near the lakes,) and told him that the branches of the lakes were claimed by the French, but that all the branches of the Ohio belonged to them and their brothers, the English, and that the French had no business there, and that it was expected that the other part of the Wyandots would desert the French and come over to the English interest, and join their brethren in the Elk Eye Creek, and build a strong fort and town there."

"Wednesday, 9th. This day came into town two traders from among the Piquatinces, (a tribe of the Twightwee,) and brought news that another English trader was taken prisoner by the French, and that three French soldiers had deserted and come over to the English, and surrendered themselves to some of the traders of the Picktown, and that the Indians would have put them to death to revenge their taking our traders; but as the French had surrendered themselves to the English, they would not let the Indians hurt them, but had ordered them to be sent under the care of three of our traders, and delivered at this town to George Croghan."

George Croghan was some years after deputy Indian agent to Sir William Johnson, but seems now to have been at the head of a party of traders. He and Andrew Montour, an influential man among the Delaware and Shawnee Indians, accompanied Mr. Gist in his visit to the Indian town at the mouth of the Scioto, and to the towns on the Big Miami — being of great service to him in his intercourse with the tribes which he visited.

"Saturday, 12th. Proposed a council — postponed — Indians drunk."

"Monday, 14th. This day George Croghan, by the assistance of Andrew Montour, acquainted the king and council of this nation, (presenting them with four strings of wampum,) that their Roggony, (father,) had sent, under the care of the Governor of Virginia, their brother, a large present of goods, which were now landed safe in Virginia, and that the governor had sent me to invite them to come and see him, and partake of their father's charity to all his children on the branches of the Ohio. In answer to which, one of the chiefs stood up and said that their king and all of them thanked their brother, the Governor of Virginia, for his care, and me for bringing them the news; but that they could not give an answer until they had a full or general counsel of the several nations of Indians, which could not be until next spring; and so the king and council shaking hands with us, we took our leave."

"Tuesday, 15th. We left Muskingum and went west five miles to the White Woman's Creek, on which is a small town. This white woman was taken away from New England, when she was not above ten years old, by the French Indians. She is now upwards of fifty — has an Indian husband and several children. Her name is Mary Harris. She still remembers they used to be very religious in New England; and wonders how the white men can be so wicked as she has seen them in these woods."

"Wednesday, 16th. Set out S. W. twenty-five miles to Licking Creek. The land from Muskingum is rich and broken. Upon the north side of Licking Creek, about six miles from its mouth, were several salt licks, or ponds formed by little streams or drains of water, clear, but of a bluish color, and salt taste. The traders and Indians boil their meat in this water, which, if proper care is not taken, will sometimes make it too salty to eat."

Leaving Licking Creek, he traveled west and south west; and on Saturday, the 19th, arrived at Hockhocking, a small town of four or five Delaware families; and on Sunday he traveled south west twenty miles to Maguck, a little Delaware town of about ten families. This town is near the Scioto.

"24th—went south fifteen miles, to a town called 'Hurricane Tom's Town' on the south west of Scioto Creek, consisting of five or six families. 25th—went down on south east side of the creek, four miles to Salt Lick Creek." Traveled twenty-eight miles, and arrived on Sunday at a Delaware town of about twenty families, on south east side of the Scioto."

Here he remained a few days, held a council, and some Indian speeches were made. He says this is the last of the Delaware towns to the westward. The Delaware Indians, by the best accounts I could gather, consist of about five hundred fighting men, all firmly attached to the English interest. They are not properly a part of the six nations, but are scattered about among most of the Indians on the Ohio, and some of them among the six nations, from whom they have leave to hunt upon their land.

"Tuesday, 28th — set out five miles to mouth of Scioto Creek, opposite to the Shawnee town. Here we fired our guns to alarm the traders, who soon answered, and came and ferried us over. The Shawnee town is situated on both sides of the Ohio, just below the mouth of Scioto Creek, and contains about three hundred men. There are about forty houses on the south side of the river, and about a hundred on the north side, with a kind of state house, about ninety feet long, with a tight cover of bark, in which they hold their councils. The Shawnees are not a part of the six nations, but were formerly at variance with them, though now reconciled. They are great friends to the English interest. Big Hanoahausa, their principal speaker, replied in a good speech, and *"hoped that the friendship, now subsisting between us and our brothers, will last as long as the sun shines or the moon gives light."*

While Mr. Gist was at this town, an extraordinary festival took place, which he describes as follows:

"In the evening a proper officer made a public proclamation that all the Indian marriages were dissolved, and a public feast was to be held for the three succeeding days, in which the women, as their custom was, were to choose again their husbands. The next morning early the Indians breakfasted, and after, spent the day dancing until the evening; when a plentiful feast was prepared. After feasting they spent the night in dancing. The same way they spent the two next days until the evening. The men dancing by themselves, and then the women in turns, around fires, and dancing in their manner and in the form of the figure eight, about sixty or seventy of them at a time. The women, the whole time they danced, sung a song in their language, the chorus of which was, "I am not afraid of my husband, I will choose what man I please. The third day, in the evening, the men, being about one hundred in number, danced in a long string, following one another, sometimes at length, at other times in a figure of eight, quite around the fort, and in and out of the long house where they held their council, the women standing together as the men danced by them, and as any of the women liked a man passing by, she stepped in and joined in the dance, taking hold of the man's shroud or blanket, whom she chose, and then continued in the dance until the rest of the women stepped in and made their choice in the same manner, after which the dance ended, and they all retired to consummate."

Tuesday, February 12th. Mr. Gist, in company with George Croghan, Andrew Montour and Robert Kallender, set out for the Indian town on the Miami, and arrived on Sunday to the Big Miami River, opposite to the Twightwee town. This town is situated on the northwest side of the river, about one hundred and fifty miles from the mouth thereof. It consists of about four hundred families, and is daily increasing. It is accounted one of the strongest Indian towns upon this part of the continent. The Twightwee are a very numerous people, consisting of many different tribes, under the same form of government. Each tribe has a particular chief; one of which is chosen indifferently out of any tribe, to rule the whole nation, and is invested with greater authority than any of the others. They are accounted the most powerful nation westward of the English settlements, and much superior to the six nations, with whom they are now in amity. At this town they remained some time. The following are extracts from the marginal notes:

"Big Miami River, land very rich — variety of timber, abundance of game. Ohio abounds in fish — smokes the pipe of peace—is kindly received by the Twightwee king."

By the aid of Croghan and Montour, with several presents, articles of peace and amity were drawn up and ratified between this nation and the English, notwithstanding the exertions of four Indian agents of the French, who also brought presents to the king. After this was accomplished, he returned to the mouth of the Scioto, and from thence passed down the Ohio River, on the south east side, to within a few miles of the falls. From thence returned home by way of North Carolina, and arrived there in May, 1751— being absent on this tour more than six months.

General Harrison, a man familiar with the history of the western tribes, in his discourse before the Historical Society of Ohio, says that the Shawnee tribes were originally natives of Alabama or the country south of the Tennessee, and were driven out from their possessions by their enemies about the year 1740, or near the middle of the eighteenth century. They applied for protection and a home among the tribes on the Miami, were accepted, and given possession of lands on the Scioto River. They would the more readily have been accepted, as friends and allies, from being at war with tribes who had for many years been their enemies, as it is well known that battles were often fought between the tribes living north of the Ohio, and those inhabiting the country south of that river. The Shawnee were a very warlike and brave people, being considered the Spartans of the western tribes; from which it seems probable that they had lived only a few years at the mouth of the Scioto. Not long after Gist's visit, they left the mouth of that river and established themselves higher up the stream, and on the waters of the Miami, building towns, known by the name of Old and New Chillicothe. They were steady friends of the English, until the period of Dunmore's war, in 1774; after which, finding the whites bent on dispossessing them of their lands, they became their most inveterate and formidable enemy. At the period of signing the treaty with General Wayne, when all the other tribes had ceased to resist, they still continued to harass the frontiers of Virginia and Kentucky with war parties, being the first to wage war and the last to make peace.

After the return of Mr. Gist, the Ohio Company proceeded to take possession of their lands on the Ohio River, by erecting a trading house at Logstown, an Indian village below the forks of the river. This establishment the French attacked and destroyed in 1753, "seizing their goods and skins to the amount of £20,000, and killing all the traders but two, who made their escape"—thus showing their determination to make good their threat, of not suffering any traders but their own, within their territory*.

*It is doubtful whether this statement is correct. Washington's Journal, of 1753, makes no reference to it. A fort erected by English traders, on the Great Miami, was destroyed by the French and Indians in 1752. Extracts from the papers of the day, relative to it, are before us; but the papers say nothing of the attack of 1753. (Hist. Soc.)

"In the summer and fall of the same year, accounts were received that a considerable French force had arrived at Presque Isle, on their way to the Ohio. In October of that year, George Washington was selected as a messenger to proceed by the way of Logstown to the French commandant, wherever he might be found, to demand information as to the object of the French troops."

Washington, accompanied by Mr. Gist, left Williamsburgh, in Virginia, immediately, and reached the present site of Pittsburgh, about the 23d of November, 1753. He examined the point, and thought it a favorable position for a fort. "He then proceeded to Logstown, and from thence to the French commandant at Le Beouf, from whom he received a very unsatisfactory reply."

Immediately after Washington's return to Williamsburgh, arrangements were made to send out two companies of men to the Ohio, and erect a fort at the forks of the river. A full account of this journey is published in the notes to Marshall's Life of Washington, vol. 2d.

"One company, under Captain Trent, being first ready, commenced their march and reached their destination. Before their arrival, it seems the French had already built a fort at Logstown,* as the following extract from the records at Harrisburg will show:

*This is, also, doubtful. See George Croghan's Journal of January and February, 1754, in Hist, of Wm. Penn. Appx. p. 50. (Hist. Soc.)

"March 12, 1754. Evidence sent to the house that Venango and Logstown, where the French forts are built, are in the province of Pennsylvania."

From the history of that period it seems that Virginia and Pennsylvania both laid claim to this disputed territory. On the 17th of April, 1754, the troops under Captain Trent were engaged in erecting a fort near the junction of the rivers. The Captain and Lieutenant being absent, Ensign Ward had the command of the company, consisting of forty-one men.

"The fort was still unfinished when, on that memorable day, the 17th of April, Monsieur Contracour made his appearance on the Allegheny River at the head of sixty batteaux, three hundred canoes, and a motley host of more than a thousand French and Indians, with eighteen pieces of cannon. Ensign Ward, after a short parley, surrendered his unfinished stockade, and was allowed to march away with his men and all their working tools."

This transaction has always been viewed as the beginning of the war which followed, and finally deprived France of her possessions in North America. The new occupants immediately proceeded to the erection of a fort, which they named Du Quesne, in honor of the then Governor General of Canada."— *Extract from Craig's Notes on Pittsburgh.*

Colonel Frye, who had command of the troops sent out by Virginia, having died on the way, Lieutenant Colonel Washington took charge of them. The retreating company of men fell in with the advancing forces at a place called the Great Meadows, on the heads of the Yohogany River. It was at this place that Fort Necessity was built, and the celebrated capitulation of the Virginia troops, to Villiers, the commander of the French army, took place. A very old copy of the articles signed by Washington, on this occasion, fell under our notice a short time since. The Hon. William Woodbridge, senator from Michigan, lives near Detroit. An aged Frenchman, of that place, had occasion to consult him, as a lawyer, on a title to some lands. Being directed to show all the old manuscripts he had in his possession, among them was this old relic, which he said had been in the family a long time; but being an ignorant man, could give no account of its origin. It is written on the coarse paper of that early day, and in the ancient French characters. The following is a copy of the original, with a translation by L. Soyer, Esq., and is deemed worthy of preservation by the Historical Society:

Capitulation accordee par M. de Villiers Captaine Commandant des Troupes de Sa Majeste" tres chretienne, a celui des Troupes Anglaises, actuellement dans le fort de Necessity qui avoit *He* construit sur les terres du Domaine du Roy.

Le 3e Juillet, 1754, a huit heures du Soir.

Scavoir.

Comme notre intention n'a jamais fit' de troubler la paix et la bonne harmonie qui regnoit entre les deux princes amis, mais seulement de venger l'assasinat qui a Ste" fait sur un de nos officiers porteur d'une sommation, et sur son escorte; comme aussi d'emp6cher aucun etablissement sur les terres du Roy mon maitre.

A ces considerations nous voulons bien acorder grace a tous les Anglais qui sont dans le dit fort aux conditions cy apres:

Art. 1. Nous accordons au commandant Anglais de se retirer avec toute sa garnison pour s'en retourner paisiblement dans son pays, et lui promettons d'empêcher qu'il lui soit fait aucune insulte par nos Français, et de maintenir, autant qu'il sera en notre pouvoir, tous les sauvages qui sont avec nous.

Art. 2. Il lui sera permis de sortir, et d'emporter tout ce qui leur appartiendra, à l'exception de l'artillerie, que nous nous réservons.

Art. 3. Que nous leur accordons les honneurs de la guerre; qu'ils sortiront tambour battant avec une petite pièce de canon, voulant bien par-là leur prouver que nous les traitons en amis.

Art. 4. Que si-tôt les articles signés de part et d'autre, ils amèneront le pavillon Anglais.

Art. 5. Que demain à la pointe du jour un détachement Français ira faire denier la garnison et prendre possession du dit fort.

Art. 6. Que comme les Anglais n'ont presque plus de chevaux ni bœufs, ils seront libres de mettre leurs effets en cache pour venir chercher lorsqu'ils auront rejoint des chevaux ; ils pourront à cette fin laisser des gardiens, en tel nombre qu'ils vondront, aux conditions qu'ils donneront parole d'honneur de ne plus travailler à aucun établissement dans ce lieu-ci, ni deçà de la hauteur des terres, pendant une année à compter de ce jour.

Art. 7. Que comme les Anglais ont en leur pouvoir un officier, deux cadets; et généralement les prisonniers qu'ils nous ont faits dans l'assassinat du Sieur de Jumonville, et qu'ils promettent de les envoyer avec sauvegarde jusqu'au Fort Duquesne, situé sur la Belle-Riviere; et que pour surete de cet article, ainsi que de ce traite Messrs. Jacob Vanbraam et Robert Stobo, tous deux capitaines, nous seront remis en Stage jusqu'a l'arrivée de nos Francois et Canadiens ci-dessus mentionn^s.

Nous nous obligeons de notre cote a donner escorte pour remettre en surete les deux officiers, qui nous promettent nos Francois dans deux mois et demi pour le plus tard.

Fait double sur un des postes de notre Blockhouse le jour, et an que dessus.

Ont signe Messieurs. Jannes Mackay, George Washington, Coullon Villiers.

Translation:

Capitulation, granted by M. de Villiers, commanding captain of the troops of his most Christian Majesty to those of the English troops now in the fort of Necessity, which had been built upon the grounds of the King's domain, the 3d July, 1754, at eight o'clock in the evening, to wit:

As our intention never has been to disturb the peace and harmony which existed between the two friendly princes, but only to avenge the murder which has been committed upon one of our officers, bearer of a summons, and upon his guard, as well also to prevent any settlement upon the domains of the king, my master.

Upon these considerations, we are willing to give favor to all the English who are in said fort, upon the conditions hereafter expressed.

Art. 1. We permit the English commander to withdraw, with all his garrison, to go back peaceably to his country, and we engage, on our part, to prevent that any insult should be committed upon him by our Frenchmen, and to hinder as much as will be in our power all the savages who are with us.

Art. 2. He will be permitted to withdraw and carry away all that belongs to them, with the exception of the artillery, which we reserve for ourselves.

Art. 3. That we accord them the honors of war; that they will go out, drum beating, with a small cannon, wishing by that to prove to them that we treat them as friends.

Art. 4. That as soon as the articles are signed on both sides, they will bring the English flag.

Art. 5. That to-morrow at the break of day a French detachment will go to cause the garrison to file off, and take possession of said fort.

Art. 6. That as the English have scarcely any horses or oxen left, they will be at liberty to hide, or secrete their goods, so that they may carry them away, when they have obtained horses; to this end they will be permitted to leave guards in such number as they think proper, upon condition that they will give parole rof honor, that they will not labor at any settlement in this place, nor beyond the high grounds, for one year, to commence from this day.

Art. 7. That as the English have in their power an officer and two cadets, and generally the prisoners which they have made at the time of the murder of Sir de Jumonville, and that they engage to send them with safe guard to Fort Du Quesne, situated upon the beautiful river, (Ohio) therefore, for the security of this article, as well as of this treaty, Messrs. Jacob Vanbraan and Robert Stobo, both captains, will be given us as hostages, until the arrival of our French men and Canadians, as above mentioned. We oblige ourselves on our part to give escort and return in safety the two officers who promised us our Frenchmen, in two months and a half at the furthest.

Made duplicate upon one of the posts of our blockhouse, the day and year as above stated.

Have signed, Messrs. Jannes Mackay, George Washington, Coullon Villiers.

The numerous bloody tragedies which were acted in the vicinity of Fort Du Quesne, while it remained in the hands of the French, from April 17, 1754, to November 24, 1758, being already well known to history, will be omitted, it being the object of the writer to treat only of such events as are unrecorded, or contained in books that are out of print, or difficult of access to the public. Before quitting the history of this interesting spot while it remained in the hands of the French, Mr. Craig's account of the perplexity of the commander, and how near he came to abandoning the fort on the near approach of Gen. Braddock, without making any defense, is well worth preserving; and shows on how trifling a pivot may turn the fate of armies.

"On the 5th of July, 1755, intelligence had been brought, by their scouts, that Braddock with his disciplined and formidable army was approaching. Fort Du Quesne was only a stockade, incapable of resisting, even for an hour, the lightest field pieces. At this crisis, when it seems the commandant had abandoned all thought of resistance, Capt. Beaujeu, a bold and enterprising spirit, well suited to such an emergency, proposed to take a detachment of French and Indians, and meet Braddock on his march. The consent of the Indians to accompany him was first to be obtained. The Captain is represented to have been a man of great affability of manners, and very popular amongst the Indians. He went amongst them, explained his plan, and urged them to go with him. They pronounced it a hopeless one, and refused peremptorily to go. A second time he applied to them, and urged them to hold a council on the subject. They did so, and again refused to go. Still not despairing, Capt. Beaujeu again went among them, used all his arts of persuasion, told them that he was determined to go, and asked them whether they would permit him to go alone to meet the enemy. This appeal proved successful. They agreed to accompany him. This was on the 7th of July, 1755, and they had information that Braddock was only eighteen miles distant. That day and the next were spent in making preparations, and early on the morning of the 9th the united forces of French and Indians departed on a seemingly utterly hopeless expedition. Along with Beaujeu were two other Captains, Dumas and Lignery, four Lieutenants, six Ensigns and two Cadets. Various estimates are given of the force of the French and Indians. The highest sets them at two hundred and fifty French and Canadians and six hundred and forty Indians; the lowest at two hundred and fifteen white men and six hundred Indians. The result of the action all know. Braddock was killed, and his army suffered a terrible defeat, to which nothing can be compared but that of St. Clair, in 1792. "The brave Beaujeu fell at the first fire, and the victory was achieved under the command of Capt. Dumas."

The following extract from Hazard's Pa. Register, 8th vol., goes to prove that the French had extensive settlements in their possession in the Mississippi, and cultivated the soil to considerable extent. The statement is from John McKinney, who was taken a prisoner by the Indians, and carried to Fort Du Quesne, in February, 1756:

"While I was at the fort, there came up the Ohio from the Mississippi about thirty batteaux and about one hundred and fifty men, laden with pork, flour, brandy, tobacco, peas, and Indian corn. They were three months in coming to Fort Du Quesne, and came all the way up the falls without unloading."

Fort Du Quesne, while in the occupancy of the French was a mere stockade of small dimensions, and not suited to resist the attacks of artillery, and some more formidable work was deemed necessary at a post so important as this. General Forbes, the captor of the fort, having died a few months after its surrender, at Philadelphia, General Stanwix was appointed to succeed him. In the following year a substantial fort was built, and a treaty held with the Indians as appears from the following letters, printed in the New American Magazine, at Woodbridge in New Jersey, in November, 1759, dated September 24:

"It is now near a month since the army has been employed in erecting a most formidable fortification — such a one as will, to the latest posterity, secure the British Empire on the Ohio."

"Upon the General's arrival, about four hundred Indians, of different nations, came to confirm the peace with the English; particularly the Ottawas and Wyandots, who inhabit about Detroit. These confessed the errors they had been led into by the perfidy of the French, — showed the deepest contrition for their past conduct, and promised not only to remain fast friends to the English, but to assist us in destroying the common enemy, whenever we should call on them to do it. They also said they would deliver up what prisoners they had in their hands to the General, at a great meeting that is to be held in about three weeks. As soon as the congress was ended, the head of each nation presented the calumet of peace to the General, and showed every token of sincerity, that could be expected, which the surrender of the prisoners will confirm. In this, as in everything that can secure the lasting peace and happiness of these colonies, the general is indefatigable."

Judge Brackenridge, in a description of Pittsburgh, published in the Gazette, in July, 1786, says the building of Fort Pitt cost the British government sixty thousand pounds.

Upon the 10th of February, 1763, peace was established between Great Britain, France, and Spain. By this treaty France surrendered to the English Canada and all her possessions east of the Mississippi River, as low down as the 31st degree of latitude; while Spain gave up Florida. In 1764, France ceded to Spain, Louisiana; thus abandoning all her territory in North America.

The Indians being now deserted by their old allies, the French, who had, for a long series of years, been their friends, and supplied them with clothing and implements of war, and environed along the lake shores by the garrisons of the English, it was thought would remain at peace, and not again molest the inhabitants of the frontier settlements. On the faith of their fair promises to General Stanwix, in the summer of 1759, traders had gone among them, with valuable assortments of merchandise to give in exchange for their peltries, little dreaming of the calamities that awaited them. While acting under these delusive appearances, during the year 1763, the Indians formed one of the most formidable alliances for the extermination of their new masters ever entered into by this brave and cunning people. It was composed of all the western tribes, from the heads of the Muskingum to Michillimackinac. At the head of this grand confederacy was Pontiac: a chief as greatly renowned for his wisdom, as he was celebrated for his bravery. They were, doubtless, instigated to this result, partly by the persuasions of their old allies, the French, who felt sore at their late defeat, as well as to resist and put a stop to the encroachments of the English settlers whose slow but gradual progress on their territories they had the foresight to perceive must, in a few years, deprive them of their whole country. They preceded their attacks on the forts by plundering and murdering the English traders, who had gone among them since the late peace. It is stated by the writers of that day, that nearly two hundred traders, and their servants, lost their lives;

while the loss of goods was estimated at more than one hundred thousand pounds sterling. A simultaneous and sudden attack was made on all the western posts. They got possession of the forts of Le Beouf, Venango, Presque Isle, Miamis on the Miami of the Lakes, St. Josephs on the river of that name, Ouachtanon on the Wabash, Sandusky, and Michillimackinac, and put the garrisons to death. Detroit was barely saved, after a long and close siege, by the Indians under Pontiac. Fort Pitt and Niagara both narrowly escaped.

CHAPTER III.

Ancient map, with a plan of Colonel Bouquet's march to Muskingum.—Indian depredations in western Pennsylvania. — Extracts from Colonel Bouquet's expedition on to the Muskingum River, in 1764, with various incidents connected therewith. — Indian treaty at Fort Pitt in 1765.

In the summer of the year 1763, the whole western frontier of Pennsylvania was ravaged by the savages; killing the inhabitants, burning their buildings, and destroying their cattle, to the vicinity of Shippensburg and Carlisle, which towns became now the frontier. It was estimated that a territory, three hundred miles long and thirty miles wide, was abandoned by the whites. This district was but thinly peopled it is true, but was occupied at various points by settlers. Fort Pitt was surrounded and cut off from all intercourse with the country east of the mountains. The fort was attacked with great spirit by the savages, who endeavored to set it on fire with lighted combustibles attached to arrows; and kept up a constant discharge at the troops, from under cover of the bank of the Alleghany River, from their rifles. But, under the command of Captain Ewyer, the soldiers, who had been strengthened by a number of traders, who had escaped the massacre of this class of men which preceded the attack on the posts, defied all their exertions and maintained the fort. Runners having been dispatched to the settlements with notice of the critical condition of the garrison, General Amherst appointed Colonel Bouquet to march to their relief, with a detachment of five hundred men, military stores and provisions. The abandoned settlements, through which he passed, presented a melancholy spectacle. On the 4th of August, when within four days march of Fort Pitt, he was attacked on Bushy run by the Indians, in great force. After two days of severe fighting, in which the Colonel displayed great military tact and coolness, the Indians were defeated, and the troops reached the fort without further interruption. The winter, following his visits to Fort Pitt, the Indians again obstructed and way-laid the road across the mountains, rendering all intercourse very dangerous. The next summer a plan was set on foot by the Governor of Pennsylvania, for invading the territory of the Indians north-west of the Ohio River, being the first attempt to attack them in that region ever made by the English colonists. The larger portion of the operations of this campaign having taken place within the territory now embraced in the state of Ohio, they become more interesting and valuable to the historical society. The volume, which contains the history of this campaign, was published in London, in the year 1766, and has now become scarce and difficult to procure. It is accompanied by the map of the country traversed, on which is delineated the location of the old forts and Indian towns. A sketch of the route and camping grounds of the army is also given, drawn by Thomas Hutchins, assistant engineer, who it seems accompanied the expedition. Plans of the order of march and of encamping are also given, which go to show that Colonel Bouquet was a commander of no ordinary military attainments. A copy of the map has been taken, and is presented to the society with these historical papers.

Colonel Henry Bouquet

Extracts from the history of Colonel Bouquets expedition into the Indian towns north-west of the river Ohio, in the year 1764.

This expedition was placed under the command of Colonel Bouquet, and consisted of fifteen hundred men. At the same time a detachment of men under Colonel Bradstreet was to make an inroad upon the towns on the southern shore of Lake Erie. Although the bill for raising the troops was passed in May, it was as late as August before they left Carlisle and the 17th of September when they arrived at Fort Pitt. While at Fort Loudon, east of the mountains, Colonel Bouquet received dispatches from Colonel Bradstreet, dated Presque Isle, August 14th, acquainting him that he had effected a treaty of peace with the Delaware and Shawnee Indians; but Colonel Bouquet at once decided, that no faith was to be put in their promises, and prepared to press onward. About the time he reached Fort Pitt, ten Indians appeared on the north side of the Ohio River, and desired a talk.

This was taken by the Colonel as a stratagem to enable them to ascertain his number, &c. Three of them at length came over to the fort; and as they could give no satisfactory reason for their visit, he detained them as spies, while their associates fled back to their towns. On the 20th of September, one of the captive Indians was sent with a talk to the hostile tribes, in which they were told that their duplicity with Colonel Bradstreet was understood, and that no mercy would be shown them unless they now came forward and complied with his just requisitions. *"First"*, he said to them, *"you are to leave the path open for my expresses from here to Detroit. And as I am now to send two men with dispatches to Colonel Bradstreet, who commands on the lakes, I desire to know whether you will send two of your people with them, to bring them safe back with an answer? If they receive any injury, or the letters are taken from them, I will immediately put to death the Indians now in my power, and will show no mercy hereafter to any of your nation that may fall into my hands. I allow you ten days to have my letters delivered at Detroit, and ten more to bring me back an answer."*

On the 1st of October, an Oneida and a Seneca Indian came to Fort Pitt, pretending friendship, and endeavored to dissuade the Colonel from proceeding against the Indians. As a particular reason, they urged upon him the small number of his army, and that if he would wait a little time; all the Indians would come and make peace with him. As to the spies he held captive, they said if he would let them go it would much expedite peace, and the coming in of the nations for that end. This was too weak a web to catch such old flies as Colonel Bouquet. He told them, no dependence was to be placed in the promises of the Delawares and Shawnee; that he should proceed forthwith to Tuscarawas, where if they had anything to say, he would hear them.

Order of March.

Colonel Bouquet, having at length with great difficulty collected his troops, formed his magazines, and provided for the safety of the posts he was to leave behind him, was ready, on the 2d of October, to proceed from Fort Pitt, with about fifteen hundred men, including drivers and other necessary followers of the camp. As a just idea of the conduct of this expedition, and the great caution taken to prevent surprise, will be best obtained from the *Order of March,* we shall insert it, with an accurate draught, taken from *actual surveys,* of the road and adjacent country through which the army passed.

In his address to the troops, he expressed the greatest confidence in their bravery, and told them that the distance to the enemy's towns, with the clearing of roads to them, must necessarily require considerable time; that in those deserts they had no other supplies to expect but the provisions and ammunition they carried with them; and that therefore the utmost care and frugality would be necessary in the use of them. He published the severest penalties against those who should be found guilty of stealing or embezzling any part of them.

The Order of march was as follows:

A corps of Virginia volunteers advanced in front, detaching three scouting parties — one of them furnished with a guide, marched in the center path, which the army was to follow. The other two extended themselves in a line abreast, on the right and left of the aforesaid party, to reconnoiter the woods. Under cover of this corps the axe men, consisting of all the artificers, and two companies of light infantry, followed in three divisions, under the direction of the chief engineer, to clear three different paths in which the troops and the convoy followed, viz: The front face of the square, composed of part of the forty-second regiment, marched in a column, two deep in the center path. The right face of the square, composed of the remainder of the forty-second and of the sixtieth regiment, marched in a single file in the right hand path. The first battalion of Pennsylvanians composed the left face, marching in like manner in the path to the left of the center. The corps of reserve, composed of two platoons of grenadiers, followed the right and left faces of the square. The second battalion of Pennsylvanians formed the rear face of the square, and followed the corps of reserve, each in a single file, on the right and left hand paths; all these troops covering the convoy, which moved in the center path. A party of light horsemen marched behind the rear face of the square, followed by another corps of Virginia volunteers, forming the rear guard. The Pennsylvania volunteers, dividing themselves equally, and marching in a single file, at a proper distance, flanked the right and left faces of the square. The ammunition and tools were placed in the rear of the first column, or front face of the square, followed by the officers' baggage and tents. The oxen and sheep came after the baggage, in separate droves, properly guarded. The provisions came next to the baggage, in four divisions, or brigades of pack horses, each conducted by a horse master. The troops were ordered to observe the most profound silence, and the men to march at two yards distance from one another. When the line or any part of it halted, the, whole were to face outward; and if attacked on their march, they were to halt immediately, ready to form the square when ordered. The light horse was then to march into the square, with the cattle, provisions, ammunition and baggage. Dispositions were also made in case of attack at night.

"These arrangements being made, the army decamped from Fort Pitt, on Wednesday, October 3d, and marched about one mile and a half, over a rich and level country, with stately timber, to camp No. 2, — a strong piece of ground, pleasantly situated, with plenty of water and food for the cattle.

"Thursday, October 4th. Having proceeded about two miles, they came to the Ohio River, at the beginning of the narrows, and from thence followed the course of the river along a flat gravelly beach, about six miles and a quarter, with two islands on their left, the lowest about six miles long, with a rising ground running across, and gently sloping on both sides to its banks, which are high and upright. At the lower end of this island the army left the river, marching through good land, broken into small hollows, to camp No. 3, — this day's march being nine miles and a quarter.

"Friday, October 5th. In this day's march the army passed through Logstown, situated seventeen and a half miles, fifty-seven perches, by the path, from Fort Pitt. This place was noted before the last war, for the great trade carried on there by the English and French; but its inhabitants, the Shawnee and Delawares, abandoned it in the year 1750. The lower town extended about sixty perches over a rich bottom to the foot of a low ridge on the summit, of which, near the declivity, stood the upper town commanding a most agreeable prospect over the lower, and quite across the Ohio, which is about five hundred yards wide here, and by its majestic, easy current, adds much to the beauty of the place. Proceeding beyond Logstown, through a fine country, interspersed with hills and rich valleys, watered by many rivulets, and covered with stately timber, they came to camp No. 4, on a level piece of ground, with a thicket in the rear, a small precipice round the front, with a run of water at the foot, and good food for cattle. This day's march was nine miles, one half, and fifty three perches.

"Saturday, October 6th. At about three miles distant from this camp, they came again to the Ohio. Pursuing its course half a mile further, and then turning off, over a steep ridge, they crossed Big Beaver Creek, which is twenty perches wide, the ford strong and pretty deep. It runs through a rich vale, with a pretty strong current; its banks high; the upland adjoining it very good; the timber tall and young. About a mile below its confluence with the Ohio stood formerly a large town, on a steep bank, built by the French, of square logs, with stone chimneys, for some of the Shawnee, Delaware and Mingo tribes, who abandoned it in the year 1758, when the French deserted Fort Du Quesne. Near the fording of Beaver Creek also stood about seven houses, which were deserted and destroyed by the Indians, after their defeat at Bushy Run, (1763,) when they forsook all their remaining settlements in this part of the country.

"About two miles before the army came to Beaver Creek, one of our people, who had been made prisoners by six Delawares about a week before, near Fort Bedford, made his escape from them, and came and informed the Colonel, that these Indians had the day before fallen in with the army, but kept themselves concealed, being surprised at our numbers. Two miles beyond Beaver Creek, by two small springs, was seen the skull of a child, that had been fixed on a pole by the Indians. The tracks of fifteen Indians were this day discovered. The camp No. 5 is seven miles, one quarter, and fifty seven perches from Big Beaver Creek; the whole march of this day, being about twelve miles.

"Sunday, October 7th. Passing a high ridge, they had a fine prospect of an extensive country on the right, which in general appeared level, with abundance of tall timber. The camp No. 6 lies at the foot of a steep descent, in a rich valley, on a strong ground; three sides thereof surrounded by a hollow and on the fourth side a small hill, which was occupied by a detached guard. This day's march was six miles, sixty-five perches.

"Monday, October 8th. The army crossed Little Beaver Creek and one of its branches. This creek is eight perches wide, with a good ford; the country about it interspersed with hills, rivulets, and rich valleys, like that described above. Camp No. 7 lies by a small run on the side of a hill, commanding the ground about it, and is distant eleven miles, one quarter, and forty-nine perches from the last encampment.

"Tuesday, October 9th. In this day's march, the path divided into two branches; that to the southwest leading to the lower towns upon the Muskingum. In the forks of the path stand several trees, painted by the Indians, in a hieroglyphic manner, denoting the number of wars in which they had been engaged, and the particulars of their success, in prisoners and scalps. The camp No. 8 lies on a run, and level piece of ground, with Yellow Creek close on the left, and a rising ground near the rear of the right face. The path, after the army left the forks, was so brushy and entangled, that they were obliged to cut all the way before them, and also to lay several bridges, in order to make it passable for the horses; so that this day they proceeded only five miles, three quarters, and seventy perches.

"Wednesday, October 10th. Marched one mile, with Yellow Creek on the left at a small distance, all the way, and crossed it at a good ford, fifty feet wide; proceeding through an alternate succession of small hills, and rich vales, finely watered with rivulets, to camp No. 9,— seven miles, and sixty perches in the whole.

"Thursday, October 11th. Crossed a branch of Muskingum River about fifty feet wide; the country much the same as that described above; discovering a good deal of free stone. The camp No. 10 had this branch of the river parallel to its left face, and lies ten miles, one quarter, and forty perches from the former encampment.

"Friday, October 12th. Keeping the aforesaid creek on their left, they marched through much fine land, watered with small rivers and springs; proceeding likewise through several savannahs or cleared spots, which are by nature extremely beautiful; the second which they passed being, in particular, one continued plain of near two miles, with a fine rising ground forming a semicircle round the right hand side, and a pleasant stream of water at about a quarter of a mile distant on the left. The camp No. 11 has the above mentioned branch of Muskingum on the left, and is distant ten miles and three quarters from the last encampment.

"Saturday, October 13th. Crossed Ne-men-she-he-las Creek, about fifty feet wide, a little above where it empties itself into the aforesaid branch of Muskingum, having in their way a pleasant prospect over a large plain, for near two miles on the left. A little further they came to another small river, which they crossed, about fifty perches above where it empties into the said branch of the Muskingum. Here a high ridge on the right and the creek close on the left, form a narrow defile about seventy perches long. Passing afterwards over a very rich bottom, they came to the main branch of the Muskingum, about seventy yards wide, with a good ford. A little below, and above the forks of this river, is Tuscarawas, a place exceedingly beautiful by situation, the lands rich on both sides of the river; the country on the north-west side being an entire level plain, upwards of five miles in circumference. From the ruined houses appearing here, the Indians, who once inhabited the place, and are now with the Delawares, are supposed to have had about one hundred and fifty warriors. This camp, No. 12, is distant eight miles, nineteen perches from the former making ninety one miles, one quarter and thirty-six perches from Fort Pitt to this camp on the Muskingum River.

"Sunday, October 14th. The army remained in camp; and two men, who had been dispatched by Colonel Bouquet from Fort Pitt, with letters for Colonel Bradstreet, returned and reported: That within a few miles of this place, they had been made prisoners by the Delawares, and carried to one of their towns sixteen miles from hence where they were kept till the savages, knowing of the arrival of the army here, set them at liberty; ordering them to acquaint the Colonel that the head men of the Delawares and Shawnee, were coming as soon as possible to treat of peace with them.

"Monday, October 15th. The army moved two miles and forty perches further down the Muskingum, to camp No. 13, formed by a very high bank, with the river at the foot of it, which is upwards of one hundred yards wide at this place, with a fine level country, at some distance from its banks, producing stately timber, free from underwood, and plenty of food for cattle. The site of this camp is probably the spot where Fort Laurens was built, by General McIntosh, in the year 1778.

"The next day, six Indians came to inform the Colonel that all their chiefs were assembled about eight miles from the camp and were ready to treat with him of peace, which they were earnestly desirous of obtaining. He told them he would meet them the next day in a bower, at some distance from the camp. In the mean time, he ordered a small stockade fort to be built, to deposit provisions for the use of the troops on their return, and to lighten the convoy.

"Wednesday, October 17th. The Colonel, with most of the regular troops, Virginia Volunteers and Light Horse marched from the camp to the bower erected for the congress. As soon as the troops were stationed so as to appear to the best advantage, the Indians arrived and were conducted to the bower. Being seated, they began to smoke their pipe, or calumet, agreeable to their custom. This ceremony being over, their speakers laid down their pipes, and opened their pouches, wherein were their strings and belts of wampum. The Indians present were of the Senecas, Kyashuta chief, and fifteen warriors; Delawares, Custaloga, chief of the Wolf tribe, and Beaver, chief of the Turkey tribe, with twenty warriors; Shawnee, Ke-issinaucht-ha, chief, and six warriors. The purport of their speeches was that of making excuses for their late treachery and misconduct, throwing the blame on the rashness of their young men, and the nations living to the west of them; and suing for peace in the most abject manner, and promising severally to deliver up all their prisoners. After they had concluded, the Colonel promised to give them an answer the next day, and then dismissed them, the army returning to the camp. The badness of the weather, however, prevented his meeting them again until the 20th, when he spoke to them in substance as follows: "He recapitulated the many instances of their former perfidy; their killing or captivating the traders who had been sent among them at their own request and plundering their effects; their attacking Fort Pitt, which had been built with their express consent; their murdering four men who had been sent on a public message to them, thus violating the customs held sacred among all nations, however barbarous; their attacking the King's troops last year in the woods, and after being defeated in that attempt, falling upon our frontiers, where they continued to murder our people to this day." Many more things he also said, and concluded by telling them: *"I give you twelve days from this date to deliver into my hands, at Wakatomica, all the prisoners in your possession, without any exception; and you are to furnish them with clothing, provisions and horses, to carry them to Fort Pitt."*

The firm manner in which the Colonel addressed them, with the sight of the army that had so severely defeated them at Bushy Run the preceding year, now advanced into the heart of their country, had a powerful effect in subduing the spirits of these haughty savages. The two Delaware Chiefs, at the close of their speech on the 17th, delivered up eighteen white prisoners, and eighty-three small sticks, expressing the number of other prisoners which they had in their possession, and promised to bring in as soon as possible. None of the Shawnee kings appeared at the Congress, and Ke-issi-nautcht-ha, their deputy, declined speaking until the Colonel had answered the

Delawares, and then, with a dejected sullenness, he promised in behalf of his nation that they would submit to the terms prescribed to the other tribes.

The Colonel, however, determined to march further into their country, knowing that the presence of his army would be the best security for the performance of their promises, and required some of each nation to attend him in his march.

Thursday, October 25th. They marched six miles, one half, and sixteen perches, to camp No. 16, situated within a mile of the forks of Muskingum. This place was fixed upon instead of Wakatomica, as the most central and convenient place to receive the prisoners; for the principal Indian towns now lay around them, at the distance of seven to twenty miles, except only the lower Shawnee town, situated on Scioto River, which was about eighty miles; so that from this place the army had it in their power to destroy their towns, if they failed to fulfill their promises. Four redoubts were built here, opposite to the four angles of the camp. The ground in front was cleared; a store house for the provisions erected, and likewise a house to receive and treat of peace with the Indians, when they should return.

Three houses, with separate apartments, were also built for the reception of the captives of the respective colonies, and proper officers appointed to take charge of them, with a matron to attend the women and children. So that, with the officer's mess houses, ovens, &c, this camp had the appearance of a little town, in which the greatest order and regularity prevailed.

Soon after these preparations were made, viz, on Saturday, October 27, Custaloga sent a messenger that he was coming with his prisoners. The next day "Peter," the Caughnewauga chief, and twenty Indians arrived, of that nation, from Sandusky, with a letter from Colonel Bradstreet. The Caughnewauga reported that the Indians on the lakes had delivered but few of their prisoners. That the Ottawas had killed a great part of theirs; and the other nations had either done the same, or else kept them. Colonel Bouquet kept so steadfastly to this article of having every prisoner delivered, that when the Delaware kings, Beaver and Custaloga, had brought in all theirs except twelve, which they promised to bring in a few days, he refused to shake hands, or have the least talk with them, while a single captive remained among them.

By the 9th of November, most of the prisoners were arrived that could be expected this season, amounting to two hundred and six in the whole, besides about one hundred more in possession of the Shawnee, which they promised to deliver the following spring. The prisoners were from the following colonies: Virginia, thirty-two men and fifty-eight women and children; Pennsylvania, forty-nine men and sixty-seven women and children.

The same day the Colonel, attended by most of the principal officers, went to the council house. The Senecas and Delawares were first treated with. Kyashuta and ten warriors represented the former; Custaloga and twenty warriors the latter.

Kyashuta said, *"With this string of wampum, we wipe the tears from your eyes; we deliver you these three prisoners, which are the last of your flesh and blood that remained among the Seneca and Custaloga tribe of Delawares. We gather together and bury with this belt all the bones of the people that have been killed during this unhappy war, which the evil spirit occasioned among us. We cover the bones that have been buried that they may be never more remembered. We again cover their places with leaves that it may be no more seen. As we have been long astray, and the path between you and us stopped, we extend this belt that it may be again cleared, and we may travel in peace to see our brethren, as our ancestors formerly did. While you hold it fast by one end, and we by the other, we shall always be able to discover anything that may disturb our friendship."*

In reply, Colonel Bouquet said, *"The peace you ask for you shall have, and much more, he added; among which, that as all the prisoners could not be delivered there, he would have two hostages put into his hands by the Senecas, and two for Custaloga's tribe, as security for the return of the rest of the captives, to be kept at Fort Pitt."*

The Colonel, after promising to deliver back two of their people, Captain Pipe and Captain John, whom he had detained at Fort Pitt, took the chiefs by the hand for the first time, which gave them great joy.

November 10th. They had another conference with the Turkey and Turtle tribes of Delawares; King Beaver, their chief, and thirty warriors, represented the former, and Kelappama, brother to their chief, with twenty-five warriors, the latter. (note—The chief of the Turtle tribe, for some reason, chose to absent himself.)

November 11th. King Beaver presented five hostages to remain with Colonel Bouquet, and five deputies to treat with Sir William Johnson. This day he acquainted the chiefs present that as he had great reason to be dissatisfied with Nettowhatways, chief of the Turtle tribe, who had not appeared, he therefore deposed him, and that tribe were to choose and present another for his approbation. This they did a few days afterwards. Their submitting to this indignity clearly shows to what a degree of humiliation they were reduced. The 12th of November was appointed for the conference with them. The Shawnee were represented by seven chiefs and forty warriors. The Caughnewauga, Seneca and Delaware chiefs, and sixty warriors, were also present. The Red Hawk was their speaker, and delivered himself with a strange mixture of fierce pride and humble submission; but, as the events of the campaign are the principal things to be preserved for history, his speech is not copied. Red Hawk promised for his people, that they should in the spring bring their prisoners to Fort Pitt. That they could not before, as they had gone to a great distance to hunt, and would not return until then. He then produced the copy of a treaty held with the government of Pennsylvania in 1701, and three messages or letters from the same, of different dates, and concluded thus: *"Now, brothers, I beg we who are warriors may forget our disputes, and renew the friendship which appears by these papers to have subsisted between our fathers."*

The writer then describes the interesting scene of the delivery of the prisoners, and their meeting with their friends and relatives:

"It is impossible to paint the various scenes of joy, and sorrow, horror and disappointment, and all the most tender passions, which appeared on this occasion. Fathers and mothers recognizing their once lost infants — husbands hanging round the necks of their newly found wives — sisters and brothers unexpectedly meeting together, after a long separation, scarce able to speak the same language, or for some time to be sure that they were children of the same parents — others flying from place to place, in eager inquiries after relations not found, and trembling to receive an answer to their questions! Distracted with doubts, hopes and fears on obtaining no account of those they sought or stiffened with horror on learning their unhappy fate!

The Indians, too, as if wholly forgetting their usual savageness, bore a capital part in heightening these most affecting scenes. They delivered up their beloved captives with the utmost reluctance, shed torrents of tears over them, recommending them to the care and protection of the commanding officer, and continuing their regard to them all the time they remained in camp. They visited them from day to day, brought them what corn, skins, horses and other matters they had bestowed on them while in their families; accompanied with other presents, and all the marks of the most sincere and tender affection. Nay they did not stop here, but when the army marched, some of the Indians solicited and obtained leave to accompany their former captives all the way to Fort Pitt and employed themselves in hunting and bringing provisions for them on the road. A young Mingo went still further, and gave an instance of love, which would make a figure even in romance. He had taken so great a liking to a Virginian young woman, who was among the captives, as to call her his wife. Against all remonstrance of the imminent danger to which he exposed himself by approaching the frontiers, he persisted in following her at the risk of being killed by the surviving relations of many unfortunate persons, who had been captivated or scalped by those of this nation! Among the children who had been carried off young, and had long lived with the Indians, it is not to be expected that any marks of joy would appear on being restored to their parents or relations. Having been accustomed to look upon the Indians as the only connexion they had; having been tenderly treated by them and speaking their language, it is no wonder that they considered their new state in the light of captivity, and parted from the savages with tears. But it must not be denied that there were even some grown persons who showed an unwillingness to return. The Shawnee were obliged to bind several of their prisoners, and force them along to the camp; and some women who had been delivered up afterwards found means to escape, and run back to the Indian towns. Some who could not make their escape clung to their savage acquaintances at parting, and continued in bitter lamentations, even refusing sustenance."*

* Bouquet left the camp near the forts of Muskingum, the 18th November, and reached Fort Pitt on the 28th. Here ended the expedition, in which it is remarkable that the troops never suffered for necessaries, continuing healthy during the whole campaign, in which no life was lost, except the man who was killed at Muskingum. The Colonel received the thanks of the legislative councils of the colonies of Virginia and Pennsylvania.

The following extract from the speech of the Shawnee chief, Lawaughqua, on delivering his prisoners, is a strong proof of what is above observed concerning their tenderness and affection for the captives whom they had preserved:

"Father", says he to the English, *"we have brought your flesh and blood to you. They have been all united to us by adoption; and although we now deliver them, we will always look upon them as our relations, whenever the Great Spirit is pleased that we may visit them. We have taken as much care of them as if they were our own flesh and blood. They are now become unacquainted with your customs and manners, and therefore we request you to use them tenderly and kindly, which will induce them to live contentedly with you."*

The above speech was made at Fort Pitt, the 9th of May, 1765, following the campaign, when they delivered over the rest of their prisoners in accordance with their agreement. On this occasion ten of the Shawnee Chiefs, with fifty warriors, attended with many of their women and children; a large number of the Delaware, Seneca, Sandusky, and other Indians, were also present. George Croghan, Esq., deputy agent of Sir William Johnson, was appointed to receive them from the hands of the savages. Here they brightened the chain of friendship, and gave every assurance of their intention to preserve the peace inviolable. Many interesting speeches were made on this occasion, which we believe have never been published, and were found in manuscript, among the papers of Colonel George Morgan, who acted as Indian agent for several years, during the war of the revolution, at Fort Pitt.

At this time it was remarked that the Indians called the English fathers, instead of brothers, as formerly. Several pages of the manuscript, containing the opening of the treaty, and the proceedings of the first day, are lost and torn. The sound part commences with the close of a speech by Lawaughqua, a Shawnee chief:

"Father—We will now comply with everything you have asked of us, and assure you that we are sincere in everything we have said. Here is a belt, with the figure of our father, the King of Great Britain, at one end, and the Chief of our nation at the other. This represents them holding the chain of friendship, and we hope that neither side will slip their hands from it, so long as the sun and moon give light." [A belt of seven rows.]

Custaloga, speaker for the Delawares :

"Brethren—Yesterday you put us in mind of our engagements to Col. Bouquet; we now assure you we are ready to perform every part which we have not yet complied with." [A string.]

"Brother—You desire we may again leave hostages at this place, and send other deputies to Sir William Johnson; this we will likewise do." [A string.]

He then addressed himself to the six nations:

"Uncles — Yesterday you desired us to be strong in complying with what our brethren the English might require of us. This we are determined to do, and hope you will also do everything on your parts to forward a good peace." [A belt.]

"Brother — (Addressing himself to Col. Croghan,) *as you told us you were ordered to visit the western nations, I now wipe your eyes and open your ears that you may see and hear those nations with pleasure when they speak to you. I likewise clear the way that you may have a safe passage to the place you are going."* [A belt.]

"Brother—Don't imagine that what I have said comes from my lips only; I assure you it proceeds from the bottom of our hearts; and now by this belt I remove every evil thing from your heart, and make it like those of our ancestors when they thought of nothing but peace; and I also wipe the outside of your body clean, that not the least remains of anything which might give you trouble may ever again appear; and by this belt we take fast hold of you our brethren in peace."

[Delivered a friendship belt of twenty rows, with the figure of two men, representing the English and themselves.]

Kyashuta then spoke to the Delawares:

"Nephews—You told us, your uncles, the six nations, that you were determined to do everything that was requested of you by us, and our brethren the English. We are glad to hear you are come to such a resolution, and we desire you to be strong and do so." [A string.]

"Kyashuta, addressing himself to us:

"Brethren, — I am going now to speak to you in behalf of all the nations present, and those to the sun-setting. You told us yesterday, that the General and Sir William Johnson ordered you to assure all the nations to the sun setting, that if they performed their engagements, we should enjoy a free trade and intercourse. I hope this comes from your heart, as you see your brethren the Delawares, and your children, the Shawnee, are willing to comply with everything you required of them. Now do not act as you have done for a year or two before these late troubles, when you prohibited the sale of powder, lead and rum. This conduct gave all the nations in this country a suspicion that you had designs against them; and was contrary to your first promises when you come here to settle and build this fort on our ground. You make rum and have taught us to drink it. You are fond of it yourselves, therefore don't deprive us of it, or the liberty of purchasing goods. Open the trade and let us sell our skins, which we have brought here for that purpose, otherwise we must think you speak from your lips and not from your hearts." [A belt.]

"Brethren — When you first came to drive the French from this place, the governor of Pennsylvania sent us a message, that we should withdraw from the French and that when the English were settled here, we should want for nothing. It's true you did supply us very well, but it was only when the war was doubtful; and as soon as you conquered the French, you did not care how you treated us, as you then did not think us worth your notice. We request you may not again treat us in the same manner, but now open the trade; and do not put us off by telling us you must first hear from your great man before it can be done. If you have but little goods, let us have them for our skins; and let us have some of your rum, or we cannot trust on what you tell us for the future." [A large belt.]

He then added that he did not speak for himself, but was appointed by all the nations present, and that what he said was the sentiments of the whole.

"Kyashuta spoke to the Delawares, on behalf of the English and six nations, giving them an invitation to return to their old settlements, at the same time desiring them to hold fast by the chain of friendship subsisting between the English and six nations." [A belt.]

"Then Ogista, an old Seneca Indian, spoke to the Shawnee, and invited them to return to their old settlements, where they would be near their father, the English, and their brethren, the Six Nations." [A belt.]

At a meeting with the same Indians, Fort Pitt, May 11th, 1765:

Present — Captain William Murray, and several officers of the garrison.

Brethren, of the Six Nations, Shawnees, Delawares, and Sandusky Indians —

"You yesterday answered the several speeches I delivered you the day before, from his Excellency, General Gage; and you have agreed to comply with everything he desired of you. Brethren, you have done right, in complying with the General's requests, and you may be assured, I will represent your readiness on this occasion to Sir William Johnson in a proper manner."

"Brethren—When first your brethren, the English, settled here, they kindled a council fire for all the nations of Indians to the sun-setting; but for two years past this fire has been neglected, and was near going out. Now brethren, I put some good dry wood on your council fire, that it may blaze up to the sky, so that all nations may see it, and come here to smoke with their brethren, the English, in peace."

"Brethren — Now I have kindled your council fire, and made it burn clear, I again with this belt disperse all the dark clouds that have been hanging over your heads for some time past, that you may see the sun clear."

"Brethren — You have now appointed a deputation to go to Sir William Johnson, of your several nations, to confirm a lasting peace as you promised Colonel Bouquet, last fall. You have made a good choice. I am well acquainted with your tribes, and I know those to be chiefs and men of consequence in your nation, and approve of them; therefore, brethren, I now make the road smooth and easy to their feet, and remove any logs that may have fallen across it that you may travel safe to Sir William Johnson."

"Brethren, the Shawnees — You yesterday delivered to Captain Murray and me a number of our own people, agreeable to your promises, and say the

few remaining, which were out a hunting, should be brought here as soon as possible. Your conduct in this is very agreeable, and convinces us of your sincerity; and you may be assured I will represent it properly to the General and Sir William Johnson; and I desire you will as soon as possible bring in those you left behind."

"Brethren — Yesterday you made two speeches concerning our past conduct in trade. I must observe to you, that had we a mind to recapitulate injuries, we could convince you that we have much more reason to complain of your conduct, than you have of ours; but we have thrown away from our remembrance everything that gave us any trouble, and I hope your future conduct will give us no reason to repeat past offences. And to convince you of our sincerity, the commanding officer here, although he has no orders for it, will take upon himself to open the trade and suffer you to purchase such necessaries as are here, which is but little, owing to your own backwardness in not coming here earlier in the spring, as you promised; but as soon as the General is made acquainted with your conduct at this meeting, he will order out traders to supply you with all the necessaries you may want."

"Brethren — You desire that rum maybe sold to you. The traders here have none; but as soon as you have sold your peltry and are setting out for your own country, Captain Murray will make you a present of some."

"Brethren — I have now finished everything I had to say to you, only to acquaint you that the General, willing to convince you of the sincerity he has towards you, has ordered Captain Murray and me, on your complying with what he ordered me to require of you, to make you a present of goods to clothe your women and children, which we now deliver to your several tribes."

After the presents were delivered, Kyashuta spoke to the Delawares and Shawnees:

"Nephews, the Delawares, and younger brother, the Shawnees — You have now heard everything your father, the English, had to say to you, and as you have answered them, that you will comply with everything, be strong. We have appointed deputies to go to Sir William Johnson, and men to attend George Croghan on his journey. Here is one of our chiefs who is to stay here with his family to assist our brethren, the English, in council."

Then he addressed himself to Captain Murray and me, and appointed the chief, saying this is the man appointed to stay here until our return.

Then Custaloga spoke to the Six Nations in behalf of the Delawares:

"Uncles — You yesterday desired us to return to our old settlements and live in peace with our fathers, the English. This I assure you we will do; and you shall see us kindle our fires again at our old places." [Gave a belt.]

Then addressing himself to the English:

"Fathers—I must now call you. It's your desire that we appoint deputies. This is done, and we send such men as are best acquainted with the affairs of our nation."

Here ends the transactions at this treaty, and immediately after commences the journal of Colonel George Croghan, kept during his journey to the western tribes, and his interview with the governor or commandant at Detroit. As this was the first visit of the kind since the country came into the possession of the English, it is well worth preserving, not only as a matter of history, but also to show the strong attachment of all the western tribes to their old favorites, the French.

CHAPTER IV.

Journal of George Croghan, deputy Indian agent, while on a friendly visit to the western tribes. — Leaves Fort Pitt.— Arrives at the mouth of the Scioto.— Shawnees deliver up seven French traders.—Arrives at the mouth of the Ouabache——Encamps seven miles below, and is attacked in the night by the Kickapoo Indians.— Arrives at Post Vincent.— Reaches the Kickapoo town. —Meets an assembly of the western tribes, with the chief, Pontiac, at Weotonan.—Proceeds to Detroit.—The Ottowas and Twightwee Indians give up English prisoners.— A treaty held with the Indians at Detroit, and speeches made.—Intrigues of the French with the Indians.—Fort Chartres occupied by Captain Sterling, with part of the 42d regiment.—The Indians of the St. Joseph River make speeches to Croghan and Campbell.— Close of the journal.—Croghan arrives at Fort Stanwix.— His letter to Sir William Johnson, with his views of the policy towards the Indians, best to be pursued by the English.

"May 15. Set off from Fort Pitt and encamped at Schertree's Island. (Probably Chartier's Island)

"May 16th. Being joined by the several deputies that were to accompany me, we set off at seven o'clock in the morning.

"May 19th. I sent a message to the Shawnees, by land, for some of them to bring to me the French traders that yet remained in their country, to the mouth of the Scioto, that I might take them with me to their own country, as they were not suffered to trade there, until they had obtained permission from his Excellency General Gage and Sir William Johnson.

"May 23d. We arrived at the mouth of Scioto, where we encamped.

"May 26th. Several of the Shawnees came there, and brought with them seven French traders, which they delivered to me, those being all that resided in their villages; and told me there was yet six more living with the Delawares; that on their return to their towns they would go to the Delawares and get them to send those French traders home; and told me they were determined to do everything in their power to convince me of their sincerity and good disposition to preserve a peace.

"May 28th. We set off down the river, and on the 6th of June, we arrived at the mouth of the Ouabache, where we found a breast work put up by the Indians, and saw several trails which we suspected had been made by some Indians who might have been sent there to way-lay us; on which we proceeded six miles lower down the river and encamped.

"June 7th. I dispatched two Indians off to the Illinois, with a letter to Mr. Fraser, and another to Mr. St. Ange, by which I acquainted Mr. Fraser of my success in settling matters with the different nations at Fort Pitt. I furnished those two deputies with wampum to acquaint the nations there of what had passed at Fort Pitt, which I judged necessary in order to facilitate the good of the service, should Mr. La Guetrie be arrived there.

"June 8th. At day-break we were attacked by a party of eighty warriors of the Kickapoo and Musquatomie, who killed three of the Shawnee deputies, and wounded another. Two of my men were killed. They then plundered us of everything we had, our Indians as well as us, and then made us prisoners. After this, they told us they were sorry for what had happened; that they had been employed by the French, their fathers, who had told them it was Cherokees who were with me, and that there was no peace made with the Shawnees, Delawares, and Six Nations. They then set the Indian prisoners at liberty, taking me and my party with them.

"June 15th. We arrived at Post Vincent, where there is a French village of about eighty houses, and an Indian village of the Pyankeshas. Here I met several Indians whom I had been acquainted with, who spoke to the party I was with, and desired them to take great care of me, until the chiefs of the several nations would return from the Illinois, where they had gone in order to meet me, and reprimanded this party for their bad conduct. Here I was informed by the French, of the arrival of M. La Guetrie and M. Sinnott, at the Illinois, with an account of the ill treatment Mr. Fraser had met with, and likewise of the ill reception Mr. Sinnott met with on his arrival there.

"June 16th. The Indians allowed me to write to Mr. St. Ange, but would not suffer me to send a letter to Mr. Sinnott; nor could I get any Frenchman in that town to furnish me with pen, ink or paper, without the consent of the Indians.

"June 17th. We set off, and on the 23d arrived at the Weotonan, where this party had set out from. On my arrival at this place, I met numbers of Indians with whom I was formerly well acquainted, and who were extremely civil to me and my party.

"June 30th. The several chiefs belonging to those villages at Weotonan arrived from the Illinois, and there were with them the chiefs of several other nations, who came to see me, and expressed their great concern at what had happened.

"July 1st. A Frenchman arrived from the Illinois with a pipe and speech, from thence to the Kickapoos and Musquatamies, to have me burnt. This speech was said to be sent from a Shawnee Indian, who resides at the Illinois, and has been during the war, and is much attached to the French interest. As soon as the speech was delivered to the Indians, by the French, the Indians informed me of it in council, and expressed their great concern for what had already happened, and told me they then set me and my people at liberty, and assured me they despised the message sent them, and would return the pipe and belt to their fathers, the French, and inquire into the reason of such a message being sent them, by one of his messengers; and desired me to stay with them until the deputies of the Six Nations, Shawnees and Delawares, arrived with Pontiac at Weotonan, in order to settle matters; to which I consented.

"On the 4th, 5th, 6th, 7th, and 8th June, I had several conferences with the Waweotonans, Pyankeshas, Kickapoos, and Musquatamies, in which conferences I was lucky enough to reconcile these nations to his Majesty's interest, and obtain their consent and approbation to take possession of any posts in their country which the French formerly possessed, and an offer of their services, should any nation oppose our taking possession of it; all which they confirmed by four large pipes.

"July 11th. Mr. Maisonville arrived with an interpreter and a message to the Indians, to bring me and my party to the Illinois. Until then I had no answer from Mr. St. Ange to the letter I wrote him, of the 16th of June. As I wanted to go to the Illinois, I desired the chiefs to prepare themselves, and set off with me as soon as possible.

"July 12th. I wrote to General Gage and Sir William Johnson, to Colonel Campbell at Detroit, Major Murray at Fort Pitt, and Major Firmer on his way up the Mississippi, and acquainted them with everything that had happened since my departure from Fort Pitt.

"July 13th. The chiefs of the Twightwee came to me from the Miamis, and renewed their ancient friendship with his Majesty and all his subjects in America, and confirmed it with a pipe.

"18th. I set off for the Illinois with the chiefs of all those nations, when we met with the deputies of the Six Nations, Delawares and Shawnees, which accompanied Mr. Fraser and myself down the Ohio, with Pontiac, with speeches and deputies from the four nations living in the Illinois country, to me and the Six Nations, Delawares and Shawnees; on which we returned to Weotonan, and there held another conference, in which I settled all matters with the Illinois Indians. Pontiac and they agreed to everything the other nations had done, and confirmed it by pipes and belts ; but told me the French had informed them, that the English were intending to take their country from them and give it to the Cherokees to settle on ; and that if ever they suffered the English to take possession of their country, they would make slaves of them; that this was the reason of their opposing the English hitherto from taking possession of Fort Chartres,* and induced them to tell M. La Guetrie, and Mr. Sinnott, that they would not let the English come into their country ; but being informed, since Mr. Sinnott went away, by the deputies of the six nations, Delawares and Shawnees, that every difference subsisting between them and the English was now settled, they were willing to comply, as the other nations, their brethren, had done; and desired that their father, the king of England, might not look upon his taking possession of the forts which the French formerly possessed, to give his subjects a title to their country, as they never had sold any part of it to the French, and that I might rest satisfied that whenever the English came to take possession, they would receive them with open arms.

*FORT CHARTRES.

This fort was originally built by the French in the year 1720, to defend themselves against the Spaniards, who were then attempting to make settlements near the mouth of the Mississippi. The location was half a mile from the river, in the northwest corner of the present Randolph County, Illinois. It was rebuilt in 1756, and was said to be the most complete and perfect work of the kind in North America. The material was stone, laid up in regular masonry, with walls two feet thick and fifteen feet high. The form was an irregular quadrangle, four hundred and ninety feet in circumference. There were loop holes at intervals for musketry, with two port holes for cannon, in each face, and two in the flanks of each bastion. The entrance was through a handsome rustic gate. All the cornices and casements were of free-stone, worked smooth. Large buildings were erected within the walls for the accommodation of the officers and men, — with store-houses, &c., all of solid masonry. In 1765, when the English took possession of the country, it was in a perfect condition. The French Commander, Mons. De St. Ange, marched his troops to St. Louis and took the command of that post, from which time it became the capital of Upper Louisiana. Fort Chartres was the seat of government for Illinois, while under the French, and afterwards the head quarters of the English commanding officer for this region. In the village of Fort Chartres, there were forty French families, when ceded to King George, who all left the homes of their childhood and emigrated to St. Louis. For many years the fort has been in ruins, and the forest is fast regaining possession of the site. Kaskaskia was founded as early as 1690, by the French, on the right bank of the Kaskaskia River, four miles from the mouth."—*Hall's Sketches.*

"25th. I set off for Detroit, having settled everything with those several nations to the westward, and was accompanied by several chiefs of those nations, which were going to Detroit to meet Colonel Bradstreet, agreeable to his invitation to them last winter, by Mr. Maisonville. As I passed by the Twightwee villages and the Ottawa's villages, on the Miami River, they delivered me all the English prisoners they had, and I found, as I passed by those villages, that several of the Indians had set off for Detroit to meet Colonel Bradstreet.

"August 17th. I arrived at Detroit, where I found several small tribes of Ottawas, Pottawatomie, and Chippewas, waiting, in consequence of Colonel Bradstreet's invitation to see him. Here I met Mr. Dequanee and Waobecomica, with a deputation of Indians from Niagara, with messages from Sir William Johnson to Pontiac, and those western nations.

"23d. Colonel Campbell and I had a meeting with the Twightwee, Waweotonans, Pyankeshas, Kickapoos and Musquatamies; when they produced the several belts sent them by Colonel Bradstreet, in consequence of which invitation they came here. Then they spoke to the Six Nations, Delawares and Shawnees, on several pipes and belts, begging in the most abject manner, that they would forgive them for the ill conduct of their young men; to take pity on their women and children, and grant them peace.

They then spoke to the Colonel and me on several pipes and belts, expressing their great satisfaction at a firm and lasting peace being settled between their brethren, the English, and the several Indian nations in this country; that they saw the heavy cloud that hung over their heads for some time past was now dispersed, and that the sun shined clear and bright; and that as their father, the King of England, has conquered the French in this country, and taken under his protection all the Indian nations, they hoped for the future they would be a happy people; and that for the time to come, they should always call the English their fathers, and begged we would take pity on their women and children, and make up the difference subsisting between them and the Shawnees, Delawares and Six Nations; and said, as we are come here in consequence of Colonel Bradstreet's invitation, and that as he had not met them, they hoped their fathers would pity their necessity and give them a little clothing, and a little rum to drink on the road, as we have come a great way to see you, our fathers. Then the Wyandots spoke to the Shawnees and all the western nations, on several belts and strings, by which they exhorted the several nations to behave themselves well to their fathers, the English, who had now taken them under their protection; that if they did they would be a happy people; that if they did not listen to the councils of their fathers, they must take the consequences, having assured them that all nations to the sun rising had taken fast hold of their fathers, the English, by the hand, and would follow their advice, and do everything they desired them, and never would let slip the chain of friendship now so happily renewed.

"24th. We had another meeting with the several nations, when the Waweotonans, Twightwee, Pyankeshas, Kickapoos, and Musquatamies, made several speeches to Colonel Campbell and me, in presence of all the other nations, when they acknowledged themselves to be the children of the king of Great Britain; and further acknowledged that they had, at Weotonan, before they came here, given up the sovereignty of their country to me for his majesty, and promised to support his subjects in taking possession of all the posts given up by the French, their former fathers, to the English, now their present fathers; all which they confirmed with a belt.

"25th. We had another meeting with the same Indians, when Colonel Campbell and I made them several speeches in answer to theirs of the 23d and 24th. Then delivered them a road belt, in the name of Sir William Johnson, baronet, to open a road from the rising to the setting of the sun; which we charged them to keep open through their country, and cautioned them to stop their ears against the stories or idle reports of evil minded people, and continue to promote the good works of peace; all which they promised to do in a most sincere manner.

"26th. Colonel Campbell and I made those nations some presents, when, after taking leave of us, they set off for their own country, well satisfied.

"27th. We had a meeting with Pontiac and all the Ottawa tribes, Chippewas and Pottawatomie, with the Hurons of this place, and the chiefs of those settled at Sandusky and the Miami River, when we made them the following speeches —"

The speeches are brief, and relate chiefly to their keeping the peace in sincerity and good faith. On the following day, or the 28th August, they had another meeting with the Indians, when Pontiac made the following speech, which is worth preserving, as coming from so celebrated a man:

"Father — We have all smoked out of this pipe of peace. It is your children's pipe, and as the war is all over, and the Great Spirit and Giver of Light, who has made the earth, and everything therein, has brought us all together this day for our mutual good, to promote the good works of peace, I declare to all nations that I have settled my peace with you before I came here, and now deliver my pipe to be sent to Sir William Johnson, that he may know I have made peace, and taken the king of England for my father, in presence of all [the nations now assembled, and whenever any of those nations go to visit him, they may smoke out of it with him in peace. Fathers, we are obliged to you for lighting up our old council fire for us, and desiring us to return to it; but we are now settled on the Miami River, not far from hence; whenever you want us, you will find us there ready to wait on you. The reason why I choose to stay where we are now settled is, that we love liquor, and to be so near this as we formerly lived, our people would be always drunk, which might occasion some quarrels between the soldiers and our people. This, father, is all the reason I have for our not returning to our old settlements ; and where we live is so nigh this place, that when we want to drink, we can easily come for it. [Gave a large pipe, with a belt of wampum tied to it.]

"Father — Be strong and take pity on us, your children, as our former father did. It is just the hunting season of your children. Our fathers, the French, formerly used to credit his children, for powder and lead to hunt with. I request, in behalf of all the nations present, that you will speak to the traders now here, to do the same. My father, once more, I request that you tell your traders, to give your children credit for/a little powder and lead, as the support of our families depends upon it. We have told you where we live, not far from here, that whenever you want us, and let us know, we will come directly to you. [A belt.]

"Father—You have stopped up the rum barrel, when we came here, until the business of this meeting was over. As it is now finished, we request you may open the barrel that your children may drink and be merry."

There were present at this treaty about thirty chiefs and five hundred warriors. A list of the tribes is given, and the names of the chiefs. This was the last public transaction, in which Pontiac was engaged with the English. The year following, in a council with the Indians on the Illinois, this noted chief was stabbed to the heart, by an Indian who had long followed him for that purpose.

"29th. A deputation of several nations set out from Detroit, for the Illinois country, with several messages from me to the Wyandots, Six Nations, Delawares, Shawnees, and other nations, in answer to theirs, delivered me at Weotonan.

"30th. The chiefs of the several nations who are settled on Ouabache returned to the Detroit, from the river Roche, where they had been encamped, and informed Colonel Campbell and me they were now going for their own country; and that nothing gave them greater pleasure than to see, that all the western nations and tribes had agreed to a general peace, and that they should be glad how soon their fathers, the English, would take possession of the posts in their country, which had formerly been in possession of their late fathers, the French, to open a trade for them; and if this could not be done this fall, they desired that some traders might be sent to their villages, to supply them for the winter, or else they would be obliged to go to the Illinois, to apply to their old fathers, the French, for such necessaries as they might want.

"'They then spoke on a belt, and said: *Fathers, everything is now settled, and we have agreed to your taking possession in our country. We have been informed that the English, wherever they settle, make the country their own; and you tell us that when you conquered the French, they gave you this country. That no difference may happen hereafter, we tell you the French never purchased a foot of our country, nor have they a right to give it to you. We gave them liberty to settle, and they were always very civil to us, when they had it in their power; but as they now are become your people, if you expect to keep those posts as your own property, we will expect to have equivalent made us, for such parts of our country as you may want to possess.*" [A belt.]

"September 2d. The Chiefs of the Wyandots, or Hurons, came to me and said they had spoke last summer, to Sir William Johnson, at Niagara, about the lands on which the French had settled near Detroit, belonging to them, and desired I would mention it again to him; that they never had sold it to the

French, and expected their new fathers, the English, would do them justice, as the French was become one people with us. [A belt.]

"4th. Pontiac, with several chiefs of the Hurons, Chippewas and Pottawatomie, likewise complained that the French had settled part of their country, which they never had sold to them, and hoped their fathers, the English, would take it into consideration, and see that a proper satisfaction was made to them; that their country was very large, and they were willing to give up any part of it that was necessary for their fathers, the English, to carry on trade— provided they were paid for it, and a sufficient part of the country left for them to hunt on. [A belt.]

"6th. The Saginaw Indians came here and made a speech on a belt of wampum, expressing their satisfaction on hearing that a general peace, was made with all the western nations and with Pontiac. They desired a little powder and lead, to enable them to hunt on their way home, and a little rum, to drink their new father's health." [A belt.]

N. B. The transactions of the 9th and 11th are written with such poor ink, and so faded, that they cannot be deciphered.

"12th. The Grand Sauton, and a party of Ottawas and Chippewas, from Chicago, sent me word they would come in the morning and see me.

"13th. The Grand Sauton came, with his band, and spoke as follows:

"Father—You sent me a belt from the Miami, and as soon as I received it I set off to meet you here. On my way, I heard what has passed between you and the several tribes that met you here. You have had pity on them; and I beg, in behalf of myself and the people of Chicago, that you will have pity on us also. It is true, we have been foolish, and listened to evil reports and the whistling of bad birds. We, red people, are a very jealous people; and, father, among you, white people, there are bad people also, that tell us lies and deceive us, which has been the occasion of what is past. I need not say much on this head. I am now convinced I have been wrong led for some years past. But there are people that have behaved worse than I and my people, and you have pardoned them. I hope you to do the same to us, that our women and children may enjoy the blessings of peace, as the rest of our brethren, the red people; and you shall be convinced, by our future conduct,

that we will behave as well as any tribe of your children in this country." [A belt.]

"He then said, *"The St. Joseph Indians would have come along with me, but the English prisoner, which their fathers want from them, was some distance off a-hunting. As soon as they could get him, they would deliver him up, and beg forgiveness of their fathers."* as they did at present.

"14th. I had a private meeting with the Grand Sauton, when he told me he was well disposed for peace last fall, but was then sent for to the Illinois, where he met with Pontiac; and that then their fathers, the French, told them, if they would be strong, and keep the English out of the possession of that country but this summer, that the King of France would send over an army next spring, to assist his children, the Indians; and that the King of Spain would likewise send troops, to help them to keep the English out of the country; that the English were a bad people, and had a design to cut off all the Indian nations in this country, and to bring the southern Indians to live and settle there. This account made all the Indians very uneasy in their minds; and, after holding a council among themselves, they all determined to oppose the English, and not suffer them to take possession of the Illinois; that, for his part, he behaved as ill as the rest to the British officers that went there this spring; but since, he has been better informed of the goodness of the English, and convinced the French told them lies for the love of their beavers. He was now determined, with all his people, to become faithful and dutiful children to their new fathers, the English, and pay no regard to any stories the French should tell him in future.

"15th. Colonel Campbell and I had a meeting with the Grand Sauton, at which we informed him of everything that has passed with the several nations and tribes; and told him we accepted him and his people in friendship, and would forgive them as we had the rest of the tribes, and forget what was past, provided their future conduct should convince us of their sincerity. After which we gave them some presents, for which he returned thanks, and departed very well satisfied.

"19th. I received a letter from Colonel Reed, by express, acquainting me of Captain Sterling setting out from Fort Pitt, with a hundred men of the forty second regiment, to take possession of Fort Chartres, in the Illinois country.

"20th. I sent off Aaron Andrew, express to Captain Sterling at the Illinois, and with messages to the several nations in that country and those on the Ouabache, to acquaint them of Captain Sterling's departure from Fort Pitt for the Illinois country.

"25th. The chiefs of the St. Joseph Indians arrived, and addressed themselves to Colonel Campbell and me, as follows:

"Fathers—We are come here to see you, although we are not acquainted with you. We had a father formerly, with whom we were very well acquainted, and never differed with him. You have conquered him some time ago; and when you came here first, though your hands were all bloody, you took hold of us by the hands, and used us well, and we thought we should be happy with our brethren. But soon an unlucky difference happened, which threw us all into confusion. Where this arose we do not know, but we assure you we were the last that entered into the quarrel. The Indians of this place solicited us often to join them, but we would not listen to them. At last they got the better of our foolish young warriors, but we never agreed to it; we knew it would answer no end, and told them, often, they were fools, and if they succeeded in killing the few English in this country, they would not kill them all, because we knew you to be a great people."

Fathers — You have, after all that has happened, received all the several tribes in this country for your children. We from St. Joseph seem to be the last of your children that came to you to beg mercy. We are no more than wild creatures to you, fathers, in understanding; therefore we request you to forgive the past follies of our young people, and receive us for your children. Since you have thrown down our former father on his back, we have been wandering in the dark, like blind people. Now you have dispersed all this darkness, which hung over the heads of the several tribes, and have accepted them for your children, we hope you will let us partake with them the light, that our women and children may enjoy peace. We beg you to forget all that is past. By this belt we remove all evil thoughts from your hearts." [A belt.]

"They added further: *"Fathers — When we formerly came to visit our fathers, the French, they always sent us home joyful, and we hope you, fathers, will have pity on our women and young men who are in great want of necessaries, and not let us go home to our towns ashamed."*

" Colonels Campbell and Croghan made them a favorable answer, and added presents of powder, lead, vermillion, clothing, and two kegs of rum, ending the interview with these remarks:

"Children — I take this opportunity to tell you that your fathers, the English, are gone down the Ohio from Fort Pitt, to take possession of the Illinois, and desire you may acquaint all your people of it on your return home; and likewise desire you to stop your ears against the whistling of bad birds, (meaning the French,) and mind nothing but your hunting, to support your families, that your women and children may enjoy the blessings of peace."

"26th. I left Detroit and arrived, October 3d, at Niagara. Here I met some Senecas with whom I had a meeting, and informed them of my transactions with the several nations; and desired them to inform their people of it on their return home, which they promised me they would.

"October 11th. Set off from Niagara, and arrived the 17th at Ontario, where I met the Bunt and several sachems of the Onondagas, with whom I had a meeting, and informed them what had passed between me and the western nations.

"19th. I set off from Ontario, and arrived at Fort Stanwix the 21st."

At the close of the journal is annexed the report of his proceedings, and his views of the ultimate results of the connection just formed between the Indians and their new fathers, the English.

"Sir—Having now returned from the services I was sent upon by his Excellency General Gage, namely, the obtaining the Indians' consent to our possessing the important posts at the Illinois, I present your honor with a journal of my transactions with the several nations and tribes in that country, for your perusal.

"In the situation I was placed at Weotonan, with great numbers of Indians about me, and no necessaries, such as paper and ink, I had it not in my power to take down all the speeches made by the Indian nations, nor what I said to them, in so particular a manner as I could wish; but hope the heads of them, as I have taken them down, will meet your approbation.

"In the course of this tour through the Indian country, I made it my study to converse in private with Pontiac and several of the chiefs of the several nations, as often as opportunity served, in order to find out their sentiments of the French and English. Pontiac is a shrewd, sensible Indian, of few words, and commands more respect among his own nation than any Indian I ever saw, could do among his own tribe. He and all the principal men of those nations seem at present to be convinced that the French had a view of interest in stirring up, the late difference between his majesty's subjects and them, and call it a beaver war; for neither Pontiac, nor any of the Indians I met with, ever pretended to deny that the French were at the bottom of the whole, and constantly supplied them with every necessary they wanted, as far as in their power. And notwithstanding they are at present convinced that it was for their own interest, yet it has not changed the Indians' affection for them. They have been bred up together like children in that country, and the French have always adopted the Indian customs and manners, treated them civilly, and supplied their necessities, generally, by which means they gained the hearts of the Indians, and commanded their services, and enjoyed the benefits of a very advantageous fur trade. They well know if they had not taken these measures they could not enjoy these advantages.

"The French have in a manner taught the Indians in that country to hate the English, by representing them in the worst light they could, on all occasions; in particular they have made the Indians there believe, lately, that the English would take their country from them, and bring the Cherokees there to settle and enslave them; which report they easily gave credit to, as the southern Indians had lately commenced a war against them. I had great difficulty in removing this suspicion, and convincing them of the falsity of the report, which I flatter myself I have done in a great measure.

"It will require some time, and a very even conduct in those that are to reside in their country, before we can expect to rival the French in their affections. All Indians are jealous, and from their high notions of liberty, hate power. Those nations are jealous and prejudiced against us, so that the greatest care will be necessary to convince them of our honest intentions by our actions.

"The French sold them goods much dearer than the English traders do at present. In that point we have the advantage over the French, but they made that up in large presents to them, for their services, which they wanted, to support their interest in the country; and although we want none of their services, yet they will expect favors, and if refused, take it in a bad light, and very likely think it done to distress them, for some particular advantage we want to gain over them. They are by no means *so sensible a people as the Six Nations,* or other tribes this way; and the French, for their own advantage, have learned them a bad custom; for, by all I could learn, they seldom made them any general present, but as it were fed them with necessaries just as they wanted, tribe by tribe, and never sent them away empty, which will make it difficult and troublesome to the gentlemen that are to command in their country, for some time, to please them and preserve peace, as they are a rash, inconsiderate people, and do not look on themselves as under any obligation to us, but rather think we are obliged to them for letting us reside in their country.

"As far as I can judge of their sentiments, by the several conversations I have had with them, they will expect some satisfaction made them by us, for any posts that may be established in their country for trade. But you will be informed better by themselves next spring, as Pontiac and some chiefs of every nation in that country, intend to pay you a visit.

"The several nations on the Ouabache and towards the Illinois, St. Josephs, Chicago, La Baye, Saginaw, and other places, have applied for traders to be sent to their settlements. As it was not in the power of any officer to permit traders to go from Detroit, or Michillimackinac, either English or French, I am of opinion the Indians will be supplied chiefly this year from the Illinois, which is all French property; and if trading posts are not established at proper places in that country soon, the French must carry the best part of the trade over the Mississippi. This they are determined to do, if they can; for I have been informed that they are preparing to build a strong trading fort, on the other side of the Mississippi, about sixty miles above Fort Chartres, and have this summer, in a private manner, transported twenty-six pieces of small cannon up the river for that purpose.

"I am with great esteem and regard, your honor's most obedient and most humble servant,
"GEO. CROGHAN.

"To the Honorable Sir William Johnson, General, his Majesty's sole agent for Indian affairs."

This letter has no date, but was probably written soon after Colonel Croghan's arrival at Fort Stanwix, which was October 21st, 1765; as it is attached to his Journal of transactions.

N. B. The above journal is copied from an original manuscript, among Colonel Morgan's papers, and not from Butler's History of Kentucky, which had not been seen by the writer at that time.

CHAPTER V.

After the treaty with the Indians, in 1765, the country on the Monongahela and on the Ohio Rivers, some distance below, began to be settled, as it enjoyed comparative security from Indian depredations. In the year 1767, a settlement at Red Stone, Old Fort, was begun. In 1770, Wheeling was settled by a number of men from the south branch of the Potomac, among who were Ebenezer, Silas and Jonathan Zane, with Colonel Shepherd, all prominent men in the colonization and establishment of that place. Soon after which, locations were made on Buffalo and Short Creek, above Wheeling, where the town of Wellsburgh now stands, then called "*Buffalo*" and afterwards Charleston.

This state of quiet continued, with little or no interruption on the part of the Indians, until the year 1774. A free and social intercourse was kept up between the red men and the white—the former often visiting their settlements, and numerous traders of the latter frequenting the Indian towns with goods, in exchange for peltries. This friendly feeling would have probably continued for some time longer, but for the depredations committed by the whites on the Indians; it being the opinion of nearly all the writers of early western history that the Indians were not the first aggressors, but that it arose out of the unprovoked attack made on the family and connections of Logan, a celebrated Mingo chief, at Baker's Station, opposite the mouth of Yellow Creek—a place about midway between Wheeling and Fort Pitt. This murderous outrage, with several others that followed, at the instigation of Doctor Connolly, was fully avenged by Logan the summer after, in the numerous fatal attacks on the whites of western Virginia, as he acknowledges, in his celebrated speech to Lord Dunmore, in October following.

These repeated assaults of the Indians on the frontiers induced the governor of Virginia and the House of Burgesses to plan an expedition into the Indian country, on the Scioto River, as the only effectual mode of checking these marauding parties, chiefly fitted out at the towns in that vicinity. The army was to consist of three thousand men, and as a portion of it marched through a district of country which for a number of years was attached to Washington County, and as it is the only instance of any considerable body of men in hostile array passing over this portion of Ohio, an account of that campaign will be given, so far as its obscure history can be traced. The troops were assembled in two divisions: one at Camp Union, now Lewisburgh, in Greenbrier County, under General Andrew Lewis; the other at Pittsburgh, under the command of Governor Dunmore, in person—a proof of his bravery and desire of military fame. Few men, situated, like him, at the head of a rich and powerful colony, with all the comforts and luxuries of life around him, would leave them to traverse a wilderness, the distance of more than five hundred miles, into an enemy's country, for the love of glory. However much we may censure his subsequent conduct, he deserves unlimited praise for his great personal sacrifices in defense of the people under his government.

The division of General Lewis marched by land to the mouth of the Big Kanawha, while the other descended the Ohio River, in canoes and other craft, to the same point where they were to unite their forces and march to the Indian towns. Lewis reached his destination on the 6th of October,* and on the 10th of October was fought one of the longest and hardest contested battles ever enacted on the borders of the Ohio, between the red men and the white. The numbers engaged on each side were nearly equal— eleven hundred Virginians, and one thousand Indians, chiefly Shawnees, under the command of Cornstalk.

* Various dates have been given; we follow the contemporary accounts, those of persons present, in Am. Archives, 4th Series, I, 774, &c.

For reasons, no doubt satisfactory to himself, Governor Dunmore landed his division at the mouth of the Big Hockhocking, instead of the Kanawha, a point but little, if any, further from the Indian towns, and commenced cutting away the forest trees and erecting a fortified camp of considerable extent. He also built a strong block-house, in which to deposit the surplus stores of provisions and ammunition in a place of safety, during the absence of the troops in their march to the Scioto. While occupied here with these preparations, he sent notice to General Lewis of the alteration in his plan, by Simon Girty, one of his principal guides, and a man named Parchment * with orders for him to cross the Ohio and join him near the Indian towns. This order was received the evening before the battle, or the 9th day of October.

Within a few days after the battle, the troops under General Lewis crossed the Ohio, and proceeded by the way of the Salt Licks, now Jackson, to join the division of Lord Dunmore, at or near old Chillicothe.

In the mean time his lordship, after leaving a strong guard to protect the stores at Fort Gower, as he called the block-house built at the mouth of Hockhocking, proceeded up the river to near the falls, where he left that stream and marched across the country to attack the Indian towns. In the course of the third day, he was met by a noted Indian trader, named Elliot, bearing a white flag, with proposals of peace, and requesting him to withdraw his troops and appoint commissioners to meet their chiefs at Fort Pitt and agree on the terms of a treaty. This the Governor declined, but said he was willing to make peace, and as he was already so near their towns, and the chiefs already near him, it was better to hold a treaty at this time than at a future day. He then selected a spot where he would encamp and attend to their propositions. Orders were sent to General Lewis to halt his troops and proceed no further in the direction of the Indian towns, as he had concluded an armistice, and was about to arrange the terms of a treaty.

The two divisions were now within a few miles of each other. For Lewis, disregarding the commands of his lordship, continued to advance until the Indians, fearful of the destruction of their towns and crops, by the enraged men under his command, again applied to Dunmore, who went in person to Lewis's command, and persuaded him to halt his men and retire. To this, with great reluctance, he finally consented, as it was an abandonment of the sole object of the campaign — the destruction of the crops and towns of the Indians. Dunmore's conduct, at this time, was thought by many to be very strange and mysterious; and his subsequent transactions in Virginia, during the early years of the Revolution, seemed to demonstrate and confirm the suspicions then generated, of his inimical and hostile feelings to the inhabitants of Virginia. Mr. Withers, the author of the "Chronicles of Border Warfare," and from whom many of the facts in relation to this campaign are gathered, is fully of the opinion that he was actuated, at this time, by the same spirit which afterwards led him to plot with the Indians to sack and destroy some of the best portions of Virginia. But at this late period, seventy years after the event, to our view, his conduct on this occasion wears a very different aspect. The Indians, already humbled by their unsuccessful attack on General Lewis, and the loss of many brave warriors, were fearful of total destruction, when the army of Lord Dunmore should be united with the other, as both of them would more than double the number of their own men, who had all been engaged in the battle of the 10th of October. Under these alarming prospects, though urged by the heroic Cornstalk to die before the fires of their wigwams, and sacrifice their wives and children, rather than submit to their enemies, yet the majority preferred life with a little disgrace, to the destruction of the nation, and so deputed an agent to sue for peace. When asked by a humble and prostrate foe, what brave man would refuse to him life and peace? Lord Dunmore was both brave and generous; and if he could bring about a peace, with promised security to the frontier inhabitants from future aggression, it was all he desired, and did not seek the destruction of a brave people because they had been his enemies.

It was during this treaty at Camp Charlotte, within eight miles of the Indian town of Chillicothe, that Logan, through Colonel Gibson, delivered his celebrated speech to Lord Dunmore. The noble minded chief, Cornstalk, who led the Indians at the battle of Point Pleasant, and afterwards in 1777, was basely murdered by the whites at the same place, was present and delivered a speech, which for manly eloquence, was fully equal to the best speeches of Patrick Henry, or Richard Henry Lee, in their best days; so says Colonel Benjamin Wilson, who had heard both these celebrated men. A strong block-house, strengthened with pickets, was erected by the men under General Lewis, at the mouth of the Kanawha, and manned with a sufficient garrison. This post was kept up during the war of the revolution, and for several years subsequently.

Immediately after the treaty was concluded, that division of the army under Lord Dunmore returned to the mouth of the Hockhocking, by the same route in which it went out. Here the troops were disbanded, and sought their way home to Virginia, west of the Blue Ridge, where the most of them resided, by way of Clarksburgh; while a few, with the Governor, proceeded by water up the Ohio to Fort Pitt, or Fort Dunmore, as Dr. Connolly, a bold, reckless man, appointed to the command of this place, had named it in honor of his patron. This post was forcibly seized upon by Dunmore, the winter preceding, as lying within the boundaries of Virginia; while Pennsylvania, for many years before, considered it as a part of her territory, and Governor Penn had commissioned officers to direct and take charge of the civil affairs.

These conflicting claims caused much difficulty and distress to the well disposed inhabitants, and were not finally adjusted until some years after the flight of Lord Dunmore from the colonial government of Virginia. It is stated by the citizens of Pittsburgh, in their letters of that day, published in the 1st Vol. Amer. Archives, to Governor Penn and council, that the war of 1774 was brought about through the agency of Dr. Connolly, by a circular letter addressed to the inhabitants and land jobbers on the Ohio, in which he directs them to attack and kill the Indians wherever they meet them. This advice they were often too ready to follow.

On the 17th September, 1774, Lord Dunmore, while on his way *to* the Indian towns, was at Fort Pitt and issued a proclamation, claiming the disputed territory as a part of Virginia, and forbidding the execution of any act of authority on behalf of the province of Pennsylvania; and that strict regard be paid to the laws of his majesty's colony of Virginia, under his administration. The proclamation is dated at Fort Dunmore; thus endeavoring to supplant the rightful name of Fort Pitt, which it had held since 1758. It is probable he left this place soon after, as he must have been at the mouth of Hockhocking by the last of September.

On the 12th of November following he was again at Fort Pitt, full of his characteristic energy, holding a court on Mr. Scott, one of Governor Penn's justices, for refusing to obey his proclamation of the 17th of September.

On the 4th of December he reached his home at Williamsburgh, Virginia, and under the same notice we learn that, in his treaty with the Indians, they agreed to deliver up all white prisoners, with the horses and other plunder taken from the inhabitants. They also promised not to hunt south of the Ohio, and not to molest any travelers upon that river. (1 Vol. 4th series, Amer. Archives, 1170.)

After the return of Lord Dunmore to his palace at Williamsburgh, congratulatory addresses were showered upon him from various quarters, for his successful campaign against the Indians; to all which he returned modest and sensible answers. As a specimen of the estimation in which he was held by the people of Virginia, the following resolution was passed by the members of the convention, on the 25th March, 1775, then sitting at Richmond, and composed of the best men in the colony, viz:

"Resolved, unanimously, that the most cordial thanks of the people of the colony are a tribute justly due to our worthy Governor, Lord Dunmore, for his truly noble, wise and spirited conduct, on the late expedition against our Indian enemy; a conduct which at once evinces his Excellency's attention to the true interests of this colony, and a zeal in the executive department which no dangers can divert, or difficulties hinder, from achieving the most important services to the people, who have the happiness to live under his administration."

A vote of thanks was also passed to the officers and soldiers of the expedition: (Amer. Arch. Vol. 2, page 170 and 301, &c.) Before the close of that year, we find him driven forth from the loyal colony of Virginia, and the people in arms against him, while he is equally inveterate against them. They were both acting from correct and honorable principles; he for the king, his master, whose sovereignty and interest he was sworn to support and defend ; and they for the protection of their own rights and liberties, which were in danger of being wrested from them. The result is well known to history. Subsequent events proved, that through the agency of Connolly, the arch mover of mischief, attempts were made to organize a confederacy, composed of Tories and Indians, to invade the colony of Virginia, on the north and west, while the British troops attacked them on the sea-board, placing them between two fires. The attempt failed; and being driven from his strong hold, near Norfolk, by General Lewis, his former friend and companion, he shortly after left the coast, and proceeded to Florida, where he was employed by the king, and appointed Governor of New Providence Island. We find him engaged in the year 1781, in an enterprise with the Creek Indians, persuading them to attack the Americans. (Arch. Am., vol. 5.) When or where he died is to us unknown, but that he ranked among the most able, enterprising, and energetic of the colonial governors at the period of the Revolution, there can be no doubt. Twenty years after this period, when the settlers of the Ohio Company took possession of their lands at the mouth of the Big Hockhocking, the outlines of Dunmore's camping ground were easily distinguished. A tract containing several acres had the appearance of an old clearing, grown up with stout saplings. In plowing their fields for several years after, mementos of the former occupants were often found, consisting of hatchets, gun barrels, knives, swords and bullets, brought to light in the upturned furrow. In one place, several hundred leaden bullets were discovered, lying in a heap, as if they had been buried in a keg or box. A tolerably perfect sword is now to be seen in the museum of the University, at

Athens, Ohio, which was found on the west side of the river, near the roots of a fallen tree.

From the year 1774, to 1794, the Indians, especially the Shawnees, carried on a continual warfare with the settlers on the frontiers, from the falls of the Ohio to Fort Pitt. It is true, there were several treaties made with the different tribes, within this time, and there were short intervals of what was called peace, but there was no year in which depredations were not committed on the lives and property of the whites.

1775.

In the spring of this year, Fort Randolph was built by troops from Virginia, at the mouth of the Great Kanawha, under the command of Captain Arbuckle. In September of this year, commissioners appointed by Congress met at Fort Pitt, to treat with the western Indians. Arthur St. Clair, at that time Prothonotary of Westmoreland County, Pennsylvania, was one of the commissioners.

CHAPTER VI.

Transactions at Pittsburgh in 1776, 1777 and 1778 during the war.— Colonel Morgan, Indian agent. — His character.—Moravian Indians friendly to United States.—Commissioners meet to treat with the western tribes.—Difficulties. — Report of Mr. Wilson, the messenger sent to visit their towns.— Letter of Colonel Morgan to John Hancock, President of Congress Indian murder, near Washington, Pa.— Transactions at Fort Pitt. — Letter of Captain Arbuckle.—Speech of Colonel Morgan to the Shawnees.— Delawares arrive at Fort Pitt.—Thirty large boats built for the transport of troops, &c.—Indian banditti.— Letter of Captain Morehead. — Indian letter. — Proceedings at Fort Pitt—Price of provisions.—Letter to the Tories— Strength of the western tribes.—Fort McIntosh.—Boundary of Delawares, &c. &c. — Extracts from the Journals of Colonel George Morgan, kept at Fort Pitt, in the years 1776,1777 and 1778.

Colonel Morgan was appointed Indian agent for the middle department, the head quarters of which office were at Pittsburgh, by Congress, in April, 1776. He was a man of unwearied activity, great perseverance, and familiar with the Indian manners and habits; having for several years had charge of a trading post in the Illinois, after that country was given up by the French, owned by a commercial house in Philadelphia. His frank manners, soldierly bearing, generosity, and, above all, his strict honesty in all his dealings with them, won their fullest confidence; and no white man was ever more highly esteemed than was Colonel Morgan, by all the savages who had any intercourse with him. He was a native of Philadelphia, in Pennsylvania, and, at the, time of his appointment, held the post of colonel in the army of the United States. Such extracts as will throw any light on the history of that period in the west, and the condition and feelings of the Indians and frontier inhabitants towards each other, will be copied.

It had early been the settled policy of Congress, and which was continued through this unnatural contest between the mother country and the colonies, to persuade the Indians to remain neutral, and not take up the hatchet on either side. It was a war in which they had no concern, and they were desired to keep quiet. The British government, however, pursued a very different course, and urged them, on all occasions, to side with them, and assist in subduing their rebellious children. For this purpose, they supplied them with arms and ammunition, and paid them a bounty on scalps: one of the most cruel and inhuman kinds of traffic ever entered into by a civilized people.

The main object of all the treaties with the Indians by the United States, during the war, was to keep them quiet, and persuade them not to molest the border inhabitants. For this purpose, they received many presents, at the close of these treaties, of clothing, blankets, &c, but little or no ammunition or arms.

The British, on the other hand, supplied them with all these articles, in four fold quantities, for the purpose of attaching them to their interests; while the Congress, from their poverty, and their absolute inability to furnish them with foreign goods in large amounts, rather sunk in the estimation of the Indians. They had the shrewdness to perceive the poverty of the United States when compared with the wealth and grandeur of their old father, the king of Great Britain; and during the whole contest acted either openly or covertly on that side. A large portion of the Delaware Indians, in addition to all those who had been converted to Christianity by the agency of the Moravian missionaries, continued to be steadfast in their friendship to the Americans, and on all occasions these Christian Indians sent timely notice, if in their power, of the marching of war parties to attack the border inhabitants of Pennsylvania and Virginia.

These friendly acts were, no doubt, promoted by the kind offices of the missionaries, Ziesberger and Heckewelder, whose names will occasionally appear in the course of these extracts. Their friendship for the United States drew upon them the ill will of all the heathen tribes, which finally led to open violence, and the Christian Indians were forcibly removed to Sandusky, where they suffered greatly from starvation. They also fell under the displeasure of the frontier inhabitants of Western Pennsylvania and Virginia, who accused them of harboring the war parties of the hostile Indians, when they returned from their murderous inroads into the settlements, and secreting for them their stolen goods. Thus placed between two fires, they finally fell a sacrifice to an exasperated party of whites, for whom they had ever professed a sincere friendship, and were destroyed at the massacre of Gnadenhutten, by the hands of those they had never injured.

Congress perceived, at an early period of the war, the importance of securing the friendship of the Indians, at least so far as to prevent their acting in concert with their enemies; and appointed commissioners to hold treaties with them at the different agencies. For the middle department, the commissioners were Thomas Walker, John Harvey, John Montgomery, and Jasper Yates. These gentlemen met at Fort Pitt in July, but were not able to assemble the different tribes until the month of October. In the meantime they were busily engaged in holding communications with the Indians, by means of letters, and by agents sent to Indian towns. The Ottawas and Pottawatomie, living nearer to the British posts, were greatly influenced in their councils by the agency of Governor Hamilton of Detroit They were also powerful tribes, and their opinions and advice had great weight with the Shawnees and Delawares. Owing to these conflicting views of the different nations, the commissioners found great difficulty in reconciling them, so far as to agree to meet them at Fort Pitt. At one time

in September, they came to the conclusion, founded on the best testimony they could obtain, that a general Indian war was inevitable; they accordingly issued orders for the assembling of all the western militia, that could be spared, at Fort Pitt for its defense. During this state of suspense and agitation, William Wilson, who was sent out in June to invite the Wyandot tribe of Indians to the treaty, returned and made the following report, the 26th of September:

"Sometime in June last, 1776, I was sent by Mr. George Morgan, agent for Indian affairs in the middle department, to the Shawnees to prevent their going to Detroit to a treaty, until he arrived there and spoke to them. Upon my reaching the towns, I found them ready to set off for Detroit; but on my delivering Mr. Morgan's message, they agreed to stay until he came to their towns. When Mr. Morgan came and spoke to them, they referred him to the Wyandots to fix the time of holding the treaty, as they had great influence over the western tribes. I continued in the Shawnee town with Mr. Morgan whilst he stayed. Sometime in July I left the towns in company with the Cornstalk, the Hardman, and several others, in order to go to the Wyandot towns, with a message from Mr. Morgan inviting them to a treaty, to be held at Pittsburgh the last of August; but Mr. Morgan directed me to settle some other time for holding the treaty, if I should find it was not convenient for them to attend then.

"We proceeded to a small Shawnee town, about ten miles from the principal towns, the first day, and continued there ten days, waiting for some of the chief warriors to join us. I grew impatient and prevailed on the Cornstalk to set off with me. The Hardman, and the others, promised to follow the next day. The following morning a couple of runners were sent to us to inform us that the Hardman had heard the Shade was at Pittsburgh, on his way from Niagara, and that he would wait four days for him, to hear the news from the treaty held there. We then proceeded to Pluggystown. There were very few people in the town, and we agreed to encamp there that night. We were detained the next day by an Indian, who said he had some news, which he wanted to inform us of. It turned out to be nothing more than that he had understood the Shade was arrived at the Shawnee towns, and that we might expect the Hardman, and others which we left behind, to overtake us in a few days.

"That evening we were alarmed by an Indian, who came in with the alarm halloo, from the Shawnee towns. The Cornstalk went to him immediately, to hear the news. He soon returned and informed me that the white people over the big river had fired on a party of Shawnee and Cherokees; that one of the party had got into the towns, who said that one of the Shawnee was certainly killed, and he did not know but more of them were, for there were a great many guns fired at them. I told the Cornstalk that I imagined the white people had sufficient reasons, or they would not have fired on them. He said he was of the same opinion; and on hearing the news, he told the Mingoes it was they who had killed his young men, and not the white people; that the mischief was done in consequence of the prisoners they took from Kentucky.

"Some time afterward the Mingoes assembled together at a house belonging to a French Smith, and began to council. The Frenchman overheard them, and told me that they had determined to take Joseph Nicholson and myself prisoners to Detroit the next day; that perhaps they might attempt to amuse us by speaking in a friendly manner, but he advised us to pay no regard to them, but to make our escape that night. Sometime after night, the Mingoes came to where we were encamped, and said they wanted to speak to us. They produced a string, and spoke to the following effect: They desired the Shawnees and Delawares not to be displeased at their laying hold of their two white brothers and detaining them for two days; that they had sent messengers to the Wyandot chiefs, and that within that time, they and all the neighboring chiefs were expected to assemble there, and that all the speeches were to be told over. I told them, that as they desired me to continue with them for two days I would do so; on which they went off, seemingly satisfied.

"I advised with the Cornstalk, and Delawares, what was the most prudent step for me to take, and what they thought of the before mentioned speech. The Cornstalk said they only wanted to deceive me; and he and the

Delawares recommended to us to make our escape that night, and endeavor to get to Coochocking, a Delaware town. We did so, after engaging a Delaware man to go to the Shawnee towns to hear the news which the before mentioned person brought, and to discover the temper they were in. I thought it expedient to continue at Coochocking, until the return of the messenger I had sent to the Shawnee. He returned in four days, and informed that the party of Shawnee and Cherokees, before mentioned, had killed two men and taken a woman prisoner on the Kentucky; that the white people pursued them, came up with them the next day, and killed two of the Shawnee and rescued the prisoner; that the Cherokees had sent a tomahawk belt, with two scalps tied to it, to the Shawnee, informing them that they had struck the white people; and it was his opinion that the Shawnee would join, provided the other nations did. He further said that the Hardman intended to proceed to the Wyandots with the messages from Mr. Morgan, and would meet me at Sandusky.

"I thought it advisable to engage some of the Delaware chiefs to go with me to the Wyandot towns. I therefore assembled the Delawares, and desired they would appoint some persons for that purpose. They pitched upon Captain Killbuck and two young men to accompany me. After I had made the necessary preparations for my journey, King Newcomer spoke to me and said, he thought it was dangerous for me to pursue my intended journey, as it was probable the Mingoes might way-lay the road and kill me; that he would send a message of his own to the Wyandots, with Mr. Morgan's, and advised me to continue at Coochocking, and let Captain Killbuck proceed with the messages, and to send Joseph Nicholson to Mr. Morgan to inform him what I had done. I took his advice. Killbuck returned in eleven days, with the messages sent by him, and a message from the Wyandots to me, signifying that those who lived on this side of the lake were not able to give an answer without consulting their chiefs on the other side; that I must come with my message myself; that I need not apprehend any danger from them; that if my heart was good towards them, I would come; if it was not, I would stay away.

"On receiving this message, I determined to go, and Killbuck and two young men were again appointed to accompany me. We traveled about ten miles from Coochocking, when Killbuck w-as taken sick, which obliged us to return. I then applied to Captain White Eyes to go with me, who very readily consented. At Winganous Town, about six miles from Coochocking, I met with John Montour, whom I employed to go with me, and a Wyandot man, who told me that he imagined that Cornstalk and other Shawnee, and the Wyandot chiefs, had left Sandusky, and that he would pilot me a nearer way, to where the chiefs were. Nothing material happened until we arrived at a Wyandot village, opposite to Detroit, where the chiefs were assembled. They received me in a very kind and friendly manner, and thanked me for coming among them in consequence of their invitation. They said they had heard many bad reports from the Big Knife; but my coming among them was a convincing proof that they were false. One of the Wyandots refused to shake hands with me. On the others asking the reason, he said he would not do it, for he did not love the Big Knife. I asked them if all the chiefs were then present, and if they chose to hear my message at that time. They said they were all present, and were willing to hear me immediately. I first spoke to them on a string, telling them that in consequence of the message sent to me from Sandusky, I had visited them; that I put myself under their protection, and that they should determine how long I should continue among them. I then produced the belt and speech, sent me by Mr. Morgan. The purport of it was to ask their assistance in brightening and strengthening the chain of friendship with all the western tribes of Indians, and inviting them to a treaty to be held at Pittsburgh, in twenty-five days from that time, which was the 2d of September.

"Captain White Eyes then spoke to them and said, that as the path to their towns appeared to be somewhat dim, he had accompanied me, that I might not lose myself. He assured them that the Big Knife desired nothing more than to live in peace and friendship with all the Indians. They answered that they were convinced the Indians desired to be in friendship with the white people, and as far as their influence extended, they would endeavor to promote the good work of peace. They then withdrew to consider of my speech. After some time, they returned and told me they were glad their brother, the Big Knife, thought so much of them as to ask their assistance in brightening the chain of friendship. They assured me they would use all their influence with the other tribes to preserve peace; and desired that I would remain with them two days, to hear them explain my speech to the other nations who were assembled at Detroit.

"Next morning they sent to the Governor of Detroit, informing him that I was in their town, and if he desired to speak to me in a friendly manner, he might have an opportunity of doing so. They made me acquainted with this message. On the return of their messenger they delivered back the belt they received from me, and said they thought it best I should deliver it in public council at Detroit; to which I agreed. I imagine they were directed by the governor to return the belt. Captain White Eyes, John Montour, myself, and the Wyandot Chiefs, went to the council house at Detroit, together. After the Indians and the Governor met, one of the Wyandot Chiefs got up and informed the other nations, that they had met with one of their brothers, the Big Knife, which might delay the business they were upon. Then addressing himself to the Governor, he said, he thought that he, as their father, was the proper person to inquire of me the business I came upon.

"The Governor then asked from whence I came, and what business I was upon. I told him I came from Pittsburgh with a message from Mr. Morgan, agent for the colonies, to the Wyandots; and told him of the message I had received from the Wyandots from Sandusky, and that, in consequence of that message, I had come to the Wyandot village. He then asked if I had my message in writing. I told him I had. He desired to see it, and I delivered it to him. After perusing the speech, he addressed himself to the Indians and said that after the message was explained to them they should consider of a proper answer to make to it; and that he would join them in their answer. The speech was then interpreted to the Indians present, and I delivered the belt to a Wyandot chief. He gave it to the Governor, telling him that he was their father, and knew best what to do with it.

"The governor then spoke to the Indians as follows: *"Children—I am your father and you are my children. I have always your good at heart. I am sent here to represent the great king over the waters, and to take care of you. Those people, from whom you received this message, are enemies and traitors to my king; and before I would take one of them by the hand, I would suffer my right hand to be cut off. When the great king is pleased to make peace with his rebellious children in this big island, I will then give my assistance in making peace between them and the Indians, and not before."*

"With that, he tore the speech and cut the belt to pieces, and contemptuously strewed it about the council house. He then told the Indians it was not customary with the English to detain or injure a public messenger, and that, therefore, I must be suffered to return unmolested; at which the Indians seemed to be greatly pleased. He then asked me if I had anything more to say to the Indians; that if I had, to speak out. I told him I had nothing further to say to them. He then ordered me to leave the place immediately, and said he would order us ten days' provisions each to take us home. I told him I came in a canoe belonging to a Wyandot man, and could not go until he was ready. He said he would furnish me with a canoe. I then told him that my blankets and shirts were at the Wyandot village, and that I must go over for them. He said he would furnish me with blankets and shirts likewise. However, at last, he suffered me to go to the village.

"While I was in the council house, the governor spoke on a tomahawk belt to the Wyandots; but as he delivered the speech in French, to the interpreter, I did not know what he said upon it. The Wyandot Chief delivered the belt to the Cornstalk. The Governor asked him if he knew what that belt meant. The Cornstalk answered, he did not. He said he would tell him in a few words. He then informed him that that belt was put into the hands of the Wyandots last March, desiring them to request the nations who lived next the river, from Presque Isle downwards, to be watchful; and if they discovered any army attempting to cross the river to let him know it; but that it now had a greater meaning; and referred him to the Wyandots for an explanation of it; and told the interpreter to tell the Cornstalk to show that belt to the Cherokees, for they had joined the English in the general cause. He then asked the nations present if any of them had anything to say at that time.

"The Mingoes then produced a black belt, telling the other nations that, the spring before last, they received that belt of Guy Johnson, informing them that he was going over the big water; that they must hold themselves in readiness against his return, and, until then, to sit still and listen to no one. They said they thought he was approaching near them, for they perceived the waters to shake. They then produced a white belt, which was sent by the Mingoes at Niagara, with the Shade, (a Shawnee,) to the Shawnee towns, telling them they intended to have sent a messenger with it to them; but as they had met with one of their brothers at Niagara, they thought proper to send it by him. They told them they had their words among them, (meaning the tomahawk,) and desired them to take them up and send them among all their friends. These speeches were explained to me by John Montour.

"The Governor then spoke to the Indians, and said he was extremely pleased with the belts produced by the Mingoes.

"While we were in the council, the Governor told me he had inquired no news of me, nor did he want to hear any. For your part, says he to Montour, I knew your father well. He was a good man. I don't know how you came to join with those people. If you should come this way again, (though not upon the same errand,) I will give you something. He told White Eyes he knew his character well, and so did all the nations present. He ordered him to leave Detroit before the sun-set, as he regarded his head; that he would lose the last drop of his blood, before he would suffer any one nation to come there and destroy the union, which was brought about by so many nations.

"White Eyes made no reply at that time, but after we had left the place, he said the Governor was a fool; that he did not know what he scolded him for; that he had never done him any injury, nor any other white man, since he had made peace with them, nor never would unless they injured him; that if he had a mind to join the Buckskins, he would soon make him tremble for his head; and if he joined either side, it would be the Buckskins .

"After we left the council house, the Governor came up to me and said he would be glad, if I would inform the people on my return of what I had seen; that all the Indians I saw there at the treaty were of the same way of thinking; and that he would be glad if the people would consider the dreadful consequences of going to war with so terrible an enemy, and accept the King's pardon while it could be obtained. He then informed me that an army of twenty thousand men were landed in Canada, and had driven the rebels entirely out of that government, and were pursuing them to the southward; that twenty thousand more were landed at New York, and the same number to the southward, with the completest train of artillery that ever came out of Europe on any occasion; and that the King must be sure of success, or he would not have sent so large an army against the Americans. He then ordered William Tucker, one of his interpreters, with whom I had a small acquaintance, to go with me and get provisions for me.

"On our way I asked Tucker his opinion of the dispositions of the Indians at Detroit, and if he thought they would strike soon. He hesitated for some time, but at last told me, that without matters took a very sudden turn, it was his opinion they would.

"On receiving my provision, I left Detroit, in company with the Hardman and others, on our way to the Wyandot village. I told the Hardman that

Governor Hamilton had informed me that all the Indians who were at Detroit were of the same way of thinking, and that I expected they would all strike the white people very soon. He said he did not doubt but the governor wished them to be of the same way of thinking, but it was not in his power to make them so, unless they chose it; that for his part he came there in search of good, and he should not put evil in his heart; and desired me to tell all his white brothers, that his heart was good towards them.

"I wanted to leave the village that evening, but the Wyandots insisted on my staying longer with them. They said they would consider my message, for as yet I had seen nothing that was good. That night they all got drunk. The next morning, White Eyes and myself grew impatient to get off, but the head chief of the Wyandots still insisted on our staying, and gave us the strongest assurances that no injury should be done to us. He and some others, in company with White Eyes, went over to Detroit and returned in the evening. He told White Eyes that his errand was to obtain the governor's leave for us to stay a few days among them, but that he would not suffer it; so that we must leave the village directly. The Governor saw White Eyes, and threatened to put him in irons and send him to Niagara, if he did not leave Detroit immediately.

"We left the Wyandot village in company with a Wyandot man, and proceeded that evening as far as his house. The next day one Isaac Zane came to see me. In the course of conversation he told me that in talking with the Half King of the Wyandots, he asked him if the Governor had not delivered him a tomahawk belt. He said he had. That the Big Knife had threatened them for some time past, so that they could not mind their hunting, and that now they would threaten them. I asked him if it was his opinion that the Wyandots would join generally. He said it was almost certain that one half of them would not.

"The next day Zane and a Wyandot man came to where we were. We conversed a good deal on the subject of the quarrel between Great Britain and the colonies. I asked the chief what the Indians promised themselves by joining the King's troops? I told him that perhaps while the contest continued, they might be furnished with clothes and such like; but when it was over, they must return to their former way of living; that if the Americans should be successful, they would be so incensed against the Indians who fought against them, that they would march an army into their country, destroy them, and take their lands from them. He said it was very true.

"There," said he;" is my tomahawk. I will never lift it, nor shall any of my family fight against the Big Knife, if I can help it, unless they come into my own house."

"John Montour, and the Wyandot man who piloted me to Detroit, came up with us. Montour continued at Detroit two days after I left it. He told me that after I came away, he was drinking in company with the half king of the Wyandots, and that when he got a little in liquor, he told him that the Big Knife need never expect him to be friends with them again; and that for his part, he should follow nothing but breaking their heads wherever he met with them.

"We set out for Coochocking. Nothing material happened on our journey. White Eyes appeared to be a good deal chagrined, as well at the reception he met with from the Governor, as from the more western tribes of Indians. He said the Delawares, he thought, were equally as liable to be struck by the western tribes, as the Big Knife was; that they kept everything secret from them; and that, as soon as they found they were determined for war, he would collect all his people together, and would apply to his American brothers to send men to him, and erect a strong fort; that then he should not regard them, for the western tribes were but very indifferent warriors, and if they struck he would soon return the blows. Then, said he, the governor of Detroit will need to take care of his head; and the people of the great falls of Niagara shall tremble, too. It was his opinion, if that should be the case, a number of the Shawnee would join him; for that one of their chiefs told him at Detroit, that his sentiments were the same as his, respecting Great Britain and the colonies."

From such sources as the above, the commissioners could hardly fail of procuring correct intelligence as to the intentions of the western tribes; and from the report of Mr. Wilson they had little favor to expect from any of them. The most they could calculate upon was a division in some of the tribes, as to whether they should actually engage in war with the United States; but nearly all agreed in holding friendly views toward their father, the king of England.

Soon after Wilson's return, they received a message from the Delawares at Coochocking, on the Muskingum, (this is now called Coshocton, by the whites,) that on the 20th of September, a party of eighteen Wyandots, two Mingoes, and one Ottawa warrior, had passed the "Standing Stone," (now Lancaster,) on their way down the Hockhocking, for the purpose of making an inroad on the Big Knife, or Virginians. The commissioners immediately sent notice of the same to the frontier inhabitants that they might be on their guard. In this way many of the war parties of the hostile tribes were disappointed in their expectations of falling by surprise on the inhabitants, from the timely notice of the friendly Delawares. Nevertheless, in case of an actual war with the United States, more than half of this tribe, it was thought, would fight against them. Mr. Morgan continued to exert himself unweariedly, in attempting to gain the friendship of the western tribes, and to induce them to attend the treaty. He was necessarily absent, in Philadelphia and Baltimore a part of the summer, on business for the commissioners; but towards the last of October, he succeeded in collecting some of the tribes at Fort Pitt. But the Ottawas, Wyandots, Chippewas, and Mingoes, could not be persuaded either to attend or to send deputies to the treaty. They were stationed too near the British forces at Detroit, and were entirely devoted to their interests.

On the 8th of November, Colonel Morgan wrote to John Hancock, the President of Congress, as follows:

"Sir—I have the happiness to inform Congress that the cloud which threatened to break over this part of the country appears now to be nearly dispersed. The Six Nations, Delawares, Munsies, Mohicans, and Shawnee, who have been assembled here to the number of six hundred and forty-four, with their principal chiefs and warriors, have given the strongest assurance of their resolutions, to preserve inviolate the peace and neutrality they have engaged in with the United States. About sixty or seventy families, composed of most of the different tribes of the Six Nations, and a few of the Lake Indians, but principally of the Senecas, who removed from near the mouths of cross creeks, on the Ohio, a few years ago, and are now seated on the heads of the Scioto, have been the perpetrators of all the mischief and murders committed on the frontiers of Virginia, since the last treaty. The murders which have come to my knowledge, are of two women at the mouth of Fish Creek (where one boy is missing), one man, opposite Hockhocking, where four others were wounded, and two soldiers, who were killed and

scalped within half a mile of Fort Randolph, at the mouth of Great Kanawha, all on the banks of the Ohio. Two days before the last mentioned happened, the Shawnee made it their business, as they frequently have done, to inform the commanding officer at Kanawha that a party of Mingoes, as these people are generally called, were in the neighborhood, with hostile intentions. Before any of these murders were committed, our frontier inhabitants were generally flown from their farms and evacuated the country, for two hundred miles in extent, except at particular places, where some of them forted and proposed to make a stand. This flight was occasioned by the false alarms we received in the months of August and September last, respecting the great assemblies of Indians to attack this post, and of a general war being inevitable. In order to put a stop to the conduct of the banditti above mentioned, the Six Nations have now deputed a principal chief and several warriors to go and remove the whole of them to the Seneca country; or at least to make them sensible of their error, and engage them to desist. In case of a refusal, they are to threaten them with a total extirpation, as disturbers of the general peace; in which several chiefs of different nations have assured me they will unite. Several principal men of the different nations having accepted the invitation of Congress to visit them, is a further proof of the peaceable disposition of their tribes. The Indians having frequently complained of our surveying their lands, and having now pointed to a recent instance thereof in public council, will give Congress a good opportunity to convince them of the sincerity of our professions on that head. For the particulars of every transaction here, I beg leave to refer to the commissioners who wait upon Congress with their report."

The following is an extract from a letter of Colonel Dorsey Pentecost, dated Catfish Camp, Tuesday, Nov. 19, 1776.

"On Monday morning last, within four hundred yards of the garrison at Grave Creek, was killed and scalped the eldest son of Adam Rowe; and the younger, who was with him, is missing."

"Catfish Camp," was so named after an old Indian, who lived there for some years after the whites came into the country, and is the spot where the town of Washington, in Pennsylvania, now stands.

The winter of 1776-7 was spent in comparative quiet. It seems that the garrison at Fort Pitt contained one hundred men, under the command of

Major Nevill; and the Fort Randolph, at Kanawha, one hundred and sixty-six men, under the command of Captain Arbuckle. In December, Colonel Morgan purchased about five thousand dollars worth of clothes, blanketing, powder, lead, &c, from two traders, from Detroit, then at Cuyahoga, for the use of the United States. He also proposed that a large stock of provisions should be laid in at Pittsburgh, for the use of the troops and volunteers, should it be necessary, from the hostility of the Indians, to make an inroad into their country, to attack their towns. At the same time, he sent to Congress a statement of the condition of the British navy and garrison at Detroit.

An order was passed for collecting provisions for two thousand men for six months; four hundred bushels of salt were ordered from Baltimore, the transport of which then was twenty-six shillings a hundred. Much of the flour was also brought on pack horses over the mountains, packed in half barrels, each horse carrying two of them. The price, east of the mountains, at that time, was from thirty-three to thirty-five shillings. Considerable quantities of flour and meal were, even at that early day, manufactured in Westmoreland County—as appears from the contracts with certain millers. A dollar was seven shillings and sixpence, in Pennsylvania.

On the 26th December, 1776, Captain Arbuckle, the commander at Fort Randolph, wrote to Major Nevill in relation to the affairs of that station. He says:

Cornstalk arrived the 29th November, in company with Mr. Wood. The White Fish's son, Kee-we-tom, left the Kanawha that day for the Shawnee towns; but, meeting three Indians, (whom he says are Mingoes, but the Cornstalk, Delawares,) he returned with them and encamped opposite the fort, with Cornstalk. All got drunk that evening. In the night, two of the new comers crossed over the river above the fort. The next morning, Captain Arbuckle crossed over to Cornstalk's camp. The stranger gave him a string of wampum. Kee-we-tom called him a damned Mingo. Cornstalk said, no; he was a Wyandot. The stranger showed signs of fear.

Captain Arbuckle then crossed back to the fort, and found that Mr. Clark, one of his soldiers, was taken prisoner. The Indians were seen and pursued, but without effect. He, however, sent over the river to make prisoner of the stranger; but Cornstalk endeavored to secrete him, and said he had ran off.

But, on searching, the party found him and made him prisoner; and Captain Arbuckle detained him until Clark was returned, which was about the 19th December. He was brought back by White Fish and five other Shawnee. They informed Captain Arbuckle that thirty Mingoes crossed the Ohio, at Little Kanawha, for the settlements, a few days before.

Early in March following, Colonel Morgan sent the following speech to the commandant of Fort Randolph, to be forwarded by him to Ke-sha-wa-ta-tha, a chief of the Shawnee:

"The United American States to their brethren, the Shawnee,

"Brothers—I was glad to hear, by the message your good old wise chief sent to me by Chitteman, that our young brothers remember the good council which we had last fall, and that they are determined to keep fast hold of our friendship.

"Brothers—If any of your young people should be so foolish as to listen to bad enemies, I desire your wise men will set them right, and not suffer the evil spirit to interrupt our good works.

"Brothers—You may depend we will hold fast to our promise, and not forget the wise councils of our ancestors, who have directed us, their children, to live in constant friendship with our Indian brethren. This our fathers agreed upon when they first met in this island and smoked together under the tree of peace; now brothers, don't let us forget our old covenant.

"Brothers—Whenever you see a white man, let him come from where he will, be sure to treat him kindly, as we do you—this will make our friendship last forever.

"Brothers—I have spoken to our brothers the Mingoes very often. I intended to send a messenger and speak to them once more. Then if they will not listen to what is good, I shall not speak again to them. Be strong brothers and let us strive to disperse that cloud, and then we shall have clear day light." [Four hundred white wampum.]

On the 4th of March, 1777, several of the Delawares arrived at Fort Pitt, with the following intelligence, which they communicated to Colonel

Morgan, or Taimenend, a name which they had bestowed upon him, and means "The White Deer", and by which they always address him.

"About twenty days ago, two Chippewa Indians, two Six Nation Indians and two white men came to the Munsey town in fourteen days from Niagara. The Indians made no delay there, but the two white men, who were very tired, staid there. The Indians proceeded directly to the Kittanning, and there took one of your people, (Mr. McFarlane,) and have carried him to Niagara. They told our young people and the women, for none others were at home, that the commanding officer at Niagara sent them for the above purpose, in order to hear the news in these parts. They were directed not to hurt him. Had our head men been at home we should have brought him back, for we will not allow this bad work to pass through our towns." Kittanning was a station on the Alleghany River, about forty miles above Fort Pitt.

On the 23d February, 1777, fourteen boat carpenters and sawyers arrived at Pittsburgh from Philadelphia, and were set to work on the Monongahela, fourteen miles above the Fort, near a saw mill. They built thirty large boats or batteaux that were forty feet long, nine feet wide, and thirty-two inches deep. These were intended to transport provisions and troops, should it be necessary to invade the Indian country.

In a letter to President Hancock, of March 15th, 1777, Colonel Morgan speaks of the hostility of the border inhabitants to the Indians. He says:

"Parties have even been assembled to massacre our known friends at their hunting camps, as well as messengers on business to me; and I have esteemed it necessary to let those messengers sleep in my own chamber for their security. It is truly distressing to submit to the injuries we have and are frequently receiving along the frontier settlements and out-posts, from the Mingo banditti and their associates; but it must be extremely injurious to the interests of the United States at this critical time to involve ourselves into a general Indian war, which I believe may still be warded off, by pursuing the wise measures intended by Congress. It is not uncommon to hear even those who ought to know better, express an ardent desire for an Indian war, on account of the fine lands those poor people possess. But I fear the dreadful consequences of a general Indian war; and I believe it is more necessary to restrain our own people and promote good order among them, than to think of aweing the different nations by expeditions into the country, which may

involve us in a general and unequal quarrel with all the nations, who are at present quiet, but extremely jealous of the least encroachments on their lands."

Colonel Morgan was unwearied in his exertions to preserve peace with the Indian nations, especially at this critical period of our contest with Great Britain. With a formidable force of civilized foes on the Atlantic border and the addition of these savage hordes along our extended frontier, the liberties of the country would have been in imminent danger. It was, therefore, of the first importance to avert this threatened catastrophe.

In a letter to the agent for Indian affairs in the northern department, he says:

"The peace of this country has been greatly disturbed for many months past, by a banditti of the Six Nations, of every tribe, but principally of the Senecas of Alleghany. They consist of sixty families at most, but have gained some adherents by intermarriages with the Wyandots, Delawares, and Shawnee, and by assuming the air and authority of the Six Nation council. Their whole number does not exceed eighty men, and even they are divided in sentiments. Yet they have, by sending out one or two small parties every month or six weeks, kept the frontiers of Virginia in a perpetual alarm, and occasioned an immense expense in garrisoning a number of posts. Were these people situated by themselves, they might easily be chastised; but they are seated in the midst of several nations whose friendship it is our interest to cultivate, and avoid every possible risk of injuring in any respect. Several attempts have been made to induce the Senecas to remove these relations of theirs, but to no effect. Sir William Johnson and his agents made several efforts in his time, for that purpose; but without avail. They have many years practiced horse-stealing and robbery, on every occasion which offered itself. Yet I apprehend, if a serious deputation, of six or eight principal men of the Six Nations' council, could be sent to them, and to insist on their removal, it might be accomplished; but they pay no regard to the Senecas, who, indeed, appear very little desirous, at present, to remove or restrain them, though they have made many promises."

In March, an express arrived from the friendly Delawares at Mahoning, that a large body of northern Indians passed by Coochocking, where they left their canoes, on their way to attack Kittanning, and to fall on the frontier inhabitants of Westmoreland. This timely notice enabled them to be prepared for the attack, and so for the present it was averted.

On the 21st of March, 1777, Captain Morehead, the commandant at Kittanning, wrote to Colonel Morgan: *"Sunday morning my brother and Andrew Simpson left here to go home. Myself left it (for Twelve Mile run) on Tuesday, and found on the road, Simpson killed and scalped; my brother either killed or taken; a war mallet left on the road, and a tomahawk, with a letter, of which I have sent you a copy, enclosed.*

Copy of the letter.

"Niagara, February 2d, 1777." A message from the chiefs of the Mohawks, Onondagas, Cayugas, Senecas, Tuscarawas, Missasagoes, and Chippewas—Serehowand, speaker —

"To the Virginians and Pennsylvanians now at Venango, You have feloniously taken possession of part of our country on the branches of the Ohio, as well as the Susquehanna. To the latter we have some time since sent you word to quit our lands, as we now do to you, as we don't know we ever gave you liberty, nor can we be easy in our minds, while there is an armed force at our very doors; nor do we think you or anybody else would. Therefore, to use you with more lenity than you have a right to expect, we now tell you, in a peaceful manner, to quit our lands wherever you have possessed yourselves of them, immediately, or blame yourselves for whatever may happen. Your pretence, of Colonel Butler coming into your country, you have no foundation for, as you know there is no army there; therefore, we look upon it, that your design is against us; but whether or not, nothing will make us easy in our minds, but your immediately leaving our country. We desire you not to make any excuses, by pretending to acquaint your congress, &c, of our behavior. The lands are ours, and we insist on your quitting them immediately." [A belt.]

In a letter to President Hancock, Colonel Morgan supposes that Colonel Butler was the instigator of the letter, for the purpose of exciting the indignation of the Indians. He also acknowledges that their complaints were true, and that we had encroached on their lands, but not at Venango. Small parties of the Mingoes, and other outlaws, continuing to harass, murder, and plunder the people on the frontiers; especially those of Virginia, against whom the Indians had more just cause of complaint than those of any other of the frontiers, they attacking them whenever and wherever they could find them.

In consequence of these repeated hostilities, Patrick Henry, Governor of Virginia, in council at Williamsburgh, the 12th March, 1777, resolved to order an expedition of three hundred men under the command of Colonel David Shepherd and Major Henry Taylor, to be raised in the counties of Monongahela, Yohiogany, and Ohio, for an inroad into the country west of Ohio, to chastise the Indians living at Pluggystown, on the heads of the Scioto. At the same time he wrote to Colonel Morgan and Colonel John Nevill, the commandant at Fort Pitt, as follows :

"Gentlemen — You will perceive, by the papers which accompany this, that the Indians at Pluggystown are to be punished in an exemplary manner. When you apply to the Shawnee and Delawares on the subject, it may not be amiss to observe to them, that these villainous Indians, by their frequent mischiefs, may breed suspicions against innocent friends and allies, for it is often difficult to tell what nation are the offenders. Willing to cultivate that good understanding which subsists between Virginia and their nations, the Shawnee and Delawares cannot take umbrage at the march against Pluggy's people, more especially as the latter march through the country of the former when they attack us. He then goes on to request him to give notice to the Delaware and Shawnee chiefs of the intended expedition, and that it be kept as secret as possible from the ears of the Indians at Pluggystown. The soldiers are enjoined to spare the women and children in the attack, and as many of the men as submit.

This communication was received at Fort Pitt on the 1st of April, and notice was immediately sent to Colonel Shepherd and Major Taylor, to meet him on the 8th of the month, that they might decide on the best means of carrying the order of the governor of Virginia into effect. At the same time they wrote to his Excellency, Patrick Henry, Esq., as follows:

"Sir — We had not the honor to receive your orders and the minutes of the 12th ult., until this day. We immediately wrote to Colonel Shepherd and Major Taylor to meet us here, the 8th inst., to confer thereon, and determine the most effectual steps to carry the same into execution; and your Excellency may be assured we will leave nothing in. our power undone, that

may tend to promote the interest of our country in general, or the success of this enterprise in particular; not regarding the strict line of duty in our respective departments, but the promotion of the service on the most liberal plan. We, nevertheless, wish we were left more at liberty to exercise our judgments, or to take advice on the expediency and practicability of the undertaking at this critical time; for although we are persuaded, from what has already passed between Colonel Morgan and our allies, the Delawares and Shawnee, that they would wish us success therein; yet we apprehend the inevitable consequences of this expedition will be a general Indian war, which we are persuaded it is the interest of the state at this time to avoid, even by the mortifying means of liberal donations to certain leading men among the nations, as well as by calling them again to a general treaty. And if the state of Pennsylvania should judge it prudent to take some steps to gratify the Six Nations in regard to the encroachments made on their lands on the north-western frontier of that state, of which they have so repeatedly complained, we hope and believe it would have a very salutary effect. The settlement of the lands on the Ohio, below the Kenhawa and at Kentucky, gives the western nations great uneasiness. How far the state of Virginia may judge it wise to withdraw or confine those settlements for a certain term of years, or during the British war, is too delicate a matter for us to give our opinion on; but we have reason to think that the measures we have (though perhaps out of the strict line of our duty) presumed to hint at, would not only tend greatly to the happiness of this country, but to the interest of the whole state; more especially if care be taken to treat the different nations in all respects with justice, humanity and hospitality; for which purpose, and to punish robberies and murders committed on any of our allies, some wholesome orders or acts of government may possibly be necessary; for parties have been formed to massacre some who have come to visit us in a friendly manner, and others who have been hunting on their own lands, the known friends to the commonwealth. These steps, if continued, will deprive us of all our Indian allies, and multiply our enemies. Even the spies who have been employed by the county lieutenants of Monongahela and Ohio, seem to have gone on this plan, with a premeditated design to involve us in a general Indian war; for, on the 15th of March, at day-break, five or six of these spies fired on three Delaware Indians, at their hunting camp, which they afterwards plundered of peltries to a considerable amount, and brought them off. This was committed about twenty miles on this side the Delaware town, between that and Wheeling, and out of the country or track of our enemies.

Luckily all the Indians escaped, only one of whom was wounded, and that slightly in the wrist.

"We enclose to your Excellency the copy of a speech or message, found near the body of a dead man who had been killed and scalped two days before, near the Kittanning, on the north-western frontier of Pennsylvania, where another man was taken prisoner. We suppose the party of Indians, who left this message and perpetrated the murder, to have been hired for that purpose by the British officer at Niagara, in order to promote an open rupture between the Six Nations and the United States, as we had intelligence of such a party being out and having come from there. In consequence whereof, and on considering the present situation of this country, a council of field officers and captains met here, and gave their opinion on certain matters, of which your Excellency is doubtless, ere now, fully informed.

"Among other things, Colonel Crawford was requested to make a return of the stores requisite to be sent here, and an estimate of the expense of repairs to make the fort defensible against any body of troops which may be brought against us, by the way of Presque Isle and the Alleghany; that being the route by which this fort will be attacked, if ever an expedition should be formed against it from Canada, and not, as has been intimated to your Excellency, from Detroit and Sandusky; there being no post at the latter place, and as we are informed, but sixty-six soldiers at Detroit, from whence by land to Fort Pitt is near three hundred miles, impassable for artillery; and all that country we are told could not furnish, to an army of one thousand men, sufficient provisions or horses for such an expedition.

"Your Excellency cannot but be already informed that many persons among ourselves wish to promote a war with the savages, not considering the distress of our country on the sea coast. This disposition, with the conduct of a banditti, consisting of sixty or eighty savages, at the heads of the Scioto, may possibly create a general quarrel; yet we flatter ourselves that, by prudent measures, it is possible to avoid it. But if, as seems the inclination of some, all Indians without distinction, who may be found, are to be massacred, and even when visiting us as friends, a general war cannot be avoided, and we fear the consequences would be fatal at this critical time. But should it please God to bless us with victory to overcome our British enemies on the sea coast, we shall have it in our power to take ample satisfaction of our Indian enemy. In the interim, we are humbly of opinion,

that the most pacific measures, with liberal presents, if in our power to make them, will be attended with much happier consequences with the savages, than an armed force can produce.

"Nevertheless, we beg leave again to assure your Excellency, that nothing in our power shall be wanting to promote and insure success to the expedition now ordered to be executed. But as it will be impossible to have the men raised and armed before the 1st day of June next, we shall have sufficient time to receive your Excellency's further instructions on that head; and we shall in the interim take every possible precaution to prevent intelligence reaching the enemy, so as to defeat the wise intentions of government.

We are, &c. &c.

"GEORGE MORGAN", "JOHN NEVILL."

"P. S. By Lieutenant Holliback, who left the Kanawha last month, all is quiet there, and no murders or Indian incursions have been made into the inhabitants, that we have heard of, since last December, when one man was killed on the Indian side of Ohio, opposite to the fort at Wheeling, and one taken prisoner. They were out as spies."

Captain Pipe, one of the principal chiefs of the Delawares, arrived at Fort Pitt on the 5th of April, and after a long speech to Colonel Morgan, relating to the affairs of the nation, he closes, by saying:

"But I wish you had goods to send to our towns to trade and supply us with, for our skins. Great stress is laid on your inability to supply our wants, and we are ridiculed by our enemies for being attached to you, who cannot even furnish us with a pair of stockings or a blanket; this obliges us to be dependent in a great measure on them. But what convinces me that I ought to listen to the United States is, that their advice is agreeable to my own reason; and when they recommend to me to love peace, and to treat all white people kindly, it proves to me your hearts are good, and I am resolved to follow your advice." [Four strings white wampum.]

By Captain Pipe he sent very friendly speeches to the Munsies and Delawares, with belts, &c.; also, a speech to the Indians who killed the man, and left the letter at Kittanning. After Captain Pipe returned home, the Delaware tribe was assembled, and speeches sent to the Wyandots, Ottawas, Chippewas and Pottawatomie, which are written and preserved in the record of the agency; also to their grand-children, the Shawnees, in which they strongly urge upon them the propriety of keeping at peace with the United States; and there can be no doubt that their advice had a powerful effect in keeping them quiet.

On the 10th of April he wrote to Colonel William Crawford:

"Last Monday a messenger arrived from the Delaware town, and informed that a party of eighteen Mingoes were out, and it was supposed would divide themselves into two parties, and strike nearly at the same time between Yellow Creek and this place. Yesterday afternoon an express arrived from Captain Steel, by which we learn that the first mentioned party had divided as supposed, and killed one man just below Raccoon Creek, and burned two cabins, viz, Muchmore's and Arnot's ; the body of the latter was found — his wife and four children are supposed to be burned in the cabin, or carried off prisoners."

"This day an express arrived from Wheeling, with an account that one Roger McBride was killed and scalped, about ten miles up that creek, and alarms had arrived from several other quarters. I do think, sir, that you will find it necessary to take some measures, in consequence of these murders, and that your presence here is requisite."

The 10th of April he wrote to two of the contractors, Joshua Wright and Gabriel Cox:

"Gentlemen—The governor and council of Virginia having directed Colonel Shepherd to call on me for ammunition and provisions, necessary for a secret expedition, against the enemies of this country, I must beg that you will exert yourselves to procure and send to this place, at as reasonable a price as you can, all the well dried bacon you can procure, without delay. I must also beg you will complete the quantity of flour I formerly ordered, with all possible dispatch. I hope no friend of his country will continue to hold back what he can spare, or complain of the price, of one ninth of a dollar a pound, delivered here; but that everyone will exert himself to promote the service, or the country will undoubtedly suffer. Had I not ordered provisions

from over the mountains, the garrisons at Kanawha and this place must have deserted the forts, for they have not now an ounce of flour but what I have supplied from thence; all owing to the backwardness of the inhabitants in bringing in their produce. If they continue to do so, I fear they will see their error when it is too late. For their own sakes, and for the safety and protection of their women and children, I exhort them to be expeditious in sending to the public magazine here, for the support of the troops, and carrying on expeditions against our enemy, all the salted provisions and flour they can spare."

From April, 1777, to January, 1778, the journal is missing; the book in which the entries were made is lost. There is no account of an invasion from other sources into the Indian country, as contemplated by Patrick Henry, the Governor of Virginia. But in September, of this year, 1777, the Indians, in great force, made an attack on Wheeling— killing no less than twenty-three men of the garrison, who were out to reconnoiter. They also killed nearly all the cattle and hogs; but were not able to get possession of the fort. A full detail of this affair is given in the "Border Warfare." After this failure, no serious attack was made on any of the frontier posts by the Indians during the year.

In January, 1778, provisions became scarce in the region about Fort Pitt, and flour rose to sixty shillings a hundred weight, Pennsylvania currency, or sixteen dollars a barrel.

In March, 1778, Daniel Sullivan, who had been employed by the state of Virginia, under the direction of Colonel Morgan, to act as a spy in the Indian country and at Detroit, in the spring of 1777, returned and made a statement of his discoveries. It seems that he had been taken prisoner, when a boy, by the Delawares, and lived among them nine years, but was released about the year 1773. His attachment, however, to the ways and manners of the Indians induced him to return and live with them again. He was directed by Colonel Morgan to attach himself to one of the Indian traders, who sold goods at Cuyahoga, and, in the capacity of a servant, go with him to Detroit. This he succeeded in doing. At that period, it took a batteaux eight days to coast from Cuyahoga to Detroit.

He wore the Indian dress, and was questioned by Governor Hamilton as to his business there. He also inquired of him the strength of the garrison at

Fort Pitt. He gave him liberty to stay as long as he pleased, and to walk about the place. A white man, named Tucker, one of Governor Hamilton's interpreters, took him home to his house and treated him well. His wife, it seems, was a Virginia woman, who had been a prisoner with the Indians, and knew Sullivan's family. This woman told Sullivan that Governor Hamilton used all his influence with the Indians to induce them to massacre the white inhabitants of the frontiers of Virginia and Pennsylvania—paying them very high prices for all the scalps they would bring. That he also paid for prisoners; but would not redeem them, so long as the war continued.

One day, as he was walking round the town, looking at the defenses and strength of the place, he was recognized by a son of the notorious banditti chief, Pluggy. He immediately applied to Governor Hamilton to have him arrested, on account of his killing his brother-in-law, at the Kanawha, in the fall of 1776. John Montour also testified to the same thing. He was arrested and put in irons, and sent down to Montreal and Quebec. From here, as a white man, he was sent round, with other prisoners, to New York, and set at liberty on parole.

His testimony only confirms that of many others as to the fact of Governor Hamilton paying the Indians for all the scalps of the Americans which they could bring. This policy was, no doubt, the cause of the death of many poor women and children, whom the Indian clemency might have spared but for this odious bounty.

The unfortunate murder of the celebrated Shawnee Chief, Cornstalk, in the autumn of 1777, at Fort Randolph, by some of the incensed soldiers of that station, came near involving the country in a general Indian war. Every suitable concession was made to that tribe, by Congress and by Colonel Morgan, to allay their anger. New commissioners were appointed, and they were invited to a treaty, to be held at Fort Pitt. The commissioners also sent them a speech and invitation by James Girty, a brother of the notorious renegade, Simon Girty; with suitable presents.

In March, Colonel Morgan received a communication from Captain White Eyes and John Killbuck, Delaware Chiefs, in relation to their affairs. In this, he gives an account of a visit he made to the governor of Detroit, last December, at the request of Colonel Morgan. He relates the speeches that passed between them, and concludes that the forces at that post are too few to cause any uneasiness as to their attacking Fort Pitt.

White Eyes also gives notice of a party of thirty warriors of the Wyandots, who had passed his village on their way to the settlements about Red Stone. He says he had spoken to the Shawnee, as to the matter of killing of their chief, Cornstalk, and that the portion of the tribe to which he belonged would still continue friendly to the United States. He also adds, *"A man from Detroit, his name Edward Hazle, came here with some writings from the governor of Detroit, and desired us to send some Indians with him, to bring them into the inhabitants of the white people; but we declined it, and told him we would not meddle with such affairs. Writings of the same kind were also sent to the Shawnee, to leave them where they should kill any white people, which they delivered to me. Both I send to you, and you will see the contents thereof.* The following is a copy of the writings:

"Detroit, January 5th, 1778.

"Notwithstanding all endeavors to apprize his majesty's faithful and loyal subjects, dispersed over the colonies, of his gracious intentions towards them, signified to them at different times, it is to be feared the mistaken zeal of the deluded multitude, acted upon by the artful and wicked designs of rebellious counselors, has prevented many from profiting of his majesty's clemency. This is to acquaint all whom it may concern, that nothing can give greater satisfaction to those persons who command for his majesty at the different posts, than to save from ruin those innocent people who are unhappily involved in distresses they have no ways merited. The moderation shown by the Indians who have gone to war from this place, is a speaking proof of the truth; and the injunctions constantly laid upon them on their setting out, having been to spare the defenseless and aged of both sexes, show that compassion for the unhappy is blended with the severity necessary to be exercised in the obstinate and perverse enemies of his majesty's crown and dignity.

"The persons under-named are living witnesses of the moderation and even gentleness of savages shown to them, their wives and children; which may, it is hoped, induce others to exchange the hardships experienced under their present masters, for security and freedom under their lawful sovereign.

"The bearer hereof, Edward Hazle, has my orders to make known to all persons whom it may concern, that the Indians are encouraged to show the same mildness to all who shall embrace the offer of safety and protection, hereby held out to them; and he is further to make known, as far as lies in his power, that if a number of people can agree upon a place of rendezvous, and a proper time for coming to this post the Miamis, Sandusky, or post Vincennes, the properest methods will be taken for their security, and a safeguard of white people, with an officer, and interpreter, sent to conduct them.

"Given under my hand and seal at Detroit.

"Signed, Henry Hamilton, (Seal.)

"Lieutenant Governor and Superintendent.
"God save the King."

"We who have undersigned our names, do voluntarily declare that we have been conducted from the several places mentioned opposite our names to Detroit, by Indians accompanied with white people; that we have neither been cruelly treated or in any way ill used by them; and farther that on our arrival we have been treated with the greatest humanity, and our wants supplied in the best manner possible.

"George Baker, for himself wife and five children—now here, from five miles below Logstown.

"James Butterworth, from Big Kanawha.

"Thomas J. (X- his mark) Shoers, from Harrodstown, Kentucky.

"Jacob Pugh, from six miles below the fort at Wheeling.

"Jonathan Muchmore, from Fort Pitt.

"James Whitaker, from Detroit, taken at Fish Creek.

"John (X- his mark) Bridges, from Detroit, taken at Fish Creek.

Notwithstanding the efforts of Governor Hamilton, by his proclamations, and other means, to seduce the frontier inhabitants from their allegiance to the United States, and to come over and join his Britannic majesty; it does not appear that any other than those named in the above list took advantage of his offers.

No portion of the United States furnished more trusty hearts in the cause of freedom, than the inhabitants of the western frontiers. Very few, if any, Tories were to be found among them, and almost every man, and woman too, entered with their whole energies into the cause of their country and of liberty, turning out more soldiers, according to their numbers, than any of the old settlements on the Atlantic board.

The following list of the number of warriors in the different tribes, who could at any time within a few weeks be assembled to fall upon the frontiers, will show how important it was for the United States to keep on friendly terms with them. It was made by Colonel Morgan, and is probably a very accurate estimate of their strength:

The Six Nations consist of,

Mohawks,	100	
Oneidas and Tuscarawas,	400	
Cuyahoga,	220	
Onondagas,	230	
Senecas,	650	
		1600
Delawares and Munsies	600	
Shawnees of Scioto,	400	
Wyandots, of Sandusky and Detroit,	300	
Ottawas, of Detroit and Lake Michigan,	600	
Chippewas, of all the lakes, said to be,	5000	
Poltewatemies, of Detroit and Lake Michigan,	400	
Pyankeshas, Kickapoos, Muscoutans, Vermillions, Weotonans, &c.,		
on the Ouabache,	800	
Miamis, or Picts,	300	
Mingoes, of Pluggystown,	600	
	Total,	10,060

The notorious renegade, Simon Girty, who had acted as interpreter for the United States, in all their treaties with the Six Nations, at Pittsburgh, fled from that place, in company with some others, on the 28th of March, 1778. Ever after this period, he attached himself to the Indians, and became one of the most cruel and inveterate foes to the whites. Through his instigation, it is well known that many prisoners were burnt at the stake, who otherwise might have been adopted into some Indian family, and their lives saved. His brother, James Girty, who was at that time employed by the commissioners, on a message to the Shawnee, was also induced to desert the cause of his country, and attach himself to the interests of Simon.

In March, the commissioners for Indian affairs ordered six large boats to be built for the defense of the navigation between the military posts on the Ohio. Each boat was to carry a four-pound cannon, and to be so constructed as to be formidable either in defense or attack.

In April, Colonel Morgan addressed a letter to Don Bernardo De Galvez, Governor General of Louisiana. In it, he says:

"On the 24th of February, I had the honor to receive your letter, dated the 9th of August last. Not having the happiness to understand the Spanish language, I immediately transmitted your letter, by express, to Congress; but unfortunately not a member of that body understands it, nor has any person been yet found, capable and worthy of trust, to translate it. Wherefore, his Excellency, the President, has directed me to present his compliments to you. He laments this disappointment, and will do himself the honor to write to you the moment he can procure a translation of your Excellency's letter."

In the above incident there are two things which strike us as very singular. One is, the great length of time it took at that day to transmit intelligence between New Orleans and Pittsburgh. The other is, that no member of Congress should be familiar with the Spanish language. It shows the simple hearts and domestic manners of the people of that day; how little intercourse they had with any foreign nation, except the mother country, their trade being almost if not entirely prohibited, while colonies, with any other kingdom. The French language must have been much more familiar to many of the officers and soldiers of the last war, as numbers of them had been prisoners in Canada.

Colonel Morgan proceeds in his letter to give a detail of the principal events of the war during the past year, and especially the surrender of General Burgoyne. It is full of patriotic zeal, and bespeaks a mind ardently attached to the cause of his country.

The projected invasion into the enemy's territory, in the year 1777, having been abandoned; the plan was again renewed on a much larger scale, early in the spring of 1778. As it would take several months to collect the provisions, pack-horses, and boats necessary for an army of three thousand men, preparations were commenced in April, by purchasing cattle, flour, &c. The state of Virginia was to furnish nearly all the men. Twenty-seven hundred came from the counties east of the mountains, and three hundred from those on, the west side. Fifteen hundred were to march through Green Brier, down the Big Kanawha to Fort Randolph, and as many more were to assemble at Fort Pitt, and descend the Ohio to that post. From this point the assembled forces were to invade the Indian country, and destroy their towns and crops. Colonel Morgan was directed to make an estimate of the quantity of provision necessary for the support of three thousand men for three months; the number of pack horses, beef cattle, &c. The amount is so great, that we are led to look with wonder and admiration at the courage and patriotism of the brave men of that day, whose heroism led them to make such sacrifices on the altar of their country's liberties. The stock to be laid in, amounted to six hundred and ten thousand pounds of flour, and seven hundred and thirty-two thousand pounds of beef, requiring three thousand eight hundred and twelve horses for the transport of the flour, and two thousand four hundred and forty head of cattle, which were to be driven on foot, and slaughtered as needed.

It also required one hundred and thirty-six horses to transport the single article of salt. The food for the horses and cattle was to be chiefly furnished by the native growths of grass, vines, &c., found in abundance at that day, during the summer months, on the rich lands of the west. The whole expense of this expedition was estimated at six hundred nine thousand five hundred and thirty-eight dollars. The cattle cost at that time ten pounds, or thirty-three dollars and thirty-three cents a head; the horses cost twenty-five pounds, or eighty-three dollars and twenty-five cents each. Flour was fifty shillings a hundred, or six pence a pound, equal to sixteen dollars a barrel. The price of a common woodman's axe was thirty shillings, or five dollars, and the price of a pack saddle was the same. Salt was six pounds a bushel, or twenty dollars. It was all brought from the sea coast, and imported; none of any consequence being made in the country. Provisions of all kinds were at this time extremely scarce and dear. These prices are not estimated in a depreciated paper currency, but in silver dollars, or something equivalent. Who at this day could be made to believe, that culinary salt, which is abundant at the low price of thirty cents a bushel, could ever have commanded the exorbitant rate of twenty dollars? and yet there is no doubt of the fact. So enormous and great were the privations and sufferings of our worthy ancestors, who toiled and bled for the freedom of the land, which we, their descendants, now enjoy in peace and quietness! We never have, and probably never shall, fully appreciate their worth; or the value of the inheritance they so nobly won.

While these preparations were making by Colonel Morgan for provisioning the troops, General McIntosh was appointed to the command of the western district, and crossed the mountains in the spring, with a body of five hundred men. Soon after this he directed the building of a fort, on the alluvial plain near the mouth of the Big Beaver Creek. It was intended as a covering point, for the formation of any inroads that might be necessary into the Indian country, and as a protection for the troops in case of a retreat or defeat. It was a regular stockaded work, with four bastions, and defended by six pieces of artillery, and was called Fort McIntosh.

Before proceeding with the projected invasion, it was thought prudent to convene the Delaware tribe of Indians, at Pittsburgh, and obtain their consent for marching through their territory. This was accordingly done the 17th of September, 1778, by Andrew Lewis and Thomas Lewis, commissioners on the part of the United States, and signed in presence of Lach. McIntosh, Brigadier General, Commandant of the Western Department; Daniel Broadhead, Colonel of the 8th Pennsylvania Regiment; William Crawford, Colonel; John Gibson, Colonel 13th Virginia Regiment; A. Graham, Brigade Major; Lach. McIntosh, junior, M. Brigade; Joseph L. Finley, Captain 8th Pennsylvania Regiment; John Finley, Captain 8th Pennsylvania Regiment, with several other gentlemen not in the army.

In the course of the following month, General McIntosh assembled one thousand men at the newly erected fort, at the mouth of the Beaver, and marched into the enemy's country. The season was so far advanced that the troops only proceeded about seventy miles west of Fort McIntosh, and halted on the west bank of the Tuscarawas River, a little below the mouth of Sandy Creek. Here, on an elevated plain, it was concluded to build a stockaded fort, which was named Fort Laurens. It was garrisoned with one hundred and fifty men and left under the command of Colonel Gibson, and the army returned to Fort Pitt. The other branch of the expedition, intended to be assembled at the mouth of the Big Kanawha, was never collected, although no opposition was made to the progress of the army under General McIntosh, as the hostile Indians were hardly aware of his presence, before he had again retreated; yet in January following, the Shawnee and Wyandots collected a large body of warriors and invested the fort, cutting off all intercourse with Fort McIntosh, and suffering no one to go in or to come out; watching it so closely that it became very hazardous to procure either wood or water. The blockade was kept up for several weeks, and was only intermitted for the purpose of procuring food. During its continuance, a number of the garrison were killed, and they suffered a good deal from sickness as well as from a lack of provisions. The distance was so great to pack the supplies, and the dangers of the road so imminent, from the attack of the Indians, requiring a large body of men to guard a small number of pack-horses, that the post was finally evacuated in August, 1779, about ten months after it was erected.

The plan of building a fort in the enemy's country, without any means or ability to maintain it there, seems to have been an unwise measure. It cost a large sum of money to the country, as well as several useful lives, without producing the least benefit in return.

In January, 1779, provisions became very scarce and dear, west of the mountains. The employing of so many men in the public service required a large supply, and the main portion of it was brought from the east side of the mountains on pack-horses. Bacon, at Pittsburgh, was seven and six pence a pound, or one dollar of Pennsylvania money. Many other articles rose in the same proportion. During the winter months, when the roads were at the worst, the carriers demanded and received twenty pounds per hundred weight for the transport of flour from Cumberland to Pittsburgh. The price of salt, also, rose to sixteen pounds a bushel. It cost, by the quantity, eight dollars a bushel in Maryland, near the sea coast; but falling into the hands of a private dealer or speculator, it was advanced to this enormous rate. Wheat rose to six dollars a bushel, and in a letter of Colonel Morgan's to Benjamin Kirkendall, a miller on Peter's Creek, he says he has forwarded three thousand dollars to purchase five hundred bushels, at that rate. This is doubtless the actual price, in paper money, as it is estimated at from forty to forty-five shillings, "Pennsylvania currency."

Colonel Morgan was absent at Philadelphia, on public business, at the time of the treaty with the Delaware tribe, and did not return until the 20th of January, 1779. During this time, the affairs of that department had been under the direction of General McIntosh, in whose hands they became much deranged. In a letter which he wrote on the 25th of January, to the council of inquiry, then sitting at Pittsburgh, who had called on him for information, he says:

"On reference to the proceedings of the late general court martial, for the trial of Colonel Steel, you will find some of the reasons why great part of this flour (eight thousand kegs) has never yet been brought to this place. But the principal reasons, as I apprehend, not only for this disappointment, but also the present scarcity of provisions, have been the ignorant, absurd and contradictory conduct and orders of General McIntosh, throughout the whole campaign. When this gentleman's conduct comes to be canvassed before a proper court, I shall afford such lights as may be necessary. Until then, I hope to be excused from being more particular."

In a letter of the 31st January, to Colonel Broadhead, the commander at Fort McIntosh, among other public matters, he speaks of the treaty held in September, and says:

"There never was a conference with the Indians so improperly or so villainously conducted as the late one at Pittsburgh. I am only surprised it has not had worse effects."

In February, 1779, the Delaware Nation was invited to send delegates to Congress, to settle several matters for the mutual interest of their people and the United States of America. In a message to them by Colonel Morgan, he says:

"Brothers — I have appointed Captain John Dodge and Mr. Daniel Sullivan to accompany you there, and I shall go before, to prepare matters for your reception. When you arrive at Philadelphia, you are to come immediately to my house, where your horses, &c., shall be taken care of; and

I will provide lodgings near to me, that we may constantly see each other during our stay in Philadelphia."

From the tenor of a message sent by Captain Killbuck, one of the principal chiefs of the Delawares, in which he complains of the deceptions practiced upon him by General McIntosh, and the commissioners, at the treaty held at Fort Pitt, in October, 1778, we learn the high estimation in which Colonel Morgan was held by the Indians. After recapitulating several articles of the treaty, he says:

"Brother Taimenend — I likewise remember, by examining the last treaty, as if it had been desired by me that Colonel John Gibson should be appointed agent, and in the room of my much beloved Taimenend. This makes me very sorry and uneasy, as my wish always has been, and now is, that I never may be robbed of him; as I am very well convinced that he (brother Taimenend) is the wisest, faithfulest and best man I ever had anything to do with. He always has dealt honestly and fair with me, which occasions the great regard I have for him. I also own that, by the assistance of him and his frequent good messages, I have been kept firm and steady in that which is good. He is the cause of our friendship with the states, which, in working and helping to perform, he has always been very diligent."

The delegates from the Delawares assembled at Princeton, New Jersey, on the 10th May, from whence they addressed Congress, in a paper setting forth their friendship and good will for the United States, and stating the relation in which they stood to each other by the articles of former treaties. At the close, they give the boundaries of their country, as then claimed by the nation, as follows, viz:

"From the mouth of the Alleghany River, at Fort Pitt, to Venango; and from thence, up French Creek, and by Le Beouf, along the old road to Presque Isle, on the east. The Ohio River, including all the islands in it from Fort Pitt to the Ouabache, on the south; thence up the river Ouabache, to that branch, Opecomeecah and up the same to the head thereof; and from thence to the head waters and springs of the Great Miami, or Rocky River; thence across to the head waters and springs of the most northwestern branches of the Scioto River; thence to the head westernmost springs of Sandusky River; thence down the said river, including the islands in it, and in

the Little Lake, to Lake Erie, on the west and northwest. And Lake Erie, on the north"

"These boundaries contain the cessions of lands made to the Delaware nation, by the Wyandots and other nations, and the country we have seated our grandchildren, the Shawnee, upon, in our laps; and we promise to give to the United States of America such a part of the above described country as will be convenient to them and us, that they may have room for their children's children to sit down upon."

At the same time they brought and delivered up three of the children of their principal men to Colonel Morgan, for the purpose of being educated at the charge of the United States. The deputies probably visited General Washington, at his camp in Middlebrook, as his answer to them is dated at that place on the 12th of May, 1779. His letter is in the most friendly style, in which he gives them much good advice, and highly commends the encouragement they have given to the missionaries among them, and their support of schools, and attempts at civilization. In a letter to his Excellency, John Jay, Esq., President of Congress, dated at Princeton, the 16th May, after stating the progress of the mission, Etc., he ceases by saying: *"I am satisfied that the Delaware Nation are disposed to give Congress such a tract of land, as in my opinion would satisfy the troops of the United States; or if set up to sale, would pay a great proportion of our national debt."*

Soon after this event, Colonel Morgan resigned his post of Indian agent.

On the frontiers, and especially among the Indians, the value of property was estimated in bucks, instead of dollars, or pounds — a buck was valued at one dollar. A copy of the following certificate, recorded in Colonel Morgan's journal, among several others of the same tenor, is well worth preserving:

"I do certify, that I am indebted to the bearer, Captain Johnny, seven bucks and one doe, for the use of the states, this 12th April, 1779.
Signed, Samuel Sample, assistant quarter master.

The above is due to him for pork, for the use of the garrison at Fort Laurens.

"(Signed) JOHN GIBSON, Colonel."

Colonel Gibson was commander of this post. These certificates were redeemed at Fort Pitt, by the Indian agent, or the commandant of the place.

At the siege of Fort Laurens, in January, 1779, (it was stated to Colonel Morgan by the Delaware chiefs), the attacking party consisted of one hundred and eighty Indians, composed of Wyandots, Mingoes, Munsies, and only four Delawares, who were outcasts, or deserters from the tribe. Among them were John Montour and his brother. At the second investment in the summer, the besieging party was composed of forty Shawnee, twenty Mingoes, twenty Wyandots and twenty Delawares, who were chiefly disaffected persons. By the interference of the Delaware chiefs, they were persuaded to abandon the siege, without firing a gun. "It is well known the Delawares saved Fort Laurens."

From the year 1780, down to near the time of the ordinance of Congress for the survey of the seven ranges, in the newly acquired territory, north-west of the river Ohio, the sufferings of the frontier inhabitants from the ravages of the Indians are already before the public, in the works of Doddridge and Withers.

The journals of John Mathews and General Buell will bring down the events on this frontier to the settlement of the Ohio Company, at the mouth of the Muskingum, whose transactions will be fully recorded.

Note. The distances of the following posts and stations from Fort Pitt, will be interesting, as taken from the journal of Colonel Morgan:

From Fort Pitt to Venango, by water, 130 miles—by land, 80 miles.
Thence to Le Beouf, by water, 86 miles—by land, 45 miles.
Thence to Old Fort Le Beouf, by water, 4 miles—by land, 4 miles.
Thence to Presque Isle, by land, 18 miles.
Thence along the lake to Fort Erie, - by water, 80 miles.
Thence to Little Niagara Fort, - - by water, 18 miles.
Thence to the Great Falls, by water, 1 mile.
Thence to Fort Niagara, - - - by water, 9 miles.

CHAPTER VII.

Journals of Joseph Buell and John Mathews, on the frontiers of the Ohio, from 1785 to 1788 —Cession of the North West Territory.—Seven Ranges, &c.

Extracts from the journal of Joseph Buell, while acting in the United States Service, from September, 1785, to October, 1788.

He was a native of Killingworth, Connecticut, and held the post of orderly sergeant in Capt. Strong's company and Col. Harmar's Regiment. These notes, although brief, and written from day to day, for his own satisfaction, and without any expectation of their being useful to anybody else, have now become valuable as records of the history of the first attempt of the United States to take possession of the North West Territory; and, with those of Mr. Mathews, will afford a sketch of the events which took place on the western frontiers, from the year 1785 to 1788, in the region of country from Fort McIntosh to Post Vincent, on the Wabash. They also contain notices of the weather, the rise and fall of the water, with the closing and breaking up of the ice in the Ohio River.

Mr. Buell had been stationed at West Point since the 6th of October; when, on the 17th of November, Major Wyllis arrived from New York, with orders for the troops to march immediately for the western frontiers. On the 20th they left that post, and reached Fort Pitt the 21st of December, 1785. He speaks of that village as very pleasant and more comfortable than he expected to see in the wilderness; but complains of the extravagant prices demanded for merchandise and such articles as they needed. After resting four days, the detachment marched for Fort McIntosh, and reached that post, below the mouth of Big Beaver Creek, on the 26th, at sunset. The weather was severe, and the ground covered with snow.

Being now fairly on the frontiers, the extracts will commence at this point. Many of the details relating to the discipline of the men will be omitted, and only such as throw light on the history of the times be preserved. _I_ may remark that the treatment of the private soldiers was excessively severe, and that flogging the men, to the extent of one and two hundred lashes, was an almost daily occurrence. Their offences were chiefly drunkenness and desertion. They seem to have been selected from the most worthless and depraved remnants of the revolutionary soldiers; men too lazy and idle to engage in any laborious employments, and as their wages were only three dollars a month, no sober industrious man would engage in the service. These facts may, in some measure, account for the trials, mortification and defeat of St. Clair, in the campaign of 1791.

"December 25th, 1785. We crossed the Alleghany River, and marched ten miles into the woods, and halted for the night. It snowed, and we made a large fire by the side of an oak tree.

"26th. Marched at daybreak for Fort McIntosh, and arrived at sunset. Went into the old barracks, which are very ruinous, being without roofs or floors. Here we closed the month of December in repairing our barracks, and trying to make ourselves comfortable for the winter. The troops are raw and unacquainted with duty; the officers very strict, punishing the men for the smallest offences.

"January 1st, 1786. We began the new year with desertion. A man by the name of Alger deserted. A sergeant and five men were sent to Fort Pitt after him. Of these men only three returned. Court Martials are continually sitting, and the men very uneasy.

"25th. Corporal Davis, John C. Dittman, Joel Guthrie, and Alexander Patterson, crossed the river, on a pass (or with permission). The corporal returned, and reported that the men refused to return with him. They were immediately pursued by Sergeant Fitch and three men, who overtook them, and they surrendered without any resistance, and were brought prisoners into the garrison. Major Wyllis, who commanded the fort, without waiting for the formality of a court martial, ordered out a file of men, and directed them to be shot within one hour after their return."

Mr. Buell remarks, that this order of Major Wyllis was the most inhuman act he ever saw, and moreover, that Sergeant Fitch was ordered to shoot them all to death, the moment he came up with them, but being a humane man, he disobeyed the order. All the three were young men, and the finest soldiers in the company. "Fitch, for his disregard of the order, was reduced." The affair was reported to the Secretary of War, and in the course of the summer, a court martial was ordered at Fort Pitt, for the trial of Major Wyllis. The result was his acquittal. In the campaign of 1790, under General Harmer, Wyllis was killed by the Indians, fighting bravely at the head of his men.

"February, 1786. This month passed without any extraordinary events; court Martials still common.

"March 12th. Generals Parsons and Butler arrived here from the treaty at Miami.

"24th. The winter has been remarkably moderate; but little snow, not over four inches at any time—the air clear, and troops healthy.

"27th. The weather warm and pleasant, with the prospect of an early spring.

"April 1st. The snow fell upwards of a foot deep.

"3d. Major Wyllis and Captain Hamtramck, with his company, went down the river on command, to disperse the frontier people settling on the Indian shore (or right bank of the Ohio).

"9th. Weather so warm as to be disagreeable standing in the rays of the sun.

"12th. An express arrived from Fort Pitt, and informed that a number of Indians had come in there the night before; their design unknown. Captain Zeigler set out immediately to learn their intentions.

"14th. Captain Strong discovered a number of Indians with their arms at a little distance from the garrison, but did not speak with them. By their behavior, we imagined they designed some mischief. They set the woods on fire in several places, and we expected them to fall on the garrison in the smoke, and were alarmed lest the fort should take fire; the wind, however, became more calm, and we received no damage. Captain Strong ordered out a party to pursue them, but they had disappeared.

"May 1st. This being May Day is kept by all the western and southern people with great glee. A pole is erected and decorated with flowers, around which they dance in a circle, with many curious antics, drinking and carousing, and firing guns in honor of St. Tammany, the patron of this festival.

"4th. Captain Zeigler's and Strong's companies embarked for Muskingum.

"8th. We arrived at Muskingum, where we encamped in the edge of the woods, a little distance from the fort.

"10th. Captain Zeigler's company embarked for the Miami, and our company moved into the garrison, where we were engaged for several days in making ourselves comfortable.

"12th. Began to make our gardens, and had a very disagreeable spell of weather, which continued for twenty-two days, raining in succession. (The fort was at this time under the command of Major Doughty).

"25th. Ingraham, of Captain Hart's company, died; which is the first man we have lost by sickness.

"31st. Employed in working my garden, which begins to be pretty forward.

"June 5th. Major Fish arrived here from New York, with an order to arrest Major Wyllis for shooting the three men, without trial, at Fort McIntosh.

"7th. Major Fish and Hamtramck left here for McIntosh.

"9th. Two boats arrived from Miami and report that the Indians had murdered several inhabitants this spring. We are getting short in meat for the troops.

"10th. Five frontier men came here to hunt for the garrison, and brought with them a quantity of venison.

"19th. News arrived that the Indians had killed four or five women and children, at Fish Creek, about thirty miles from this garrison.

"23d. Lieutenants Bradford and Tratt, arrived from Fort Pitt, and brought with them Captain Tunis, an Indian trader. They report the arrival of the commandant at Pittsburgh, together with Captains Furguson and McCardy's companies, and that twenty men had deserted from each company.

"26th. Major Wyllis arrived here from the Miami.

"29th. Major Wyllis and Captain Strong embarked for Pittsburgh, where he is to be tried by a court martial.

"July 4th. The great day of American independence was commemorated by the discharge of thirteen guns; after which the troops were served with extra rations of liquor, and allowed to get drunk as much as they pleased.

"9th. We discovered some Indians crossing the Ohio in a canoe, below the garrison, and sent a party after them, but could not overtake them.

"8th. We are brought to half rations, and have sent out a party of men to hunt. They returned without much success, although game is plenty in the woods. Sergeant Munsell came near drowning, by the upsetting of his canoe, in crossing the Ohio. He could not swim; and, after sinking two or three times, accidentally caught hold of the side of the canoe, and was saved.

"10th. Ensign Kingsbury, with aparty of men, embarked for Wheeling, in quest of provisions.

"12th. Captain Strong arrived from Fort Pitt.

"16th. We were visited by a party of Indians, who encamped at a little distance from the garrison, and appear to be very friendly. They were treated kindly by the officers, who gave them some wine, and the best the garrison afforded.

"17th. Our men took up a stray canoe, on the river. It contained a pair of shoes, two axes, and some corn. We suppose the owners were killed by the Indians. Same day, Lieutenant Kingsbury returned, with only a supply of food for six or seven days.

"18th. Captain Strong's company began to build their range of barracks, to make ourselves comfortable for winter. It contains six rooms, under one roof, and forms one of the five curtains or sides of the fort, between the bastions.

"19th. This day buried the fifer to Captain Hart's company. Our funerals are conducted in the following manner. The men are all paraded without arms, and march by files in the rear of the corpse. The guard, with arms, march in front, with their pieces reversed; and the music in the rear of the guard, just in front of the coffin, playing some mournful tune. After the dead is buried, they return in the same order, playing some lively march.

"21st. A boat arrived from Fort Pitt with intelligence of a drove of cattle being at Wheeling for this garrison.

"22d. Lieutenant Pratt, with a party of men, went up by land to bring down the cattle.

"23d. Colonel Harmer arrived at the garrison. The troops paraded to receive him, and fired a salute of nine guns.

"26th. Captain Hart went with a party of men to guard the Indians up the Muskingum.

"27th. Lieutenant Pratt arrived with ten head of cattle, which revived our spirits, as we had been without provisions for several days.

"29th. Three hunters came into the fort and informed that they had seen a party of Indians lying in the woods. We sent out some men, but discovered nothing.

"August 2d. Our garrison was alarmed. Captain Hart was walking on the bank of the river and said he saw Indians on the other side of the Ohio, and saw them shoot one of our men, who was out hunting, and beheld him fall. Colonel Harmer immediately sent the captain, with a party of men, after them. They crossed the river, and found one man asleep on the ground, and another had been shooting at a mark. They had seen no Indians.

"4th. Ensign Denny arrived from the Miami and reports that their men desert very much.

"5th. Major North arrived from New York with pay for the troops.

"10th. Lieutenant Bradford embarked for Fort Pitt, to bring down two field pieces for the defense of this garrison.

"11th. Captain Hart's Company was ordered" to encamp in the open ground outside the fort, as the men are very sickly in the barracks.

"23d. Captain Hart, with his company, embarked for Wheeling, with orders to escort and protect the surveyors in the seven ranges.

"September 1st. Captain Tunis, the Indian, came to the fort and reported that the Indians designed to attack our garrison, and that they were bent upon mischief. We were all hands employed in making preparations to receive them; lining the bastions, and clearing away all the weeds and brush within a hundred yards of the fort. We likewise cut up all our corn, and broke down the bean poles, to prevent their having any shelter within rifle shot distance.

"6th. Captain Tunis left the garrison to return to his nation, and bring us further information.

"7th. The troops received orders to parade at the alarm post at day break, and continue under arms until after sun rise.

"12th. Still busy making preparations for the Indians, and expect them every day.

"19th. Lieutenant Ford and Mr. Cowdry arrived here on express — the particulars kept private.

"29th. The Ohio rose ten feet in five hours—kept the men up several times in the night to secure the boats. It is a singular freshet, as we have had no rain here for ten days.

"21st. Ensign Kingsbury was ordered to take a party of men into the commandant's house, and put it in the best order for defense, and to remain there during the night.

"26th. The troops are again brought to half rations. I went with a party of men after a raft of timber to build our barracks.

"27th. Lieutenant Smith embarked in quest of provisions. We are on short allowance, and expect the Indians every day to attack us. Our men are very uneasy, laying various plans to desert, but are so closely watched that it is very difficult for them to escape.

"October 2d, 1786. Lieutenant Smith returned with provisions, sufficient only for a short time. We are busily occupied in erecting the barracks.

"10th. Major Doughty and Captain Strong left here for New England.

"11th. The Indians made us a visit, and stole one of our horses as it was feeding in the woods.

"16th. Captain Tunis called again at the fort, and says the Indians had repented of their design to attack the garrison.

"21st. Finished shingling our barracks.

"24th. Sergeant Shamburg returned from his voyage to Pittsburgh, with Major Doughty and Captain Strong, occupying fourteen days.

"26th. We this day finished building the chimneys to the barracks.

"27th. Lieutenant Pratt ordered out the men for timber to build him a house. The officers' houses were two stories high, and built in the bastions.

"November 2d. Captain Sheets arrived with a new barge for the colonel, built at Pittsburgh.

"3d. Captain Tunis and a number of Indians, with two squaws, came into the garrison. At night they got very drunk, and threatened the guard with their tomahawks and knives.

"5th. Uling, a trader on the river, arrived with provisions.

"9th. The hunters brought in about thirty deer, and a great number of turkeys.

"24th. There fell a considerable snow.

"25th. Captain Hart's and M'Curdy's companies came in from the survey of the seven ranges. They had a cold, wearisome time — their clothes and shoes worn out, and some of their feet badly frozen.

"December 3d. Uling arrived with twenty kegs of flour and ten kegs of whisky, and some dry goods.

"4th. Major Wyllis was cleared by the court martial, and ordered to resume his command at the rapids of the Ohio.

"8th. Our rations now consist of a little venison, without any bread; as a substitute we have some corn and potatoes. The weather is very cold, and the river full of ice.

"13th. Lieutenant Pratt embarked in a boat for "Flinn's Station,"* distant thirty miles below the garrison, for a load of corn and potatoes. The troops are in great distress for provisions. About twelve miles below they landed on account of the storm, and their boat was carried off by the ice, with a considerable amount of goods in it.   * Since called Bellville.

"14th. The Ohio has been rising rapidly, and we were obliged to be up several times in the night to secure the boats from the floating ice.

"16th. A number of boats came floating down in the ice, carried away by the flood. Some of them had rich loads of goods on board.

"19th. Weather more moderate. Ensign Kingsbury embarked for "Flinn's Station," to make another trial for provisions.

"22d. Ensign Kingsbury returned, with about sixty bushels of corn and twenty of potatoes.

"24th. We drew for our rations about a peck of frozen potatoes. As Christmas is so near, we are making all the preparation in our power to celebrate it.

"25th. This being Christmas day, the sergeants celebrated it by a dinner, to which was added a plentiful supply of wine.

"27th. The men killed a deer, as it was floating down on a cake of ice.

"28th. Uling arrived with a boat load of provision.

"January 4th, 1847. In the evening a furious tornado tore the roofs from our barracks, and did us considerable damage.

"7th. The Ohio River rose about thirty feet, to the top of its banks.

"8th. Major Wyllis embarked for the falls of the Ohio

"17th. Sergeant Hartshorne embarked for Wheeling, to purchase vegetables for the troops.

"26th. Hartshorne returned with a load of potatoes, &c.

"27th. A severe cold day.

"31st. Hamilton Kerr, our hunter, began to build a house on the island a little above the mouth of the Muskingum, and some of our men were ordered out as a fatigue party, to assist him, under the command of Lieutenant Pratt.

"February 11th. The weather has been very fine, and there is a prospect of an early spring.

"16th. Hamilton Kerr moved his family on to the island.

"19th. Captain Beatty arrived, with pay and clothing for the troops.

"25th. Colonel Harmar embarked for Pittsburgh, and Major Finney arrived from "the rapids."

"March 8th. Began fencing our gardens, and laying them out very large.

"15th. Sergeant Judd went with a party of men to assist some inhabitants to move their families and settle near the garrison. (Probably from Fish or Grave Creek.)

"18th. Several families are settling on the Virginia shore, opposite the fort.

"24th. Isaac Williams arrived with his family to settle on the opposite shore of the river. Several others have joined him, which makes our situation in the wilderness much more agreeable.

"26th. Colonel Harmar returned from Fort Pitt.

"27th. Major Hamtramck arrived from Fort Steuben, in order to muster the troops. The same day some of the hunters brought a buffalo into the fort that was eighteen hands high and weighed one thousand pounds.

"29th. The troops were mustered and paid up to the 1st January, 1787.

"April 1st. The Indians came within twelve miles of the garrison, and killed an old man and took a young boy prisoner.

"3d. We began to lay out the ground in our gardens, and to dig up the earth.

"5th. Lieutenant Smith went out with a party of men on a scout, and discovered four Indians on a hill within half a mile of the garrison.

"9th. Ensign Kingsbury went on command with a party to bring in one of our hunters, fifty miles up the Muskingum, for fear of the Indians, who we hear are bent on mischief.

"10th. Captain Hart embarked with his company to build a fort at Venango. (This was the name of an old Indian town, situated at the mouth of French Creek, on the Alleghany River; a post was established soon after a few miles below and called Fort Franklin.)

"12th. Ensign Kingsbury returned from his trip after Hamilton Kerr.

"15th. Colonel Harmar embarked in his new barge to visit the post at the falls of the Ohio.

"17th. Major Hamtramck arrived and took the command of the garrison. He is a severe disciplinarian, and turned out the troops twice a day for exercise.

"25th. One of our men discovered two Indians endeavoring to steal our horses a little distance from the fort. The weather is now warm and pleasant.

"May lst. This is St. Tammany's Day, and was kept with the festivities usual to the frontiers. All the sergeants in the garrison crossed the Ohio to Mr. Williams', and partook of an excellent dinner.

"6th. Thirteen boats bound for Kentucky, landed at the fort, loaded with families, goods, cattle, &c.

"7th. Twenty-one boats passed, on their way to the lower country. They had on board five hundred and nine souls, with many wagons, goods, ifcc.

"8th. Colonel Harmar returned this evening from the rapids of the Ohio.

"14th. John Stockley, a fifer in Captain Strong's company, deserted. He was pursued and overtaken twelve miles from the garrison, brought back and ordered to run the gauntlet eleven times through the troops of the garrison; then stripped of his continental clothing and drummed out of the fort with a halter round his neck; all of which was punctually executed. (The usual punishment for desertion was whipping, from one hundred to several hundred lashes; the same for drunkenness; and the record of these events is found on almost every page.)

"15th. Major Hamtramck embarked to return to his post at Steuben, and Captain Beatty for New York, after pay and clothing for the regiment.

"17th. Captain King arrived with an express from Congress.

"21. This evening I sent a young man, who cooked for me, to Kerr's Island, about half a mile above the fort, after some milk; he was seen to jump into the river, near the shore, when about a third of a mile from the garrison.

We supposed some of the people were playing in the water. He did not return that evening, which led me to fear he had lost his canoe. In the morning a party was sent after him. They discovered fresh signs of Indians, and found his hat. They followed the trail but did not find them. We afterwards heard that they killed and scalped him. The Indians were a party of Ottawas.

"23d. Captain Strong was ordered to get his company ready to embark for the rapids at a minute's warning.

"25th. Lieutenant Kersey arrived with a part of Captain Mercer's and Smith's companies.

"26th. Captain Strong with his company embarked at ten o'clock, A. M., on board of two keelboats, for the falls, with a warm sunshine and pleasant breeze.

"27th. At six in the morning reached the mouth of Big Kanawha, ono hundred and twelve miles, where we landed and took breakfast at Colonel Lewis's. Here the men bought liquor, got drunk, and refused to be silent when ordered — whereupon I was forced to give several of them a severe whipping, which produced quiet, and we proceeded on our passage.

"28th. We arrived at Limestone, one hundred and seventy-five miles below Kanawha, at four o'clock, P. M., and passed the night. This is the main landing for the Kentucky emigrants.

"29th. In the morning resumed our passage. About twenty miles below Limestone discovered an elegant horse on the Indian shore. The captain was apprehensive of danger, and would not suffer the men to land and take it. We remained all the night on the river. In the morning there was quite a storm of wind and rain.

"30th. Arrived at Kentucky River about three o'clock, P. M. Made a short halt and pursued our course.

"31st. Arrived at Fort Finney, at the falls of the Ohio, at ten o'clock, A. M., distance five hundred and thirty-three miles from Muskingum. Here we landed our men and marched up to the fort, forming our camp a little distance from it. This garrison is pleasantly situated on the Indian shore, opposite a beautiful town called Louisville.

"June 1st. Nothing worth notice happened, except our troops moved into the fort.

"5th. Made a visit to Louisville, in company with Sergeant Wilcox. We drank two bowls of punch and paid two dollars; which I then thought extravagant, but they were reasonable people when compared with the inhabitants of Post Vincent.

"6th. An express arrived at the garrison, with information that the Indians had cut off a boat's crew fifteen miles below the falls. A command was immediately sent after them, who found the dead bodies, all scalped, but did not discover the Indians.

"9th. Captain Mercer arrived with his company, from Muskingum, in the evening.

"10th. Captain Smith arrived with his company.

"11th. Colonel Harmer and Major Hamtramck landed at the fort.

"18th. The military stores were guarded over the falls, so that we expect a movement soon.

"19th. All the keelboats were piloted over the falls.

"20th. The two soldiers, who were discharged on the 4th instant, returned to the falls, and reported that the Indians attacked their boat near the mouth of the Miami; that they fought them for some time, but were worsted and obliged to return.

"July 2d. The second battalion were ordered to embark and encamp below the falls.

"3d. The first battalion joined us early in the morning.

"4th. The day of independence. Nothing was done worth notice. We were busy preparing to embark for the Post Vincent. The troops had an extra gill of liquor served out to them.

"8th. Our regiment embarked at six o'clock, A. M., on board of boats, with their baggage, horses, and cattle. I tarried at the rapids until afternoon, to bring on one of the contractor's boats. We floated all night, and overtook the fleet the next day about ten o'clock, A. M.

"10th. We arrived at Pigeon Creek, one hundred and eighty miles below the falls, at one o'clock, P. M. Sent off our boats with an escort of one hundred men, to transport the baggage up the Wabash River. In the mean time, we were busy in making preparation to march through the wilderness. Here the troops drew sixteen pounds of flour to each man, and have to transport it on their backs,' in addition to their arms, &c., through the woods.

"11th. Commenced our march early in the morning. The weather is extremely hot, and the men weary and faint. Many of them threw away their flour. During the first day, I carried my load of flour; but after that put it on a pack horse. We were seven days on the march, and had a fatiguing, tedious tour of it—suffering much for the want of water. The troops marched in four columns, in the most perfect order, with a drummer at the head of each; to give and answer signals for the halting and forward movements of the divisions.

"19th. We arrived at Post Vincent, distant sixty miles from the place of landing. Marched through the town and encamped near the old fort.

"20th. A command was sent to meet the boats, and the regiment moved up the Wabash about half a mile and encamped on the bank of the river, at a very pleasant spot.

"25th. Major Hamtramck arrived, with the boats and baggage. One man was drowned on the passage, and a package of two hundred shirts sunk in the river.

"26th. Lieutenant Armstrong embarked with a party of men, to bring up some baggage that was left at the mouth of the Wabash.

"27th. An express arrived, and informed us that the Indians had attacked one of our boats, and killed one man of Captain Zeigler's company and a number of the inhabitants.

"28th. Two canoes of Indians came down the river with their flag flying, landed on the opposite shore, fired their guns, whooped and yelled a few times, and went into the town.

"29th. Went into the village with Sergeant Wilcox, and spent the day. Found all kinds of goods and liquors very dear.

"August 2d. Old Mr. Owens came an express here through the wilderness. The weather is very hot, and we have had no rain for a long time. The men begin to be sickly, and although this is called a healthy place, we expect the troops will suffer a good deal, as the climate is very different from that in which they have formerly lived. Post Vincent is a beautiful place, was it settled with respectable people; but they are a mixture of all nations. The principal inhabitants are French, intermarried with Indians, and pay but little regard to religion or law. They are under the guidance of an old Roman Catholic friar, who keeps them in ignorance as much as he can, and fills them full of superstition. The people give themselves up to all kinds of vice, and are as indolent and idle a community as ever composed one town. They might live in affluence if they were industrious. The town has been settled longer than Philadelphia, and one half of their dwelling houses are yet covered with bark like Indian wigwams. The inhabitants are quite numerous, and people from all parts of the United States are emigrating to this place.

"4th. In the evening a party of men were ordered out to disperse a band of Indians, who were lying in ambush to attack our boats as they ascended the river.

"5th. The party returned without seeing any Indians.

"7th. Two canoes came down the river from Detroit, loaded with peltry and Indian goods, which we thought to make a prize of.

"9th. Colonel Harmer left here attended by a strong guard, for Kaskaskia; distant one hundred miles from the post.

"11th. The troops began to erect batteries on the flanks of our encampment.

"19th. There was a violent storm of rain, which broke down our boweries and much incommoded the encampment.

"23d. Several men have died, and Captain Strong was carried into town sick of a fever.

"27th. At this time our troops are very sickly; nearly half of them are down.

"September 3d. Colonel Harmer returned from Kaskaskia.

"5th. The Pyankesha Indians came down the river in canoes, with their white flag hoisted. When they were within a mile of our encampment, they began a running fire, and continued until quite near it. A guard was ordered out and fired three vollies as a welcome. They landed and came up to our camp, when the music was ordered to play them a salute. They were painted in fine style; some black with streaks of white, others red and eyes white. To us they seemed hideous, but in their own estimation no doubt very fine. They made but a short visit, when they embarked in their canoes, returning our parting salute with a running fire as before, and went into the town.

"7th. The Indians visited our camp to drink whisky. The music saluted them as they came in and went out.

"9th. The Indians came again to our camp. A band of warriors marched in front painted for battle, and perfectly naked, except their breech clouts, and commenced a dance round our flag staff. Their music consisted of a drum made of a small keg, covered at one end with a skin, and beat upon with a stick. After performing their antics for some time round the flag staff, they went to the Colonel's marquee, and danced in the hot sun, drinking whisky at the same time, until all were as drunk as they could be and stand on their feet. They then staggered into town, where I saw them fighting and dragging each other through the mud and dirt of the streets.

"11th. Sergeants Fitch and Hartshorne were sent to the hospital: three of my messmates are now in town sick with the fever, and there are only two of us left.

"12th. The Indians left Post Vincent to return to their towns.

"14th. Sergeant Fitch, my messmate, died; which I lament greatly, as he was my most intimate friend.

"15th. Mr. Britt, the contractor, arrived from the Illinois, and reported that one of our men had left him and gone to the Spaniards. Mr. Bradshaw arrived with a drove of cattle from the falls of Ohio.

"26th. Several of the sick have recovered and returned to duty.

"October 1st. Captain Zeigler's and Strong's companies marched at eleven o clock A. M., for the rapids of the Ohio, through the wilderness. The tour was much more pleasant than in July.

"4th. In our march to day, came across five buffaloes. They tried to force a passage through our column. The general ordered the men to fire on them. Three were killed, and the others wounded.

"7th. We arrived at the rapids a little before sunset, after a fatiguing march.

"22d. Major Wyllis came in with Captain Finney's and Mercer's companies, from "the post."

"25th. Captain Zeigler's and Strong's companies received orders to be in readiness to embark for Muskingum.

"28th. General Harmer left here for Muskingum.

"29th. The two companies embarked at eleven o' clock A. M., for Fort Harmer.

"31st. Reached Kentucky River, and encamped on the Indian shore.

"November 1st. We continue on our passage, and make about fifteen or twenty miles a day up stream. Every night we encamp on the shore, and embark early in the morning.

"3d. Reached the Big Miami, and encamped on the Kentucky side.

"4th. We killed two buffaloes, as they were crossing the river.

"5th. Passed the Little Miami, with a fine breeze.

"7th. Came within five miles of Limestone and encamped.

"8th. Reached Limestone, and tarried until three o'clock, P. M., then pursued our voyage and encamped.

"11th. Passed the mouth of Scioto River.

"13th. Passed Big Sandy.

"14th. Passed the Guyandotte.

"16th. Reached the Big Kanawha, and tarried all night.

"18th. The hunters killed several buffaloes. Passed "Letart," or " Little Falls."

"19th. Came to Bellville and passed the night. Bought a quantity of vegetables for the winter.

"20th. Reached the Little Kanawha and encamped on the Indian shore. Had a stormy night.

"21st. We had a fine breeze, and reached Muskingum at ten o' clock A. M., and took possession of our old quarters. The upward voyage was accomplished in twenty-four days. The downward one in five days. The distance is five hundred and thirty-three miles.

"December 7th, 1787. Captain Mercer and Ashden embarked for the falls of the Ohio.

"8th. Captain Beatty left here for New York, after money and clothing for the regiment.

"12th. Mr. Melcher, a cadet, came here from Philadelphia.

"22d. Information was received that the contractor's boat had grounded at Middle Island.

"23d. Sergeant Pratt, with a party of men, left here in a severe storm to assist the boat.

"25th. Christmas day. We passed this day in a melancholy mood, having but little either to eat or drink.

"28th. Lieutenant Kingsbury returned with provision.

"31st. Two men arrived from Venango.

"January 3d, 1788. Mr. Cochrane left here for Pittsburgh, and General Harmer for Venango. The weather is extremely cold, and the Ohio frozen over so as to afford good crossing on the ice.

"10th. The weather at this time is fifteen degrees below extreme cold.

"15th. The recruiting officers received orders for enlisting soldiers.

"16th. Weather moderate, with rain, and a prospect of the ice breaking in the Ohio.

"17th. Weather clear and cold.

"20th. The ice gave way in the Ohio, and came down with great force.

"22d. A detachment of pack horses came in with provisions.

"24th. There fell a great body of snow.

"February 1st. Fine, moderate weather.

"4th and 5th. Quite cold, and fourteen degrees below extreme cold; and very variable. Our provisions very poor.

"10th. More moderate. The ice broke up in the Muskingum. Two Indians and a white man arrived from Sandusky. Their object is to get permission to trade with the garrison. They remained some time, and were supplied with rations.

"15th. News arrived that Ulin's boat, loaded with provisions for the fort, was stove at the islands called the "Three Brothers."

"16th. Lieutenant Schuyler, with a party of men, went up with a boat to bring down Ulin's cargo.

"18th. The Lieutenant returned with the provisions.

"25th. The larger portion of the soldiers, whose time had expired, have re-enlisted again.

"March 1st. Cold weather. The Ohio River has again frozen over.

"8th. Captain Pipes, the chief of the Delaware nation, made us a visit, with some of his tribe.

"11th. The Indian warriors held a war dance in Captain Strong's room, and made a noise like so many devils.

"12th. The Indians left the fort for their camp up the Muskingum.

"23rd. The contractor's large boat arrived, with provisions and whisky.

"30th. A number of Indians came into the fort with furs to trade.

"April 6th. General Harmer embarked in his barge for Venango. Day stormy.

"7th. General Putnam arrived at this place with fifty men, to begin a settlement on the east side of the Muskingum. They commenced with great spirit, and there is a prospect of it becoming a flourishing place in a short time.

"8th. Captain M'Curdy's company went on scout in the woods after some frontier men, who were said to be lying in the woods for the purpose of attacking the Indians as they returned from the garrison to their towns. They returned without finding them.

"11th. The Indians left us to return to their hunting grounds.

"12th. Colonel Meigs arrived from Connecticut; and Captain Ziegler's company went on scout into the woods.

"14th. The scouts returned. Many Kentucky boats pass daily.

"19th. Several new arrivals for the Ohio Company. This morning there was a severe frost, and weather cold.

"22d. Our old friend Captain Tunis, with a number of Indians, made us a visit. They were treated hospitably.

"25th. The troops in the fort are mustered twice a day for exercise.

"27th. I crossed the Muskingum to view the new city.

"28th. Sergeant Sprague, with a party of men, went out as an escort for the Ohio Company's surveyors.

"May 1st. St. Tammany's day was kept as usual. A party of the sergeants went up to the island, and had a dinner provided at old Mr. Kerr's.

"5th. Kentucky boats pass continually; ten or twelve every day.

"16th. Captain Strong went out with his company to reconnoiter the country, about thirty miles up the Muskingum.

"17th. After leaving our last night's camp, we pursued a south-east course, to strike the Ohio.

"18th. We fell on an Indian trail, and pursued it until it crossed our trail of the 16th. The streams are high, and we had to ford them, which made our march uncomfortable. At evening we reached the garrison in the midst of a hard thunder shower. This excursion brought on me the fever and ague.

"26th. General Parsons, Major Sargent, and a number of other settlers, arrived at Muskingum, belonging to the Ohio Company.

"27th. Lieutenant Armstrong and Ensign Spear arrived from the rapids, and lost two men from the party, killed by the Indians.

"28th. General Harmer arrived from Venango. I was attacked with a fever.

"June 2d. Two hunters were fired at by the Indians, a little distance from the fort.

"3d. Lieutenant Armstrong, with a party, went out in search of the Indians, but saw nothing of them. Captain Beatty arrived with pay for the troops.

"12th. The contractor busily engaged packing up stores for the Indian treaty.

"15th. Major Doughty embarked with a command, to go up and demolish Fort McIntosh; and to escort Governor St. Clair to this place.

"July 4th. This day was celebrated with thirteen rounds from the six pounder, and repeated again at four o'clock. The troops received an extra allowance. For my part, I had a turn of the fever and ague on me.

"8th. Captain Bradford returned from a recruiting tour at New York.

"9th. Governor St. Clair arrived at the garrison. On landing he was saluted with thirteen rounds from the field piece. On entering the garrison the music played a salute; the troops paraded and presented their arms. He was also saluted by a clap of thunder and a heavy shower of rain as he entered the fort; and thus we received our governor of the western frontiers.

"13th. An express came in from the falls of Muskingum, about ninety miles from this garrison, where it is designed to hold the treaty, with news that the Indians had attacked our party, who were guarding the stores and provisions, and killed four men and wounded several more.

"14th. Sent off a command to reinforce them at the falls, and bring back the stores and goods to this garrison.

"20th. Ensign McDowell returned with the command from the falls of Muskingum, and brought as prisoners six Indians, supposed to belong to the band who fired on our men.

"28th. Early this morning the garrison was alarmed by the firing of the sentry, and we thought there was an attack by the Indians to rescue their friends, who were prisoners. But it turned out to be occasioned by the escape of two of the Indians; who, although chained together, found means to break loose and get off safe.

"August 1st. Nothing very interesting to notice at present. There is but little prospect of a treaty at present.

"2d. Old King Pipes came in with a few Delawares, but staid only a few days. Governor St. Clair sent him, with one of the Indian prisoners, to the tribes, to invite them to the treaty.

"3d. I crossed the Muskingum to hear a sermon. (The preacher is not named, but was probably the Rev. Mr. Breck.)

"6th. Lieutenant Kingsbury returned from Fort Pitt, and lost all his baggage the night before, by the sinking of his boat.

"17th. Captain Hart arrived from Venango, and Captain Strong left for Connecticut, to remove his family to this country.

"19th. General Tupper arrived with his family.

"27th. Judge Symmes, of New Jersey, landed here, on his way to Miami, with a number of families. I purchased four hundred acres of land from him, lying in the reserved township, at fifty cents an acre. Paid him one hundred dollars, the balance in a year.

"September 2d. Major Doughty and Captain Hart left for Fort Pitt.

"3d. Captain Zeigler arrived with his company from Philadelphia, accompanied by a number of Seneca Indians. We saluted them with our field piece, which they returned by a running fire from their rifles.

"11th. An express arrived from the falls of Ohio, informing us that the Indians had attacked one of our boats, on its way to "the post," with provisions, and killed seven or eight men, and wounded a number more.

"22d. Ensign Hartshorne arrived from Connecticut with twenty-nine men.

"October 4th. Captain McCurdy embarked for Miami, with forty-four men, as a guard for Captain Hutchins, the United States geographer.

"5th. The Indiana had a drunken frolic, and drowned one of their men by dragging him in the river. The prospect of a treaty with them is very discouraging.

"17th. The two Indians arrived who were sent with speeches by the governor to their towns. It is reported they intend making war.

"21st. Four canoes landed from Kentucky, loaded with ginseng, and report that the Indians had attacked a party of men with Judge Symmes, and killed one of his surveyors. Also had fired on Captain Armstrong's boat, and wounded two of his men.

"21st. Weather very stormy and disagreeable."

About this time Mr. Buell obtained his discharge from the army, and returned to Connecticut, where he arrived on the 27th of November. The following winter was spent in teaching a school, and in making preparations to return to the North West Territory. On the 25th of May, 1789, he commenced his return journey, accompanied by his brother, Timothy Buell, then quite a youth, and afterwards, for several years, sheriff of Washington

County. On the 15th June he reached Fort Harmer. From thence he embarked for Miami, and landed at North Bend, the 26th of the month, where the journal ends. Mr. Buell soon after returned, and located himself in Marietta, and became one of the leading men in civil, political, and military affairs. At his death, in 1812, he held the post of associate judge in the court of common pleas, and major general in the militia.

NORTH-WESTERN TERRITORY CEDED TO THE UNITED STATES.

On the 1st day of March, 1784, the state of Virginia, by deed, ceded to the United States her right and title to the territory north-west of the river Ohio. This right she claimed partly under her charter, and partly by right of conquest, under Colonel George Rogers Clark, in the year 1778, while it remained under the jurisdiction of Great Britain. The states of New York and Massachusetts also made a cession of western territory to the United States.

The 20th day of May, 1785, Congress passed an ordinance for the survey and disposition of that portion of the territory which had been purchased by treaty from the Indian inhabitants. For carrying this ordinance into effect one surveyor was appointed from each of the states, and placed under the direction of Thomas Hutchins, the geographer of the United States. The territory was to be surveyed into townships of six miles square, by lines running due north and south, and others crossing these at right angles. "The first line running north and south as aforesaid, shall begin on the river Ohio, at a point that shall be found to be due north from the western termination of a line which has been run as the southern boundary of the state of Pennsylvania, and the first line running east and west shall begin at the same point and shall extend throughout the whole territory. The townships were to be numbered from south to north, beginning with No. 1, and the ranges to be distinguished by their progressive numbers to the westward; the first range extending from the Ohio to Lake Erie, being marked No. 1. The geographer was to attend personally to running the first east and west line, and to take the latitude of the extremes of the first north and south line, and of the mouths of the principal rivers. Seven ranges of townships, in the direction from south to north, were ordered to be first surveyed, and plats thereof transmitted to the Board of Treasury, and so of every succeeding seven ranges that should be surveyed.

After these lands had been advertised for sale, they were to be sold at a rate of not less than one dollar per acre, with an addition of the expenses of survey, estimated at thirty-six dollars a township. Four lots, numbered 8, 11, 26, and 29, were reserved for the United States, out of every township. These lots were mile squares of six hundred and forty acres. Lot No. 16 was reserved for the benefit of schools within the township.

In May, 1786, the state of Connecticut ceded to the United States her claim to western lands, with the reservation of a strip *"beginning at the completion of the forty-first degree of north latitude, one hundred and twenty miles west of the western boundary line of the commonwealth of Pennsylvania, as now claimed by the said commonwealth, and from thence by a line to be drawn north parallel to, and one hundred and twenty miles west of, the said west line of Pennsylvania, and to continue north until it comes to forty-two degrees two minutes north latitude."* This arrangement with Connecticut put a stop to the continuation of the ranges northwardly to Lake Erie, and ended them at the termination of the forty-first degree of latitude.

On the 27th of May, 1785, Congress proceeded to the election of surveyors, and chose one for each state, as follows, viz:—Mr. Nathaniel Adams, for New Hampshire; Rufus Putnam, Massachusetts; Caleb Harris, Rhode Island; William Morris, New York; Adam Hoops, Pennsylvania; James Simpson, Maryland; Alexander Parker, Virginia; Absalom Tatum, North Carolina; William Tate, South Carolina; and on the 18th of July, Isaac Sherman, for Connecticut. General Putnam being engaged in the survey of Maine, for the state of Massachusetts, could not attend to the duty, and General Benjamin Tupper was appointed in his place, *"until Mr. Putnam shall actually join the geographer, and take the same upon himself."* Caleb Harris having resigned, Colonel Ebenezer Sproat was chosen in his place. Nathaniel Adams, of New Hampshire, also resigned, and Winthrop Sargent, afterwards secretary of the Northwest Territory, and governor of Mississippi, was chosen in his place.

Colonel Ebenezer Sproat

At a treaty held with the Indians at Fort McIntosh, in January, 1785, the boundary line between the United States and the Wyandot and Delaware nations was agreed, on as follows:

"Article 3d. Beginning at the mouth of the river Cuyahoga, and run thence up the said river to the portage between that and the Tuscarawas branch of Muskingum; thence down the said branch to the forks at the crossing place above Fort Laurens; then westwardly to the portage of the Big Miami, which runs into the Ohio, at the mouth of which branch the fort stood which was taken by the French in 1752; then along the said portage to the Great Miami, or Ome River, and down the south-east side of the same, to its mouth; thence along the south shore of Lake Erie, to the mouth of Cuyahoga, where it began.

"Article 4th. The United States allot the lands contained within the said lines to the Wyandot and Delaware nations, to live and to hunt on, and to such of the Ottawa nation as now live thereon, saving and reserving for the establishment of trading posts, six miles square at the mouth of Miami, or Ome River, and the same at the portage on that branch of the Big Miami which runs into the Ohio, and the same on the Lake of Sandusky, where the fort formerly stood, and also, two miles square on each side of the lower rapids of Sandusky River; which posts and the lands annexed to them shall be to the use and under the government of the United States.

"Article 6th. The Indians who sign this treaty, as well in behalf of all their tribes, as of themselves, do acknowledge the lands east, south, and west of the lines described in the third article, so far as the said Indians formerly claimed the same, to belong to the United States, and none of their tribes shall presume to settle upon the same, or any part of it."

At a conference, held in Princeton, New Jersey, at the house of Colonel George Morgan, Indian agent, the 10th of May, 1779, between several of the leading chiefs of the Delaware nation, and Lewis Morris, John Dodge, and Daniel Sullivan, commissioners, *they claim as their sole property, all the lands they have long inhabited and hunted on, contained within the following boundaries, viz.: from the mouth of the Alleghany River, at Fort Pitt, to Venango; and from thence up French Creek and by La Beouf along the old road to Presque Isle, on the east; the Ohio River, including all the islands in it, from Fort Pitt to the Wabash, on the south; thence up the river Wabash to that branch Opecomeecah, and up the same to the head thereof; and from thence to the head waters and springs of the Great Miami, or Rocky River; thence across to the headwaters and springs of the most north-western branches of Scioto River; thence to the head westernmost springs of Sandusky River; thence down the said river, including the islands in it, and in the little lake, to Lake Erie, on the west and north-west, and Lake Erie on the north. These boundaries contain the cessions of lands made to the Delaware Nation by the Wyandots and other nations, and the country we have seated our grand children, the Shawnee, upon in our laps. And we promise to give to the United States of America, such a part of the above described country as will be convenient to them and us, that they may have room for their children's children to sit down upon.*"

This conference seems to have been held on the part of the Delawares, chiefly for the purpose of inducing Congress to supply them with goods and merchandise in exchange for their peltries and skins. They had faithfully promised to do this in their treaties at Pittsburgh, in 1775, '76, and '77, but had entirely failed to perform; and as the savages had remained true to their promises not to trade with the English, they were now in a suffering condition for blankets, &c. These goods Congress probably could not furnish, as they were unable to supply their own soldiers during several years of the war with suitable clothing. They also complained of having been cheated and deceived by General McIntosh, and the commissioners, in a treaty made with them in the year 1778, which caused a great division in their councils, and induced two hundred of their tribe to go over into the neighborhood of the English, at Detroit — while on their part all their contracts were kept with good faith.

In all the interruptions and annoyances experienced subsequently by the agents of Congress, in making the surveys of the public lands, it will be found, as a general thing, that the Delawares were innocent, and that the mischief was accomplished by the Wyandots, Mingoes, Shawnee, &c. They could not brook the thought of the white man entering upon and taking possession of their hunting grounds, which their people had enjoyed unmolested for ages. They well knew that wherever the surveyor with his chain and compass penetrated, the settler and backwoodsman would follow, and the smoke of the white hunter would soon drive them from their long cherished homes. Who, then, shall condemn them for trying to put off the evil day that boded their destruction?

INCIDENTS CONNECTED WITH THE SURVEY OF THE SEVEN RANGES.

Sometime in July, 1786, the surveyors appointed by Congress, under the direction of Thomas Hutchins, geographer of the United States, assembled at Pittsburgh. Mr. John Mathews, of New Braintree, in Massachusetts, then quite a young man, and afterward a surveyor for the Ohio Company, had also come on, with the intention of being employed in the survey, and to view the new region west of the mountains. Extracts of a journal which he kept at the time will show the progress of the survey, and some of the difficulties which attended it in the autumn of that year.

"Saturday, 29th July, 1786. Arrived at Pittsburgh about three o'clock, P. M. Found the surveyors had gone down the Ohio to Little Beaver Creek. Received directions from General Tupper, by Colonel Sherman, to go down the river. The colonel being to set off immediately for Beaver, we crossed the Monongahela River and rode about a mile and a half, and put up for the night.

"Sunday, 30th. Proceeded down the southeast side of the Ohio River, and put up within four miles of the camp.

"Monday, 31st. Arrived at the camp, on the east bank of the Ohio, this morning; where the surveyors were waiting for the troops, from Mingo, which are to escort them in the survey."

"Mingo" was the common name for a post or garrison established at the upper end of a broad extensive tract of bottom lands, once occupied by a band of Mingo Indians, and known as the "Mingo Bottom." The garrison was called "Fort Steuben," and stood on the spot where the town of Steubenville has since been built. It was evacuated the following year, and the troops sent to Muskingum or Fort Harmer.

"Saturday, August 5th. The troops arrived from Mingo, crossed the river and encamped on the other side."

Mr. Mathews staid in camp until the 15th—his journal giving daily the state of the weather and the water in the Ohio River, which had been unusually high for this season of the year. On this day, he commenced the survey of the second range of townships, under the superintendence of Captain Adam Hoops, the surveyor from Pennsylvania, camped that night five miles from the river, on the east and west line. In his journal, he gives daily the progress made, and an accurate description of the land passed over—as to soil, timber, and its apparent capability for crops.

"September 1st. Captain Hoops having been for some time in a bad state of health, and growing worse, concluded this morning to leave the line and return to camp at Little Beaver."

They arrived the next day at three o'clock, P. M., "and found the surveyors had all left camp, excepting General Tupper, Captain Morris and Mr. Duffey." Who this Mr. Duffey was does not appear, as his name is not found in the appointments by Congress.

"Wednesday, September 6th. Made arrangements to go out with General Tupper, on the survey of the seventh range of townships.

"7th. Crossed the river with our horses and baggage at two o'clock, P. M., and started for the woods. Camped at night four miles from Beaver Creek.

"On the evening of the 9th, camped at the end of the fourth range.

"Sunday, 10th. Camped near the end of the fifth range. Major Sargent, who surveys the fifth range, came to our camp, and informed us that one of his hands had left him, which much embarrassed the progress of his work. General Tupper not being ready to begin work, as the geographer had not yet completed the sixth range, I went with Major Sargent to assist him for a few days, and General Tupper proposed to send his son Anselm, who had gone to the geographer's camp, also, the next day to assist us. On my journey from Beaver to this place, after leaving the second range, I found a great part of the third range, poor and uneven land — the timber pitch pine and small oaks. The fourth range is very good wheat land generally. The fifth is excellent for wheat, with many large glades that will make fine meadows.

"Monday, 11th. Anselm Tupper came to our camp about ten o'clock, and he and myself carried the chain.

Major Anselm Tupper

"13th. Completed the west boundary of the first township in fifth range.

"14th. Mr. Anselm and myself with a hunter, left Major Sargent's camp, in order to fall in with General Tupper on the geographer's line, whom we found encamped near the end of the sixth range. In traveling from Sargent's camp, we passed through the first township of the sixth range. Land broken with large bodies of fallen timber.

"15th. Decamped and moved to the westward five miles, where we joined the geographer's camp on Sandy Creek, a large branch of the Tuscarawas.

"Sunday, 17th. This morning I went to a camp of Indians, who were returning from Fort McIntosh to their town. It was eighty rods above us on the creek. They were about eight in number, men and women. They had rum with them, and had a drunken frolic the night before, but appeared decent and friendly.

"18th. General Tupper began his range, and our camp moved to the west about three miles, to a large branch of the Tuscarawas, called Nine Shilling. After running on the line three fourths of a mile, an express arrived from Major Hamtramck's camp at Little Beaver, with word that the Indians were assembling at the Shawnee towns, and intended making a general attack on the surveyors. Captain Hutchins and General Tupper thought it unsafe to proceed any further. Notice was immediately sent to Captain Morris, who had got about one mile and a half on the west boundary of the seventh range, and we all returned to the ground we left this morning, and passed the night.

"19th. At nine A. M. decamped and marched for Little Beaver. Our party consisted of about fifty men, thirty-six of whom were troops, under the command of Lieutenant Percy. Encamped at night near the first mile post on the sixth range.

"20th. Encamped at night near the first mile post on the fourth range.

"21st. Decamped and marched to the eastward. At one o'clock, P. M. met Major Hamtramck with the whole of his detachment, on their way to meet us, near the third mile post on the third range, where we encamped on an eminence by the line.

"22d. Decamped at three, P. M., and marched about three miles to the east.

"23d. Marched and encamped at evening on the Ohio, five miles below Little Beaver, at Hamtramck's Station, where we are to wait until the surveyors return from their respective ranges.

"Sunday, 24th. Mr. Simpson returned from his range, which was the sixth.

Tuesday, 26th. The surveyors not having returned, and business in suspense, I left the camp and crossed the river in order to go down to Mr. William Greathouse, who lives opposite the Mingo bottom, and with whom I had become acquainted in the woods, and there wait until I know what is to be done. Put up at night with Mr. Croxen, about eighteen miles below Beaver.

"27th. Arrived at Greathouse's about one P. M. The country through which I passed is hilly, but rich lands. It is thinly settled, but the inhabitants have in plenty the immediate necessaries of life.

"Wednesday, October 4th. This day I went to Esquire McMahan's, who lives about six miles below Greathouse, and found that the surveyors were principally collected there and determined to continue part of the ranges, and were to be escorted by the whole of Major Hamtramck's detachment. 1 concluded to go with Major Sargent to the fifth Range.

"Wednesday, 11th. Having made the necessary preparations for resuming the survey, we crossed the Ohio at ten, A. M., one mile below the old Mingo town, and took the route of " Crawford's Trail," which leaves the river at the upper end of " Mingo Bottom," and encamped at night about two miles from the Mingo town. Our party consisted of the surveyor and his assistants, with a captain and twenty-five men as an escort. The Mingo Bottom contains some thousands of acres of very fine land. Indian Cross Creek runs through it.

"12th. Decamped and proceeded still on the route of "Crawford's Trail," in nearly a north-west course. At five P. M. encamped; having made, as nearly as we could judge, about six miles of westing. The trail keeps the dividing ridge, between Cross Creek and the creek that falls into the Ohio above the "Mingo Bottom." The surface is uneven, but the ridge nowhere steep, and the greater portion of the soil as rich as the Ohio bottoms.

"13th. Decamped at six A. M. and moved before the troops, as they were not ready, and Major Sargent is anxious to get to business. At ten A. M. we left "the trail," it tending too much to the south-west, and steered to the north-west and came on the boundary of the third range, one mile and three quarters on the line of the third township. Encamped at night at the south-east corner of the second township, fourth range, and found that the troops were ahead of us.

"14th. Decamped at seven A. M. and proceeded to the west on the south boundary of the second township, fourth range. About two o'clock, P. M. overtook the troops at the south-west corner of the second township, fourth range.

"Sunday, 15th. At sunrise Major Sargent and myself, with two men, left the party to find the west boundary of the fifth range, at a point eight miles south of the geographer's line. (It will be recollected that Mr. Hutchins was directed to run the east and west line through the ranges.) At ten A. M. we struck the line seven and a half miles south of the geographer's. After striking the line, we followed it south to the second mile post on the second township, where we began work. Run one mile and returned to camp, which was pitched about eighty rods east of the line."

For many succeeding days, Mr. Mathew's notes with much care the state of the weather and the temperature of the air by Mr. Sargent's thermometer, at three periods of the day, which it would be interesting to preserve, were it not for the fear of being tedious and prolix to the reader.

"Monday, October 30th. Cloudy and rained all day. We lay still in our camp. About noon our pack-horsemen returned from looking after their horses, and informed us that they were not to be found, and that the Indians had stolen them, with the exception of one poor horse, which was evident from several corroborating circumstances. The Indians were about six in number. They lay part of the night within eighty rods of our camp, and we suppose took our horses about eleven o'clock in the evening. They also stole a buckskin out of a brook within a hundred yards of us. It was evident they had been watching us for several days. When the commander of the escort, Captain Hart, was informed of the loss of our horses, he immediately commenced building a block-house on the most advantageous ground in the vicinity of our camp.

"31st. We this morning dispatched a man for Major Hamtramck's camp, on Wheeling rivulet, informing him of our situation, and requesting more horses, so that we might proceed on our range. Although we were apprehensive of danger, we finished the west boundary of the seventh township this day. On our return to camp, we found the blockhouse in such a state as to afford a good shelter in case of an attack from the Indians.

"November 1st. Major Sargent, thinking it improbable that horses would be sent out sufficient to enable him to go on with the range, determined to run the south boundary of the seventh township on our way in. We run two miles of it this day, and returned to camp at the blockhouse at night.

"2d. Tarried in the camp all day waiting a return from Major Hamtramck, which did not arrive.

"3d. The man who was sent to the major returned, with only three horses, which will not be sufficient to move our baggage without going twice.

"4th. Major Sargent this morning concluded to leave the woods as soon as he can run the south boundary of the seventh township.

"5th. We finished the remainder of the south boundary of the seventh township, but fell short of the west bounds of the fourth range, two chains and ninety links, and came on the line fifteen chains and ten links north of the southwest corner of the seventh township, fourth range. Our camp has moved on to the fourth range, where we expect to wait until more horses arrive to carry in our baggage.

"Monday, 6th. This morning Major Sargent concluded to load a part of our baggage on one horse, and proceed to Major Hamtramck's camp, which from the best information we can get is in the south-east part of the third township and third range. At eight o'clock left Captain Hart's camp; kept on the south bounds of the seventh township to the south-east corner of it; thence we kept a north-east course, and in about four miles fell on to a large rivulet, which we supposed to be the main branch of Indian Wheeling, and followed it down, expecting to strike the camp. Night coming on, and finding, we began to think, we were on Mr. Mahan's rivulet, we built a fire and lay all night near the south boundary of the seventh township, third range, but were uncertain whereabouts on the line we were.

"Tuesday, 7th. Discovered this morning that we were two miles west of the south-east corner of the seventh township, and on Mr. Mahan's rivulet. From thence we traveled in a north course, and struck Wheeling Creek five miles below the camp; which proves that we were misinformed as to the major's situation. When we struck the creek we met with some soldiers, who informed us that Captain Hutchins was gone into Wheeling; upon which we proceeded immediately to the river, and crossed over to Esq. Zane's, where we found Captain Hutchins. After dinner left Wheeling in his company to go to Esq. McMahan's, which is about sixteen miles above. Proceeded about half a mile, and tarried all night.

"Wednesday, 8th. At eight o'clock, A. M. embarked in a canoe, and proceeded up the river. At sunset arrived at the mouth of Buffalo, one mile from Esq. McMahan's, and tarried all night.

"Thursday, 9th. Went to day to Mr. Greathouse's, my old quarters.

"Friday, 10th. Attended a sermon delivered by a Methodist preacher."

From the above fact, it appears that this zealous and enterprising sect had commenced their labors of love at an early period in the wilderness region west of the Alleghany. A scene which Mr. Mathews soon after witnessed, and is by him quite graphically described, would lead us to conclude that their services were as much needed to rebuke the vices of the residents of the border west of the mountains, as those of the older settled portions of the country near the Atlantic coast.

"Saturday, November 11th. Being disappointed in my expectation of teaching a school this winter, I went to Harman Greathouse, the father of my friend William. Here I found a number of the neighbors seated in social glee around a heap of corn. The inspiring juice of rye had enlivened their imaginations, and given their tongues such an exact balance, that they moved with the greatest alacrity, while relating scenes of boxing, wrestling, hunting, &c. At dusk of evening the corn was finished, and the company retired to the house, where many of them took such hearty draughts of the generous liquor, as quite deprived them of the use of their limbs. Some quarreled, some sang, and others laughed; while the whole displayed a scene more diverting than edifying. At ten o'clock, all that could walk went home, but left three or four round the fire, hugging the whisky bottle, and arguing very obstinately on *religion;* at which I left them and went to bed.

"Sunday, 12th. In the morning, found the neighbors who had tarried all night still at their cups; and, at eleven o'clock, others came in to assist in drinking up the whisky that remained from the carousal of last night. I left them and returned to William Greathouse's.

"14th. Went to Esq. McMahan's and settled my account with Major Sargent.

"15th. This morning, engaged with Mr. Simpson, to assist him in protracting his survey.

"Wednesday, 22d. This day, General Tupper left this place for Massachusetts.

"Sunday, December 3d. This day, Colonel Sproat and Mr. Simpson left this for their respective homes: Colonel Sproat for Providence, in Rhode Island, and Mr. Simpson for York County, Pennsylvania."

Mr. Mathews concluded to spend the winter at Greathouse's, and pursue his studies in surveying.

On the 5th, he notes the snow to be eighteen inches deep. The weather was cold and stormy; and, on the 10th, he says the snow was thirty inches deep.

On the 18th, he notes, *"I am this day twenty-one years of age, and free, by the laws of my country. I am nearly six hundred miles from my native home, and poor enough — the whole pittance that I can call my own does not exceed fifty dollars. But while I have my health, I feel no anxiety about getting a living, and hope by honest industry to support that independency of spirit which is requisite to happiness."*

And full well did this noble spirited man carry out in after life his youthful resolves. He became one of the most useful, active, and clear-headed men that Ohio ever claimed as a citizen. Soon after the close of the Indian war, in 1796, he married a daughter of Judge Woodbridge, of

Marietta, purchased a large tract of land on Moxahala Creek, in Muskingum County, and erected a large flouring mill. Here he became a scientific cultivator of the soil, and an early propagator of the finest fruits—having introduced an extensive variety of the most valuable kinds from the nurseries east of the mountains, as early as 1806. But to return to the journal, from which I shall make occasional extracts, to show the hostility of the Indians to the encroachments of the whites.

"Saturday, January 27th, 1787. Captain Hutchins, the United States geographer, left here for New York.

"February 3d. This evening I received a letter from Major Hamtramck, requesting me to come and take charge of the commissary department at Fort Steuben, which is three miles above the mouth of Indian Cross Creek, on the west side of the Ohio.

"Sunday, 4th. I went to Fort Steuben, in company with Mr. Ludlow, one of the surveyors, and engaged to be ready to take charge of the stores on Wednesday next.

"Fort Steuben, Thursday, 8th. This morning Mr. Peters delivered the stores in his charge to me. I am now entering on business with which I am unacquainted, but hope that use will make it familiar to me. I have to issue provisions to about one hundred men."

From this time to the 10th of April, his journal is made up with remarks on the weather, the state of the river, and the progress of vegetation.

On the 10th, he writes, *"Captain Martin and Mr. Ludlow left this for the woods, to continue and complete the survey of the ranges.*

"17th. Mr. Smith left this place for the woods.

"21st. Mr. Simpson left here for the woods." Mr. Simpson was the surveyor for Pennsylvania.

"May 8th. This day three of the surveyors and their assistants or parties arrived from the woods, viz.: Captain Martin, Mr. Simpson and Mr. Ludlow; they arrived at Wheeling the 5th instant. Their coming in was in consequence of information from Esq. Zane, that the Indians had killed three persons at Fishing Creek, and taken three more prisoners, on the 25th day of April. Mr. Smith is yet in the woods, and nothing has been heard from him since he left this place, as he did not come up with Mr. Ludlow on the seventh range as was expected; but, by comparing circumstances, I apprehend no misfortune has befallen him.

"Thursday, 10th. Mr. Smith and party returned from the woods, and all is well.

"12th. We have intelligence this day, that the Indians had murdered a family on the night of the 11th, about fifteen miles below this place. On my way to Esq. McMahan's, I saw several persons from Wheeling, who informed me that there was one man and two children killed, and two children taken prisoners, and the woman badly wounded.

"14th. Left McMahan's for Pittsburgh, in company with Messrs. Ludlow, Simpson and Crane. Passed the night at Elliott's, about a mile below Pittsburgh.

"15th. After breakfast went to Pittsburgh, and saw Colonel Sherman who had just arrived. He brings no news of importance from below, only that Congress are determined to go on with the surveys this season.

"16th. Left Pittsburgh in company with Mr. Sherman, Ludlow and Simpson, and arrived at the fort on the 17th.

"Wednesday, 23d. I was ordered by Major Hamtramck to engage a number of pack horses to go into the woods with the surveyors and escorts, to carry the provisions. Went up Buffalo Creek about ten miles, in search of horses. There are several mills on the creek, and the best farms I have seen in this country.

"24th. Rode to the court house in Ohio County. There is a town laid out here, and about twenty of the lots occupied.

"25th. About two, P. M., arrived in the fort, not having very good success in procuring horses, but a prospect of completing what I want. A part of the troops stationed at Steuben had left here during my absence, being ordered to

Muskingum, and the remainder immediately to follow. Their further destination is not known. Major Hamtramck informs me that the stores in my charge will be moved to Wheeling, and I am to go with them. This place will probably be the rendezvous of the surveyors and their escorts this summer.

"30th. A party of the troops left this post for Muskingum, and I have made arrangements to go to Wheeling in the morning.

"31st. At ten o'clock, A. M., left fort Steuben, with a canoe deeply laden, and no one on board but myself. At two o'clock, was obliged to lie by on account of the wind. At four it abated, and I got as far as the mouth of Short Creek. Here I found Mr. Wheaton and Mr. McFarlane, and was induced to stay all night.

"June 1st. We embarked and arrived at Wheeling at nine A.M. Landed the provisions and proposed pitching my tent near Esq. Zane's store.

"Saturday, 2d. The surveyors all arrived on the other side of the Ohio, and pitched their tents near the mouth of Indian Wheeling Creek, where they are waiting for their escorts to arrive from Muskingum, or Fort Harmer.

"5th. Rode into the country, up Wheeling Creek and between that and Short Creek, in search of pack horses and saddles.

"6th. The troops arrived from Muskingum.

"Friday, 8th. The surveyors all left the Ohio about sundown, and encamped two miles up the creek, fully supplied with pack horses, &c., excepting the lack of one man and horse, which I shall forward in the morning.

"9th. Went in the morning with the man and horse to the surveyor's camp, and about twelve o'clock they all got under march for their respective ranges.

"23d. The troops from Fort McIntosh passed this place on their way down the river. The Indians have lately done mischief about ten miles above Wheeling; they have also been seen near here; and from many circumstances I fear the summer will be a troublesome one."

From the 23d of June to the 30th of July, Mr. Mathews omitted to keep a journal, or else it is lost. On the 30th he was at Wheeling, and says that on the 9th of that month he went to Pittsburgh to settle his accounts, as commissary, with the contractors; but Mr. Britt, agent for the company, was absent. From thence he returned to McMahan's and spent eight or ten days with the surveyors, who, it seems, a part of them at least, had returned from the woods. While at Wheeling, he notes in his journal: *"The Indians have been seen in this quarter lately, and have stolen several horses. About ten days past, the signs of a party were discovered near Short Creek, and were followed by a party of our people, who came up with them four miles below Wheeling — killed one and wounded two more of the Indians, who were eleven in number. Our party consisted only of eight men. The Indians were attacked unexpectedly in their camp, and fled with precipitation, leaving their blankets and moccasins behind them. It is supposed they were Chippewas."*

On the 31st he returned to McMahan's.

"August 4th. About one o'clock, P. M., the people living on the bank of the river against this place were alarmed by the screaming of a person begging for life, and the report of two guns. A party of men armed themselves immediately and crossed the river where they found one man killed and scalped at the lower end of "Mingo bottom." The Indians were pursued, but could not be overtaken. The party consisted of only two Indians, who were seen by some people engaged in fishing at the mouth of Cross Creek.

"5th. Mr. McMahan, with a party of volunteers, about twenty in number, crossed the Ohio River, intending to come up with the Indians who killed the man. They are determined to range the Muskingum country, where they hope to fall in with some party of Indians, or come to their trail and follow them into their settlements.

"6th. At nine o'clock, A. M., embarked on board of a boat, for Muskingum, in company with Captain Mills, Lieutenant Spear, and Doctor Scott. Twelve o'clock, stopped one mile above Short Creek, on the north-west side of the river. At this place are about ten families collected, and are determined to stand it out against all opposition, either from the Indians or the troops. (N. B. Squatters were forbidden to settle on the lands of the

United States, and the troops had been ordered to remove them.) After a drink of good punch, proceeded on our way. At six arrived at Wheeling and tarried all night. Here we were informed that five Indians were seen last evening between this place and Ohio Court House.

"7th. Left Wheeling at six o'clock. At nine o'clock, the mouth of Grave Creek, twelve miles below. At twelve, Captina Creek on the west side of Ohio. At sundown, cloudy and rainy. Stopped one mile below the mouth of Fishing Creek. The rain makes our lodging uncomfortable— four of us sleeping under a narrow awning in the stern of the boat.

"8th. At one o'clock this morning we were suspicious that the Indians were about us; on which account we pushed off our boat and rowed moderately down the river. At daylight entered the "Long Reach" — morning foggy and shower at nine A. M. At three P. M. passed the mouth of Little Muskingum on the north-west side of the Ohio; at five o'clock arrived at Fort Harmer. The Ohio was very low; in many places not more than three feet deep, the whole way across, which rendered the navigation inconvenient. The Ohio often rises thirty feet above its present stage; consequently a vessel drawing twenty or twenty-three feet, will pass without difficulty at such a time. Fort Harmer is built just below the mouth of Muskingum. The fort is a regular pentagon, whose sides are made of log barracks, for the accommodation of the troops, and has a picket bastion at each corner.

"9th. Day showery. Spent a part of the day in viewing the garrison and gardens contiguous. The gardens are well stored with culinary and ornamental plants, which flourish with great luxuriance. The officers have an abundance of melons in fine perfection.

"10th. Clear and warm."

From this period to the 23d, the journal is missing. On that day, he notes, "Captain Mills left this place for post St. Vincent. Nothing material has taken place since I came here. I have not accomplished the business on which I came, and am now waiting for a boat to return up the river. I went with a hunter, Mr. Carr, about three miles into the country, between Duck Creek and the Muskingum River; the land is rich and finely timbered. Went to view the Indian works which are about a mile from the fort. They extend for about half a mile on the second bottom; are covered with as large timber as any part of the country. The walls of the works are of earth, fifteen feet thick, and five or six feet high. In the eastern part is a mound, about thirty-four feet high. About twenty yards from the foot of the mound is a ditch and breastwork encircling it. The Indians can give no account respecting them, and say their fathers do not know how they came. Doubtless, when the country is settled, and lands cultivated, many discoveries will be made that will throw light upon the subject, and help historians and philosophers to form reasonable conjectures about the original inhabitants of this country.

"31st. Since the 23d there has been a good deal of rain and the Ohio River high for the season. At six, A. M., left Muskingum in a boat bound up the river, in company with Captain McCurdy, Doctor Scott and Mr. Cochrane — the river in good order for going up it. At twelve it began to rain, and continued moderately all the afternoon until sundown. In the evening we encamped on an island in the "Long Reach," having made about thirty miles. Immediately after lying down, there came on a heavy rain, which continued all night; from which we had no shelter but the bushes.

"September 1st. Morning cloudy and cool. We were in a very uncomfortable condition. The water has risen nearly two feet during the night. Left the island before sunrise. The water continued to rise, which much impeded our progress. Just after sundown, encamped five miles below Fishing Creek, having made about twenty-four miles. We kindled a good fire, dried our clothes and blankets, and made ourselves very comfortable.

"2d. Proceeded on our voyage before sunrise; the waters falling. At eight o'clock reached the mouth of Fish Creek. Here Mr. Willis and Mr. Carr, two men that were along, and myself left the boat, and walked about four miles. We passed several plantations that were deserted, which are some of the lowest between Wheeling and Muskingum. At twelve o'clock we left the boat again at the lower end of "Round Bottom," four miles below the mouth of Grave Creek by land, and seven miles by water. This bottom lies on the southeast side of the Ohio, contains about one thousand acres, and belongs to General Washington. Stopped and refreshed ourselves at Mr. Williams' house, from which he moved last spring. Above the mouth of this creek is a noble body of flat land, upwards of two miles square. On this flat are many marks of ancient civilization and an amount of population far exceeding the present race of Indians. There are many mounds of various sizes; the largest is about seventy feet in height and between two and three hundred yards in circumference; the top is about forty feet across, and settled down, which forms a basin. It is supposed to have been their grand receptacle for the dead, as some bones have been dug from the sides of the mound. It is doubtless a subject which the curious will thoroughly investigate."

N. B. About forty-five years after this period, the great mound was thoroughly explored by Mr. Towlinson, the owner of the land, and many curious things discovered; an account of which was published in the "Pioneer," a work devoted to the early history of the west.

"At sundown, arrived within six miles of Wheeling, and put up at a Mr. McMahan's, who was here making preparations to move his family down from Wheeling, where they had been for a long time, on account of danger from the Indians.

"Monday, 3d. Started at two, A. M., and arrived at Wheeling before sunrise. Took breakfast at Esq. Zane's, at nine o'clock. Left Wheeling soon after; river still rising. At twelve o'clock, reached Woodford, four miles above. The river is so rapid that it is very difficult to make progress with the boat. Under these circumstances, I left the water and walked as far as Esq. McMahan's, reaching there about sunset. Here I learned that Messrs. Simpson and Ludlow had left this place the week before, for their homes. Messrs. Wheaton and Smith were to leave in a few days.

"Tuesday, 4th. Went to Mr. Crawford's, where the boat was to stop. It arrived about eleven o'clock, A. M. Dined and spent a few hours with the gentleman who came up in the boat. About two o'clock they set out for Pittsburgh."

From this time to the 20th of the month he remained at Esq. McMahan's. A small party then proposed to cross the Ohio, and go out into the woods for a few days to dig ginseng. In those early times when the plant was plenty, it was a source of profit to the frontier inhabitants, who had few articles to give in exchange for money, or the more valuable articles of merchandise brought out by the traders. It proved to be rather a hazardous trip, as the Indians were hostile, and killed all the white men they could, especially if found on their hunting grounds.

"A little before sunset the squire and myself crossed the Ohio, and went about two miles and tarried all night at a house which was left by the inhabitants.

"21st. At eight o'clock, four men joined us and we set off by "Williamson's Route" or Trail, a little before sunset. We encamped half a mile beyond the "Big Lick," on the head waters of Short Creek, in the ninth township of the fourth range.

"22d. Left our camp at sunrise, and moved about five miles to the west, and encamped about half a mile to the east of the dividing ridge, between the waters of Muskingum and Short Creek. Here we dug ginseng until Thursday, 27th. It grew here in great abundance. Men accustomed to the work, could dig from forty to sixty pounds a day. The roots were generally very large. The biggest grow where the land is very rich and open to the sun. Many roots of ginseng of a medium size appear to be twenty or thirty years old, which is ascertained from the number of joints, or escars, on the top of the root, every year producing one; but I found roots of a good size not more than three or four years old. From the fact of it being found the largest in open lands, I am led to think that cultivation would be friendly to it, and that a few years, with proper attention, will bring it to maturity. I have collected a considerable quantity of the seed, and am determined to try it. Our camp is on the head of Short Creek, in the fifth township, fifth range, in the north-east part of township. It is an excellent body of land, and extends eight or ten miles north and south, along the east boundary of the fifth range, and about two and a half miles to the west of it.

"28th. Collected our horses and prepared to start for the river. At one o'clock, completed their loading. At sun-set encamped within about sixteen miles of the Ohio.

"29th. Arrived at the river about three o'clock, P. M. We were much surprised to hear that three men had been killed and one taken prisoner by the Indians, about ten miles up Cross Creek, who were out after ginseng on Sunday last. Two of the party made their escape. They had also killed a family the week following, up Wheeling Creek, and done considerable other damage. While we were out, we were very careless and came on their trail, but very fortunately they did not fall in with us. I feel very happy that I have reached my old quarters, and will give them liberty to take my scalp if they catch me after ginseng again this year.

"October 12th. This evening McMahan returned from over the river, where he had been with a party of men in pursuit of some Indians, who yesterday morning killed an old man near Fort Steuben. He did not discover them, but by the signs; thought them to be seven or eight in number.

"November 30th. A part of this month I have been on the west side of the Ohio, with Mr. Simpson and Colonel Martin, assisting them in the survey of the lands they bought at the public sales in New York. Last evening I returned from Pittsburgh, where I have been to settle my accounts with Britt & Co., which I have accomplished. While there, I saw Colonel Meigs, of Connecticut, who has lately come on to this country. He belongs to the Ohio Company, and informs me that the surveyors, workmen, &c., will be on this winter. I was gratified to learn that, by the resolve of the company, I had been appointed one of the surveyors."

January 1st, 1788. He speaks of the weather as very cold and snowing. Also on the 2d. On the 28th, he notes: "Since the 2d of this month, the weather has been remarkably cold, and snow deep. Set out this morning for Washington, and was informed at Southerland's mill that a number of the mechanics (of the Ohio Company) had arrived at the mouth of the Yohiogany River, from New England." He remained at Washington with Mr. Anselm Tupper, until the 1st February, completing some plats of the late surveys, when they left for mouth of "Yoh."

"February 2d. A fine day. Crossed the Monongahela at Parkerson's Ferry, and arrived at Sumrill's Ferry on the Yoh at evening, where we found Major White, with twenty-two men from New England. He informs that General Putnam, with about thirty more men, will be on by the 10th of this month.

"3d. Rainy in the morning; snow in evening. Left Sumrill's for Pittsburgh."

From this to the 6th the weather was very cold, and river so full of ice, that it was with great difficulty he got across to Pittsburgh. On the 8th, the river was frozen over so strong that horses crossed on the ice. From thence he went to Greathouse's, his first resting place. By the 13th the weather had become mild, and the creeks very high. This afternoon I left Greathouse to go to Sumrill's ferry, where I expect to find General Tupper and Colonel Sproat, with a party arrived from New England.

"14th. Went to the store houses at Mingo and Coxes' Bottom, to make inquiries as to the price of provisions, that I might give information to the New England party. Tarried all night at Esquire McMahan's.

"15th. Cloudy and snowy. Rode to Washington. Mr. Tupper will go with me tomorrow to Sumrill's Ferry.

"16th. Day warm. Just as we reached Devore's Ferry, on the Monongahela, the ice began to come down with amazing rapidity, so that we could not cross. Tarried all night at Parkerson's.

"17th. It was twelve o'clock before we could cross the river. In the afternoon arrived at Sumrill's, where I had the pleasure of seeing my honored uncle, General Putnam, by whom I received a number of letters from my friends.

"18th. Set out for Pittsburgh in company with Esquire Foster, who belongs to Brookfield, Massachusetts. He is sent out by General Putnam to purchase provisions, and I am requested to attend on him, and consider myself in the company's employ.

"19th. Found great difficulty in crossing the river, on account of floating ice.

"20th. Went to Washington, but could make no contract for provisions, and left there for the country on Buffalo Creek and the Ohio River. At Absalom Wells' mill made a partial contract for flour, and with Spear & Sutherland for six thousand pounds of pork, to be delivered on the Ohio, at four dollars fifty cents per hundred. Also for sixty barrels, probably for flour, at two shillings and sixpence, or forty-two cents."

Mr. Foster returned to Sumrill's, while Mr. Mathews remained to see to the collection and delivery of the articles, and to make contracts for flour. On the 25th contracted with Mr. Buchanan for three thousand weight of flour, two thousand of which was at nine shillings a hundred, and one thousand at ten shillings, or one dollar sixty-six cents. He also bought of Mr. Wells seven thousand pounds, at one dollar sixty-six cents per hundred and several bushels of beans at one dollar per bushel. On the 26th, received a letter from Mr. Foster, saying the party would not be down under twelve or fifteen days.

27th. Clear and very cold. The month of March was very cold, as he notes in his journal, which is "omitted until the 2d of April; when he notes as follows:

"A fine pleasant day; the snow is not yet all melted. The month of March has been remarkably cold. Since the 27th February I have been employed in collecting provisions in this quarter, and have had the stores all ready for three weeks past, daily expecting the party down the river. This day Colonel Sproat and Mr. Foster arrived at my quarters, and informed that the boats will be down on the morrow.

"Thursday, April 3d. Cloudy morning. From ten o'clock, A. M., until night, hard rain. General Putnam arrived with boats at the mouth of Harman's Creek, before sunrise; and not being acquainted, fell some below the landing. Esq. Foster and myself attended to getting the provisions to the river, and a very disagreeable time we had of it, on account of the rain. I am to take General Putnam's horse by land to Buffalo on the morrow.

"Friday, 4th. I left Greathouse's in the morning. Found Colonel Sproat at McMahan's, and rode with him to Wells' Mills, and hurried on the provisions to the landing. From thence we went to the mouth of Buffalo, where the boat had arrived. She will not be loaded today; therefore I returned to McMahan's and staid all night with Colonel Sproat.

"Saturday, April 5th. Clear and warm in A. M. At one o'clock a shower with thunder and a heavy thunder shower in the evening. Our boats tarried all day in the mouth of the creek, and we have everything to put on board in the morning. They also took in here a quantity of poplar boards for the erection of temporary huts, until more substantial buildings could be built.

"Sunday, 6th. Cloudy and rainy all day. At half past eight o'clock, A. M., everything on board, and we started for Muskingum, with one large boat of fifty tons, a flat, and three canoes.

"At four o'clock, P. M., came too at "Round Bottom," and propose waiting until nine or ten o'clock in the evening, in order to arrive at Muskingum in the forenoon tomorrow. At half past nine got under way, and run all night without meeting with any accident.

"Monday, April 7th. Cloudy and rain a part of the day. At twelve o'clock arrived at Muskingum, and encamped on the upper side of its mouth. Our whole party consists of forty-two men, surveyors and all. We found about seventy Delaware and Wyandot Indians, including women and children, who are here to attend the treaty, and appear very friendly.

"Tuesday 8th. High wind and scattering clouds from the south-west. The party busy all day in unlading the boats, making shelters to live in, &c. Colonel Sproat and myself are to begin surveying on the morrow."

Here we shall close the extracts from the journal of Mr. Mathews, although it is continued for some time longer, but only relates to the incidents of the survey in the eighth range, and not to the history of the progress of the Ohio Company. Many of the sentences already quoted may seem trivial, and of little account to some persons; but in the dearth and paucity of the written records of the proceedings of the early adventurers of the Ohio Company after reaching the head waters of the Ohio, anything in the form of a manuscript, and written daily on the spot, is of real value and ought to be preserved. His details of the settled hostility, and marauding propensities of the Indians, are interesting records that may be trusted in as facts in the early history of the west.

The large boat which was built at Sumrill's Ferry, under the direction of Captain Jonathan Devoll, was forty-five feet long and twelve feet wide. She had a deck roof, and her model was that of a galley, raking at the bows, so that she could be sailed, or rowed up stream. During the following summer she, by the aid of sail and oars, made two or three voyages to Buffalo, or Charleston, as it was soon after called, to bring down emigrant families. Subsequently running boards were built on the sides of the boat, so as to push her up stream with poles, similar to a keel boat; which mode was found to be much more expeditious, than trusting to the uncertain and variable nature of the winds in the numerous bends of the Ohio. She was called the "Adventure Galley" by the first pioneers, but was afterwards named the "Mayflower," in remembrance of the "forefathers'" little bark at Plymouth.

CHAPTER VIII.

First notice for formation of Ohio Company.—First meeting, March, 1786, at Boston, Mass Names of the Delegates. — Committee appointed to draft Association. — Articles adopted.—Second meeting of the company, 1787. — Three directors chosen.—Dr. Cutler employed to contract with Congress for land. — One and a half millions at sixty-seven cents.—Location of purchase.—Boundaries.—Reservations. — Winthrop Sargent aids Dr. Cutler in the purchase. — Meeting of Company.—Dr. Cutler's report. — A city to be laid out at Muskingum.—Four surveyors appointed, and company of men to go oat and take possession. — General Putnam to be superintendent. — Early provision for schools and religious instruction.—Rev. Daniel Story employed.—Party leave Massachusetts, December, 1787.—Boats built at Surarill's Ferry.—Embark on the river.—Downward voyage.—Land at Muskingum, 7th April, 1788.— Names of the first pioneers.

Extracts from the records of the Ohio Company.
Origin of the Ohio Company.

"On the 25th day of January, 1786, appeared in the public prints a piece styled "Information;" with signatures of the Generals Putnam and Tupper, of the late American army, in substance, as follows:

INFORMATION.

"The subscribers take this method to inform all officers and soldiers, who have served in the late war, and who are by an ordinance of the honorable Congress to receive certain tracts of land in the Ohio country, and also all other good citizens who wish to become adventurers in that delightful region; that from personal inspection, together with other incontestable evidences, they are fully satisfied that the lands in that quarter are of a much better quality than any other known to New England people. That the climate, seasons, produce, &c., are, in fact, equal to the most nattering accounts which have ever been published of them. That being determined to become purchasers, and to prosecute a settlement in this country; and desirous of forming a general association with those who entertain the same ideas, they have to propose the following plan, viz: That an association by the name of the *Ohio Company* be formed of all such as wish to become purchasers, &c., in that country (who reside in the commonwealth of Massachusetts only, or to extend to the inhabitants of other states, as shall be agreed on).

"That in order to bring such a company into existence, the subscribers propose, that all persons who wish to promote the scheme should meet within their respective counties (except in two instances hereinafter mentioned), at ten o'clock, A. M. on Wednesday the 15th day of February next; and that each county or meeting, there assembled, choose a delegate, or delegates, to meet at the Bunch of Grapes tavern, in Boston, Essex. At Captain Webb's, in Salem, Middlesex; at Bradish's, in Cambridge, Hampshire; at Pomeroy's, in North Hampton, Plymouth; at Bartlett's, in Plymouth, Barnstable, Dukes and Nantucket counties; at Howland's in Barnstable, Bristol; at Crocker's, in Taunton, York; at Woodbridge's, in York, Worcester; at Patch's, in Worcester, Cumberland and Lincoln; at Shattuck's, in Falmouth, Berkshire; at Dibble's in Lenox.

"Rufus Putnam,
"Benjamin Tupper.

"Rutland, January 10th, 1786.

"In consequence of the foregoing, on the 1st day of March, 1786, convened at the Bunch of Grapes Tavern, in Boston, as delegates from several of the counties of the commonwealth of Massachusetts, to consider of the expediency of forming an association or company to purchase lands and make a settlement in the western country, the gentlemen whose names are underwritten:

"County of Suffolk — Winthrop Sargent, John Mills.
"County of Essex — Manasseh Cutler.
"County of Middlesex — John Brooks, Thomas Cushing.
"County of Hampshire — Benjamin Tupper.
"County of Plymouth — Crocker Sampson.
"County of Worcester — Rufus Putnam.
"County of Berkshire — John Patterson, Jahlaliel Woodbridge.
"County of Barnstable — Abraham Williams.

"Elected General Rufus Putnam, chairman of the convention, and Major Winthrop Sargent, clerk.

"From the very pleasing description of the western country given by Generals Putnam and Tupper, and others, it appearing expedient to form a settlement there, a motion was made for choosing a committee to prepare the draught or plan of an association into a company to the said purpose, for the inspection and approbation of this convention. Resolved in the affirmative.

"Also, resolved, That this committee shall consist of five. General Putnam, Mr. Cutler, Colonel Brooks, Major Sargent, and Captain Cushing were elected.

"On Friday, the 3d of March, the convention met, and the committee reported as follows:

"Articles of agreement entered into by the subscribers, for constituting an association by the name of the Ohio Company. "The design of this association is to raise a fund in continental certificates, for the sole purpose, and to be appropriated to the entire use of purchasing lands in the Western Territory (belonging to the United States), for the benefit of the company, and to promote a settlement in that country.

"Article 1st.—That the fund shall not exceed one million of dollars, in continental specie certificates, exclusive of one year's interest due thereon (except as hereafter provided), and that such share or subscription shall consist of one thousand dollars, as aforesaid, and also ten dollars in gold or silver, to be paid into the hands of such agents as the subscribers may elect.

"Article 2d.—That the whole fund of certificates raised by this association, except one year's interest due thereon, mentioned under the first article, shall be applied to the purchase of lands in some one of the proposed states, north-westerly of the river Ohio, as soon as those lands are surveyed, and exposed for sale by the commissioners of Congress, according to the ordinance of that honorable body, passed the 20th of May, 1785; or on any other plan that may be adopted by Congress, not less advantageous to the company. The one year's interest shall be applied to the purpose of making a settlement in the country, and assisting those who may be otherwise unable to remove themselves thither. The gold and silver is for defraying the expenses of those persons employed as agents in purchasing the lands, and other contingent charges that may arise in the prosecution of the business. The surplus, if any, to be appropriated as the one year's interest on the certificates.

"Article 3d.—That there shall be five directors, a treasurer, and secretary, appointed, in manner and for the purposes hereafter provided.

"Article 4th.—That the prosecution of the company's designs may be the least expensive, and at the same time, the subscribers and agents as secure as possible, the proprietors of twenty shares shall constitute one grand division of the company; appoint their agent, and in case of vacancy by death, resignation, or otherwise, shall fill it up as immediately as can be.

"Article 5th.—That the agent shall make himself accountable to each subscriber for certificates and monies received by duplicate receipts (one of which shall be lodged with the secretary); *that* the whole shall be appropriated according to those articles of association, and that the subscriber shall receive his just dividend according to quality and quantity of lands purchased, as near as possibly may be, by lot drawn in person or through proxy; and that deeds of conveyance shall be executed to individual subscribers, by the agents, similar to those he shall receive from the directors.

"Article 6th.—That no person shall be permitted to hold more than five shares in the company's funds, and no subscription for less than a full share will be admitted; but this is not meant to prevent those who cannot, or choose not, to adventure a full share from associating among themselves, and by one of their number subscribing the sum required.

"Article 7th.—That the directors shall have the sole disposal of the company's fund, for the purposes before mentioned; that they shall, by themselves, or such person or persons as they may think proper to entrust with the business, purchase lands for the benefit of the company, where, and in such way, either at public or private sale, as they shall judge will be most advantageous to the company. They shall also direct the application of the one year's interest, and gold and silver mentioned in the first article, to the purposes mentioned under the second article, in such way and manner as they shall think proper. For those purposes, the directors shall draw on the treasurer from time to time, making themselves accountable for the application of the moneys, agreeably to this association.

"Article 8th.—That the agents, being accountable to the subscribers for their respective divisions, shall appoint the directors, treasurer and secretary, and fill up all the vacancies which may happen in these offices respectively.

"Article 9th.—That the agents shall pay all the certificates and moneys received from subscribers into the hands of the treasurer, who shall give bonds to the agents, jointly and severally, for the faithful discharge of his trust; and also, on his receiving certificates or moneys from any particular agent, shall make himself accountable therefore, according to the condition of his bonds.

"Article 10th.—That the directors shall give bonds, jointly and severally, to each of the agents, conditioned that the certificates and moneys they shall draw out of the treasury shall be applied to the purposes stipulated in these articles; and that the lands purchased for the company shall be divided among them within three months, from the completion of the purchase, by lot, in such manner as the agents or a majority of them shall agree; and that, on such divisions being made, the directors shall execute deeds to the agents respectively for the proportions which fall to their divisions, correspondent to those the directors may receive from the commissioners of Congress.

"Article 11th.—Provided, that whereas a sufficient number of subscribers may not appear to raise the fund, to the sums proposed in the first article, and thereby the number of divisions may not be completed, it is therefore agreed that the agents of divisions of twenty shares each shall, after the 17th day of October next, proceed in the same manner as if the whole fund proposed had been raised.

"Article 12th.—Provided, also, that whereas it will be for the common interest of the company, to obtain an ordinance of incorporation from the honorable Congress, or an act of incorporation from some one of the states in the Union (for which the directors shall make application), it is therefore agreed, that in case such incorporation is obtained, the fund of the company (and, consequently, the shares and divisions thereof), may be extended to any sum, for which provision shall be made in said ordinance or act of incorporation, anything in this association to the contrary notwithstanding.

"Article 13th.—That all votes under this association may be given in person, or by proxy, and in numbers justly proportionate to the stock holden, or interest represented."

After adopting the articles of association, which constituted the Ohio Company, a committee of three was appointed, *"to transact the necessary business of the company until the directors are chosen."*

The next meeting of the associates was held at Bracket's Tavern in Boston, on the 8th March, 1787, called by special advertisement. At this meeting it appeared that two hundred and fifty shares had been subscribed in this *"company's funds,"* and *"that many in the commonwealth of Massachusetts, Connecticut, Rhode Island, and New Hampshire, are inclined to become adventurers, who are restrained only by the uncertainty of obtaining a sufficient tract of country, collectively, for a great settlement."* It was resolved that three directors be appointed for the company, who shall make immediate application to Congress, for a private purchase of lands. General Samuel H. Parsons, General Rufus Putnam and the Rev. Manasseh Cutler were chosen. Major Winthrop Sargent was elected secretary. The other two directors and treasurer were postponed until the next meeting.

This board of directors employed Doctor Cutler, to make a contract with the "Continental Congress," for a tract of land in the "Great Western Territory of the Union." In July following, the Doctor visited New York, where the American Congress were then sitting; and after a tedious and lengthened negotiation, succeeded in contracting for a million and a half of acres for the Ohio Company, at two thirds of a dollar per acre. From the failure of some of the associates to pay for their shares and other causes, they finally became possessed of only nine hundred and sixty four thousand, two hundred and eighty five acres. By the advice of Thomas Hutchins, Esq., "Geographer of the United States," this tract was located on the Ohio and Muskingum Rivers; he considering it *"the best part of the whole western country,"* and he had visited it from Pennsylvania to Illinois. The boundaries of this purchase are as follows, viz:

"From the seventh range of townships, extending along the Ohio south-westerly to the place where the west line of the seventeenth range of townships would intersect that river; thence northerly, so far that a line drawn due east to the western boundary of said seventh range of townships would, with the other lines, include one million and a half of acres of land, besides the reserves."

One half the purchase money, or five hundred thousand dollars, was to be paid at the time of the purchase, and the other moiety of the million of dollars, the sum to which the land amounted, one month after the outlines of the tract should have been surveyed in behalf of the United States, *'in gold or silver, or in securities of the said United States."*

The reserves, above noticed, were as follows, viz:

Two full townships of land for the benefit of a university. Section, or mile square, lot of six hundred and forty acres, number sixteen, in every township, or fractional part of a township, was given perpetually for the support of schools within said township. Section number twenty-nine in the same manner for the support of religion. While sections, or lots, number eight, eleven and twenty-six, were reserved for the future disposition of Congress. In the North American Review, No. 113, will be found a very interesting narrative of this negotiation from the original manuscript journal of Dr. Cutler.

Winthrop Sargent, the secretary of the Ohio Company, was associated with Mr. Cutler, in consummating the contract, which was finally executed by the board of treasury, the 27th of October, and the first half million of dollars paid. At a meeting of the Ohio Company in August, at the Bunch of Grapes Tavern, in Boston, Mr. Cutler made a report of the verbal contract he had entered into with the board of treasury. On the 30th of that month it was voted, that a tract of five thousand seven hundred and sixty acres of land, near the confluence of the Muskingum and Ohio Rivers, be reserved for a city and commons. The city was to be laid off in sixty squares, four of which were reserved for public uses. The size of the squares and city lots was subsequently altered, and the reserve for a city reduced to four thousand acres. Resolutions were passed for the construction of houses for the use of the settlers, and also to encourage the erection of mills. At this meeting General James M. Varnum, of Rhode Island, was elected a director, and Richard Platt, of New York, treasurer.

At a meeting of the agents and directors of the Ohio Company, held at "Cromwell's Head Tavern", in Boston, the 21st day of November, 1787, it was resolved, among other things, that *" the house lots shall consist of ninety feet front and one hundred and eighty feet in depth,"* and *"that the centre street crossing the city be one hundred and fifty feet wide."* At this meeting it was ordered that no more subscriptions for shares be received after the first of January; and that they adjourn to the first Wednesday in March next, to meet at Providence, Rhode Island, for the purpose of drawing the eight acre lots, which are directed to be surveyed by that time.

"At a meeting of the directors of the Ohio Company, at Bracket's Tavern, in Boston, November 23d, 1787, it was ordered, that four surveyors be employed, under the direction of the superintendent, hereinafter named; that twenty-two men shall attend the surveyors; that there be added to this number, twenty men, including six boat builders, four house carpenters, one blacksmith, and nine common workmen, in all forty-eight men. That the boat builders shall proceed, on Monday next, and the surveyors rendezvous at Hartford, the 1st day of January next, on their way to the Muskingum; that the boat builders and men, with the surveyors, be proprietors in the company; that their tools, and one axe and one hoe to each man, and thirty pounds weight of baggage, shall be carried in the company's wagons, and that the subsistence of the men on their journey be furnished by the company; that upon their arrival at the place of destination, and entering upon the business of their employment, the men shall be subsisted by the company, and allowed wages at the rate of four dollars (each) per month, until discharged; that they be held in the company's service until the 1st of July next, unless sooner discharged; and if any of the persons employed shall leave the service, or willfully injure the same, or disobey the orders of the superintendent, or others acting under him, the person so offending shall forfeit all claim to wages; that their wages shall be paid the next autumn in cash, or lands, upon the same terms as the company purchased them; that each man furnish himself with a good small arm, bayonet, six flints, a powder horn and pouch, priming wire and brush, half a pound of powder, one pound of balls, and one pound of buck shot. The men so engaged shall be subject to the orders of the superintendent, and those he may appoint as aforesaid, in any kinds of business they shall be employed in, as well for boat building and surveying, as for building houses, erecting defenses, clearing land, and planting, or otherwise, for promoting the settlement. And as there is a possibility of interruption from enemies, they shall also be subject to orders as aforesaid in military command, during the time of their employment. That the surveyors shall be allowed twenty-seven dollars per month and subsistence, while in actual service, to commence upon their arrival at the Muskingum; that Colonel Ebenezer Sproat, from Rhode Island, Mr. Anselm Tupper, and Mr. John Mathews from Massachusetts, and Colonel R. J. Meigs from Connecticut, be the surveyors; that General Rufus Putnam be the superintendent of all the business aforesaid, and he is to be obeyed and respected accordingly; that he be allowed for his services forty dollars per month and his expenses, to commence from the time of his leaving home."

To enable General Putnam to execute the business of the company, the directors furnished him with a commission, embracing full power to do and transact all matters necessary for the progress of the settlement. A meeting of the directors and agents was held on the 5th day of March, 1788, at Rice's Tavern, in Providence, Rhode Island.

The agents then present represented one thousand shares, and they proceeded to draw for the eight acre lots, which had been surveyed in the vicinity of the new city, at the mouth of the Muskingum River. At this meeting it was resolved, that a committee, composed of Rev. Mr. Cutler, General Varnum and Colonel May, *"consider and report upon the expediency of employing some suitable person as a public teacher, at the settlement now making by the Ohio Company."* They reported — *"That the directors be requested to pay as early attention as possible to the education of youth, and the promotion of public worship, among the first settlers; and that for these important purposes, they employ, if practicable, an instructor eminent for literary accomplishments, and the virtue of his character, who shall also superintend the first scholastic institutions, and direct the manner of instruction, and to enable the directors to carry into execution the intentions expressed in this resolution, the proprietors, and others of benevolent and liberal minds, are earnestly requested to contribute by voluntary donation to the forming a fund to be solely appropriated thereto."*

Under this resolution the directors authorized Mr. Cutler to search out and employ some suitable person to fulfill the intentions of the company. He engaged the Rev. Daniel Story, then a young man who had been but a short time in the ministry, to go on to Marietta, as a preacher of the gospel, where he arrived in the course of the next year. Further notice will be taken of this good man, among the brief biographical sketches of the most eminent of the early settlers. In this resolution we see the spirit of the primitive fathers of New England, sparkling forth in the acts of their descendants. They held that religion and learning went hand in hand, and were absolutely necessary in the foundations of civil society. This meeting of *the "directors and agents, was adjourned to the first Wednesday in July next, then to meet at the settlement upon the Muskingum."* After this period the subsequent meetings of the company were held at Marietta.

In pursuance of the orders of the directors of the Ohio Company, a party consisting of twenty-two men, under the command of Major Haffield White, assembled at Danvers, in Massachusetts, early in December. In this advance guard were included the boat builders and mechanics. After a tedious and toilsome journey at this inclement season of the year, Major White reached his destination at Sumrill's Ferry, on the Yohiogany River, at a point about thirty miles above Pittsburgh, toward the last of January, and immediately commenced preparations for boat building. The surveyors, and the remainder of the pioneers, assembled at Hartford, in Connecticut, early in January, 1788, and commenced their march under the command of General Putnam, who was aided in the more immediate supervision of the men by Colonel Ebenezer Sproat. When the party reached the mountains, the roads were found impassable for wagons, by the great depth of snow. Sledges, or sleds, were constructed, and the baggage transported over the Alleghenies to the place of destination. When General Putnam arrived at Sumrill's, about the middle of February, owing to the uncommon severity of the weather, and the depth of snow, he found that little progress had been made in the construction of the boats. With this additional force of men, and under the immediate eye and direction of the superintendent, a man in the vigor of life, and bred up to mechanical employments, new spirit was infused into the workmen, and the labors of the boat yard progressed rapidly.

By the 2d day of April the large boat was ready to descend the river, and the company of pioneers left Sumrill's Ferry in the afternoon of that day. The "Adventure Galley," as she was called by the builders, was afterwards named the "Mayflower." She was forty-five feet long and twelve feet wide, with an estimated burthen of fifty tons. Her bows were raking or curved like a galley, strongly timbered, and covered with a deck roof. She was intended to run up stream as well as down; but was found to be rather unwieldy and only used a few times on voyages of this kind. As the galley would not carry all the men, in addition to a large quantity of provision for the future support of the company, a flat boat and three canoes were added to the flotilla. After several stoppages by the way, the pioneers of the new settlement came in sight of Kerr's Island, a little after sunrise. It was a cloudy, rainy morning, and as they neared the foot of the island, Captain Devoll observed to General Putnam, *"I think it time to take an observation; we must be near the mouth of the Muskingum."* In a few minutes they came in sight of Fort Harmer, which was seated just opposite to the junction of that river with the Ohio. The banks of this stream were thickly clothed with large sycamore trees, whose lofty tops and pendant branches leaning over the shores obscured the outlet so much, that a boat in the middle of the Ohio, in a cloudy day, might pass without observing it at all. Before this mistake could be corrected, they had floated too far to gain the upper point, and were forced to land a short distance below the fort. With the aid of ropes and some soldiers from the garrison, sent to their assistance by the commander, the boat was towed back and crossed the Muskingum a little above the mouth, landing at the upper point about noon, on the 7th day of April, 1788. They immediately commenced landing the boards brought from Buffalo, for the erection of temporary huts, and setting up General Putnam's large marquee. Under the broad roof of this hempen house, he resided and transacted the business of the colony for several months, until the blockhouses of Campus Martius, as their new garrison was called, were finished.

The following list embraces the names of the pioneers who first landed at the mouth of the Muskingum, the 7th day of April, in the year of our Lord one thousand seven hundred and eighty-eight:

General Rufus Putnam, superintendent of the settlement and surveys.

Colonel Ebenezer Sproat, Colonel R. J. Meigs, Major Anselm Tupper, and Mr. John Mathews, surveyors. Major Haffield White, steward and quarter master. Captain Jonathan Devoll, Captain Josiah Munroe, Captain Daniel Davis, Captain Jethro Putnam, Captain William Gray, Captain Ezekiel Cooper, Peregrine Foster, Esq., Jarvis Cutler, Samuel Cushing, Oliver Dodge, Isaac Dodge, Samuel Felshaw, Hezekiah Flint, Hezekiah Flint, jr., Amos Porter, Josiah Whitridge, John Gardner, Benjamin Griswold, Elizur Kirtland, Theophilus Leonard, Joseph Lincoln, William Miller, Jabez Barlow, Daniel Bushnell, Ebenezer Corey, Phineas Coburn, Allen Putnam, David Wallace, Joseph Wells, Gilbert Devoll, jr., Israel Danton, Jonas Davis, Earl Sproat, Josiah White, Allen Devoll, Henry Maxon, William Maxon, William Moulton, Edmond Moulton, Simeon Martin, Benjamin Shaw, Peletiah White, amounting to forty-eight persons.

N. B. Colonel Meigs did not arrive until the 12th of April.

CHAPTER IX.

At the time of the landing of the first settlers, Captain Pipes, a principal chief of the Delawares, with about seventy of his tribe, men, women and children, were encamped at the month of the river. They had come in a few days before, for the purpose of trading their peltries with the settlers, at the garrison of Fort Harmer. They received the newcomers very graciously, shaking hands with them, and saying they were welcome to the shores of the Muskingum, on the heads of which stream they resided.

The contrast in the appearance of vegetation between the region they had left three or four days before, where patches of snows still lingered in the hollows, and that of the bottoms on the Ohio, at their new home, was very striking, and was a theme of remark for many years after. The pea vines, and buffalo clover, with various other plants, were nearly knee high, and afforded a rich pasture for their hungry horses. The trees had commenced putting forth their foliage, the birds warbled a welcome song from their branches, and all nature smiled at the approach of the strangers.

On the 9th of April, two days after the landing of the pioneers, Colonel Sproat and Mr. Mathews, with thirteen men, were sent out by the superintendent to survey the eight acre lots for the company. They were commenced thus early for the convenience of the new settlers, who were expected on immediately, and would commence clearing them for cultivation. They were located on the bottom lands, a few miles above the new city, both on the Ohio and Muskingum Rivers. The people not engaged in surveying were occupied in cutting down the trees, and erecting log houses, for the shelter of the provisions, and dwellings for themselves. By the 12th of the month, they had cleared about four acres of land, at the junction of the Muskingum with the Ohio.

The settlers seemed much delighted with their new home, and spoke highly in its praise, as appears by one of their letters, of May 18th, addressed to a citizen of Worcester, Massachusetts, and dated at "Adelphi," as the new city was called; and retained this name until the 2d of July, when the directors changed it to Marietta. He says:

"This country, for fertility of soil and pleasantness of situation, not only exceeds my expectations, but exceeds any part of America, or Europe, I ever was in. The climate is exceedingly healthy; not a man sick since we have been here. We have started twenty buffaloes in a drove. Deer are as plenty as sheep with you. Beaver and otter are abundant. I have known one man to catch twenty or thirty of them in two or three nights. Turkeys are innumerable; they come within a few rods of us in the fields. We have already planted a field of one hundred and fifty acres in corn."

Another writer of July 9th says, *"the corn has grown nine inches in twenty-four hours, for two or three days past."*

Much has been said and written as to the wisdom of the Ohio Company, in selecting their purchase as they did, in the hilly and broken region of country on the borders of the Ohio River, at and below the mouth of the Muskingum, when they might have chosen a more level and fertile region.

Some circumstances then existed, which influenced them in the matter, that have since been done away. One was the danger of hostility from the Indian tribes, few of whom lived within a hundred miles of their purchase, and were therefore the less to be dreaded. Another was the proximity of Fort Harmer, garrisoned by a battalion of United States troops, whose walls might protect them in a time of danger, and serve as a check to the daring of the savages. General Parsons, one of the directors of the Ohio Company, had visited the country bordering the Ohio River, in the year 1785, as low down as the mouth of the Big Miami, in the capacity of a commissioner to treat with the Shawnee Indians. From that place, dated Fort Finney, December 20th, 1785, he wrote to Captain F. Hart, of Fort Harmer, as follows:

"Since I left the Muskingum, I have been as far as the falls of Ohio, one hundred and fifty miles below this place. From the Muskingum to the falls, the lands preserve a great uniformity in appearance and quality. The first place that drew my attention for a settlement, after I passed your post, was

the Great Kanawha, in latitude thirty-nine degrees, about one hundred and twelve miles below you. This is a fine river, navigable about eighty miles, which will bring us within one hundred miles of the Virginia settlements. The lands on the Indian shore are preferable to those on the Kanawha. The next place for settlements is this spot. The Miami is a large fine river, on which the Shawnee, and other nations, live. The lands are very fine." He concludes by saying, *I have seen no place since I left you, that pleases me so well for a settlement, as Muskingum."*

Doctor Cutler, who negotiated the purchase, before completing the contract, consulted Thomas Hutchins, the geographer of the United States, *where to make the location.* He gave him the most ample information of the western country, from Pennsylvania to Illinois, and advised him, by all means to make the location on the Muskingum, which was decidedly, in his opinion, the best part of the whole western country. Colonel Ebenezer Zane, a man well acquainted with the territory north-west of Ohio, also coincided with this advice. Had the counsel of Mr. Hutchins been strictly followed, and the purchase selected from lands on the Muskingum above the mouth of Licking Creek, at the forks of the Muskingum, a country with which Mr. Hutchins was familiar, having visited that region in 1764, as engineer for the army under General Bouquet, the selection would have been far superior to that at the mouth, and along the margin of the Ohio. This would have brought them into the vicinity of the most powerful tribes, and further removed from the older settlements in western Pennsylvania, and the hope of aid from any of the military posts, which were generally near the Ohio River. When we take into consideration the early period of the settlement, and all other matters connected therewith, the purchase was not so bad a one. The lands were not bought with a view to speculation, but for actual settlement, by a large portion of the share holders, and nothing prevented its speedy accomplishment, but the breaking out of the Indian war. At the close of that disastrous period, the current of emigration was diverted from Muskingum, to the vicinity of Fort Washington, and the more fertile region of the Miami and Scioto.

The following description of that portion of the company's lands, lying in the south-east part of the tract, as given by an intelligent settler, will show that the pioneers were well satisfied with the quality of the soil:

"From the eastern boundary to the Muskingum, the distance of about five miles, the intervales, or what are called in the west, "bottoms", are from one-half to three-fourths of a mile wide, and of the richest quality of soil. Adjacent to these lie the second bottoms, which are elevated plains, of a thinner soil, and of a more loamy or sandy character. Back of the second bottoms the country rises into hills, clothed with a heavy growth of timber, principally oak. In many places the sides of the hills are covered with beech and sugar tree, and the tops with chestnut or some variety of oak. The hills are not high; from one hundred and fifty to two hundred feet above the water in the Ohio. They are separated by deep hollows, in which flow small streams of water, many of which are fed by springs. The uplands afford a fertile, clayey soil, well adapted to the culture of wheat and all the small grains, grazing, &c. In this distance there are two large creeks, tributaries of the Ohio, called Little Muskingum and Duck Creek. These are bordered with rich bottom lands, and the hill sides afford suitable tracts for farming.

"We have found several salt licks within our surveys, and are assured there is a salt spring about forty miles up the Muskingum, from which a sufficient quantity of salt, for the supply of the country, may be made. Some gentlemen at Fort Harmer doubt this information, but think a supply may be made at a spring on a branch of the Scioto."

As a specimen of the fertility of the new country, the following fact is given:

"About a dozen families moved to this place a year ago last March, and settled opposite to Fort Harmer, on the Virginia side of the Ohio. Their lands were the same as ours, and entirely new. They raised one thousand bushels of corn last season; and although the winter was very severe, they wintered, without any hay, making use of the husks and stalks, with some corn, between sixty and seventy head of neat cattle and horses; fattened a sufficient quantity of pork for their own consumption; besides wintering a large number of swine."

In laying out and plowing the grounds for the new city, the main streets were made to conform to the course of the Muskingum River, which is north, forty degrees west, and extends up that stream one mile one hundred and twenty rods. They are ninety feet wide and crossed by others at right angles, which are seventy feet wide. The main streets are designated by numbers, and the cross streets by the name of some distinguished person. One of these streets, a little north of the centre of the plat, is one hundred and twenty feet wide, and called Washington. They are about half a mile in length. Broad and extensive public grounds, for commons, were reserved on the bank of the Muskingum. And as the city included the ancient remains of a fortified town, the most interesting portion of these were preserved by including them in squares, appropriated to the public use. These consisted, first, of an advanced work containing a conical mound of earth, the base of which is three hundred and seventy-six feet in circumference, and thirty feet in perpendicular height. It is surrounded by a parapet, or bank of earth, five hundred and eighty-six feet in circumference, and fifteen feet thick, within which is a ditch, fifteen feet wide and three feet deep. On the north side next the old town is an open space, without wall or ditch, as a gateway.

They also reserved in the same manner the two truncated pyramids or elevated squares, which lie within the principal fortifications. They are similar in form to those since discovered in Central America, and described by Stephens. These are of earth, while those are built of stone, and were the elevated sites of public buildings. One of them is nearly square, and is raised about six feet above the surface of the high plain on which it stands. The sides measure one hundred and fifty-three by one hundred and thirty-five feet. The top is perfectly smooth and level, and is reached on three of the sides by regularly graduated ascents, about twenty feet wide; while on the fourth, or south side, is an indented recess of the same width. The other elevated square lies on the north-west side of the old town. It is two hundred feet long by one hundred and twenty-four wide, and is six feet in height. The graduated ascents are alike on all the sides. To the latter was attached a public square containing three acres and one third, or ten city lots; to the former two acres and two thirds, or eight city lots. These reservations are lasting monuments of the good taste of the directors of the Ohio Company.

The first meeting of the directors and agents, west of the mountains, was held on the 2d day of July, 1788, and continued by adjournment to the 14th day of August, on the banks of the Muskingum, and near the confluence of that river with the Ohio. It was, doubtless, convened under the marquee of General Putnam, as no building was then erected, of sufficient dimensions to hold them. There were present at this meeting, as follows: Generals Samuel H. Parsons, Rufus Putnam, and James M. Varnum, directors; Colonel John May, Winthrop Sargent, Colonel Archibald Crary, Major William Corlis,

Colonel Return J. Meigs, Captain Aaron Barlow, Colonel Ebenezer Sproat, Major Haffield White, and General Rufus Putnam, agents. The shares represented amounted to six hundred and sixty-nine. They passed the following resolution as to the name of their new city:

"That the city near the confluence of the Ohio and Muskingum be called Marietta; that the directors write to his Excellency, the Count Monstiers, informing him of their motives in naming the city; and request his opinion whether it will be advisable to present to her majesty of France a public square."

The name is an abbreviation of Marie Antoinette, the fair queen of France, a lady who had treated the minister of the young American republic, the venerable Franklin, when at the court of Louis XVI, with all the respect and kindness due to her own father; and who had done more to appropriate and enlist the feelings of the king in favor of the Americans, than any other person, not excepting even La Fayette. It was a natural gush of feeling in the hearts of these old officers, to remember with gratitude their kind benefactress, and to perpetuate her name by connecting it with their infant city. The veneration of the directors for the classics is discovered in the names they bestowed on some of the most prominent objects in the ruins of the ancient town. The smaller square was named *"Capitolium,"* the larger one *"Quadranaou"* and the broad, graded road, with high embankments on each side, leading up from the river Muskingum to Quadranaou, was called *"Sacra Via."* The new garrison, with blockhouses at the corners, was named *"Campus Martius"* as if in anticipation of the Indian war which soon commenced, and continued for five years, during which period it was strictly a military camp. At this time a board of police was appointed for drafting a set of rules for the government of the settlement. It was composed of the directors, who were to lay the system before the proprietors for their adoption.

These regulations for the government of the inhabitants at present, until Governor St. Clair and the judges of the court, two of whom by the way were also directors, could prepare a more perfect code, were written out and posted up on the smooth trunk of a large beech tree, near the mouth of the Muskingum, on the 4th of July, 1788. This day was duly celebrated, in the usual manner, by the firing of thirteen cannons from Fort Harmer, in the morning, and at evening. A sumptuous dinner was provided by the inhabitants, and eaten under a bowery which stretched along on the bank of the Muskingum. General Varnum, one of the judges, delivered an oration, which was the first political address ever made in what is now the state of Ohio. The officers of the garrison attended, and many patriotic toasts were drank. The table was supplied with venison, bear meat, buffalo, and roasted pigs, procured from Williams' settlement, with a variety of fish. Among the latter, was a pike, which weighed one hundred pounds, and when suspended from a pole from the shoulders of two tall men, its tail dragged on the ground. It was the largest ever taken in the Muskingum by white men. Judge Gilbert Devoll and his son, Gilbert, caught it in the mouth of that stream, after a severe chase in a light canoe, being able to follow it by the wake of its course in the water. It soon became fatigued, and, running along side, was captured with a gig, or fish spear.

Campus Martius, Marietta
From the West

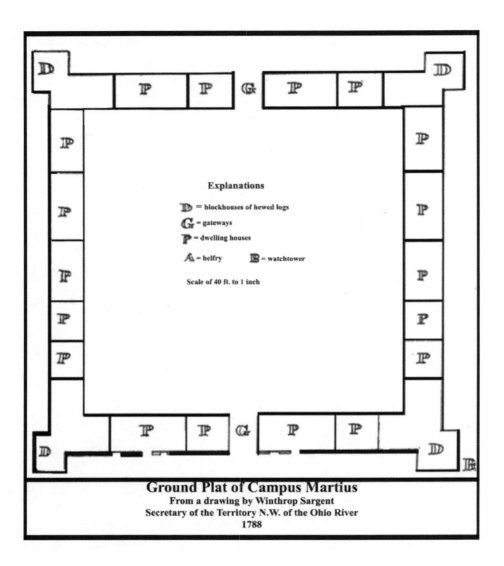

Explanations

D = blockhouses of hewed logs

G = gateways

P = dwelling houses

A = belfry   B = watchtower

Scale of 40 ft. to 1 inch

Ground Plat of Campus Martius
From a drawing by Winthrop Sargent
Secretary of the Territory N.W. of the Ohio River
1788

Winthrop Sargent
Secretary of the Northwest Territory
1788

On the 9th day of July, Governor St. Clair arrived at Fort Harmer, escorted by a detachment of troops under Major Doughty, who had gone up to Pittsburgh some days before for that purpose. He was received with military honors, and a salute of fourteen guns. The 15th of July, as appears from the journal of Paul Fearing, was agreed on for his first appearance before the citizens of the territory. At five o'clock, P. M., he came over from Fort Harmer in the government barge, escorted by the officers of the garrison, and the secretary, Winthrop Sargent, Esq. He was received in the bowery by General Putnam, the judges of the territory, and the principal inhabitants of the new colony. The secretary read the ordinance of Congress forming the Northwest Territory, the governor's commission, the judges', and his own. He was then congratulated on his welcome arrival at the seat of government by General Putnam, and three cheers closed the ceremonies of the day.

As these were the first commissions issued by Congress to the governor and judges of the new territory, and the journals of that period are accessible to but few, it may be proper to record them here as a portion of the early history of the colony.

Commission of the Governor.

"The United States in Congress assembled to Arthur St. Clair, Esq.

"We, reposing special trust and confidence in your integrity, prudence and ability, have constituted and appointed, and by these presents do constitute and appoint, you, the said Arthur St. Clair, Governor, in and over the territory of the United States of America, northwest of the river Ohio; and Commander-in-Chief of the militia therein; to order, rule, and govern the same, conformably to the ordinance of the 13th July, 1787, entitled, "an ordinance for the government of the territory of the United States, northwest of the river Ohio," which is hereto affixed; and we do hereby give and grant to you, the said Arthur St. Clair, all the powers, authorities and prerogatives assigned to the governor of the said territory in and by the said ordinance. And we do strictly enjoin all persons to pay due obedience to this our commission. This commission to take effect from the 1st day of February, 1788, and to continue in force for the term of three years thereafter, unless sooner revoked by Congress. In testimony, &c."

Commission of one of the Judges.

"The United States in Congress assembled to Samuel Holden Parsons, Esq.

"We, reposing special trust and confidence in your wisdom, uprightness and integrity, have constituted and appointed, and by these presents do constitute and appoint, you, the said Samuel Holden Parsons, one of the judges in and over the territory of the United States north-west of the river Ohio, with full power and authority, in conjunction with one or more of the judges of the said territory, to form a court, with all the powers and authorities incident to a court having a common law jurisdiction, and to exercise all such powers, and perform and execute all the duties directed by the ordinance of the 13th July, 1787, entitled "an ordinance for the government of the territory northwest of the river Ohio," which is hereto affixed; giving to you, the said S. H. P., all the powers and authorities assigned to a judge of the said territory, in, and by the ordinance aforesaid; and we do enjoin all persons to pay due obedience to this our commission. This commission to continue and be in force, during good behavior, or during the existence of the government established by the ordinance aforesaid. You residing within the said territory. In testimony, &c."

The other two judges, were James Mitchell Varnum, from Philadelphia, and John Cleves Symmes, of New Jersey. Mr. Symmes had not arrived, but was expected on soon. Winthrop Sargent, secretary of the territory, was a native of Boston, but latterly a citizen of New Hampshire.

The judges who succeeded these in the territory, were S. H. Parsons and J. C. Symmes, re-appointed by the president, with the advice and consent of the senate, and William Barton, in place of J. M. Varnum, deceased, August 20th, 1789. In September, 1789, George Turner was appointed, Mr. Barton having declined the office. In March 31, 1790, General Rufus Putnam succeeded S. H. Parsons, deceased. Joseph Gilman was made a judge in place of General Putnam, who had received the office of surveyor general United States lands, in December 22d, 1796; February 12th, 1798, R. J. Meigs, jr., in the place of G. Turner, resigned. The judges Symmes, Gilman and Meigs, were in office when the general assembly of the territory convened, in September, 1799. (Chase's Stat, of Ohio).

The first laws for the government of the territory were published by the governor and judges at Marietta. The more important of these early acts, were *"a law regulating and establishing the militia," July 25th, 1788"*; also *"a law for establishing general courts of quarter session of the peace (and therein of the powers of single justices), and for establishing county courts of common pleas (and therein of the powers of single judges, to hear and determine upon small debts and contracts)"*; also, *"a law for the establishing the office of sheriff, and the appointment of sheriffs."*

The court of quarter session was held four times in a year in each county, and was composed of the justices of the peace, nominated and commissioned by the governor. Not less than three, nor more than five of these justices, were especially named in a general commission, for holding the said courts of quarter session. Three of them might hold special courts when required, one of them being of the quorum. In the year 1790, the number of justices was increased to nine in a county, and it received authority to divide the counties into townships, to appoint constables, overseers of the poor, clerks of townships, and to establish public roads.

The county courts of common pleas were composed of not less than three nor more than five persons, commissioned by the governor, and authorized to hold and keep a court of record. This court convened twice a year, in each county, at the places where the quarter sessions were held. In 1790 the periods were increased to four in a year and the judges to seven. A sheriff was appointed by the governor for each county, who took the oath of allegiance to the United States, and of office, and gave a bond of four thousand dollars. He had ample authority to suppress riots, keep the peace, arrest criminals, &c. (Pub. Aug. 23, 1788.) A court of probate was established, composed of a single judge, for the settlement of estates, recording of wills, &c. This court was opened four times in a year, and oftener if necessary. (Pub. Aug. 30, 1788.)

"A law for fixing the terms of the general court.

'The general court, for the territory of the United States, north-west of the river Ohio, held four sessions in a year for civil and criminal suits, at such points in the territory as the judges deemed most conducive to the public good, they giving timely notice of their sitting. The periods were the first Mondays of February, May, October, and December. Process, both civil and criminal, could be returned to this court at any place in the territory, where they might be convened. They were not obliged to hold more than one court a year, in any one county. (Pub. at Marietta, Aug. 30, 1788; Chase's Stat, of Ohio.)

The law respecting crimes and their punishment, published on the 6th of September, 1788, shows that the principles of justice, morality, and good order, were deeply impressed on the hearts and minds of the governor and judges. The section for the suppression and prevention of profanity, irreverent and obscene language, with the closing one for the sacred observance of the Christian Sabbath, are worthy of all praise, and the particular notice of modern law makers. In accordance with the usage of that period, the punishment for theft and minor offenses consisted of fines, whipping, confinement in the stocks, and binding out to hard labor for a limited time, where the offense had been often repeated and the offender unable or refused to make restitution. For this purpose every county was provided with a pillory, whipping-post, and stocks, in addition to the jail. These emblems of justice were continued in Marietta, as a terror to evil doers, as late as the year 1812, or until the period of the introduction of the present penitentiary system.

CHAPTER X.

The latter part of June, a party of thirty men, under the command of Lieutenant McDowell, of Fort Harmer, was sent up by water, with provisions and presents of goods to the falls of Muskingum, in preparation for the approaching treaty, which was expected to be held with the Indians on the arrival of Governor St. Clair. The place chosen for this transaction is about sixty miles from the mouth, on the right bank of the river, where the town of Taylorsville now stands. They were ordered up by Colonel Harmer, to erect a council house, and build huts for the comfort of the men, and the security of the goods against the weather. This remote spot was selected by the Indians, in preference to Fort Harmer, as being nearer their own homes, a well known and favorite locality, and not under the influence of a military post. They had commenced assembling from the different tribes, especially in large numbers from the Delawares. Among them was a band of Chippewa, and other Indians, outcasts from different tribes, amounting to about twenty. On the night of the 12th of July, these desperadoes crept slyly around the tent containing the goods, and fired on the sentries, ten in number, with the intention of plundering them. By this discharge two men were killed, and one or two wounded. The sentries returned the fire, and the rest of the guard running to their assistance, the Indians retired without accomplishing their object. One of the assailants was killed, and one wounded. The same night they killed and scalped a mulatto man, servant to Major Duncan, a trader, who was waiting for the assembly of the tribes, with goods to barter for their skins and peltries.

The fall was soon after named "Duncan's Falls," which it retained until the slack-water improvement on the Muskingum obliterated the rapid at this place.

209

The next day, on examining the dead Indian, the Delawares pronounced him to be a Chippewa, and that they had no knowledge of, or concern in, the attack. As a test of their innocence, the Delawares came fearlessly into the camp, bringing with them their women and children. In addition, they seized upon six of the offending band, tied them with thongs, and handed them over to the commandant of the troops, to be dealt with as they might deserve. They were brought down to Fort Harmer by the reinforcement which went up the next day, and kept in irons for some time, but were finally allowed to escape, either by design, or the carelessness of their guards. The large boat belonging to the Ohio Company was sent up, and the goods, stores and troops transported to Fort Harmer.

This untoward event postponed the treaty for several months. The Indians, however, still continued to linger in the vicinity of the garrison, hunting and destroying all the deer and wild game within fifteen or twenty miles of Marietta; stripping off the skins, and leaving the meat to rot and decay on the ground, or be eaten by the wolves, with the exception of the small quantity needed for their own use. When questioned on their object in this destruction of the game, they answered, *"To keep it from the white hunter."* They considered all the wild animals as their own property, to which the new comers had no right. They often visited the inhabitants, to trade their peltries for goods, tobacco, and whisky. Captain Pipes, a noted chief of the Delawares, with several of their leading men, dined a number of times with General Putnam, and expressed great friendship for their new neighbors. They, however, were not pleased with their building houses, clearing lands, and preparing for a permanent residence, until after the expected treaty was made and signed. In answer, they were told that it was necessary to plant some corn for the support of their women and children, and that the lands they occupied were ceded to the United States, several years before, as they well knew, at the treaty of Fort McIntosh.

At a council held among the tribes, after the affair at Duncan's Falls, the Ottawas and Chippewas were opposed to making any treaty; but were for war, unless the whites would confine themselves to the south side of the Ohio River. The Delawares, and Indians of the Six Nations, told them that they should then fight their own battles in their conflict with the whites, for they would not assist them. Finally, on the 2d of August thirteen of their chief men came into the garrison on horseback, in procession, bearing the flag of the United States, and pretending to be friendly, but it was only pretense. (Mass. Spy, Aug., 1788.)

On Sunday, the 20th of July, the Reverend William Breck, a New England man, and one of the Ohio Company, delivered, on the banks of the Muskingum, the first sermon ever preached to white men in the present state of Ohio. The Moravian missionaries, and among them the venerable Heckewelder, had many years before, on the banks of the Tuscarawas, preached to the Delaware Indians. His text was from Exodus, xix chap., 5th and 6th verses — *"Now therefore, if ye will obey my voice indeed and keep my covenant, then ye shall be a peculiar treasure unto me above all people; for all the earth is mine, and ye shall be unto me a kingdom of priests, and an holy nation."*

The text was a very appropriate one to a people who were just beginning to lay the foundations of civil society in a wilderness land, encouraging them to the practice of holiness, truth, and justice; with the promise that by so doing, God would especially bless them. This sermon was delivered in the hall of the north-west blockhouse in Campus Martius.

The first county organized in the territory was called Washington, in honor of the man who had done so much for his country. The order for its erection and boundaries is as follows:

"By his Excellency, Arthur St. Clair, Esq., Governor and Commander-in-Chief of the territory of the United States, north-west of the river Ohio —

"A proclamation,

"To all persons to whom these presents shall come, greeting: Whereas, by the ordinance of Congress of the 13th of July, 1787, for the government of the territory of the United States north-west of the river Ohio, it is directed that for the due execution of process, civil and criminal, the governor shall make proper divisions of the said territory, and proceed from time to time, as circumstances may require, to lay out the part of the same, where the Indian title has been extinguished, into counties and townships subject to future alterations as therein specified. Now, know ye, that it appearing to me to be necessary, for the purposes above mentioned, that a county should immediately be laid out, I have ordained and ordered, and by these presents

do ordain and order, that all and singular the lands lying and being within the following boundaries, viz: Beginning on the bank of the Ohio River, where the western boundary line of Pennsylvania crosses it, and running with that line to Lake Erie; thence along the southern shore of the said lake to the mouth of the Cuyahoga River; thence up said river to the portage between that and the Tuscarawas branch of the Muskingum; thence down the branch to the forks, at the crossing place above Fort Laurens; thence with a line to be drawn westerly to the portage of that branch of the Big Miami, on which the fort stood that was taken by the French in 1752, until it meets the road from the lower Shawnee town to the Sandusky; thence south to the Scioto River; thence with that river to the mouth, and thence up the Ohio River to the place of beginning; shall be a county, and the same is hereby erected into a county, named and to be called hereafter the county of Washington; and the said county of Washington shall have and enjoy all and singular, the jurisdiction, rights, liberties, privileges and immunities whatever to a county belonging and appertaining, and which any other county, that may hereafter be erected and laid out, shall or ought to enjoy, conformably to the ordinance of Congress before mentioned. In witness whereof, I have hereunto set my hand, and caused the seal of the territory to be affixed, this twenty-sixth day of July, in the thirteenth year of the Independence of the United States, and in the year of our Lord, one thousand seven hundred and eighty-eight.

"(Signed,)   *A. ST. CLAIR."*

At a meeting of the directors and agents of the Ohio Company, in July, the subject of encouraging persons, not members of the company, to settle in the new purchase, was brought up. Large numbers of emigrants were daily passing Marietta on their way to the new settlements in Kentucky and the region below, many of whom were desirous of remaining at this place, if they could get possession of lands for farms; but as the directors had no authority either to sell or to give away the lands of the company, they were obliged to pass on to where their wants could be supplied. At this meeting a committee, consisting of General Rufus Putnam, S. H. Parsons and Colonel Archibald Crary was appointed to draft an address to the share holders on this important matter. They say, *"within twelve months, more than ten thousand emigrants have passed this place to Kentucky and other parts of the Ohio and Mississippi Rivers; upwards of seven thousand of which have gone down since we began our settlement. Much the greater part of these are not the*

212

owners of any lands in the countries to which they have emigrated, but expect to become purchasers; and we are confident very many of these would have become settlers on this purchase, if they could have had any encouragement to stay with us; but under our present arrangements we have no lands to give or to sell. Many applications have been made to us on this subject, but we have not had the means of giving them satisfaction."

"We are of opinion that giving a part of the lands to industrious people, on performing certain duties in settling, clearing, &c, will be very much for the interest of the proprietors."

A meeting of the proprietors, by their agents, to consider of this subject, was appointed to be held at Marietta on the first Wednesday in December, 1788. The notice, or address, is dated August 17th.

In a letter from General Putnam to the printer of the Massachusetts Spy, dated at Marietta, October 22, 1788, we learn the progress of the colony during that summer. The city lots were ninety feet wide by one hundred and eighty in length, and with the streets and commons, covered a space extending one mile on the Ohio River, and one mile one hundred and twenty perches on the Muskingum.

"A substantial bridge was built over the creek which falls into the Muskingum in the southern part of the city, called "Tyber Creek." This bridge was twenty-five feet high, ninety feet long, and twenty-four feet wide, covered with hewn plank, four inches thick. Three other bridges were also built over smaller streams; which rendered the intercourse between the different portions of the city easy and pleasant. A road was cut through the forest from the mouth of Muskingum up to the spot selected for the site of Campus Martius. By the 5th of May the work in the woods necessary for making the plan of the eight acre lots was completed, and I made a proposition to the people in the company's employ, that as many as chose might go to clearing and planting on their own account, and make up the time after their present contract expired. To this proposition many of them agreed, and began the same day to prepare lands for planting, by cutting away the small, and "girdling" the larger trees.

"Near the same time Colonel May, Colonel Stacey, and a number of other adventurers arrived, who, with the others, began to clear and plant the

land intended for the city, with the risk of giving it up whenever it should be claimed by the owners." (This field lay on the elevated plain east of Campus Martius, was rather a thin, light, soil, but free of underbrush, as were the woods generally at that day, being annually burnt over for a long series of years, by the autumnal fires of the Indians.)

"So great was the industry of the people, that by the 20th of June one hundred and thirty-two acres of land were planted with corn, besides a large quantity of potatoes, beans, &c."

"About thirty-five acres of the corn land was either plowed or harrowed; the rest of the field was planted with the hoe. But the great misfortune was that the leaves of the beech and poplar trees, which formed a considerable portion of the growth, did not wither by the girdling, and so shaded the corn as to injure the crop very considerably. The prospect in the fore part of the season was so discouraging, that some of the planters did not hoe their corn at all, while others hoed but once. However, under all these adverse circumstances, there is a great deal of corn and forage raised. The crop will average from twenty to thirty bushels an acre on the plain. A piece of bottom land on the bank of the Ohio, belonging to Mr. Corey, has been harvested and measured one hundred and four bushels of ears to the acre. Some of these ears yield a pint and a half of shelled corn each, and when fully dried, a bushel weighs sixty-two pounds. In short, the quality of the corn of this country is in all respects fully equal to that of New England. As for beans, turnips, pumpkins, squashes, cabbages, melons, cucumbers, &c., they are in flavor the finest I ever tasted, and the great production is truly surprising."

Campus Martius.

The annexed plate shows the appearance of this noted garrison, after it was fully completed and enclosed with pickets after the commencement of the Indian war, in the year 1791. The ground plat and front view of the face, next the Muskingum River, was engraved and published in the Columbian Magazine, from a plan made by Winthrop Sargent, Esq., The present drawing is copied from that, with additions from Mr. Horace Nye, of Putnam, Muskingum county, Ohio, who was an inmate of the garrison during the period of the war, and for some time after.

"Campus Martius is the handsomest pile of buildings on this side the Alleghany Mountains, and in a few days will be the strongest fortification in the territory of the United States. It stands on the margin of the elevated plain on which are the remains of the ancient works, mentioned in my letter of May last, thirty feet above the high bank of the Muskingum, twenty-nine perches distant from the river, and two hundred and seventy-six from the Ohio. It consists of a regular square, having a blockhouse at each angle, eighteen feet square on the ground, and two stories high; the upper story on the outside or face, jutting over the lower one, eighteen inches. These blockhouses serve as bastions to a regular fortification of four sides. The curtains are composed of dwelling houses two stories high, eighteen feet wide, and of different lengths. The blockhouses and curtains are so constructed by high-roofs, &c., as to form one complete and entire building. The timber of which they are built is either sawed or hewed, four inches thick, so that the walls are very smooth, and when the seams are pointed with mortar, will be very warm and comfortable. On the top of three of the blockhouses are very handsome watch towers, which are to be made musket proof; and are large enough to hold four men, their arms, &c. On the top of the fourth (in the North West corner), above the watch tower, is a balcony with a cupola, spire, &c., for the reception of a bell, which we are told is coming on as a present from a gentleman at Boston. The chimneys will be mostly of bricks; several kilns have already been burnt, and more ready to set. All the blockhouses, and part of the curtains, are built at the expense of the company. The blockhouse, intended for the bell, with a part of the adjacent curtains, has a hall appropriated to public use, where three hundred people may assemble. The open space within the square of buildings is one hundred and forty-four feet, on each side, in the center of which a well is now digging. (This well is upwards of eighty feet deep.) *The blockhouses are all up, the gates and a greater part of the curtains, and I expect the whole will be completed by the 1st of December. In all the buildings of this square, there will be seventy two rooms of eighteen feet and upwards, exclusive of the lofts and garrets, which, at twelve persons to a room* (a moderate proportion in case of necessity), *will lodge eight hundred and sixty-four people."*

Soon after, the Indian war broke out, and the garrison was put under the discipline of a regular camp. It was found that the watch towers on the roofs of the blockhouses were at such an elevation as to render it inconvenient ascending and descending from them at night, in changing the guards. As a substitute, square bastions or sentry boxes were erected on four stout posts, sixteen feet high, at the corner of each blockhouse, into which the guard could enter from the upper story by a single step, through a door cut for that purpose. These boxes were about six feet square, and six feet high, made of plank, proof against musket balls. Around the inside, above the floor, ran a slight elevation, or *"banquette"* on to which when the sentry stepped, his head appeared above the bulwark. They were open to the weather on top, and furnished with loop holes and embrazures for the discharge of fire arms. In the south-west and north-east bastions, was placed a small cannon or four pounder, which was fired as an alarm, when Indians were discovered in the neighborhood, to call in the people who might be in the fields at work, or to be used in defense, in case of an attack. The roofs of the buildings were covered with well made oak shingles, fastened with nails, instead of roof pools, as was common to all the log houses on the frontiers.

At one time during the war, soon after the attack on the garrison at Waterford, it was thought advisable to cover the roofs with a coating of clay mortar, two or three inches thick, to protect them against combustible missiles, that might be thrown on them by the bows and arrows of the Indians. Happily for the inhabitants this experiment was never put to the test, and a few heavy showers of rain demolished this earthen coat of mail, that had cost them so many days of hard labor. In the west and south fronts were strong gateways, and over that, in the center of the west front, was a chamber surmounted by a tower. This room projected over the gateway like a blockhouse, and was intended for the protection of the gate underneath in time of assault. It was occupied for several years by Hon. Winthrop Sargent, secretary of the territory, as an office. The south-west blockhouse was appropriated to the use of Governor St. Clair and his family. The north-east was devoted to the use of the directors of the Ohio Company, and for a store house, the south-east to private families and house of entertainment, the north-west, as before stated, to religious worship, and for the sitting of the courts during the first years of the settlement. In the year 1791, other defenses were added. Running from corner to corner of the blockhouses, was a row of palisades sloping outwards, resting on stone rails. Twenty feet in advance of these was a row of very large and strong pickets, set upright in the earth, with gateways for the admission of the inhabitants. A few feet in advance of the outer palisades was placed an additional defense or *abbatis,* made from the tops and branches of trees sharpened and pointing outwards, so that it would have been very difficult for an enemy to have penetrated even within their outworks.

Suitable plats for gardens were laid out between the garrison and the river, for the officers and for private families, who lived in Campus Martius. The appearance from without was grand and imposing; at a little distance resembling one of the military palaces or castles of the feudal ages.

The writer goes on to state, *"besides these buildings at Campus Martius, twenty very comfortable houses, made of round logs, for families, and covered with long shingles, are already erected in the town, and several more are going forward. Nor is this all the labor we have done. Large quantities of land have been cut over and fitted for wheat and rye; besides which, several persons have begun to prepare land for planting next spring. And what is very extraordinary, very few of us have been able to work on our own land, and our labor must in the end contribute more to the general emolument of the company, than to the particular advantage of those who have performed it. However, I hope the December meeting will conclude with such encouragement to industrious adventurers, as will be promotive of the interest of the proprietors in general, and sufficient reward for those who encounter the risks and fatigues always incident to a new and savage country."*

By the 20th of August the north-west blockhouse was so far completed, that the directors of the company on that day gave a dinner to Governor St. Clair and the officers of Fort Harmer. On this occasion the judges and all the principal inhabitants attended, with the wives of a number of the officers, and several ladies of General Tupper's and Major Goodale's families, who had ventured thus early into the wilderness. A line barge, rowed by twelve oars, brought the company from the fort up the Muskingum and landed them on the bank opposite the new garrison.

The gardens at this time attached to the fort were under fine cultivation, and already produced the finest peaches from pits planted by Major Doughty at its first establishment. So rapid was the growth of the peach in the light, rich, virgin soil of the Ohio, that fruit was sometimes produced the second, and always the third year after planting. There is a fine variety of that fruit now in Marietta, descended from this early stock, and called the "Doughty Peach."

On the 24th of August, the second sermon ever delivered in the territory, was preached at the hall of the north-west blockhouse, by the Rev. Manasseh Cutler. He was one of the directors of the Ohio Company, and was now on a visit to Marietta, to see the country of which he had heard so much. His home was in Ipswich, Massachusetts. He was the principal agent in negotiating the purchase with Congress for the Ohio Company, and stood deservedly high as a man of acute intellect and highly cultivated mind. He was an accomplished botanist as well as a faithful preacher of the gospel; a man of great observation and critical research. In science he was far in advance of the age and country in which he lived, as will appear from various articles from his pen in the early transactions of the "American Philosophical Society."

Rev. Manasseh Cutler

The first court.

The first court of common pleas in the Northwest Territory, was opened at Marietta, on Tuesday, the 2d day of September, 1788. A procession was formed at "the point," composed of the inhabitants, and officers from the fort, who escorted the judges of the court of common pleas, with the governor and supreme judges of the territory, to the hall in the north-west blockhouse of Campus Martius. The procession was preceded by the sheriff, with his drawn sword and wand of office, the whole making quite an imposing appearance, and exciting the admiration of the friendly savages, a number of whom were loitering about the new city. When all were assembled, the duties of the day were opened with prayer by the Rev. Manasseh Cutler. The court was then organized by reading the commission of the judges, the clerk, and the sheriff; after which it was opened for business by the proclamation of the sheriff. The first judges were General Rufus Putnam, General Benjamin Tupper, and Colonel Archibald Crary; the clerk was Colonel R. J. Meigs; and the sheriff, Colonel Ebenezer Sproat. Paul Fearing, Esq., was admitted an attorney, and was the first lawyer in the territory. R. J. Meigs, jr., was admitted some months after. There being no business before the court at this term, it was adjourned without day. A law was published at this time by the governor relating to oaths of office. In the year 1790, Joseph Gilman, Esq., was appointed a judge in place of Colonel Crary, resigned. In 1792, Dudley Woodbridge, John G. Pettit, Daniel Loring and Robert Oliver were added to the bench.

First court of general quarter sessions.

On the second Tuesday of September, which was the ninth day, this court sat for the first time. It was held in the south-east blockhouse, occupied by Colonel E. Battelle. The court was opened with the usual proclamation of the sheriff, after the general commission appointing the judges was read by the clerk. By this commission General Rufus Putnam and General B. Tupper were constituted justices of the quorum, and Isaac Pearce, Thomas Lord, and Lt. J. Meigs, assistant justices. Colonel Meigs was clerk. Paul Fearing was admitted an attorney to plead in all courts of record in Washington County. He was also appointed by the court counselor for the United States in said county.

The grand jury was then called, and William Stacy appointed the foreman. The names of the jurors were, William Stacy, Nathaniel Cushing, Nathaniel Goodale, Charles Knowles, Anselm Tupper, Jonathan Stone, Oliver Rice, Ezra Lunt, John Mathews, George Ingersoll, Jonathan Devol, Samuel Stebbins, Jethro Putnam, and Jabez True.

The charge was given with much dignity and propriety by Judge Putnam. At one o'clock the grand jury retired, and the court adjourned for thirty minutes. At half past one the court again opened, when the jurors entered and presented a written address to the court, which after being read was ordered to be kept on file. Judge Putnam made a reply to the address. There being no suits before the court, it was adjourned without pay. Thus closed the first court of quarter sessions in the new territory. This court was one of the greatest importances to the people, as in addition to its civil and criminal jurisdiction, it had the power of laying out public highways, establishing the bounds of townships, and appointing the township officers; with a general supervision of the county, similar to that of the present county commissioners. In 1789, Griffin Green, Esq., was appointed by the governor, one of the assistant justices.

In 1790, Joseph Gilman was appointed a judge of the quorum, in place of General Putnam, resigned. Robert Oliver was also appointed one of the quorums, after the death of Judge Tupper, in 1792. These courts continued to transact the law business of the county, until the territory became the state of Ohio. They were held for a number of years in the hall of the north-west blockhouse. The jail used by the early courts before the war, was a strong log cabin that stood at the foot of the plain, near the south-west corner of Campus Martius. During the continuance of the war, and for several years after, a blockhouse in the garrison at the mouth of the Muskingum was used for a jail, and may be seen in the plate representing that garrison.

The first death.

The first death in the new city was that of a female child of Major N. Cushing, aged thirteen months, on the 25th of August, 1788.

In August, eight families arrived from New England, amongst them were those of General Tupper, Major Cushing, Major Goodale, Major Coburn, and Mr. Ichabod Nye; and in the course of the year there were fifteen families in all, with eighty-four men, which with the forty-eight who first landed on the 8th of April, enlarged the number to one hundred and thirty-two, in the year 1788. At the close of this year, Marietta was the only white settlement in the territory, now constituting the state of Ohio.

Progress of the treaty.

In the month of September, the Cornplanter, a principal chief of the Seneca tribe, with about forty Indians, arrived at Fort Harmer, escorted by a company of soldiers from Fort Pitt, under the command of Captain Zeigler. This chief was an influential man with the Six Nations, and very friendly to the United States. Much good was expected from his assistance in bringing about a treaty with the western tribes, several of which still appeared cold and averse to any amicable adjustment of existing difficulties. So valuable were the services of this enlightened savage, that the Ohio Company, in the month of December, voted him a mile square of land, to be located within the purchase.

A son of the celebrated Brant, with two hundred warriors, was at the falls of Muskingum in November, and sent a messenger to Governor St. Clair, with a request that the treaty might be held at that place. He returned a mild but decided refusal; on which Brant, with a large portion of his followers, retired to their towns, and, it is supposed, persuaded the Shawnee not to visit Fort Harmer, as very few of them were present in January.

On the 13th of December, about two hundred Indians, from the different tribes, arrived at the garrison. They marched down the banks of the Muskingum, many of them on horseback, with the flag of the United States displayed in their front; and as they approached the fort, fired their rifles into the air as a token of friendship. The salute was returned by the cannon and musketry of the soldiers for several minutes, sounding so much like a real engagement of hostile bands, that the old officers at Campus Martius were quite animated with the sound. A guard of soldiers, with music escorted them into the garrison in military style, which much pleased the chiefs, who expressed their thanks to the governor in a set speech, at their cordial reception. They also expressed their desire to meet him at the council fire. The governor answered, that he was glad to see them, and as he had been waiting a long time for them, hoped they would be expeditious in finishing the treaty.

The following day the council fire was kindled in the council house, which was a large log house that stood near the north-east bastion, on the outside of the fort. As the Indians are proverbial for transacting all their civil concerns with great deliberation, the time was protracted to the 9th of January following, before the articles were all adjusted and agreed to on the part of the tribes. Governor St. Clair was quite ill with an attack of the gout, to which he was subject, during the course of the treaty, and was carried daily by the soldiers, in a large chair, to the council. General Butler assisted, as a commissioner, at this treaty, which was finally closed, to the apparent satisfaction of all the parties. The Rev. John Heckewelder, an old Moravian missionary, by his kind offices and salutary advice to the Delaware and other

Indians, whose language he spoke with fluency, contributed largely to the final success of the treaty. He was held in great veneration by all the Christian Delawares, and highly respected by the most heathen portion of them all. Their intercourse with General Putnam and the new settlers, during the summer, who treated them with uniform kindness and hospitality, often inviting them to eat with them, won greatly on their favorable opinion of the new comers. They were also represented by those who saw them, to the other Indians, as an entirely different people from the long-knives and backwoodsmen of Kentucky, with whom they had heretofore had intercourse, being a pacific and brotherly community, who loved the red men, and not of a blood-thirsty and revengeful disposition. These favorable impressions, no doubt, inclined them the more readily to treat, although very few of them did it freely or with a sincere good will; and no doubt they operated more or less on their minds during the following war, as they did not attack the settlements of the Ohio Company with that determined spirit of revenge so common to the Indians, but oftentimes were known to pass by them unharmed, in their marauding parties into the western counties of Virginia, the territories of their inveterate foes, "the long-knives "— a name by which they were familiarly known to all the western tribes.

An abstract of the treaty

Made at Fort Harmer the 9th of January, 1789, between Governor St. Clair, and the sachems and warriors of the Six Nations.

The treaty was signed by twenty-four of their chief men, and they agreed to renew and confirm all the engagements and stipulations entered into with the United States at the treaty of Fort Stanwix, the 22d day of October, 1784. By this treaty they relinquished all claim to lands in the western territory, lying west of the following boundaries, viz:

"Beginning at the mouth of a creek about four miles east of Niagara, called O-non-wa-ye-a, or Johnson's Landing Place, upon the lake named by the Indians Os-we-go, and by us Ontario; from thence southerly in a direction always four miles east of the carrying place, between Lake Erie and Lake Ontario, to the mouth of Te-ho-se-ro-ron, or Buffalo Creek, upon Lake Erie; thence south to the northern boundary of the State of Pennsylvania; thence west to the end of the said north boundary; thence south along the west boundary of the said state to the river Ohio."

For thus renewing the treaty they received a present of three thousand dollars in goods. The Mohawks did not attend, but were allowed to be considered as parties, if they desired so to do within six months. A separate article was attached to the treaty, by which it was agreed that if any murders were committed by the Indians on the whites, or the whites killed any Indian, the guilty persons should be given up to be punished agreeably to law. So also if any horses were stolen, they should, if found, be reclaimed by either party.

Treaty with the Wyandots, Etc.

On the same day a treaty was made by Governor St. Clair, with the Wyandots, Delawares, Chippewas, Pottawatomie and Sac nations. The Indians had been invited to come in to a treaty in the summer of 1788, and had begun to assemble for this purpose and to trade with the whites as early as the month of April. But from various causes, a part of which have been narrated in the foregoing pages, nothing definite was accomplished until January, 1789. Many of the Indians were not disposed to treat on any terms, and generally they felt reluctant to give up any more of their territory and hunting grounds to the whites; foreseeing that the day was rapidly approaching when they would be forced to abandon all their country in the valley of the Ohio to the United States. They, therefore, entered into the treaty reluctantly, and with no sincere and decided intention of abiding by its stipulations any longer than they found it for their advantage to do so.

By the first article, the tribes confirmed the treaty made at Fort McIntosh in January, 1785, and agreed to give up all white prisoners in their hands to Governor St. Clair at Fort Harmer, as soon as they conveniently can.

Art. 2d. Describes the boundaries of the lands belonging to the said tribes, as follows, viz.:

"Beginning at the mouth of the Cuyahoga River, and running thence on said river to the portage between that and the Tuscarawas branch of the Muskingum; thence down the said branch to the forks at the crossing place above Fort Laurens; thence westerly to the portage on that branch of the Big Miami River which runs into the Ohio, at the mouth of which branch the fort stood that was taken by the French in the year 1752; thence along the said portage to the Great Miami, or Ome River, and down the south-east side of

the same to its mouth; thence along the southern shore of Lake Erie to the mouth of the Cuyahoga, where it began."

At the same time, in consideration of six thousand dollars, paid them in goods and other presents at former treaties, the Indians ceded and quit-claimed all right to the lands east, south, and west of the lines above described, so far as the said tribes formerly claimed the same, to the United States forever.

Art. 3d. The United States relinquished and quit-claimed to the tribes aforesaid, all the lands included in the boundaries described in article 1st; but forbid their selling it to any foreign power, or to the private citizens of the United States.

Art. 4th. Grants to the Indians liberty to hunt on the lands ceded to the United States, while they conduct peaceably.

Art. 5th. Stipulates to give up murderers, mutually.

Art. 6th. Relates in the same way to horse thieves.

Art. 7th. Relates to trade with the Indians; no one to be allowed to trade without a license from the Governor of the Northwest Territory, or his deputy.

Art. 8th. The parties agree to give notice to each other of any hostile intentions, or movements of their enemies.

Art. 9th. Forbids any white man to settle on the lands of the Indians; if so, they may punish them.

Art. 10th. Enumerates the reserves of lands in the Indian territories, for trading posts.

Art. 11th. A strip six miles wide, from Detroit to Lake St. Clair, reserved for the use of the United States.

Art. 12th. Michillimackinac, and twelve miles square around it, is reserved for the United States.

Art. 13th. Renews the treaty and friendship made at Fort McIntosh; and the tribes acknowledge themselves under the protection of the United States, and no other power whatever.

Art. 14th. Includes the Pottawatomie and Sacs, in the privileges and agreements of the present treaty.

Art. 15th. Defines more definitely the boundaries across the portage of the head of the Big Miami.

This treaty was signed by the sachems and warriors of the Sacs, Chippewa, Ottawa, Pottawatomie, Delaware, and Wyandot tribes of Indians.

Memorandum

"Be it remembered, that the Wyandots have laid claim to the lands that were granted to the Shawnee at the treaty held at Miami, and have declared that as the Shawnee have been so restless, and caused so much trouble, both to them and to the United States, *"if they will not now be at peace, they will dispossess them, and take the country into their own hands; for the country is theirs of right, and the Shawnee are only living on it by their permission. They further lay claim to all the country west of the Miami boundary, from the village to the Lake Erie, and declare it is now under their management and direction."*

N. B. The Wyandots have two villages in the reserve above Detroit, which they are to retain without being disturbed by the United States.

In proof of the fact that the western tribes generally were opposed to the treaty, and, especially, the Shawnee, it may be stated that, in April, the following year, or 1790, Antoine Gamelin was sent from Fort Knox, at Vincennes, by Major Hamtramck, to the tribes on the Wabash and Miami, with a speech from Governor St. Clair. While at the Miami village, Le Gris, the principal chief of that tribe, in a private conversation, asked Gamelin, *"What chief had made a treaty with the Americans at Muskingum?*

"I answered him that their names were mentioned in the treaty. He said he had heard of it some time ago; but they are not chiefs, neither delegates, who made that treaty. They are only young men who, without authority and

instruction from their chiefs, have concluded that treaty, which will not be approved. They went to that treaty clandestinely, and they intend to make mention of it in the next council to be held." (1 Vol. U. S. Indian Affairs.)

How often has that thing been acted over again since that time! And the Indians defrauded out of their lands by the unauthorized act of a few worthless men of the tribe, who would sell their birthright for a mess of pottage.

This treaty was closed on the 9th, and ratified by a mutual exchange on the 12th. The inhabitants of the new colony had been a long time in anxious suspense as to its results, and felt a great load taken from their minds at its favorable conclusion. They now thought there was no danger of a war, and that they could go on with their settlements in safety. On this occasion, a feast or great dinner was provided in the hall at Campus Martius, to which the principal chiefs were invited, with the officers of the fort and gentlemen of the Ohio Company. The following is a copy of the letter of invitation, as preserved in the Massachusetts Spy:

"To Messrs. Nicholson, Williams and La Chappelle, Indian interpreters at Fort Harmer.

"You are requested to inform the Wyandots, Delawares, Chippewas, Ottawas, Miamis, Pottawatomie and Sacs, with the Senecas and such of the Five Nations as are present, that we are desirous of celebrating the good work which the Great Spirit has permitted our father, the governor, with our brother, General Butler, and their sachems and chiefs, so happily to accomplish; for which purpose we will prepare an entertainment on Monday next, at two o'clock; and our brothers, the sachems and chiefs, to whom we now send tokens, are requested to attend at that time; that we may in friendship, and as true brothers, eat and drink together, and smoke the pipe of everlasting peace; and evince to the whole world how bright and strong is the chain which the thirteen United States hold fast at one end, and the Wyandots, &c., at the other. We are very sorry that we cannot entertain all our brethren together, with their wives and children; but as we have come into this country a very long way, some of us forty or fifty days' journey toward the rising sun, and could not bring much provision along with us, it is now out of our power. We trust the Great Spirit will permit us to plant and gather our corn, and increase our stores, and their children and children's

children may be told how much we shall all rejoice to make glad their hearts when they come to see us."

At this feast, the writer says, *"the Indian chiefs behaved with very great decorum, and an admirable harmony prevailed throughout the day. After dinner we were served with good wine, and Cornplanter, one of the first chiefs of the Five Nations, took up his glass and said:*

"I thank the Great Spirit for this opportunity of smoking the pipe of friendship and love. May we plant our own vines, be the fathers of our own children, and maintain them."

The day following the feast, the Indians began to disperse and return to their towns, apparently well satisfied with the treaty and their new friends.

Transactions of the Ohio Company,
To the close of the year 1788,
From their manuscript journal.

To accommodate the settlers with land for cultivation until they could occupy their own, and also to have the city grounds cleared for buildings, the agents and proprietors voted to lease the commons, and portions of section number twenty-nine, for a term of ten years. A tract for the convenience of the officers was reserved around Fort Harmer, and fifteen acres given to Governor St. Clair. Lots in the market square were leased to individuals for gardens. This square was near the Muskingum, and had been reserved for the benefit of the city as public ground; but as the section, or mile square number twenty-nine, devoted to the support of the gospel, happened to fall at the mouth of the Muskingum, so as to cover a large portion of the land selected for the city, it was given up, as were all the city lots within this section, and others laid out for the proprietors at the mouth of the Great Hockhocking, and at a place opposite the mouth of the Big Kanawha, greatly to the disappointment of the share holders. An exchange for other lands was proposed to Congress, but could not be effected. The reserved squares, Quadranaou, Capitolium, and Sacra via, fell north of section twenty-nine. The great mound was reserved by the ministerial trustees of Marietta at an early day, and leased to the town, with about four acres of ground as a public burying ground. This ancient relic has thus far been carefully preserved, a monument of the good taste of its builders, and an ornament to the city.

To encourage the building of mills, a lot was offered for twenty years to anyone who would build a wind mill, near the mouth of the Muskingum. Preparation was made for this object but none completed, probably from the varying and vacillating state of the winds at this place. Boards for the floors in the blockhouses, and private dwelling houses, were made by the whip saw, in a pit erected by Captain Jonathan Devol, near the bank of the river, opposite the garrison. The yellow poplar, which grew in the greatest abundance on the plain, furnished a fine material for boards, and also for the walls of buildings. Convenient lots for gardens were laid out for the owners of houses, in Campus Martius, and between that and the Muskingum. Section number sixteen for schools, which fell near the mouth of Duck Creek, was leased in lots to individuals, to clear and have the use of for ten years.

After the 20th of September, the surveys of the purchase were discontinued, by the advice of the governor, probably on account of the dislike of the Indians, until the treaty then in train could be accomplished. In making all the surveys of the Ohio Company, the surveyors were directed to govern themselves by the ordinance of Congress, passed in 1785, for the survey of lands in the North-Western territory, as to observations on the needle, meridian, &c., Bo that their surveys for accuracy may be safely compared with those done by the United States. In December, committees were appointed and sent out to reconnoiter the lands in the purchase, of which they as yet knew but little. The immediate object was to point out and decide on suitable spots for making settlements. One was reported at the forks of Duck Creek, about fifteen miles from Marietta, and two thousand acres advised to be given in one hundred acre lots to twenty settlers. Also, a tract of six hundred and forty acres to encourage the erection of mills at a rapid on Duck Creek, about three miles north of the town.

Donation lands

In donating their lands the directors required a strict adherence to the following rules and regulations:

First. The settler to furnish lands for highways when needed.

Second. To build a dwelling-house within five years, of the size of twenty-four by eighteen feet, eight feet between the floors, and a cellar of ten feet square; a chimney of stone or brick.

Third. To put out not less than fifty apple trees, and twenty peach trees, within three years.

Fourth. To clear and put into meadow or pasture fifteen acres, and into tillage not less than five acres, within five years.

Fifth. To be constantly provided with arms, and be subject to the militia law.

Sixth. Proper defenses or block-houses to be kept upon the donation lands, of such strength as shall be approved by the committee.

The expenses of surveying the lots to be paid by the grantees.

Any settler who complied with the above rules, and kept on the land a man able to bear arms for five years, was entitled to a deed from the directors. They were allowed to issue these donation lots until the 1st day of October, 1789, to any number of persons not exceeding two hundred, making in all twenty thousand acres. They were to settle in companies or associations, of not less than twenty men, so as to be able, when assembled in their blockhouses, to defend themselves against small parties of the enemy.

This mode of settling the new lands of the purchase was one of the most admirable that could be devised, and showed the men who planned it were familiar with the cultivation of the soil as well as with military affairs. These donation settlements were generally located on the frontiers of the purchase, and served as out-posts to guard the more central parts. They formed a military as well as an agricultural people—just such as the condition of the country needed. Their requirements as to the character of the improvements on the land were such as would be most beneficial to the settler, and ultimately useful to the community. The regulation as to the fruit trees made a permanent impression on the people generally; so that no part of the State of Ohio has paid that attention to the culture of fruit that is to be seen in the County of Washington.

The winter of 1788 commenced early in December, and the Ohio filled with ice so that no boat moved either up or down until March. The inhabitants were hard pressed for provisions; no meat but venison or bear, and these very scarce from the destruction made among them by the Indians in the summer and autumn previous, while waiting to attend the treaty, so that few could be found within ten or twelve miles of Marietta.

Before the river opened, many of the people lived for weeks without bread, eating boiled corn, or coarse meal ground in the hand mill, with little or no meat of any kind. When the river opened, those who had money could purchase flour from the boats that traded in provisions from Red Stone and the country about Pittsburgh.

The new settlement at the mouth of the Muskingum had attracted the attention of the House of Burgesses in Virginia, and an appropriation of money was made to survey a route for a road from Alexandria on the Potomac to the Ohio River opposite Marietta. The commissioners found a very feasible course, and the estimated distance only three hundred miles. A road was cut out; and for many years before the building of the national turnpike from Cumberland to the Ohio, merchandize was brought in wagons to the stores in Marietta, from the port of Alexandria.

CHAPTER XI.

The year of 1789 opened with the death of the Hon. James Mitchell Varnum, which took place the day after the completion of the treaty at Fort Harmer, on the 10th of January. He landed at the mouth of the Muskingum in June, 1788, and lived only seven months in the new purchase. His health was feeble for some time previous, his disease being consumption. He was a native of Rhode Island, and an active man in forming the Ohio Company, of liberal education, refined manners, and superior abilities. In 1787, he was elected by Congress as one of the judges of the Northwest Territory, and assisted Governor St. Clair in drafting the laws published in 1788. This code of early laws was in many respects fully equal or superior to those adopted since we became a state. They were formed at a time before political party spirit had biased the mind, and made for the sole good of the people they were to govern. Although the ordinance of Congress restricted them to the mere copying of those already in use in the states, yet the code adopted was chiefly original, and as they thought, better suited to the condition of a new settled country than those of the older settlements. He was also one of the directors of the Ohio Company. His untimely death was much regretted by the inhabitants of Marietta. The obsequies took place on the 13th, when an oration was pronounced by Doctor Drowne.

During the winter, several associations were formed for settlements on the donation lands, which had been surveyed, or were in progress of survey, at the forks of Duck Creek, Wolf Creek, Plainfield, and Belpre; notices of which will be given in the separate history of the three last of these places.

On the 4th of February, 1789, during the absence of Governor St. Clair, the inhabitants of Marietta held a town meeting to determine on the propriety of forming a system of police, and to adopt a code, of laws, for the regulation of the inhabitants of the city. This was the first town meeting ever held in the territory. Colonel Archibald Crary was chosen chairman, and Colonel E. Battelle, clerk. It was voted that Colonel Crary, Colonel Robert Oliver, Mr. Backus, Major Sargent, and Major White, be a committee to form a system of police, and to draft an address to his Excellency, Governor St. Clair, and to report at the adjourned meeting.

The address to the governor was accepted and forwarded, to him in a letter, as follows:

"To his Excellency, Arthur St. Clair, Esq., governor and commander in chief of the territory of the United States north west of the river Ohio.

"We, the citizens of Marietta, assembled at Campus Martius, beg leave to address your Excellency with the most cordial congratulations upon the happy issue of Indian affairs. For this event, so interesting to the United States at large and to this settlement in particular, we hold ourselves indebted, under God, to your Excellency's wisdom and unremitted exertions, displayed during the long and tedious negotiation of the treaty. It was with pain and very affectionate sympathy that we beheld this business spun out by the Indian nations through so many tedious months, and to a season of the year which, from its inclemency must have endangered and perhaps impaired the health and constitution of a character, under whose auspices and wise administration of government, we hope to be a good and happy people. We must lament with all the feelings of men, anxious to live under the precepts of legal authority, the absence of your Excellency, and the judges of the territory more particularly at this time, ere the system of laws has been completed. We feel most sensibly the want of them, and the privilege of establishing such city regulations as we are conscious should be derived alone from the sanction of your Excellency's authority; and that nothing but the most absolute necessity can exculpate us in assuming even the private police of our settlement. But the necessity and propriety of some system, which may tend to health, the preservation of our fields and gardens, with other essential regulations, will, we flatter ourselves, apologize for our adopting it; and convince your Excellency, that we could not ever be guilty of an interference with, or encroachment upon, any of the prerogatives of government.

"With the most sincere and affectionate respect for your Excellency in the character of governor and parent of our settlement, wishing you a safe

and pleasant passage, and anxiously anticipating your speedy return, we subscribe ourselves, in behalf of the citizens of Marietta, your most obedient and humble servants."

(Signed by the committee.)

The system of police was not ready for report until the 17th March, when a code of bylaws for the government of the inhabitants was adopted, well suited to the condition and wants of the people. Men who had always been accustomed to law and good order were not content to live without any regulations, although they dwelt in the wilderness, and their city was yet covered with the trees of the forest. They were governed by this code, so far as related to the police of a city until after the war.. The first board of police was Rufus Putnam, Archibald Crary, Griffin Greene, Robert Oliver and Nathaniel Goodale. They also appointed a sealer of weights and measures, and a register of births and deaths, with fence viewers, &c.

First marriage

The first marriage took place on the 6th of February, 1789, between the Hon. Winthrop Sargent, secretary of the Northwest Territory, and Miss Rowena Tupper, daughter of General B. Tupper, by General Rufus Putnam, judge of the court of common pleas for Washington County. The certificate is now on the files of the court.

Doings of the Ohio Company

Soon after the death of General Varnum, in January, Griffin Greene, Esq., was chosen a director to fill his place, and continued to occupy that post until the lands of the company were divided, in 1796. In February, the agents and proprietors passed the following resolution:

"Resolved, That the 7th day of April be forever considered as a day of public festival in the territory of the Ohio Company, as their settlements in this country commenced on that day; and that the directors request some gentleman to prepare an oration to be delivered on the next anniversary."

This festival was observed with all due regard for many years thereafter, by the first inhabitants and their children, until there came in so many strangers, who knew nothing of the trials and hardships of the forefathers in the early days of the colony. It is now kept as a kind of holiday, or May-day, by the young people, with "picnic parties" upon Devoll's Island, excursions into the hills, or social intercourse at each other's houses. The half-century celebration, in the year 1838, was observed by an oration and dinner at Marietta and also at Cincinnati, and has been occasionally observed since by the Historical Society of Washington County. During the Indian war, the inhabitants celebrated the day by a public dinner, and spent the afternoon in athletic amusements, such as games of ball, wrestling, and foot races, in which all took a part, from the oldest to the youngest. These were healthy exercises, and fitted them the better to contend with their Indian enemies in any personal contest that might ensue.

In February, further provision was made for the erection of water mills, at the nearest suitable point on Duck Creek, and lands granted Captain Enoch Shepherd amounting to nearly a thousand acres, who took in as partners in this expensive speculation Colonel E. Sproat and Thomas Stanley, enterprising and active men. The mills were to be completed by the 1st of September, 1790; suitable defenses for their protection erected, and a guard of eight men kept on the ground. The dam and mills were put up in that and the ensuing year, and were nearly ready to go into operation, when the war broke out and put a stop to further work. The saw mill was finished in September, and had sawed some boards, when a sudden flood in the creek tore away a part of the dam. The cost of their erection proved a dead loss to their owners, as the articles of the contract were not fully complied with. A grant of lands was also made for the building of mills at Wolf Creek, about a mile from its junction with the Muskingum. Donation lots to settlers were also surveyed, around it. A more full account of this mill, as the first built in the territory, will be given in the history of the settlement at Waterford.

Not regarding the recent treaty at Fort Harmer, parties of Indians still continued to harass the settlements in western Virginia, from April to October, probably not considering their old enemies as included in the compact; killing the people, stealing their horses, and burning their houses.

Not less than twenty persons were killed or taken prisoners, as appears from the memorial of the House of Burgesses to General Washington, in December. Their depredations extended from Kentucky to Pittsburgh. The settlements of the Ohio Company remained unmolested, with the exception of one man killed at Belpre. They felt a special dislike to surveyors, whom they saw traversing their hunting grounds with the chain and compass. In August, they made an attack on a surveying party in the employ of the Ohio Company, engaged in running the western line of the purchase. The following is a history of that event, taken chiefly from the manuscript notes of Mr. Mathews.

Attack on John Mathews

Early in the summer of 1789, Mr. Mathews was employed by the superintendent of the Ohio Company to survey the lands in the lower part of the purchase. James Backus was engaged with him in the survey. During the first week he was so unfortunate as to lose two of his pack horses, which strayed away in the woods and could not be found. This weakened their force so much that a portion of their provisions was left behind, stored in a hut near the river.

By the 10th of July their flour was exhausted, and the party lived for nine or ten days on meat alone, and that of a poor quality; that part of the country having been recently hunted over by the Indians, as they discovered by the number of fresh hunting camps, and the deer killed or dispersed, so that their hunter could furnish but a scanty supply.

On the 22d of July, he had nearly completed the survey as far south as the northern boundary line of township three, in range number sixteen; but by that time their stores were so much exhausted that the party was forced to quit the work, and set out on their return to the mouth of the Muskingum.
On the 23d they left the Big Kanawha, on their way up.

On the 25th, near the outlet of Old-town Creek, (In present day Meigs County, Ohio BPC) they met the committee of the company, consisting of Judge Parsons, Griffin Green, Esq. and General Tupper, in a boat, on a reconnoitering expedition, to examine the lands on the Ohio River down to the termination of the purchase, with Colonel Meigs, one of the surveyors, to take the meanders of the river. They requested them to go back and complete the unfinished work; and, to enable them to do so, sent a messenger immediately to Marietta for provisions.

On the 31st of July, the man returned with supplies.

On the 1st of August the committee landed them at a place fifteen miles below the Big Kanawha, while the boat proceeded on down the river.

On the 2d Mr. Backus and himself left the Ohio, for the northeast corner of township three, in range sixteen.

On the 3d they commenced their work. Backus was directed to run a west line across the sixteenth and seventeenth ranges and from thence south to the Ohio, where the committee was to wait until the 12th of the month for him to join them. In the mean time, Mr. Mathews was engaged in running a south line; and by the evening of the 5th had completed the east line of the third township, and progressed two miles west on the line between the second and third townships of the same range, and that night encamped by the side of a run in a narrow valley.

On the 6th he commenced work early in the morning, taking three of the seven soldiers who accompanied him as a guard, and leaving the corporal and other three soldiers, with the pack horseman, to bring on the baggage. In the forenoon he crossed a creek, running from the northwest, on which he discovered the tracks of three horses, traveling up the creek; and as they had passed since the rain of yesterday, he knew it was within a few hours. At noon the party at the camp had not joined him; and while he was wondering at their delay one of the soldiers came up and reported that one of the horses was missing and could not be found. He at once concluded that the Indians had taken him; but decided on sending Mr. Patchen, his assistant, who was a very active young man and a good woodsman, to make further search, while he directed one of the soldiers to carry the chain in his place. After running three miles on the line, he returned to the camp he left in the morning, not very well satisfied with his day's work. A little after sunset Mr. Patchen came in, and reported that he had discovered the trail of a man and horse, passing over one of the valleys in which they had encamped, and followed it to where it united with those they had seen in the fore part of the day, and continued on the trail up the creek, until there appeared to be eight or ten horses, and that on his way back he had discovered moccasin tracks in several places. From these circumstances, he concluded that a small plundering party had been over to the old settlements on the Big Kanawha, or to a new one on Sandy River, and on their return, had discovered the surveying party, and stolen the missing horse, but would make off as fast as they could to elude pursuit. Not knowing what might be the result, before lying down at night, he directed the corporal of the guard to keep a careful watch. Regular sentries were set, and at day break, the whole turned out under arms. About sunrise, thinking the danger past, if there was any, as the Indians usually make their attacks at early day light, the soldiers came into the camp, and a part of them were lying down, or setting on their blankets, with their arms near them, while others were kindling a fire to cook their morning meal.

Mr. Mathews had awakened early, and dispatched two of his men in quest of a horse that had strayed from the camp in the night, and was sitting on his blanket undressed, about twenty yards from the soldiers, with Mr. Patchen and one other man by his side. Two guns were first discharged, nearly together, by an unseen enemy. Patchen was shot through the breast and exclaimed, "Oh God, I am killed!" As Mr. Mathews turned his head toward him, he saw the bullet hole in his breast. At this instant a whole volley was fired at the soldiers as they rose from their sitting posture, followed by one of the most appalling Indian yells. This fire killed all the soldiers but the corporal, who happened to be sitting with his back against a friendly tree between him and the savages. As they rushed in upon their victims on one side of the camp, Mr. Mathews and the three remaining men fled out on the other. A part of their murderers followed them about forty rods, when they quit the pursuit, and returned to share with their comrades in the plunder of the camp. After running a quarter of a mile or more, and seeing that the Indians were not pursuing him, he slackened his pace, and was directly joined by a man by the named Russell, who was setting near him when Patchen was killed.

He had escaped with nothing on him but his hat and shirt, having thrown away his overcoat, which was lying on his arm and had been used for a covering in the night, to facilitate his flight, while his companion happened to be more fully dressed. The brush and briars had torn his skin severely, when his comrade offered him his coat, into the sleeves of which he contrived to slip his legs, at this time very thin, from his previous privations. It was now that he discovered a hole in his shirt made by a bullet, which had just grazed the skin without hurting him.

They directed their course for the river, intending to fall in with the boat and exploring party, whom they judged by this time to be forty miles below Big Kanawha. About nine o'clock they struck the Ohio, at the thirty mile post, lately set by Colonel Meigs. This was about seven or eight miles from their camp, as they had traveled. After following down the Ohio a few miles further, the naked feet of Mr. Mathews became so much blistered and swollen that he walked in great pain. Under these circumstances they concluded to construct a raft, of old logs, fastened together with grape vines. When it was about half finished, two Kentucky boats came in sight, and took them on board, where they were much gratified to find two of his men, who had struck the river higher up. About four miles below they found the company boat, with Colonel Meigs, the committee having left for Marietta, a part of them being sick a few days before.

The corporal came in the same day, and related that as he was hurrying away from the camp, he stumbled and fell over a log, behind which he lay concealed until the Indians gave up the pursuit. From this covert he could see the movements of the Indians, while plundering the camp. They were greatly amused and amazed at the vibrations of the needle in the compass, which shifted its position like a thing of life, as they turned it from side to side. They laughed and whooped as they witnessed its movements, in great glee, no doubt thinking it "a great medicine." After scalping and stripping the soldiers of their clothing, they broke up their muskets against a tree as of no use to them. As soon as they were gone, the corporal hastened away after his companions.

To which tribe they belonged was not certainly known, but from various circumstances, and the opinion of the friendly Delawares and Wyandots, it was supposed they were Shawnee. This nation, above all others, had the greatest hatred to the whites, and were the very last to sign the treaty of peace, after their defeat by General Wayne. They were the Spartans of the Indian confederacy. On the morning of the day that Mr. Mathews was attacked, Colonel Meigs became alarmed at seeing two strange dogs on the shore, and discovered signs of Indians in the vicinity, by fresh marks on the trees. As the boat was not prepared for defense, soon after the fugitives came, he had her removed across the Ohio to the Virginia shore. That night they fell down the river to the mouth of "Twelve Pole" Creek, which is about four miles above Big Sandy, and nearly opposite to the present town of Burlington. This spot was near the termination of the seventeenth range, where Mr. Backus would strike the Ohio. On the eighth, Colonel Meigs, who was an old soldier, directed the men to commence building a small blockhouse, on the margin of the bank, to cover them in case of an attack. They applied themselves so diligently, that it was finished the same day.

During this period the other missing man came to the river, and was brought over. In this covert they remained, feasting on fat buffalo meat, which was very plenty in that vicinity, until the 10th, at noon, when they heard two guns fired below them on the river, which they hoped might be the signal of the arrival of Mr. Backus, for whom they had began to feel the most serious apprehensions, lest the Indians had attacked him also. They directly answered the guns, by firing a large blunderbuss, or wall piece, they had in the boat. They soon heard a shot in reply. A large canoe was manned and sent down, which returned before night, with Mr. Backus and his party all safe.

On the 11th, the boat moved up to Little Guyandot and on the 12th arrived opposite to the spot where he was attacked by the Indians.

On the 13th, a party of armed men went with Mr. Mathews to visit the scene of his calamity, and learn the state of his dead soldiers. He found them lying near where they fell, but could not discover the remains of Mr. Patchen. The flesh was all eaten from their bones by the wolves, except that on the palms of their hands and soles of the feet; to which parts of the human body they, as well as dogs, seem to have an instinctive aversion, as they had in the days of Jezebel.

Mr. Mathews lost all his camp equipage, surveying apparatus, field notes, and clothing. The loss of the notes was most seriously felt, as without them he could make no return of the survey, and could claim nothing for his labor and expenses. He recovered all the horses but one. That which he supposed the Indians had stolen, he found standing in the camp at the time of his visit. The spot where he was attacked is on the north line of township number two, range sixteen, two miles west of the northeast corner, and about four miles in a direct line from the Ohio River; so that the locality can be identified at this day by anyone who will take the trouble.

The party commenced their return on the 14th of August and by the combined aid of poles and oars could urge on their unwieldy craft only twelve or fourteen miles a day. The boat was a species of bateau, of a class well known at that day by the name of "a contractor's boat," and long since passed out of use on the Ohio River. It had a cabin of ten or twelve feet in the stern, for sleeping and eating, while the rest of the boat was open to the weather; and of the burthen of thirty or forty tons.

In the spring of the year 1789, the Rev. Daniel Story came to Marietta, from the state of Massachusetts, employed by the Ohio Company, as a chaplain for the new settlement, and continued to preach in Campus Martius, and in a blockhouse at the stockade at" the point," from this period to the close of the war. He occasionally preached at the settlements in Belpre and Waterford during the war, traveling by water in a canoe, accompanied by some of the inhabitants.

Regular progress was made in the clearing of land and planting of grain during this year, in the vicinity of Marietta; but not much greater than in the previous year, from the circumstance that a large portion of the farming class had removed to Belpre and Waterford. Quite a number of log houses were built; and at "the point," near the Ohio, on the corner of First Street, was erected a large two-storied frame house, for a tavern, by Joseph Buell and Levi Munsel. This was the first frame building in Marietta; the timber and boards for which were prepared at McKeesport, above Pittsburgh, by Captain Enoch Shepherd and brought down in a raft with his family. This man was a brother of General Shepherd, who commanded the troops of Massachusetts in subduing the rebellion, headed by the notorious Shays, in 1789.

On the 1st of October, there was a frost generally throughout the western country. It proved ruinous to all the late planted corn, and damaged much that was early. This frost was the source of great suffering to the new settlers in Marietta and Belpre; especially among those who had exhausted nearly all their resources in the journey out, and had not money to purchase provision from the trading boats.

In November the measles broke out among the inhabitants of Marietta, and continued through the winter, proving fatal to a number of the children. It was said to have been brought by a family from head waters. The addition to the number of inhabitants this year was one hundred and fifty-two men, and fifty-seven families.

In November, the Honorable S. H. Parsons, one of the judges of the territory, and a director in the Ohio Company, lost his life by drowning in Big Beaver Creek. He was descending that stream in a canoe, with Captain Joseph Rogers, as an assistant, and, being a fearless man, insisted on passing over a rapid or fall, not usually attempted by the navigators of that stream. In this experiment the canoe upset, and he was drowned. His companion was more fortunate and escaped with his life at that time, to be killed by the Indians in a year or two afterwards.

Judge Parsons was a citizen of Connecticut at the time of his appointment, and took an active part in the early transactions of the Ohio Company.

CHAPTER XII.

Doings of the Ohio Company. — A mill built.—Reverend D. Story to preach at Marietta, Belpre and Waterford. — Company lands explored—Salt springs.— Funds for schools. — Money loaned to settlers.—Prospect of war. — Guards raised.—Spies or rangers.—Family of Governor St. Clair.—Small pox breaks out at Marietta. — Famine of 1790. — Sufferings of the settlers. — Relief afforded by the directors. — Indian hostilities —Letter of Governor St. Clair.—Colonel Vigo. — R. J. Meigs sent on a mission to Detroit—French emigrants arrive.—Settle Gallipolis. — Grant of land by Congress.— Townships organized.

Doings of the Ohio Company

In February, 1790, liberty was granted to Robert Potts, a professional millwright, from New London, Connecticut, to build a grist mill on the company lands at Mill Creek, about two miles north of Marietta. A dam was erected and a house put up just as the war commenced, during which period the works were destroyed by Indians, and the labor and money lost.

About this time, Colonel Robert Oliver was appointed a director, in place of S. H. Parsons, deceased.

The agents and proprietors, in this month, decided, that reverend Daniel Story, who still continued in the pay of the Ohio Company, *"should preach three Sundays at Marietta, and two Sundays at Belpre and Waterford, in rotation."* This he continued to do until the war rendered his tours of duty more irregular; and when he visited these outposts a guard of armed men accompanied him.

Exploring committees were sent out during the winter, to ascertain the most suitable places for settlements along the Ohio River, in the lower part of the purchase, and reports made of several localities. Lands to the amount of fifty-seven thousand acres were allotted, forming farms for five hundred and seventy settlers. Subsequent events altered this arrangement, and donation lands were supplied by the United States, so that a large proportion of this generous outlay was saved to the company.

Salt springs

So great was the scarcity and value of salt during the first ten years of the settlement, not less than six or eight dollars a bushel, that the Ohio Company, in their final division of their lands, passed the following resolve:

"Whereas, it is believed that the great "salt springs" of the Scioto lie within the present purchase of the Ohio Company; therefore, resolved, that this sixth division of land to the proprietors is made upon the express condition and reserve, that every salt spring now known, or that shall hereafter be found, within the lands that shall fall to the lot of any proprietor, they be and are hereby reserved to the use of the company, with such quantity of land about them as the agents and proprietors shall think proper to assume for general purposes, not exceeding three thousand acres; the person on whose land they are found, to receive other lands of equal value."

It so happened that the Scioto springs were situated a few miles west of the purchase, and on the lands belonging to the United States. When Ohio became a state, these noted springs, with those on Salt Creek in Muskingum County and at Delaware, were reserved by Congress for the use of the state, with large tracts of land adjoining to furnish fuel for boiling the salt water. For many years these springs were leased to individuals, and became a source of revenue to Ohio. The state was forbidden to sell or alienate them in any way. Finally, after other waters were found, by boring wells deep into the rocky strata, of much greater strength, so that no one would lease or pay for the use of them, they were sold in the year 1826, by a special act of Congress, on the petition of the Ohio legislature; and the lands once deemed so valuable, became common farms. For many years salt has ceased to be made at any of these old and long cherished salines.

A similar reservation was also made by the Ohio Company, in relation to mines of iron ore, and encouragement given for the erection of furnaces, similar to that for mills; but no mines were found of sufficient extent to make it an object to hazard the erection of works.

In July the agents and officers of the company appropriated one hundred and fifty dollars of their funds for the support of schools in the settlements at Marietta, Belpre, and Waterford.

They also ordered money in small sums to be loaned to the sick and needy families, under the supervision of Griffin Green, Esq., until such time as they could refund it again. In this way two or three thousand dollars were distributed among the settlers, relieving them very greatly from the distressing effects of the famine that pressed sorely upon them.

The last of September, as the prospect of war thickened around them, they ordered a corps of thirty men to be raised at the expense of the company, as guards for the defense of the settlements, at eight dollars a month and rations; also, that Campus Martius be put in a good state of repair, with strong doors, windows, &c. Early in November they authorized Colonel Sproat, the commandant of the militia, to enlist six men as spies, or rangers, with such pay, rations, and services, as he should think best. The 1st of December, Colonel Sproat was directed to detail ten men at a time, to act as guards or patrols, to traverse the woods in the vicinity of the settlements. At the same time they appointed a committee to carry into effect their resolution of July, by devising ways and means of opening schools in the settlements, and to divide the money among them according to the number of children. They had always been accustomed to see schools among the people, especially in the winter, and they could not forego that valuable custom, even here in the wilderness.

The family of Governor St. Clair

The governor of the Northwest Territory moved his family to Marietta in the winter of the year 1790, and took possession of the south-west blockhouse, in Campus Martius, which had been fitted up for his express use by the Ohio Company. At the period of their removal they lived in Legonier Valley, at a place called " Potts's Grove," in Westmoreland County, Pennsylvania, where he owned a princely domain, a small portion of which only was then under cultivation. Here he subsequently erected extensive iron works, a flouring mill, &c, with convenient dwelling houses for himself and workmen. At the time of the removal, his family consisted of a son, Arthur St. Clair, jr., and three daughters, Louisa, Jane and Margaret; with a middle aged, sensible colored woman, who acted as cook and house keeper. Mrs. St. Clair did not accompany them, but remained in charge of the plantation at "Potts's Grove." Arthur was a young man of twenty-one, and afterwards settled in Cincinnati, as a lawyer. Louisa was a young woman of eighteen' or nineteen years; Jane a girl of fifteen or sixteen, of a feeble constitution, and retiring manners and habits; Margaret was a child of eight or nine years, and died that summer with a fever. Louisa was a healthy, vigorous girl, full of life and activity, every way calculated for a soldier's daughter; fond of a frolic, and ready to draw amusement from all and everything around her. She was a fine equestrian, and would mount the most wild and spirited horse without fear, managing him with ease and gracefulness; dashing through the open woodlands around Campus Martius at full gallop, leaping over logs, or any obstruction that fell in her way. She was one of the most rapid skaters in the garrison; few, if any of the young men equaling her in speed and activity, or in graceful movements in this enchanting exercise. Her elegant person and neat dress, showing too much advantage, called forth loud plaudits from both young and old. The broad sheet of ice on the Muskingum, near the garrison, for a few days in the winter, afforded a fine field for this healthy sport. She was also an expert huntress; and would have afforded a good figure of Diana in her rambles through the woods, had she been armed with *the bow,* instead of the rifle. Of this instrument she was a perfect mistress; loading and firing with the accuracy of a backwoodsman; killing a squirrel from the highest tree, or cutting off the head of a partridge with wonderful precision. She was fond of roaming in the woods, and often went out alone into the forest near Marietta, fearless of the savages that occasionally lurked in the vicinity. She was as active on foot as on horseback, and could walk for several miles with the rapidity of a ranger. Her manners were refined; her person beautiful, with highly cultivated intellectual powers, having been educated with much care in Philadelphia. Born with a healthy, vigorous frame, she had strengthened both her body and mind by these athletic exercises when a child; probably first encouraged by her father, who had spent the larger portion of his life in camps. She was one of those rare spirits, so admirably fitted to the times and the manners of the day in which she lived. After the war she returned to her early home, amidst the romantic glens of the Legonier Valley.

Small pox

In January, 1790, a boat on its way to Kentucky put on shore a sick man and his family, by the name of Welsh. He was taken to the house of Mr. James Owen, who, at that time, lived in a long, narrow log house on the corner, where the banking house of Marietta now stands. It had been built the year before by some young men from Boston who, not finding employment to suit them had left the country. It was called, for some years after, the "Boston House." Mr. Owen was from South Kingston, Rhode Island, and came on to the country with General Varnum. They landed at Marietta the 5th of June, 1788, and Mrs. Owen was the *first female* who settled in Marietta. Mr. Welsh's disease proved to be small pox. This was the first time it had appeared among the people, and was greatly dreaded. A meeting of the inhabitants was called, and a house built for the reception of the sick man, near where the college now stands. He lived but a few days after the removal.

Mrs. Owen took the disease the natural way, and was too sick to be removed. A meeting was again called, and it was decided that houses should be put up back of the plain, and the people generally be inoculated. This course was adopted, although some were inoculated in their own houses. Dr. True and Dr. Farley were the physicians who attended the sick. Of those inoculated only two died, out of a hundred and more and these quite aged women. Six died who took it by infection. Mrs. Owen recovered and lived many years afterward; and received a donation lot of one hundred acres from the Ohio Company, as a reward for her meritorious services, and her being the first female inhabitant of Marietta.

Famine of 1790

The inhabitants of Marietta had barely closed their trials and anxieties with the small pox, when they were assailed by a more obstinate and unrelenting, if not a more dangerous enemy. It was a trial in which all, whether rich or poor, were more or less involved, and that was a scarcity of wholesome food. It was as late as the fore part of June, 1789, before the inhabitants had finished fencing and planting the great cornfield on the plain. The increased number of horses and oxen had made it necessary to enclose the field with a fence, while the year before it had been without one. A brush fence, from the Muskingum to Duck Creek, had afforded a sufficient range for the support of the stock then in the country.

A frost on the 1st of October had seared the corn, when it was not fairly out of that soft and succulent state called the milk. It was gathered and put away, and supposed by many that when it was fairly dried, it would make good bread; but when tried it almost invariably produced sickness and vomiting. Even the domestic animals could not eat it with safety. The effect was similar to that of the fungus grain, or "sick wheat," as it is usually called. Eatable corn rose from fifty cents to one dollar fifty and two dollars a bushel. The poorest was a dollar.

By the middle of May the scarcity was felt generally. There were but few cows in the country to afford milk; no oxen or cattle to spare for meat, and very few hogs. The woods, which were full of game in 1788, were now nearly as bare of it as an old settled country — the Indians having killed, or driven away, nearly all the deer within twenty miles of Marietta. In this great scarcity it was wonderful how little there was of selfishness, and how generally kindness and good feeling abounded. Those who had more resources, lent, or gave, to those who had less; using, at the same time, the strictest economy themselves, that they might be more able to do so. Occasionally a turkey, or a piece of bear meat, was procured from the hunters, which was put into the kettle and boiled up with hominy or coarse meal. Those who had cows divided the milk with their neighbors, especially where there were children. Sugar, or molasses, they had little of, as they had not kettles to boil the sap of the maple, which grew in great abundance on the rich lands, and would have afforded a valuable source of nourishment in the general scarcity. The river furnished a tolerable supply of fish, and aided much in preventing starvation, especially in very poor families. Nettle tops, and the tender shoots of pigeon-berry, or *phytolacca decandria,* as soon as they appeared, were gathered up and boiled with a little flour, or meal, and salt, and eaten by many persons. Potato tops were eaten in the same way. Salt was scarce, and sold, in small parcels, for fifty cents a quart. Spice-bush and sassafras afforded an alimentary drink, in place of tea and coffee. The Ohio Company, with a liberality worthy of all praise, assisted many poor families with small loans of money, or the suffering would have been much greater: with this they could occasionally get provisions from boats descending the Ohio. Thus they struggled along, until the young beans and early squashes appeared; then green corn and potatoes, which was considered a perfect relief; and finally, the ripened corn, with a little wheat, ground in the hand mill, furnished bread that was thought a luxury. The matrons of the colony, in a little sober "chit-chat" over a cup of spice-bush tea, without any sugar, and very little milk, concluded if they lived ever again to enjoy a supply of wholesome food for their children and selves, they would never complain of their fare, be it ever so coarse and homely. The crop of that year was fine and abundant, and closed their fears for food from that day to this. It was long known to the inhabitants as "the starving year."

Indian hostilities

In the spring of this year the Indians, chiefly Shawnee and Miamis, commenced a new species of warfare, by attacking boats on the river, generally owned by emigrants on their way to Kentucky. Their chief rendezvous was near the mouth of the Scioto. One of their main devices to get possession of a boat, was to induce them to land, by means of a white man showing himself on the bank, and begging them to land and take him on board, as he had been a prisoner with the Indians and just escaped; if he fell again into their hands they would certainly put him to death. In this way many boats were induced to land, when the Indians, who lay in ambush, instantly took possession of the boat, or shot down the crew from the shore. This decoy was sometimes an actual prisoner, whom they forced to aid them in this stratagem; at others a renegade white man who had voluntarily joined them to share in the plunder.

Letter from Governor St. Clair

The following letter to the Secretary at War, dated at Marietta, September 19th, 1790, shows the state of the country during that summer. (1st Vol. Indian Affairs.)

"The depredations on the Wabash and Ohio still continue. Every day, almost, brings an account of some murder or robbery; and yesterday a number of horses were taken from this settlement. Not long ago, a boat belonging to Mr. Vigo, a gentleman from post St. Vincennes, was fired upon near the mouth of Blue River. This person the United States have been very much obliged to, on many occasions, and is in truth the most disinterested person I have ever seen. He had three men killed, and was obliged, in consequence, to fall down the river. This party it seems had been designed to intercept me, for they reported that they had had three fair discharges at the Governor's boat, and expected they had killed him. In descending the river, Mr. Vigo's boat fell in with Mr. Melchor's, returning from Tennessee, and attempted, in company with him, to ascend the Wabash. Here they were attacked again. Melchor escaped, and fell down to the Ance de la graisse; but the savages possessed themselves of Vigo's boat, which they plundered of all his and the crew's personal baggage and arms; but as she was navigated by Frenchmen, they suffered them to depart with the peltries, telling them that if they had not been in company with Americans they would not have injured them; and that if they found them in such again, they would put them to death. Captain McCurdy was also fired upon between Fort Washington and this place, and had five or six men killed and wounded."

Colonel Vigo

At the time of the conquest of Kaskaskia and the Illinois country, by Colonel George Rogers Clark, Francis Vigo was a merchant, or Indian trader, living at St. Louis. He was by birth a Spaniard, and St. Louis at that period,

July, 1788, in possession of the Spaniards, who were at peace with England as well as with the United States. As soon as Mr. Vigo heard of the capture of Kaskaskia, he visited that place, and unsolicited made an offer of his services and means to Colonel Clark, not only in keeping possession of the country, but also in the conquest of the British post at Vincennes. For this purpose he made a visit to that place, accompanied only by a single servant. Before reaching there he was taken prisoner by a party of Indians, plundered, and carried before Governor Hamilton, the Commander of "the post." Here he was detained for some time, but finally set at liberty, at the urgent request and remonstrance of the French inhabitants of that place, who were well acquainted with, and held him in high estimation. The information he took back of the strength, position, &c., of the garrison, enabled Colonel Clark to succeed so wonderfully as he did in its capture.

The honorable John Law, in his address before the Historical Society of Vincennes, in February, 1839, and from whom the most of these facts are obtained, says, *"its conquest, and subsequent attachment to the Union, was as much owing to the counsel and services of Vigo, as to the bravery and enterprise of Clark."*

Francis Vigo was born in 1747, and at the time of this attack was forty-three years old. He still continued the hazardous and laborious pursuit of a trader in peltries along the western waters, from St. Louis to Pittsburgh, and was acquainted with the officers in Fort Harmer and other frontier posts, which he often visited in his voyages up and down the Ohio River. His home was at Vincennes, where he passed the latter years of his life. He was a man whose name ought to be better known to the American people, and especially those of the western states.

The last of September, Governor St. Clair sent a dispatch to the governor of Detroit, informing him that the contemplated expedition under General Harmer was not intended to molest any of the British posts or possessions, but solely to chastise the Indians, whose outrages and cruelties had become intolerable. He also said that he expected the governor would not suffer any under his command to afford assistance to the hostile tribes by furnishing them with military stores.

This letter was committed to the care of R. J. Meigs, jr., Esq., then in the prime of life, and a practicing attorney in the courts of the territory. He possessed courage and activity, both needed in this hazardous enterprise. His companions were John Whipple, a son of Commodore Abraham Whipple and a sprightly Indian, named Charley, who had loitered in the vicinity of Marietta since the treaty. He could speak some English and a little French.

The region they had to traverse, after leaving the settlement at Waterford, was an entire wilderness. The journey was chiefly performed on foot, as they had but one horse to carry their provision and baggage, which was stolen by the Indians when about half way on the route. They proceeded, without serious molestation, to a friendly Delaware town, on the heads of the Sandusky. While there a deputation arrived from the hostile Miamis to the Delawares and Wyandots, urging them to unite with them against their common enemy, the whites; and, also, saying that General Harmer had been driven from their country, after a severe engagement with their warriors.

While here passing the night, the Miamis heard of the two white men on their way to Detroit, and threatened to kill them if they could find them; and were only prevented by the kind offices of the Delawares, who conducted them in the night out of the village, and so far on the way the next day as to be out of danger. Charley, their Indian guide, here left them, being threatened with death by the Miamis if he proceeded any further in conveying their enemies.

On their arrival at Detroit, Mr. Meigs was received with great coolness by the governor. He, however, after some time, condescended to answer the message, and kindly informed him that he could not return again in safety through the Indian Territory, as they would certainly put him to death, without any regard to the flag of truce which he had borne in his way out. At the same time, he offered him a passage down the lake to Presque Isle in a packet vessel, then about to sail.

While staying here a few days for the schooner to get ready, a young chief of the hostile tribes, learning who he was, aimed his rifle at him as he stood on the shore looking at the vessels in the harbor. Unconscious of his danger, he would certainly have lost his life had not a white man, who was standing near, observed the act, and instantly snatched it from his hands and shook out the priming, at the same time threatening him with punishment if he again made the attempt. The vessel soon after sailed, and landed them at

Presque Isle, from whence they passed down the old route by Venango, French Creek, and the Alleghany River, to Pittsburgh, and thence to Marietta.

It was an enterprise of great danger, and performed to the entire satisfaction of Governor St. Clair; but in its results was unproductive of the least good to the United States; the British agents, after this, supplying the hostile tribes with arms and ammunition in fivefold abundance; and encouraged them in every way to prosecute the war with that detested people, who had renounced their king, and threatened to deprive them of their trade with the Indians.

French emigrants

On the 16th of October, 1790, the inhabitants of Marietta were much gratified at the arrival of a large company of French emigrants, composed of men women and children, amounting in all to more than four hundred souls. Their outlandish dress, foreign language, and wooden shoes of the lower classes, were a matter of rare interest to the dwellers in the wilderness, especially as at that day the deluge of foreign emigration, which has since flooded the country, had had not commenced. They had descended the Ohio in six "Kentucky Arks", or flat boats. A large portion of them were from the city of Paris, who were equally surprised at the vast forests and broad rivers of the new world, of which they had heard, but could form no adequate conception. This company of adventurers had purchased land of Joel Barlow, the accredited agent of "The Scioto Land Company." Their agent rather prematurely sold out a portion of their lands to the French people, before they had completed their purchase from Congress. The contract ultimately failed, and the poor emigrants were left without lands for a home. Many of them were destitute of money; the little they once had being spent in the purchase, and in the voyage and journey out. In the contract with the company, they engaged to build them comfortable dwelling houses on the lands, and to furnish them a year's provision, until they could clear fields, and raise crops of their own. General Putnam was employed by William Duer of New York, the principal man in the Scioto Company, to build the houses for them, and to furnish provision. This he kindly undertook, and accomplished, at an expense of more than two thousand dollars; which money he finally lost, as Duer soon after became a bankrupt, and the company dissolved. In the summer of that year, he employed Captain William Burnham, with forty men under his charge, to perform the work of clearing the land, and putting up two long rows of dwelling houses, on the bank of the Ohio, three miles below Big Kanawha. The village of Gallipolis, as the new town was called, when the houses were whitewashed, made a very neat appearance from the Ohio, in the midst of the surrounding wilderness. The land on which the village stood belonged to the Ohio Company, who finally sold it to the occupants at a moderate price.

Very few of these emigrants were cultivators of the soil. They were generally artisans and tradesmen of different kinds, such as are found in cities; and some were broken down gentlemen, bred to no particular calling, so that on the whole they were a very helpless company. A few of the more wealthy adventurers had a number of men in their employ, whose passage money and expenses they paid, to be refunded by their labor here. Among them were a Marquis and a Viscount, his son, who were the principal leaders.

A few of the French spent the winter in Marietta, and became permanent settlers, but the larger portion went down to Gallipolis. In the spring the Marquis returned to France. They suffered much during the Indian war, which broke out that winter, from want of food and privations of various kinds. The hostile Indians learning that the new village was occupied by Frenchmen, scarcely molested them at all, having an old and lasting friendship for that people ever since the travels and adventures of La Salle, in the valley of the Mississippi, in the year 1678.

In the year 1795, Congress took notice of the wrongs of these much injured colonists, and gave them a tract of land on the Ohio River, commencing about a mile above the Little Sandy, and extending down the Ohio eight miles and back, so as to include twenty thousand acres. It was a noble act of justice, and in some measure atoned for the cupidity of their countrymen. A few of the emigrants were educated men, and have held judicial offices in the republic and seats in the halls of legislation. A number of their descendants yet live in Gallipolis, and own the cherished homes of their forefathers; while a large portion of the donation tract, or "French Grant," has passed into other hands.

Organization of townships

At a meeting of the court of quarter sessions, on the 20th day of December, 1790, they, for the first time, exercised the authority given by law, of establishing the boundaries, and organizing townships. The three following were the first established in the territory north-west of the river Ohio.

Marietta

"Resolved, that townships No. 1, 2 and 3, in the eighth range, and townships No. 2 and 3 in the ninth range, be, and they hereby are incorporated and included in one township, by the name of Marietta."

Town officers — Anselm Nye, Town Clerk; Joseph Gilman, Esq., and Colonel William Stacey, Overseers of poor; B. J. Gilman, Constable.

N. B.—Mr. Gilman declined acting, and Christopher Burlingame was appointed in his place.

Belpre

"Resolved, that townships No. 1 and 2, in the tenth range, and No. 1, in the ninth range, be, and they hereby are incorporated, and to be included in one township, by the name of Belpre.

Town officers — Colonel E. Battelle, Town Clerk; Waton Casey, Overseer of poor; Colonel Nathaniel Cashing, Constable.

Waterford

"Resolved, that the seventh and eighth townships in the eleventh range, the fourth and fifth townships in the tenth range, and mile square, No. 33, in the fourth township of the ninth range, be, and they hereby are incorporated and included in one township, by the name of Waterford.

Town officers — Captain Ebenezer Gray, Town Clerk; Noah Fearing, Overseer of poor; Dean Tyler, Constable.

CHAPTER XIII.

Indian war

The war broke out very unexpectedly to the settlers, and found them poorly prepared for such an event. Few of them had any considerable store of provisions, or money to support their families, or to go on with the clearing of their lands, during an actual state of hostilities, which they did not know how long might continue. It was a sad reverse of fortune. They had trusted in the treaty recently made, to preserve them in peace with the Indians. The policy pursued by the United States was pacific; but the frontier inhabitants of Pennsylvania, Virginia, and Kentucky, were always at war with the Indians, and killed and plundered them whenever they could find a fitting opportunity. They also disliked to see new settlements forming on the north side of the Ohio. But above all, they were now irritated and vexed at the campaign of General Harmer into the territories of the Shawnee and the Miamis. They were also encouraged to pursue the war from the disastrous termination of that campaign to the American troops. On the 2d day of January the war commenced in earnest in the Ohio Company's purchase, by the attack on the blockhouse at "Big Bottom," by which fourteen persons were killed and four carried into captivity, as will be more fully related in the history of Waterford.

The news of this startling and mournful event reached Marietta in the forenoon of Monday the 3d; the messengers sent out by Captain Rogers having deviated from the right course in the darkness of the night. The court of quarter sessions had just opened when the message arrived. As many of the jurors and witnesses were from Belpre and Waterford, it was directly adjourned that they might immediately return to their homes for the protection of their families, whom they had every reason to fear had shared the same fate, for they were living in cabins, and generally unprepared for resistance or defense. As they approached their homes, many a stout heart trembled lest they should see the smoking ruins and bleeding bodies of their wives and children. But a merciful and overruling Providence had preserved them, by inclining the minds of the savages to return to their own homes, without proceeding any further at that time against the defenseless settlers of Waterford and Belpre. The inhabitants of Marietta were in a better state of defense.

Doings of the Ohio Company in 1791

The agents and proprietors held a meeting on the 3d of January, and adjourned. On the 5th they met again, and continued daily until the 10th. At these meetings the directors, with General Putnam at their head, passed a number of spirited and salutary resolutions for the safety and protection of the colony. Governor St. Clair being absent at Philadelphia, where Congress were in session, they addressed the judges of the court, as the representatives of the governor, requesting them to represent the present defenseless condition of the country to him, and through him to the President of the United States, asking such aid of troops, &c., as the exigency demanded. They say, *"The most of our settlers are encumbered with families, many of which are numerous, and having been prevented for several years from getting subsistence by their labor, have already exhausted their property, and now can support themselves only by cultivating their lands. If they contract their settlements and garrison themselves for defense, they must eventually starve. If they do not, they are massacred. We have no resource but in the humanity of the general government, and persuade ourselves that, on a proper representation made by your honors, we shall receive such assistance as will enable us to live in quietness."*

The court met on the 7th of January, and appointed Charles Greene, Esq., to go on to Philadelphia as an express, with this address and their own views on the state of the country.

Their condition was very alarming. News had recently reached them of the disastrous termination of General Harmer's campaign, and that in place of humbling the Indians, it had only exasperated them; and that they had openly threatened, *"That before the trees had again put forth their leaves, there should not remain a single smoke of the white man north-west of the Ohio River."*

Under these trying circumstances, the old veterans of the Revolution acted with their usual firmness and discretion, by preparing themselves for the worst that might happen. They could not expect any aid at present from the adjoining states, as the Governor, who only had authority to call on them in case of necessity, was absent.

The troops at Fort Harmer had nearly all been withdrawn by General Harmer and only one small detachment remained under Captain Zeigler. With these facts before them, they turned to their own resources. The remote settlements, at the forks of Duck Creek, Wolf Creek Mills, &c., were evacuated, and the inhabitants quartered at Marietta, Belpre and Waterford; thus concentrating their strength, and establishing a regular system of defense. New blockhouses were ordered to be built at those places, and the settlers to live as compact as possible. A large portion of these defenses were built at the expense of the Ohio Company. Colonel E. Sproat was directed to detail sixty men from the militia, with proper officers, to garrison these posts, and to assist in building the new fortifications, who were to receive regular pay and rations until otherwise provided by the United States. To encourage the men to enlist, their pay was made double that of the regular service, or eight dollars a month.

Six of the best hunters, familiar with the backwoods, were employed as scouts or spies, to watch the approach of the enemy and prevent a surprise, at such pay as the commandant should be able to procure them, and was established at one dollar a day. These were divided so as to furnish two for each garrison. The directors were ordered by the agents to keep a separate and accurate account of their expenses in the defense of the colony, with the expectation of its being repaid by Congress. They spent more than eleven thousand dollars, none of which was repaid, but remained a dead loss to the Ohio Company. In March, the agents authorized Colonel Sproat to put the houses in Campus Martius in the best state of defense, and surround the works with an outer protection of palisades and abbatis.

In March, the agents and proprietors, amidst their other cares and perplexities, did not forget the ornamenting of their new city, but attended to this also, as well as to its defense. Joseph Gilman, Daniel Story, and Jonathan Hart, were appointed a committee to point out the terms for leasing and ornamenting the public squares in the city of Marietta, and reported as follows:

"The mound square to be leased to General Putnam, for twelve years, on these conditions: To surround the whole square with mulberry trees, at suitable distances, with an elm in each corner; the base of the mound to be encircled with weeping willows, and evergreens on the mound; the circular parapet, outside the ditch, to be surrounded with trees; all within this to remain undisturbed by the plow, seeded down to grass, and the whole enclosed with a post and rail fence. The squares Capitolium and Quadranaou to be ornamented in the same way, with different species of forest trees, seeded down to grass, and never disturbed with the plow."

Sacra Via, or the Covert Way, was not leased, but put into the care of General Putnam for its preservation, and seeded down to grass as a public ground. Subsequently, Rufus Putnam, Jabez True, and Paul Fearing, or either of them, were appointed trustees to take charge of these squares, and lease them to suitable persons, and carry out the intentions of the Ohio Company, until a board of corporation be appointed over the town, who may then take charge of the same. The avails of the rents were to be appropriated to the education of indigent orphan children of Marietta.

The foregoing report, in relation to the public squares, is not less creditable to the men who made it, than to the agents of the company who adopted it, and deserves the praise and thanks, not only of the people of Marietta, but of all men, of every country, who have any taste for the beautiful, or reverence for the curious remains of that ancient people who once inhabited the valleys and hills between the lakes and the Ohio River; vestiges of whose industry and greatness meet us in a thousand places, but of whom we comparatively know nothing. Investigations are, however, making, which, it is hoped, will develop the long hidden mystery, and the builders of these earthen mounds, and ruined cities, discovered and made known.

On the 8th of January, General Putnam addressed a letter to General Washington, President of the United States, on the condition of the country, dated at Marietta:

"Sir: The mischief I feared has overtaken us sooner than I expected. On the evening of the 2d instant, the Indians surprised a new settlement of our people, at a place on the Muskingum called "Big Bottom," nearly forty miles up the river, in which disaster eleven men, one woman, and two children, were killed; three men are missing, and four others made their escape. Thus, sir, the war, which was partial before the campaign of last year, is, in all probability, become general; for, I think, there is no reason to suppose that we are the only people on whom the savages will wreak their vengeance, or that the numbers of hostile Indians have not increased since the last expedition. Our situation is truly critical: the Governor and Secretary, both being absent, no aid from Virginia or Pennsylvania can be had.

"The garrison at Fort Harmer, consisting at this time of little more than twenty men, can afford no protection to our settlements; and the whole number of men in all our settlements, capable of bearing arms, including all civil and military officers, do not exceed two hundred and eighty-seven; and these many of them badly armed. We are in the utmost danger of being swallowed up, should the enemy push the war with vigor during the winter. This I believe will fully appear, by taking a view of our several settlements, and I hope justify the extraordinary measures we have adopted. The situation of our people is nearly as follows: At Marietta, about eighty houses in the distance of one mile, with scattering houses about three miles up the Ohio; a set of mills on Duck Creek, four miles distant, and another mill two miles up the Muskingum. Twenty-two miles up this river is a settlement of about twenty families; about two miles from them, on Wolf Creek, are five families and a set of mills. Down the Ohio and opposite the Little Kanawha, commences the settlement called Belle Prairie, which extends down the river with little interruption about twelve miles, and contains between thirty and forty families. Before the late disaster, we had several other settlements, which are already broken up. I have taken the liberty to enclose the proceedings of the Ohio Company, and justices of the session, and beg leave, with the greatest deference, to say, that unless government speedily send a body of troops for our protection, we are a ruined people. The removal of the

women and children, &c, will reduce many of the poorer sort to the greatest straits; but if we add to this the destruction of their corn, forage, and cattle, by the enemy, which is very probable to ensue, I know of no way they can be supported. But if this should not happen, where these people are to raise bread another year is not easy to conjecture; and most of them have nothing left to buy with. My fears do not stop here. We are a people so far detached from all others in point of situation, that we can hope for no timely relief, in case of emergency, from any of our neighbors; and among the number that compose our military strength, almost half are young men hired into the country, intending to settle by and by. These, under present circumstances, will probably leave us soon, unless prospects should brighten; and as to new settlers, we can expect none in our present situation. So that instead of increasing our strength, we are likely to diminish daily; and if we do not fall a prey to the savages, we shall be so reduced and discouraged as to give up the settlement, unless government shall give us timely protection.

"It has been a mystery with some, why the troops have been withdrawn from this quarter, and collected at the Miami. That settlement is, I believe, within three or four days' march of a populous part of Kentucky; from whence, in a few days, they might be reinforced with several thousand men; whereas, we are not within two hundred miles of any settlement, that can probably more than protect themselves. I will only observe further, that our situation is truly distressing; and I do, therefore, most earnestly implore the protection of government, for myself and friends, inhabiting the wilds of America. To this we conceive ourselves justly entitled; and so far as you, sir, have the means in your power, we rest assured that we shall receive it in due time."

On the same day, General Putnam wrote to General Knox, the Secretary of War. It was, in part, a repetition of that to the President, and closed with saying:

"I hope government will not be long in deciding what part to take, for if we are not to be protected, the sooner we know it the better; better that we withdraw ourselves at once than remain to be destroyed piecemeal by the savages; and better that government disband their troops now in the country, and give it up altogether, than be wasting the public money in supporting a few troops totally inadequate to the purpose of giving peace to the territory."

There was much truth in these remarks. The force under General Harmer was entirely inadequate to its object; it should have been three or four thousand, instead of a few hundreds. The government was not well informed on the strength and temper of the Indians, but thought to do that by negotiation, which could only be done by force of arms. This policy was continued until the defeat of General St. Clair, when they seem to have awakened and discovered the condition of the west, and the difficulties they had to contend with. It was with the greatest reluctance that the government entered into a war with the western tribes. The country had just begun to recover from the ruinous effects of the Revolution; and the people, generally, in the old states, were opposed to a war, and nothing but the necessity of the case forced them into it.

The following summer a company of United States troops was stationed at Marietta, under Captain Haskell, designed for the defense of the Ohio Company settlements. The men were distributed in squads of six or eight, under a sergeant or corporal, at the different garrisons.

Death of Captain Joseph Rogers

It is an ancient axiom, with military men, that rangers, or spies, are the eyes of an army. It proved true with respect to the new settlements. The measure of employing rangers was adopted previous to the commencement of hostilities, and they were stationed at Marietta and Waterford three months before the massacre at Big Bottom. The requisite number of rangers, for the safety of the settlements, were enlisted by Colonel Sproat, after the war began, and paid by the United States at the rate of five shillings, or eighty-four cents a day. The safety of the property and the lives of the inhabitants depended so much on the vigilance and faithfulness of the rangers, that none were employed who did not possess these qualities, with a full share of courage. Captain Joseph Rogers and Edward Henderson were the two first employed in the service, at Campus Martius. Their tour of duty lay between the Big Muskingum and Duck Creek, making a range of fifteen or twenty miles a day, varying their route as their judgment dictated. Two others were stationed at Fort Harmer, and two in the garrison, "at the point." The costume selected by the rangers was similar to that worn by the Indians, as being more free and convenient for active service in the woods. To make the resemblance more complete they sometimes added paint to their faces, but could distinguish each other by signs well known to themselves.

On Sunday the 13th of March, two days after the attack on Waterford, Rogers and Henderson sallied out of the garrison at an early hour to scout up the Muskingum. They ranged diligently all day, without seeing any Indians, or discovering signs of their being in the neighborhood.

Just at night, as they were returning to the garrison by a cow path that led along the side of the ridge that stretches up north of Campus Martius, and had approached to within a mile of home, at a point a little above the present residence of W. R. Putnam, two Indians rose up from behind a log, about fifty yards before them, and fired. Rogers being ahead was shot through the breast, and as he fell, Henderson attempted to support him, but his companion told him he was a dead man, and that he must provide for his own safety.

As he turned around to escape down the side of the ridge on to the bottom, two more Indians, who had reserved their fire, rose and discharged their rifles at him as he ran. One of the balls passed through the collar of his hunting shirt, and the other through the silk handkerchief which was bound round his head, and formed a part of the dress of a ranger, just grazing the scalp. His blanket being folded up and placed on his back in the manner of a knapsack, probably saved his life, shielding the most vital parts of the body from the passage of a rifle ball, by its numerous folds. This, the Indians well knew, and aimed at his head. After running a few hundred yards on the back track, the Indians by taking a shorter course got ahead of him. This he was so fortunate as to discover, without their seeing him. Making a short turn to the right up a ravine, he crossed the ridge, and came out into the valley of Duck Creek, unmolested.

While making this detour, he fell quite unexpectedly upon their camp, and saw an Indian busily engaged kindling a fire. He was so diligently occupied, that he did not notice Henderson. He could easily have shot him, but as his pursuers had lost the direction of his course, he thought it imprudent by firing to give them notice of his whereabouts. He reached the garrison "at the point" in the evening, and gave notice of the fall of his companion. The alarm gun was fired, and answered from Fort Harmer and Campus Martius. The story soon spread through the village, that Rogers was killed, and that the Indians had chased Henderson into the garrison, and were now besieging the gates. The darkness of the night added to the confusion of the scene. The order in case of an alarm was for every man to repair to his alarm post and the women and children to the blockhouse. The proceedings of that night will be best related in the language of an eye witness, Colonel Barker:

"The first person for admittance at the central blockhouse, was Colonel Sproat, with a box of papers for safe keeping; then came some young men with their arms; next a woman with her bed and children; and after her, old Mr. William Moulten, from Newburyport, with his leather apron full of old gold smith's tools and tobacco. His daughter Anna brought the china tea pot, cups and saucers. Lydia brought the great Bible; but when all were in, mother was missing. Where was mother? She must be killed by the Indians. No, says Lydia, mother said she would not leave the house looking so; she would put things a little to right. After a while the old lady came, bringing the looking glass, knives and forks, &c."

Messengers were soon exchanged with Campus Martius, and no appearance of hostilities discovered. In the morning all returned to their own dwellings, and order was restored. About ten o'clock, a party of men from the two garrisons went out and brought in the body of Captain Rogers. They found him scalped and stripped of his clothing. He was buried on the east side of second street, a little north of the new brick house built by Waldo Putnam, which spot was used for a burying ground until after the war.

The death of Captain Rogers was severely felt by the colonists, as he was a man of experience in Indian warfare, and who possessed the confidence of every one. He was a native of Pennsylvania, and aged about fifty years; large and well built frame, gentlemanly in his manners, brave, and humane. He served as an officer in General Morgan's rifle corps, at the taking of Burgoyne. He came early to the frontiers, with many other old soldiers of the revolution, to seek a home. It is related by an eye-witness, now living, at an advanced age, in Marietta, that the night preceding his death he had an ominous dream, which greatly depressed his spirits, and made a deep impression on his mind. The purport of it was that he would, that day, kill an Indian, or be killed himself. So much was he affected, that he could eat no breakfast. The officer of the day noticed his dejected mein, and asked if he was sick. He answered no; but related his dream, and confessed how deeply it had depressed his spirits. The officer urged him to stay in garrison that day, and he would order another ranger in his place. This he declined, saying, *"Joseph Rogers would never shrink from his duty for a paltry dream."* As he passed out of the gate, by the guard, he said, *"Well, boys, today we take a scalp, or lose one."* The result proved that dreams are not always the idle vagaries of the imagination.

Death of Mathew Kerr

One or two years before the commencement of hostilities, the settlements of the Ohio Company had extended two or three miles up the Ohio, and over Duck Creek. Among others who had planted and raised a crop above the creek, was Matthew Kerr, a native of Ireland. He had moved at an early day upon the frontiers west of the mountains, and, in 1787, settled on Devoll's, or Kerr's Island, as it was then called, just above the mouth of the Muskingum. Here Major Doughty assisted him in building a house, and he kept a few cows to supply the officers of Fort Harmer with milk. His family consisted of three sons, Hamilton, George, and Mathew, and two daughters. The first had been employed as a hunter for the fort, two or three years, and was afterwards much celebrated as a spy. One of his daughters married Peter Nisewonger, another famous hunter and ranger.

After the attack on Big Bottom, he, with others, moved his family into the garrison, at "the point," leaving their cattle, hogs, &c, with the corn and fodder, on the clearing, going up daily to feed them. This they had practiced all the winter and spring without molestation. In 1791, he planted there again, going up daily in his canoe to see to the crops. On the 16th of June, in his visit, he found a nice little black horse, tied by the halter, in an empty corn crib, which some plundering party of Indians had stolen in Virginia, and on their way back had visited the new settlement, for plunder and mischief, leaving the horse here for safe keeping.

The old man, thinking it a fair prize, took the horse down to the garrison. The next day he started again to go up in his canoe. His sons told him he had better not go, as it was likely the Indians would be watching for, and kill him. He, however, went up, and just as the canoe touched the shore in the mouth of the creek, four Indians rose up from behind the willows and fired. Three of the balls passed through his body, and he fell dead in the canoe, into which one of them sprang and scalped him. Some soldiers, employed by the state of Virginia, and stationed in a blockhouse on the island, nearly opposite, hearing the fire, ran upon the bank and saw the Indians as they ascended from the shore, swinging their bloody trophy, and yelling the shout of victory. They fired two or three shots at them, but the distance was so great that they did no other harm than hasten the escape of the Indians. After they had plundered the canoe, they pushed it out into the current, and it was taken up a little above the garrison, with the dead body in it. A party was directly sent out in pursuit, but no discovery was made of them, as they had immediately fled.

Campus Martius

The garrison at this post was kept under the strictest discipline by order of Governor St. Clair. The men were divided into squads, and called out to their posts by daylight. The bastions were occupied every night by four of these squads. After dark the sentries were set, and the watchword cried every half hour during the night. A magazine of ammunition was placed in the north-west blockhouse, in the upper loft, and long poles with iron spears kept in each of the blockhouses for the defense of the doors, should the Indians break through the inner rampart of palisades. A four pound cannon was placed in each of the bastions of the north-east and south-west blockhouses, to defend the approaches in these quarters, and especially to be fired as alarm guns, to give notice to the inhabitants of danger, when out at work in the field. This strict discipline' was kept up for about four years, or until after the victory of General Wayne.

Indians killed at Duck Creek Mills

Late in July, Major Ezra Putnam, an old man, who had lost one of his sons and an apprentice boy in the massacre at Big Bottom, and recently another son by a fever, concluded to build a barn against the coming winter. The people, commiserating his losses, turned out to assist him in getting the timber. This was cut and hewed on the ridge back of the garrison, and sentinels set in all exposed points, to watch the approach of the enemy, while the men were at work. William Smith, a lad of eighteen years, who acted as one of the guards, was posted at the foot of the ridge, near the Muskingum bottom. A little before sunset, as he was looking for a squirrel to shoot for a sick comrade, he was startled by a terrible bellowing among the cattle in the woods beyond him, which directly came rushing by him in the greatest terror. He ran up the ridge where the men were at work, but they had quit their labor and gone into the garrison, where he soon followed. On being questioned by the officer why he had not returned with the other men, he related the cause and the alarm of the cattle, suggesting the probability of there being Indians in the vicinity, who had frightened them, for even the horses and cows, as well as the dogs, gave symptoms of fear at the approach of these dreaded enemies. Search was made among the cattle, and a cow belonging to John Russell found with an arrow still sticking in the flesh of the abdomen, and dangling by her side.

The next day a party of twenty volunteers from the garrison, and as many soldiers from Fort Harmer, under a lieutenant, turned out in search of the Indians. They were led by two of the spies, Hamilton and George Kerr, as men best acquainted with the woods, and familiar with Indian warfare. The men were divided into two squads, the smaller one, under the lieutenant, marching up the Muskingum bottom, and the larger, under the two spies, going directly out to the new mills on Duck Creek. As they emerged from the woods, on the brow of the hill that overlooks the mills and the creek for half a mile or more, both above and below the dam, Hamilton's quick eye caught sight of six Indians crossing the stream, at the ripple below the mill, on to this side, where stood a cabin that the workmen had occupied for cooking and sleeping.

He instantly called a halt, and proposed that the party should remain in the edge of the woods, out of sight, while himself and his brother George crept across a little clearing of half an acre, this side the house, now overrun with weeds, and reconnoiter.

When they had approached within about seventy yards, two of the Indians, who were armed with bows and arrows, came out of the house, the door of which was next the creek, and turning round the corner, stood looking into the unfinished log chimney, which was built up only three or four feet. Another with a rifle gun soon followed, but passed round the corner of the house out of sight. This one Kerr was most anxious to get a shot at. While waiting for him to come again in sight, and listening to the Indians talking to each other in their low, guttural tones, totally unconscious of their danger, a little cur dog of Hamilton's, which he had left with the party on the hill, began to whine for his master. One of the men carelessly gave him a kick to silence him, when he yelped so loud that the Indians caught the distant sound, and were instantly on the alert to discover the cause. Fearing lest they should start and run, Hamilton rose from his crouching posture and fired at one of the Indians, while George shot at the other. The one, aimed at by Hamilton, although shot through the heart, ran twenty rods before he fell. The other also fled with the blood pouring out of his side apparently mortally wounded. By this time the men on the hill came rushing down and joined in the pursuit of the flying foe.

Just below the mill the creek makes a bend, forming a neck of land, with another ripple. Across this bend the Indians retreated, and passed the creek a quarter of a mile lower down. When about half way over the neck, they found one Indian dead, and traced the other by the blood into the water at the ford. Here the Indians flanked out to the right and left, and defended the passage so bravely that it was thought imprudent to cross at that place, but at the ripple above.

By the time the party had countermarched and got over the creek, the Indians had disappeared and borne off their wounded companion beyond the reach of pursuit. Wrapped up in the blanket of the dead Indian was found a nice halter for securing any horse that might fall in his way, and a new case knife and fork, which he had plundered from some frontier family. The halter was all in one piece, cut out very ingeniously from a buffalo skin, and was owned for many years after by Colonel Sproat. That afternoon the party went out with a horse and packed in the body of the dead Indian. It was given to the surgeons of Marietta, who hired an old soldier to boil the flesh from the bones in a kettle on the bank of the Muskingum, to make a skeleton. This disposition of the dead body came to the knowledge of the Indians, who were much vexed and astonished thereat, exclaiming in broken English, *"What! white man boil Indian?"* Whether they thought the whites ate the flesh, or did it by way of some unknown charm, it is certain that it made a deep impression on their superstitious minds, and was the cause of their venturing very cautiously into the vicinity of the fort, lest their bones, if they were killed, should be treated in the same way.

Indians killed on the Little Muskingum

From the commencement of the settlement the Sabbath was observed as a day of rest, and from and after 1789, regular religious service was kept up in the north-west blockhouse at Campus Martius. After the war commenced, and large blockhouses were built in the garrison at "the point," religious worship was held there a part of the time. The Rev. Daniel Story officiated as clergyman. The law regulating the militia required a muster of the troops every Sabbath day at ten o'clock, A. M., when they were paraded by beat of drum, the roll called, and their arms inspected; after which a procession was formed, headed by Colonel Sproat, with his drawn sword, the civil officers and the clergyman, with the fife and drum, marched to the hall for divine service. All the New Englanders being versed in psalmody, there was no lack of good singing to aid in the solemnities of the day. On these occasions nearly all the population attended. The arms of the soldiers were sitting by their sides, or kept near them, during the service, ready for use if needed.

The latter part of September, on a Sabbath morning, Peter Niswonger, one of the rangers, went up to visit a field of corn and potatoes he had cultivated on the east side of Duck Creek, near the mouth. He had some fat hogs in a pen, one of which he found killed, and a portion of the meat cut out and carried off. Several hills of potatoes had been dug, and in the loose earth he discovered fresh moccasin tracks, a proof that Indians had been there and done the mischief. He hurried back to the garrison at "the point," and gave the alarm. It was in the midst of the forenoon service, and the inhabitants were generally assembled in the large blockhouse listening to the sermon. The instant the word was heard, of "Indians in the vicinity," the drummer seized his drum and rushing out at the door, beat "the long roll," as the well known signal for every man to hasten to his post.

Among the warlike instruments of music invented by man, the drum above all others possesses the power of communicating to the human heart the sensations of alarm, or of confidence. Whoever has once heard that long roll of continuous sound, sent forth by it, in a time of danger, will never forget the impression. The shrill, sharp notes of the fife enliven and cheer us at all times, but can never convey, in sounds almost articulate, the meaning of the expressive drum.

The place of worship, so quiet and calm a few moments before, was now filled with confusion and alarm. The women caught up their little children and hastened to their homes, and the place of prayer was abandoned for that day. Anxiety and fear for the fate of their brothers and husbands, who had gone in pursuit of the dreaded Indians, banished all holy thoughts, but the silent prayer for their safe return. A party was soon mustered, made up of five or six of the rangers, ten volunteer citizens, and twelve United States soldiers from the company stationed at "the point." The men went up in canoes to the mouth of Duck Creek, where they left their water craft. The more experienced rangers soon fell upon the trail, which they traced across the wide bottoms on to the Little Muskingum. At a point about half a mile below where Conner's mill now stands, the Indians forded the creek. In a hollow, between the hills, about a mile east of the creek, they discovered the smoke of their camp fire. The rangers now divided the volunteers into two flanking parties, with one of the spies at the head of each, and three of their number to act in front. By the time the flankers had come in range of the camp, the Indians discovered their pursuers, by the noise of the soldiers who lagged behind, and were not so cautious in their movement. They instantly fled up the run on which they were encamped. Two of their number leaving the main body, ascended the point of a hill, with a ravine on the right and left of it.

The rangers now began to fire, while the Indians, each one taking his tree, returned the shot. One of the two Indians on the spur of the ridge was wounded through the hips, by one of the spies on the right, who pushed on manfully to gain the flanks of the enemy. The men in front came on more slowly, and as they began to ascend the point of the ridge, Ned Henderson, who was posted on high ground, cried out "Ham! Ham! There is an Indian behind that white oak, and he will kill some of you." Kerr instantly sprung behind a large tree, and Peter Anderson who was near him, behind a hickory, too small to cover more than half his body, while John Wiser jumped down into the ravine. At that instant the Indian fired at Anderson, and as John looked over the edge of the bank to learn the effect of the shot, he saw Peter wiping the dust of the hickory bark out of his eyes. The ball grazed the tree, just opposite his nose, and glancing off did him no serious harm, but filling his eyes with the dust, and cutting his nose with the splinters. At the same time Henderson, with others, fired at the Indian, and he fell with several balls through his body. The brave fellow who was killed lost his life in a noble effort to aid his friend, who had been wounded through the hips, and could not spring up on to the little bench, or break in the ridge, where he was standing.

While occupied in this labor of love, the rangers on his flanks had so far advanced, that the shelter of the friendly tree could no longer secure him from their shots, as it had done while his enemies were more in front of him. The wounded Indian escaped for the present; although it is probable he died soon after. The other five Indians, there being seven in the party, seeing that their enemies outnumbered them so greatly, after firing a few times, made a circuit to the right and came up in the rear of the soldiers, who were occupying themselves with the contents of the kettle of hog meat and potatoes, which the Indians in their hurry had left boiling over the fire. The first notice they had of their danger was the report of their rifles. It made a huge uproar amongst the musketeers, who taking to flight, ran in great alarm for protection to the rangers. As it happened the Indians were too far off to do much harm, and no one was injured but one poor fellow, who was shot through the seat of his trousers, just grazing the skin. He tumbled into the brook by the side of the camp, screaming at the top of his voice, "I am kill'd! I am kill'd!" Greatly to the amusement of the rangers, who were soon at his side, and dragging him out of the water, searched in vain for the mortal wound. The dead Indian was scalped, and his rifle and blanket taken as the legitimate plunder of a conquered foe. The other five retreated out of reach of the rangers, after their feat of frightening the soldiers. They returned to the garrison, well pleased that none of their men were killed, but much vexed with the soldiers, whose indiscretion had prevented their destroying the whole of the Indians, had they encircled them as first arranged by the leaders of the party. It served as a warning to the Indians not to approach too near the Yankee garrison as their rangers was brave men, whose eyes and ears were always open.

Doings of the Ohio Company

In March, the agent directed Colonel Sproat to enlist another company of men, equal to that ordered in January, to serve three months from the first of April. The Directors were notified to pay the troops and all other debts incurred by the war, as speedily as possible. There being little or no specie in the country, these orders for the pay of the troops, being generally in small sums, served as a circulating medium for the colony, in place of money, during the war. They were drawn on the treasurer at Philadelphia, and were taken in payment for debts by the people, or at the store for provisions and merchandise. They served all the purposes of the old continental currency, without its disastrous termination, as they were all promptly paid. To encourage the young men who were now here to remain in the country, and others to come in, it was resolved that whoever shall continue here during the present Indian war, and defend the purchase, either at Marietta, Belpre, or Waterford, shall receive a hundred acres of land equal in quality to that already bestowed.

This notice, spread abroad through Pennsylvania and Virginia, brought in a number of able bodied men in the midst of the war, whose services were very valuable in the defense of the country. Had the settlement at Marietta commenced like most others in the western country, since that period, it would doubtless have been destroyed or broken up. But the wealth, wisdom, and firmness of the agents, and directors, backed by the council of so many old officers of the revolution, with General Putnam at their head, preserved it in safety amidst all the horrors and dangers that surrounded it. The greatest regularity and order was preserved in all their transactions, like those of a well ordered government. In March a non-commissioned officer, one drummer, and eleven privates were added to the guards at Marietta, and one drummer and four privates to the garrison at Belpre, all under the pay of the Ohio Company.

Funds were also voted for the support of the Rev. Daniel Story, as a preacher of the gospel, and twenty dollars to Colonel Battelle for religious instruction at Belpre; thus providing for the welfare of the souls, as well as the safety of the bodies, of the inhabitants under their care.

In the spring of 1791, Colonel Ichabod Nye erected buildings and laid down vats for a tannery and dressing of leather, on the outer margin of the plain, distant about three furlongs from Campus Martius. It was in quite an exposed situation, as it lay near the border of the forest, where an enemy could lie concealed. Although the Indians often visited the establishment, pulling the hide* out of the vats, and cutting up the leather for their own use, yet no one was ever killed, or attacked while working the yard. This was doubtless the first attempt to manufacture leather in Ohio.

In April a committee was appointed to report on the mode of furnishing the settlements with future religious instruction. On their report it was resolved that the sum of one hundred and sixty dollars be appropriated for that purpose, as follows: eighty-four dollars for Marietta, fifty dollars for Belpre, and twenty-six dollars for Waterford, on condition that Marietta support a teacher one year, Belpre seven months, and Waterford three months and a half. Should either of these places not comply with the above, such place shall not receive the money allotted to it. One hundred and twenty dollars of the above sum was to be paid out of the interest of the money loaned to the inhabitants, and forty dollars from the treasury of the company. Committees were to be appointed in each settlement to carry these designs into operation, and to engage teachers of such a character as shall be approved of by the directors. General Putnam and Robert Oliver were the directors at this time.

Surgeons for the troops were also appointed, and provided with instruments and medicines. They received their pay and rations from the same liberal source — Dr. Jabez True at Marietta, Dr. Samuel Barnes at Belpre, and Dr. Nathan McIntosh at Waterford.

The war having put a stop to the use of the mills built by Captain Shepherd, on Duck Creek, all the corn meal needed for bread was ground in hand mills. It was a laborious and slow process, requiring two men to grind half a peck an hour. The flour used by the inhabitants, and for the troops, was procured "at head waters." For these reasons encouragement was given to Mr. Charles Greene and associates to build a floating mill on the Muskingum River, opposite to the garrison, within the protection of the guns of Campus Martius. One of this kind was now building at Belpre by Captain Devoll. It was completed in the course of the year, with a substantial timber wharf for the landing of goods, and buildings for the convenience of the mill. A lease of an adjacent lot on the commons was given him for twenty years, as an encouragement to the work. It proved, however, to be of very little use the greater portion of the year, the current in the river being too slow to move the machinery. During the summer months the mill was towed up the Muskingum, about three miles, to a rapid called "rocky ripple," and fastened with a grape vine to a tree. At this point it could grind a little; but for the larger portion of the time before and during the Indian war, nearly all the corn meal was made on the hand mill, that primitive implement so often mentioned in the Scriptures, and still in use among many of the eastern nations.

The news of Governor St. Clair's defeat by the Indians, which took place on the 4th of November, did not reach Marietta until the 5th of December. The word was brought by Major Denny, quarter-master in the army, as he was on his way to Philadelphia. (At this period there was no regular intercourse between the different posts. All the traveling was done on the river in keel boats or barges, especially upstream. Expresses by land could not be sent on account of the Indians. They sometimes traveled across the country by "the crab orchard" route, through North Carolina and Virginia. In a year or two after, a regular line of packet row boats was established by the secretary of war, J. Pickering, from Pittsburgh to Fort Washington, as will be more fully noticed in the events of that year.)

On the receipt of this news, a special meeting of the agents was called, and two expresses sent to notify Mr. Ludlow and his party of the defeat He was engaged in the woods, running the line defining the northern boundary of the purchase, and since known as "Ludlow's Line." This adverse and unexpected event for a while filled the inhabitants with consternation and alarm, fearing lest the Indians now assembled in large numbers and flushed with victory, should attack all the posts of the company, and execute in earnest the threat of *"putting out every white man's fire north of the Ohio."*

So greatly alarmed were a portion of the settlers that they began to talk of evacuating the country. In a few days, however, these evil forebodings began to subside, and by the calm deportment and resolute counsel of the more influential and experienced men, a better spirit prevailed, and they determined to defend their families and possessions to the uttermost; and sooner be buried under the ruins of their homes, than abandon them to the savages. In a day or two the party under Mr. Ludlow arrived in safety.

In December, Judge Gilman and his son, B. J. Gilman, erected a blockhouse on the west side of the Muskingum, on the lands attached to Fort Harmer, near the spot now occupied by the dwelling of L. Barber. A number of families had lived here since the removal of the troops in 1790; and considerable tracts of land were cleared and cultivated within a quarter of a mile of the fort. Several families arrived this winter from Nova Scotia, who had lands allotted to them for building and cultivation, in the vicinity of the fort, until they could occupy their donation lots. Among them were the Olneys, Seamans, &c, who lived after the war on the Muskingum, in the townships of Union and Adams. In December, Commodore Abraham Whipple had a lot of land assigned to him on the commons, west of the land leased to Charles Green, for the purpose of building thereon a horse-mill for grinding corn, and Peletiah White a small lot for an earthen ware pottery; which was probably the first establishment of the kind north of the Ohio. The commodore's mill did but little in the way of grinding; the main dependence of the people for bread still being the hominy block and hand mill.

Abraham Whipple

Providential escape

During the continuance of the war, the inhabitants were obliged to work in their fields as the Israelites did at the rebuilding of the walls of Jerusalem, every man with his weapon in his hand. All their food was procured at the risk of life. Whether in seed time or in harvest, they worked in parties of fifteen or twenty men, three or four of whom were posted as sentries in the edge of the woods or around the more exposed portions of the field. Without these precautions they were almost certain to be killed, as several were who carelessly exposed themselves alone. They were obliged to plow and plant for the sustenance of themselves and families, or starve. Famine on the one side and the tomahawk on the other; there was no alternative.

In July, 1791, a party of this kind had been engaged in harvesting a field of flax and oats for General Putnam, lying adjoining to, and east of the mound square. The square itself was planted with corn, then in the tassel. The work was nearly finished, except the binding of a few oats. The next morning, the job being so small, it was decided that the whole need not go out again, but that the General's two sons, William Rufus and Edwin, with William Browning, his son-in-law, and Augustus Stone, then a boy of ten or twelve years, who lived in the family, should finish the work, thinking there would be no danger from Indians, as none had been seen lately, and it would occupy but a short time.

Directly after breakfast Mr. Putnam's sons and Stone were ready to go to the field, but on calling for Browning, found he had gone to "the point" on some important errand. The others did not choose to go without him, and he did not return until ten o'clock, when they all started for the field. On their arrival, they thought it prudent to reconnoiter the ground. Edwin, a lad of fifteen, was posted on the fence between the field and the low ground east of it. Augustus was sent to the top of the mound to look out for Indians; the others traversed the cornfields around it. The corn had recently been hoed, and the track of a man in the loose earth was readily seen. They directly discovered signs of Indians made since the last night, and following on; found where they had stood between the mound and the field for a long time, by the number of their tracks, about fifty yards or a short rifle shot distance from the oats. They also saw where two had stood on the outer margin of the corn, near the spot where the path came into the field, as if watching for their approach. The party now called in their out-posts and retreated unharmed to the garrison. There is no doubt the savages had seen them at work the day before, but thought the party too strong to attack. When they were gone, by seeing how the work was unfinished, they knew that some of them would be back next morning, and made their arrangements by posting themselves around the margin of the field. Had this small band gone out early in the morning, as intended, there is little doubt they would have been killed or taken prisoners.

But a gracious and overruling Providence so ordered this small matter of Browning's delay at "the point," that they were detained, much against their wills, until their enemies had left the ground, thinking it was now so late in the day, they had given up the work. There were among these Indians two whose foot prints were well known to the rangers. One of them left a track eleven inches long, the other not more than seven or eight. They were known as the big and little Indian. They were men of great subtlety and caution; often seen together by the spies, yet never but once within reach of their rifles. Joshua Fleehart, a noted hunter, and as cautious and cunning as any savage, got a shot at the big Indian as the two lay in their camp below Bellville. The ball cut loose his powder horn, which Joshua took as a prize, and wounded him in the side, but he escaped.

The year 1791, was more fruitful in tragic events than any other during the war, in the vicinity of Marietta. After that period the attention of the Indians was more occupied with the troops assembled on the borders of their own country, or already penetrating to the vicinity of their villages. The United States troops stationed at the posts within the new settlements drew a considerable portion of their meat rations from the inhabitants of the western branches of the Monongahela, about Clarksburgh, especially their fresh beef. Several droves had been brought from that region of country in 1790 and '91, and sold to Paul Fearing, Esq., who had been appointed commissary to the troops. A considerable number of cattle, especially milk cows, were also sold to the inhabitants of Marietta. Among those engaged in this employment was Nicholas Carpenter, a worthy, pious man, who had lived many years on the frontiers and was well acquainted with a forest life. He left Clarksburgh the last of September, with a drove, accompanied by his little son of ten years old, and five other men, viz.: Jesse Hughes, George Legit, John Paul, Barns, and Ellis. On the evening of the 3d of October, they had reached a point six miles above Marietta, and encamped on a run half a mile from the Ohio, and since called "Carpenter's Run." The cattle were suffered to range in the vicinity, feeding on the rich pea vines that then filled the woods, while the horses were hoppled, the leaves pulled out from around the clappers of their bells, and turned loose in the bottom. After eating their suppers, the party spread their blankets on the ground and lay down with their feet to the fire. No guard was set to watch the approach of an enemy. Their journey being so near finished, without discovering any signs of Indians, that they thought all danger was past.

It so happened that not far from the time of their leaving home, a party of six Shawnee Indians, headed as was afterwards ascertained by Tecumseh, then quite a youth, but ultimately so celebrated for bravery and talents, had crossed the Ohio River near Bellville, on a marauding expedition in the vicinity of Clarksburgh. From this place they passed over the ridges to "Neil's Station," on the Little Kanawha, one mile from the mouth, where they took prisoner a colored boy of Mr. Neil, about twelve years old, as he was out looking for the horses early in the morning. It was done without alarming the garrison, and they quietly proceeded on their route, doing no other mischief; pursuing their way up the Kanawha to the mouth of Hughes's River, and following the north fork, fell on to the trail from Clarksburgh to

Marietta. This took them about three days. There was no rain and the leaves so dry that their rustling alarmed the deer, and they could kill no game for food. Their only nourishment for that period was a single tortoise, which they divided among them, giving Frank, the black boy, an equal share. As he was much exhausted and discouraged, they promised him a horse to ride on their return. These circumstances were related by Frank after his escape.

Soon after leaving the north fork of Hughes's River, they fell on to the trail of Carpenter's drove, and thinking it made by a caravan of settlers, on their way to the Ohio, they held a short council. Giving up any further progress towards Clarksburgh, they turned with renewed energy and high spirits upon the fresh large trail, which they perceived had very recently been made. So broad was the track made by the cattle and four or five horses that they followed it without difficulty, at a rapid pace all night, and came in sight of the camp fire a little before daylight. Previous to commencing the attack, they secured Frank with leather thongs to a stout sapling on the top of an adjacent ridge. The trampling of the cattle and the noise of the horse bells greatly favored the Indians in their approach, but as there was no sentinel there was little danger of discovery. Tecumseh, with the cautious cunning that ever after distinguished him, posted his men behind the trunk of a large fallen tree, a few yards from the camp, where they could watch the movements of their enemies.

At the first dawn of day, Mr. Carpenter called up the men, saying they would commence the day with the accustomed acts of devotion which he had long practiced. As the men sat round the fire and he had just commenced reading a hymn, the Indians rose and fired, following the discharge with a terrific yell, and rushed upon their astonished victims with the tomahawk. Their fire was not very well directed, as it killed only one man, Ellis from Greenbrier and wounded John Paul through the hand. Ellis instantly fell, exclaiming *"O Lord, I am killed!"* The others sprang to their feet, and before they could all get their arms which were leaning against a tree, the Indians were among them. Hughes, who had been an old hunter and often in skirmishes with the savages, in his haste seized on two rifles, Carpenter's and his own, and pushed into the woods, with two Indians in pursuit. He fired one of the guns, but whether with effect is not known, and threw the other away. Being partly dressed at the time of the attack, his long leggings were only fastened to the belt round his waist and were loose below, entangling his legs, and greatly impeding his flight. To rid himself of this encumbrance he stopped for a moment, placed his foot on the lower end, and tore them loose from the belt, leaving his legs bare from the hips downward. This delay nearly cost him his life. His pursuer, then within a few feet of him, threw his tomahawk so accurately as to graze his head. Freed from this impediment he soon left his foe far behind. Christopher Carpenter, the son of Nicholas, now living in Marietta, says he well remembers seeing the bullet holes in Hughes's hunting shirt after his return.

In the race the competitors passed near the spot where Frank was concealed, who described it as one of the swiftest he had ever seen. John Paul, who had been in many engagements with the Indians, escaped by his activity in running. Burns, a stout, athletic man, but slow of foot, was slain near the camp after a stout resistance. When found a few days after, his jack knife was still clasped in his hand, and the weeds trampled down for a rod or more around him, showing he had resisted manfully for life. George Legit was pursued for nearly two miles, overtaken and killed. Mr. Carpenter, although a brave man, was without arms to defend himself and being lame could not run rapidly; he therefore sought to conceal himself behind some willows in the bed of the run. He was soon discovered, with his little boy by his side. His captors conducted him to the spot where the black boy had been left, and killed both him and his son. What led to the slaughter, after they had surrendered, is not known. He was found wrapped up in his blanket, with a pair of new Indian moccasins on his feet, and his scalp not removed. It is supposed that these marks of respect were shown him at the request of one of the Indians, whose gun Carpenter had repaired at Marietta the year before, and had declined any compensation for the service. He was by trade a gunsmith. This circumstance was told to C. Carpenter, many years after by one of the Indians who was present, at Urbana, in Ohio. It is another proof of the fact, that an Indian never forgets an act of kindness, even in an enemy.

Tecumseh and his men, after collecting the plunder of the camp, retreated in such haste, that they left all the horses, which had probably dispersed in the woods at the tumult of the attack. They no doubt feared a pursuit from the rangers at Marietta and Williams' Station, who would soon be notified by the escape of their prisoner, Frank, who in the midst of the noise of the assault contrived to slip his hands loose from the cords, and hide himself in a thick patch of hazel bushes, from which he saw a part of the transactions. After the Indians had left the ground, he crept cautiously forth, and by good fortune took the right direction to Williams' Station, opposite to

Marietta. A party of men was sent out the next day, who buried the dead, as far as they could then be found. Frank returned to his master, and died only a few years since.

CHAPTER XIV.

Doings of the Ohio Company

On the 28th of March, 1792, the directors of the Ohio Company held a meeting of their board, in Philadelphia, for the purpose of closing their contract with Congress, and paying for the lands already in their possession. This meeting was attended by Rufus Putnam, Manasseh Cutler, Griffin Green, and Robert Oliver. On the 11th of April there was a meeting of the agents, at the same place, who represented seven hundred and fifty shares. From various causes, among which was the expense of the Indian war and the bankruptcy of their treasurer, who failed largely in their debt, the company was unable to pay for the whole amount of the contract, for one million and a half of acres; but by a reduction in the price the whole could be yet secured. For this they had petitioned Congress, who refused to make any abatement from the original price of one dollar an acre. It is true that they were allowed to make a deduction for worthless lands, and the expense of surveying, equal to one third of a dollar. They, therefore, now applied for two hundred and fourteen thousand two hundred and eighty-five acres to be paid for in "army land warrants." They also petitioned for a tract of one hundred thousand acres as donation lands to actual settlers, to be given by Congress, and thus relieve the company of the heavy charge of furnishing the donation lots from their own lands, as they had proposed in 1790, and had already, in part, actually fulfilled. By an act of Congress, passed the 21st of April, 1792, these applications were granted, thus making the actual purchase of the company amount to nine hundred and sixty-four thousand, two hundred and eighty-five acres, instead of a million and a half. The tract of one hundred thousand acres was to be located within the boundaries of the purchase first agreed for, and adjoining to the tract now belonging to the company. The donation was secured, by letters patent from the President of the United States, in fee simple to Rufus Putnam, Manasseh Cutler, Griffin Green, and Robert Oliver, in trust for the purpose of encouraging settlers within the purchase. The trustees were bound to make deeds free of expense, of one hundred acres, in fee simple, to each male person, not less than eighteen years of age, and being an actual settler, or resident within the purchase at the time of such conveyance. If any portion remained un-deeded, at the end of five years from the passage of the act, it reverted to the United States. This liberal donation from Congress was of essential benefit to the company, and greatly hastened the settling of the country by adventurers from abroad. It did not, however, make so many permanent residents as was expected. After the war ceased, many who drew donation lots sold them to others for a small sum, without any actual settlement on the land, and left the country; making it a source of individual speculation instead of a general public benefit.

The "donation tract," is about twenty two miles long by seven and a half wide; bounded east on the seventh range of townships, and stretching west across the waters of Duck Creek, and the Muskingum Rivers. The south line approaches within four miles of Marietta. It is generally a body of good farming lands.

About the time of the meeting of the directors in Philadelphia, General Putnam was appointed a Brigadier General in the service of the United States, and not far from the same period, General Washington nominated him a Commissioner, to make a treaty with the tribes of Indians living on the Wabash River. The Rev. John Heckewelder, at the request of General Putnam, was to act as interpreter.

A convenient boat, called a barge, was built that spring, of about twenty-five tons burthen, rowed with twelve oars, in which to make the voyage. It was constructed at "Farmer's Castle," in Belpre, by Captain Jonathan Devoll, from the wood of the red cedar, cut on the Little Kanawha, at the hazard of life and limb. This boat was said to be a model of beauty, and distinguished on the river for its elegant proportions, and easy progress in the water.

He left Marietta on the 26th of June, stopping one day at Gallipolis, and reached Fort Washington the 2d of July, where he expected to meet the Indians. But as they lived generally on the Wabash, a distance of two or three hundred miles by land, and double that by water, from the fort, they declined; but agreed to meet the Commissioners at Vincennes. The time agreed upon was the 20th of September. This was the first treaty made with the Wabash tribes. Liberal presents of goods and silver ornaments were taken down by the Commissioner. After a good deal of trouble, a treaty was concluded on the 27th of the month with the following tribes, viz: Eel River Indians, Ouotanons, Pottawatomie of the Illinois River, Musquitoes, Kickapoos of the

Wabash, Pyankesha, Kaskaskia, and Peoria, thus quieting the hostility of these bands for the present. Mr. Heckewelder, the interpreter, also wrote to the Delawares, with whom he had lived many years as a missionary, urging them to come to the Muskingum, or Marietta, and make a treaty.

General Putnam sent messages to the hostile Indians to come in, but they would listen to no overtures; the Delawares, Shawnee and Miamis preferring war to peace, being greatly irritated at the invasion of their country, and much elated by the defeat of General St. Clair. Soon after the close of the treaty, General Putnam was attacked with a fever, and did not reach home until late in the fall.

By this treaty the Indians agreed to be at perpetual peace with the people of the United States, and acknowledged themselves to be under the protection of the United States. They were to give up all prisoners, and in return they were to possess their lands and hunting grounds in quietness, and no part ever to be taken away without their consent, and full remuneration to be paid when any was sold to the United States. The treaty was signed by thirty Indians. They at the same time agreed to send a deputation on to Philadelphia, to see their father, the President of the United States, and fourteen chiefs reached Marietta on the 17th November, conducted by an officer of the army.

On the 18th a public dinner was given them at Campus Martius, to which the citizens of Marietta were also invited, and the officers of the garrisons. The feast was held in the hall of the northwest blockhouse; a room about twenty-four by forty feet in size. A procession was formed on the bank of the Ohio, near the boat which brought up the chiefs, and marched with military music to the northeast gate of the garrison; and as soon as the head of the column appeared, a salute of fourteen guns was fired from a six pound brass piece in the northeast bastion. The procession then moved through the gate and up into the hall, where a dinner was provided by a committee of arrangements, aided by the ladies of the garrison.

An eye witness of this feast says, *"that under all the circumstances, the entertainment was very novel, and the scene peculiarly striking. Shut up in garrison, and at war with the other tribes of the forest, shaking hands with our red guests, and the appellation of "brother" passing from one to the other.* It seemed to renew the scenes of the first year's settlement, in 1788, and *make us almost forget that war was on our borders."* (MSS. Notes of Colonel Nye.)

After the feast and ceremonies were closed, the chiefs were conducted to their boats again. The next day they were invited by several gentlemen of the stockade garrison, at "the point," to smoke the pipe of friendship at Buell and Munsell's hotel; after which they proceeded on their journey.

Condition and strength of the colony

"Previous to the commencement of hostilities there was a weekly military inspection of the settlers liable to do duty, and the commandant informed what numbers were armed and equipped to defend the settlements. Emigrants frequently arrived without arms, so that the number of guns fell short of the number of men. In the fall of 1790, Colonel Sproat was authorized by the secretary of war to enlist a company of men into the United States service, out of the settlers, to be employed in guarding and defending the settlements, and to distribute them to those points which most needed their assistance, and to appoint a commissary to supply subsistence for those troops. He was considered as commander in chief for the military, and his aid was solicited to procure arms for the citizens who were destitute. On his application the commander at Fort Pitt sent down about thirty old muskets, much out of repair. The blacksmiths put them in as good order as they could, and they were distributed where they were most needed. Ammunition was prepared, and stored in the blockhouses, ready to be distributed in case of emergency. It was not until June, 1792, when Colonel Sproat received two boxes, containing twenty-five stands each of United States muskets, with bayonets, new from the factory. These were distributed among the inhabitants and soldiers, on their giving a receipt to return them when called for. The people were now considered to be well armed. Many rifles were procured and brought into the country. The most of the eastern or New England men, previous to coming here, were unacquainted with the rifle and the woods; but by practicing on the example of those who had been educated among the woods and the Indians, they soon became good hunters and expert woodsmen. Those who were well armed and good marksmen were commonly selected as sentries for the working parties, and who were always ready to start on the discovery of an enemy, or pursue an Indian trail. Thus by being familiar with danger and inured to the hazard of a reencounter with their foes, they gained that confidence in themselves, which promised in case of meeting an Indian the odds of battle in their own favor. Many followed hunting continually; others were out with the spies, or in small parties, so that it was difficult for an Indian to make a track within five miles of a garrison without being detected. Thus a large portion of the inhabitants became fearless of danger from the Indians, and preferred some employment, or some enterprise out, to being confined in or about the garrisons."— (MSS. notes of Judge Barker.)

All the men now in the purchase able to bear arms amounted to about two hundred and fifty. But after this period they rather increased in number to the end of the war.

Backwoodsmen and rangers

"When the Ohio Company first came out, every man found in the region was a woodsman, a hunter of game, and of Indians; all knew their customs and habits of warfare, and were always ready and proud of imparting their knowledge to anyone who would listen to their teaching. The Yankees, placed in the very school for hunting and fighting Indians, were apt scholars, and soon became able to practice with skill on their precepts and examples, and to compete with their masters; so that before the close of the war we had rarely any other rangers or hunters for the surveying parties but Yankees. To the plan, early adopted, of employing rangers may be attributed the general safety and success of the first settlement of this country. It was early adopted by General Putnam and the Ohio Company, and afterwards pursued by the Ohio Company.

"The Indians finding themselves so closely watched by men, who were their compeers in their own arts of warfare, as well as more vigilant and untiring soldiers, became indifferent to enterprises where they were likely to meet with little success, and which might result in loss and disaster far exceeding any benefits to be obtained. The hope of reward is the great spring of human action. Men, who are not paid, fed, and clothed, may make good partisans for a short emergency, but their patriotism soon cools, and their courage oozes out at the ends of their fingers.

"The hope of plunder is the main stimulus with the Indians; therefore, they crossed the Ohio River below and above us, passing by the settlements, and going a hundred miles on to the waters of the Monongahela, where there was more plunder and less watchfulness. Revenge is sweet, but must not be bought too dear. Small parties who came in to attack us, of fifty or a hundred, seldom hung about more than a week, while larger bodies could not keep together only a few days for want of food.

The Turk could not repulse the Russian, nor the Arab the French, because they had no system of finance to provide for the family of the soldier, while he fights the battles of his country.

"It is estimated that, in seven years previous to the war in 1791, the Indians, on the frontiers south of the Ohio River, killed and took prisoners fifteen hundred persons, stole two thousand horses, and other property to the amount of fifty thousand dollars. This was the declared object of the party who killed Captain Carpenter, and subsequently the family of Armstrong."
(MSS. Judge Barker.)

Attack on R. J. Meigs, Esq.

Toward evening, one day late in the month of June, 1792, Mr. Meigs, with Joseph Symonds, his hired man, and Jim, a black boy, of twelve years old, his servant, were returning from work in a field, which he cultivated near Fort Harmer, to Campus Martius, where he then lived. The land about the fort was cleared up the Muskingum to a point about where the steam mill now stands; from thence upward there was a thick forest, with considerable underbrush. A narrow path led along near the bank to a spot a little below Campus Martius, which had been made by the passage of the inhabitants up and down from that place to Fort Harmer. At its termination they had fastened their canoe.

The party was all unarmed, except Mr. Meigs, who carried a shot gun, which he had taken along to kill a turkey or some pigeons, which then abounded in the woods. The field lay so near the fort, that no guard was necessary while at work, and the distance so short between the two garrisons, that no danger was apprehended from the Indians. When about half way up to the canoe, a large snake crossed their path at which he fired, and did not then reload his gun. As they walked along, Mr. Meigs in front, and the black boy behind, Symonds observed, *"We should be in a poor state of defense if the Indians came upon us."* This alarmed Jim, who looked behind him as he naturally would do, and exclaimed, *"there is two now!"* Symonds turned to see also, and at that instant the gun cracked. This motion probably saved his life, and directed the ball through his shoulder instead of his body, as the Indians were only a few paces distant.

Return Jonathan Meigs Jr.

Return Jonathan Meigs Sr.

Being a fine swimmer, he instantly ran and sprang down the bank into the river, with one of the Indians after him; but he was soon out of his reach and turning on his back contrived to keep himself on the surface, with one arm and leg, the other being sprained in the leap. The Indian, who was only armed with a tomahawk, gave up the pursuit and followed the black boy, who had fled up the path to the canoe. As Jim could not swim, he soon overtook him, a rod or two from the shore, and dragged him toward the land, trying to make him understand that he would not kill him, but make him a prisoner. Under the influence of fear, and probably not comprehending his intentions, he screamed and resisted with all his strength. The Indian, therefore, struck him down in the edge of the water and took off his scalp. He was probably partly forced to this extremity by a black man of Commodore Whipple, who was at work on the opposite shore in a little distillery, who fired at the Indian with an old musket. The guards hearing the shot and the tumult came running down and commenced firing with their rifles.

In the mean time, Mr. Meigs, after the flight of Symonds, turned round and faced the remaining Indian, who had shot Symonds, and was the only one armed with a rifle. He instantly recognized the face of the savage who had undertaken to guide him in the autumn of 1790, on his journey to

Detroit, and exclaimed, "Is that you, Charley?" At the same time he pointed his gun at him as if about to fire; but Charley knew it was not loaded and did not fear it. He now advanced upon him, with his keen black eyes fixed upon the Indian's, until he was close to him, when he struck at him with the clubbed gun, and rushed past. The Indian received the blow on his rifle, and dropping it in his path, drew his tomahawk from his belt and pushed on in pursuit. The chase was not a long one, but very keen while it lasted. In about forty rods, the path crossed a small run with pretty deep and wide banks, across which Mr. Meigs sprung at a single leap. The Indian came up to the brink, stopped, and threw his hatchet at his intended victim as he was crossing a log which lay in the path. As it missed its object, with a loud yell he gave up the pursuit and hastened back to his companion.

Mr. Meigs now ran down to the river and assisted Symonds, who was nearly exhausted, in getting to the shore. A party of soldiers from the fort was soon on the ground and carried him to the garrison, where his wound was dressed and he finally recovered.

By the time Charley got back to his companion, several riflemen had joined old Caesar at the distillery, and began to fire at the Indian in the water. As one of the guns cracked, and he was in the act of stepping up the bank, he slipped back and fell; but whether from the effect of the shot, or the slipping of his wet moccasins, was not known. It served as a matter of momentary triumph to the riflemen, who were sure they had hit him, although the distance was two hundred and fifty yards. No blood, however, was found. Charley now sprung down to his assistance, when they soon reached the top of the bank, and swinging the bloody scalp over their heads, in concert with the yell of victory, vanished into the woods.

They were hardly out of sight, when E. W. Tupper, a brave and fearless man, in spite of the remonstrance of the bystanders, sprang into a canoe with one other person, and pushed over to the body of the black boy, hoping he might yet have life in him. But he had lain in the water ten or fifteen minutes, and could not be restored.

About half an hour before these events, Mr. Bureau, one of the French emigrants and since well known to many of the citizens of Ohio, in company with Horace Nye, then a small boy, passed over the same ground. They had spent the afternoon with one of his French friends who lived close by Fort

Harmer. On their return, near the spot where Meigs shot the snake, he attempted with his rifle to shoot a pigeon. The piece only flashed in the pan. Little Horace, who had seen him load the gun, had noticed that, either from haste or carelessness, he had pushed down the ball before the powder, and now told him of the mistake. Bureau mistrusted the boy's accuracy, and made several more attempts, which all flashed in the pan. They now went up to their canoe, which lay along side of Meigs' and had barely time to cross the river and reach the gate of the garrison, without entering it, when the attack was made, and the alarm given of Indians on the opposite shore. The mother of Horace, hearing the tumult and learning the cause, rushed out of the gate in an agony of fear for the fate of her little son, who, she knew, was over the river, and met him just as he was approaching the gate.

The mistake of Mr. Bureau, which vexed and fretted him so much at the time, no doubt saved both their lives, for the report of his gun would have directly called the Indians to the spot. On so small and trifling an incident do not only our lives, but even the fate of nations, sometimes depend. A party of riflemen followed the Indians to the top of the hill, but they escaped their search.

Names of the heads of families who lived in Campus Martius
at the period of the war, and began the settlement of Marietta.

The memory of these first pioneers ought to be preserved, and will make an interesting portion of the early history of Ohio.

Governor St. Clair, son and three daughters; the youngest died of sickness in 1790.

General Rufus Putnam, wife, two sons and six daughters.

General Benjamin Tupper and wife, three sons and two daughters; one, the wife of Colonel Ichabod Nye, the other married Winthrop Sargent, Esq., secretary of the territory; General Tupper died in August, 1792.

Colonel Robert Oliver and wife; two sons, William and Robert; two daughters, Nelly, married to Thomas Lord, Esq., the other, to Captain William Burnham.

Thomas Lord, Esq., with two apprentice boys, Benjamin Baker and Amos R. Harvey.

Colonel R. J. Meigs, wife and son, Timothy. R. J. Meigs, jr., and wife. He lived the larger portion of the time at "the point" garrison.

Colonel Enoch Shepherd, wife and nine children, chiefly adults; sons, Enoch, Daniel, Luther and Calvin; daughters, Esther, Anna, Rhoda, Lorana and Huldah. He was a man of great industry and enterprise, and the author of a work on the .prophecies.

Charles Greene, Esq., wife and three children; Sophia, Susan and Charles. Miss Sheffield, sister to his wife, and afterward married to Major Zeigler, lived with him.

Colonel Ichabod Nye, wife and two or three children.
Major Ezra Putnam, wife and two daughters; one of his sons was killed at Big Bottom by the Indians, and one died of sickness, the same year.

Major Haffield White and son, Peletiah, who served as a ranger at Waterford in the latter part of the war.

Joshua Shipman, wife and three children.

Captain Strong and wife, two sons and a daughter. He was attached to the army, but his family lived in Campus Martius.

Captain Davis, wife and five children, chiefly adults.

James Smith, wife and seven children.

John Russel, who married a daughter of Mr. Smith.

Archibald Lake, wife and three sons; Thomas, Andrew and John.

Eleazer Olney, wife and fourteen children.

Major Olney and two sons; Columbus and Discovery.

Ebenezer Corey and wife.

Richard Maxon, wife and several children.

James Wells, wife and ten children. His daughters married as follows: Polly, to Richard Maxon; Nancy, to Thomas Corey; Susan, to Peletiah White; Betsy, to Jacob Proctor, and Sally, to Peleg Springer; sons, young men, David, Joseph, Thomas and Varnum. Mr. Wells, his wife and daughter, Matilda, all died of the small pox.

Major Coburn and wife, and two daughters; Polly married Gilbert Devol, jr.; Susan, to Captain William Mason; sons, Asa, Phineas, and Nicholas — the two latter were with the forty-eight who first landed at Marietta, and were alive in 1844.

Joseph Wood, Esq., wife and one child. Mr. Wood was living in Marietta in 1845, aged eighty-six years.

Captain John Dodge, wife and two sons, John and Sidney.

Robert Allison, wife and several children; Charles, Andrew and Hugh, young men.

Elijah Warren, wife and one child.

Girshom Flag, wife and several children.

Widow Kelly and four sons. James Kelly, her husband, was killed by the Indians at Bellville, and her little son, Joseph, taken prisoner in April, 1791.

The single men recollected were Major Anselm Tupper, E. W. Tupper, Benjamin Tupper, Rev. Daniel Story, Thomas Hutchinson, William Smith, Gilbert Devol, jr., Oliver Dodge, Alpheus Russell, Thomas Corey and Azariah Pratt.

There were a few other families whose names are not retained.

The descendants of nearly all these families are now living in Ohio, the most of them in Washington County. They were nearly all of them from the New England states, and were descendants of the Puritans.

Fort Harmer

This fort was erected on the right bank of the Muskingum River, at its junction with the Ohio, by a detachment of United States troops, under the command of Major John Doughty, in the autumn of the year 1785, but was not completed until the following year. The position was judiciously chosen, as it commanded not only the mouth of the Muskingum, but swept the waters of the Ohio, from a curve in the river for a considerable distance both above and below the fort. It was the first military post built within the limits of the present state of Ohio, excepting Fort Laurens, which was built in 1778. The fort stood on what is called the "second bottom," being elevated above the ordinary floods of the Ohio, while between it and the banks of the river was a lower or first bottom, depressed about six feet, on to which the descent was by a gradual slope. This regular natural glacis was continued for a quarter of a mile up the Muskingum, and for a considerable distance below on the Ohio, adding greatly to the unrivaled beauty of the spot. The outlines of the fort formed a regular pentagon, and the area embraced within its walls contained about three-fourths of an acre. The curtains or main walls of the fort were constructed of large timbers, placed horizontally to the height of twelve or fourteen feet, and were one hundred and twenty feet in length, as was recently ascertained by measurement, as the outlines of two of the bastions can be still readily traced in the earth. The bastions were constructed of large timbers set upright in the ground, fourteen feet in height, fastened together by strips of timber tree nailed into each picket. The outlines of these were also pentagonal; the fifth side or that opening into the area of the fort being occupied by blockhouses, us Ad as quarters for the officers.

The barracks or dwellings for the private soldiers were built along the sides of the curtains, with their roofs sloping inward. They were divided into four rooms, of thirty feet each, with convenient fire places; and afforded ample space for a regiment of men. The officers' houses were made of hewed logs, two stories high, two rooms on a floor, with chimneys at each end. The large house in the south-east bastion was used for a store house. From the roof of the barrack which stood in the curtain, facing the Ohio, there arose a square tower like a cupola, surmounted by a flagstaff, in which was stationed the sentinel. The room beneath was the guard house. An arsenal, built of timber and covered with earth, stood in the area of the fort near the guardhouse, and answered as a magazine, or bomb-proof, for their powder. The main gate was next the river; with a sally port on the side toward the hills, which rise abruptly from the level grounds, at the distance of a quarter of a mile.

Near the center of the fort was a well for the supply of the garrison in case of a siege, although for ordinary purposes water was brought from the river. In the rear and to the left of the fort, on the ground which had supplied the materials for building, Major Doughty had laid out fine gardens. These were cultivated by the soldiers, and in the virgin soil of the rich alluvions, produced an abundant crop of culinary vegetables, for the use of the garrison.

To the bravery and pride of a soldier, the major also possessed a refined taste for horticulture. Peaches were planted as soon as the ground was cleared, and in the second or third year produced fruit. A variety of his originating is still cultivated in Marietta, and known as the "Doughty Peach."

Fort Harmer was named in honor of General Josiah Harmer, to whose command Major Doughty was attached. It continued to be occupied by the troops of the United States until September, 1790, when they were ordered down the river to Fort Washington, now Cincinnati.

Fort Harmer in 1790
From a drawing by Joseph Gilman

During the war the barracks and officers' houses were chiefly occupied by the Ohio Company settlers, only a small detachment being stationed at the fort. The house in the south-west bastion was occupied by Paul Fearing, and for several years after the war, the fort was a great convenience to the inhabitants, affording them comfortable dwellings, as well as a protection against the Indians. There were no regular batteries built within the fort, for the mounting of cannon, as it was in no danger of attack from enemies who had the use of artillery. One or two six pound field pieces were mounted on carriages, and kept on the bank of the river near the walls. With these they could command the boats on the river. The hill from which the drawing of the fort was taken looked directly into it, and cannon on its brow could sweep every part of it. As an early post, to awe and keep the savages in check, the location was a judicious one.

Between the fort and the bank of the river there was sufficient space to muster a battalion of men. A part of the ground was occupied by three stout log buildings, for the use of the artificers attached to the garrison. The rivers have made sad inroads on the site of the old fort. At this day not only the whole space between it and the river is washed away, but more than half of the ground occupied by the walls; so that the stone wall of the well, which was near the center, is now tumbling down the bank of the river. This continual wasting of the banks has widened the mouth of the Muskingum so much, that during the summer months a sand bar or island occupies the spot that used to afford ten or twelve feet of water. Before any clearings were made, the huge sycamore trees, as they inclined over the water on the opposite shores, narrowed the mouth of the river so much, that a person passing hastily by in the middle of the Ohio, would hardly notice its outlet, so darkly was it shadowed by these giants of the forest. The hand of cultivation has greatly injured the permanency and lessened the beauty of the river banks of the streams, by cutting away the trees. The roots acted as so many ligatures and fillets of net-work in protecting the earth from the wash of the waters, while their graceful trunks and drooping branches, served to beautify the banks of "La Belle Riviere."

Names of the heads of families, who lived
in and near to Fort Harmer, during the war.

Hon. Joseph Gilman and wife.

B. J. Gilman, his son and wife, with one or two children. They kept a store of goods or merchandise, in a small frame building, where the stone store now stands, and the two families lived in a blockhouse, built where L. Barber now lives.

Paul Fearing, Esq., unmarried, lived in the south-west blockhouse of the fort, given him by Major Doughty.

Colonel Thomas Gibson, single man, from Pennsylvania, was the licensed Indian trader for Washington County, and lived and kept his merchandise in a blockhouse, near where David Putnam, Esq., now lives. He was afterwards the first auditor of the state of Ohio.

Hezekiah Flint, one of the first forty-eight pioneers; a carpenter by trade; moved to Cincinnati.

Gould Davenport, single man.

Mrs. Welch and three or four children. Her husband died of small pox in 1790. She married Thomas Hutchinson.

Preserved Seaman, wife and four sons—Samuel, Gilbert, Preserved, and Benajah. Samuel had a wife and two or three children and occupied the guard house of the fort. They emigrated from Nova Scotia, drew donation lots, and settled on the Muskingum.

Benjamin Baker, wife and one child lived in. small stone house, a few rods south of the fort.

George Warth, wife and five sons, young men, and two daughters, brought up in the backwoods: John, George, Robert, Martin and Alexander, all of them fine hunters. John and George were employed as rangers for Fort Harmer. The family lived in a log house, on the first bottom, between the garrison and the river, built by the United States troops for the artificers to work in. George married Ruth Fleehart, sister of Joshua, and John married Sally Fleehart, and lived in one of the barracks of the fort. Paul Fearing, who lived in the adjoining blockhouse, took a deep interest in the welfare of John, who possessed a kind, pleasant disposition, and a sprightly mind. Not one of the family could read or write their names. After some persuasion, he concluded to let Mr. Fearing teach him to read in the intervals of his ranging tours, and when this was accomplished he soon learned to write, in a satisfactory manner. After the peace, he settled in what is now Jackson County, Virginia, a little below Buffington's Island, and served as a magistrate for several years. He became quite a wealthy planter, and the owner of a number of slaves. His success in after life may all be attributed to his learning to read and write after he was married. His wife had been brought up on the frontiers, and possessed all the intrepidity and courage, so common to females of that class, in an eminent degree. She could fire a rifle with great accuracy; bring down a hawk on the wing, or a squirrel from the tree top, as readily as her husband.

Joseph Fletcher was a young man from New England, and married Catharine, one of old Mr. Warth's daughters, and settled in Gallia County. He was surveyor of the County, and one of the Judges of Common Pleas. He bored the first salt well in that part of the county, on Chickemanga Creek. He died in 1844.

Picket Merion, also a young man from the eastern states, married Polly Warth, the sister of Catharine. He settled in Gallia, and served several years as a magistrate.

Francis Thierry and wife, with two children, Pierre and Catharine La Lance, of his wife by a former husband. He was one of the French emigrants and had been bred as a baker and confectioner in Paris. His bake-house stood between the fort and the river, and had been built for the use of the troops, where he found an oven ready to his hand. He made sweet cakes and loaves of fine bread. When the late king of France was in exile, in the United States, he passed through Marietta; he visited Mons. Thierry's bake-house and bought several loaves of his nice bread. He also pursued the gentle art of angling, with wonderful skill and success, catching more fish than any other three men in the garrison; being in that respect a second Isaac Walton. His wife was a faithful help-mate, not only assisting him in the baking operations, but also accompanied him to his garden and little cornfield, dressed in a suit of her husband's clothes, cheering him at his work with her lively French tongue. This was probably done to deceive the Indians. Mons. Thierry lived for many years after the war, and retained his love for angling to old age. He died a few years since, leaving an estate worth several thousand dollars. Catharine La Lance married Robert Warth, who was killed by the Indians soon after. Her son, Robert, is now a merchant in Gallipolis.

Monsieur Cookie, a single man, was another of the French emigrants who remained at Fort Harmer, and was a well educated gentleman, bred to no particular calling. He was a small, short man, and noted for wearing a very tall, steeple crowned hat, similar in fashion to those worn by the cavaliers in the days of Charles II. He had a great taste for trapping, fowling, and hunting, and used to set his traps in a little run about a hundred rods from the garrison. The Indians, who often watched the movements of the inhabitants from the hill which overlooked the fort, had discovered his trail to the traps, and one day, in the summer of 1792, lay in wait for his approach by the side of the little path that wound through the papaw bushes and fallen timber to the scene of his labors. Seeing the top of his high crowned hat approaching above the bushes, they fired at it thinking the balls would hit the head within it. But in this they were deceived, for both bullets passed through the crown an inch or two above his head, doing no other harm than giving him a terrible fright. Being an active little man, he ran with all speed to the fort, escaping their pursuit, and glad to compound for his life by the marring of his favorite hat. He had been often told by the rangers that the Indians would someday kill him if he continued his trips to the traps so far from the fort. This alarm cured him, and he gave up the occupation of trapper, but continued to wear his cavalier hat a long time after, displaying the bullet holes in the crown as trophies of his lucky escape.

Mons. Le Blond, another emigrant, who carried on for a living a distillery of cordials, made from the wild native grapes, papaws, sassafras, mint, &c.; he also manufactured very nice wooden shoes, made from the soft wood of the buckeye. They were much worn by the French people at all times; and in wet, muddy states of the streets, by the other inhabitants.

Monsieur Shouman, wife and son. He followed gardening, being bred to that occupation in France. Having lost his wife, after the war he married the widow of Sherman Waterman, who was killed by the Indians in 1795 and lived at Waterford.

Monsieur Gubbeau, another emigrant, a young man of great activity and a fine waterman. In company with Pierre La Lance, Mrs. Thiery's son, they transported the mail, in the year 1795, from Marietta to Gallipolis, in a large canoe. It was made by Captain Jonathan Devol, from the trunk of a wild cherry tree, and finished as nicely as any piece of cabinet furniture. The length was forty feet and would carry twenty men; but was so nicely modeled for passing through the water, that two men could move her with poles or paddles as easily as any other canoe of half the size. The trip up and down was performed in a week, being a little over one hundred miles.

The head quarters of a company of fifty men was established at the fort, after the year 1791. The soldiers were distributed in small detachments at the different garrisons, and changed every few months, by a fresh squad. Their presence gave confidence to the inhabitants, and enabled them to devote more time to the cultivation of their fields, as they kept the guard of the garrison, while they were out at their work. Captain Haskell commanded a part of the time, and Lieutenant Morgan at another.

CHAPTER XV.

Description of the garrison at "the point."

The first dwelling houses in Marietta were erected at "the point," in a short time after the landing of the pioneers; and at the breaking out of the war in 1791, there were about twenty houses occupied by families. These houses were generally made of round logs, and did not possess the neatness and finish of the dwellings in Campus Martius. When the war began, several families from the country moved in and erected additional houses. No blockhouses, or defenses of any kind, had been built. The ground was cleared of nearly all the trees from the Ohio bank up the Muskingum to Tyber Creek, and east, to a little beyond the east side of First Street. The center of this area was lower than on the banks of the rivers, and occupied by a small run that passed obliquely across the village, discharging its water into the Muskingum a few rods below where Cram's mill now stands. The mouth of the run was without the palisades, and crossed by a bridge close to the gate, which was placed near the Muskingum blockhouse, and was the outlet to the road which communicated with Campus Martius. The town plat was encumbered with stumps and some fallen timber. When the war commenced, Colonel William Stacey was employed by the Ohio Company to superintend the erection of defenses, under the direction of Colonel Sproat. A line of palisades was set from the Muskingum River, easterly to the east side of First Street, terminating in this direction near to where lawyer Hart now lives. From thence on the east side of First Street to the Ohio River; inclosing about four acres. A piece of ground, of nearly the same size, remained unenclosed, between the northern line of palisades and Tyber Creek, for corn and garden grounds. Three or four houses stood on the outside of the defenses, near the blockhouse on the Muskingum bank, occupied by Colonel Niswonger, Jacob Wiser and Isaac Mixer, as seen in the sketch of the garrison. Two or three other buildings stood in Ohio Street, near the upper gate, outside the palisades.

Three blockhouses were immediately built: one on the Muskingum bank, at the western termination of the pickets; one in the northeast corner of the enclosure; and one on the Ohio bank. Near to the latter, and by that on the Muskingum, were strong gates, of a size to admit teams, the approaches to which were commanded by the blockhouses. These blockhouses were surmounted by sentry boxes, or turrets, the sides of which were secured with thick planks for the defense of the men when on guard. The upper room in the blockhouse number one was occupied as a school house a large portion of the time, while the lower story contained one or two families.

In blockhouse number two, in the northeast corner of the garrison, families lived in the upper story, and the lower one was used for a guard house. A sergeant's guard of Ohio Company troops, commanded by Joseph Barker, since a Colonel and Judge of the Court of Common Pleas, had charge of this building for two or more years.

Blockhouse number three stood on the bank of the Ohio. A sentry was posted on it every night. It was occupied by the family of Colonel William Stacey, a very excellent and useful man.

Blockhouse number four stood near the spot where Mr. Dunn's hatter's shop now stands. It was built in the spring of the year 1792, by a detachment of United States troops under Lieutenant Tillinghast, from Rhode Island. It was the largest blockhouse in the garrison, the lower story being twenty-six feet square, and upper one nearly thirty. The timbers were eight inches thick, hewed smooth, the joints snug and tight, with good floors, and bullet proof doors and window shutters. During the war, the upper story was occupied for a magazine; and after its close it was used for holding the county courts, while the lower room served for a jail. The building stood in the line of the pickets partly in and on the east side of First Street. During the war it was occupied by the United States troops, who kept a sentry, and assisted in guarding the garrison until sent down the Ohio to join General Wayne.

After the defeat of General St. Clair, Captain Jonathan Haskell was ordered to Marietta, and took command of the garrison, and put it under military law. The gates were closed at the setting of the sun, and sentries posted on the adjacent blockhouses, preventing any one from passing in or out until sunrise next morning. This order produced some difficulty between the military and the citizens. Several families had houses, stacks of grain and forage outside the palisades, and resided there by day, but came in at night. This made it difficult to conform to the strict police of the garrison, as the citizen had to provide his own rations, while the soldiers were fed by the public. Many incidents might arise to prevent the citizen from being within the gates at sunset. For this reason several families moved out into houses near the garrison, and remained out at the hazard of being killed by the Indians.

Considerable fields were cultivated where the court house now stands, and so round in the neighborhood of the college, and up the Ohio bank. One or two of the blockhouses were provided with small cannon, to which suitable cartridges were made, and filled with cut pieces of iron and ounce lead bullets.

Three sentries were on duty every night—one on each of the river blockhouses, and one on the north-east corner of the garrison, or No. 2, by day as well as night. The enlisted men kept one sentry day and night; the other was taken in routine by the citizens. Alarm posts were assigned within, where they were to repair in an attack or alarm. These were, first, the blockhouses, and next, such of the dwelling houses as were best fortified against any attempt of the Indians. The firing of the cannon was the signal for each one to repair immediately to his alarm post, with his arms ready for defense. The cannon was fired also in the day time, when news of Indians in the neighborhood was brought in by the rangers, to put the people on their guard who might be abroad in the fields. There were several alarms, but no serious attack, with now and then a false one, which served to keep up the activity of the inhabitants. (Col. Barker's Notes.)

One dark, rainy night in June, while John Wiser, then a youth of eighteen years, and well known to the inhabitants of Marietta at this day, was standing watch in the tower of the middle blockhouse, he saw by the aid of a flash of lightning, a dark looking body climbing over a log, which lay about fifty yards from the garrison. A report had been circulated the day before of Indians being seen in the neighborhood. This object appeared about the height of a man, and at the next flash John hailed and fired in the same instant. All remained quiet on the outside; but the report of the gun awakened those within the garrison, who came running from all quarters in great alarm, thinking the Indians were upon them, as no one ever fired without good cause. The women came hurrying along with their screaming children, and 'the men with their guns ready for defense, so that great tumult prevailed for a time. Colonel Sproat was soon on the ground, and questioned the sentry very closely as to what he had seen or heard. John was rather confused at the disturbance he had raised, without being able to state a more definite cause. He however described the dark looking object he saw standing on the log and its resemblance to a man, and how he had fired at a white spot he saw about the head, by a flash of lightning. Many surmises were made as to what it could be. Some said it must surely be an Indian, while others laughed and said John had fired at nothing to see the fun of a night alarm, as he was known to be fond of a little harmless sport. No further signs of an enemy were discovered, and no one ventured out in the dark to reconnoiter for the savages. In the morning, after the gates were opened, a party went out, and behind the log pointed out by John, was found a large, black dog, with a rifle shot through the centre of a white spot he had on his forehead. It belonged to one of the men in the garrison. John was a little cross-eyed, and always fired with both eyes open, and was a first rate shot by day or night.

Names of the heads of families in the garrison, at "the point" with the houses in which they lived in the year 1792, as numbered on the sketch of the garrison, which accompanies this catalogue.

Marietta
At the Point in 1792
From a drawing by C. W. Elliott

No. 1. William Moulton, wife, two daughters and one son, Edmond. The father and son were among the forty-eight pioneers who first landed at Marietta, in April, 1788. Anna married Dr. Josiah Hart, one of the early physicians of Marietta, in 1796, and Lydia married Dr. Leonard, an English surgeon of great eccentricity of character, a few years later. Mr. Moulton was a goldsmith by trade, from Newburyport, Massachusetts. He died about 1793. Edmond was noted for his oddities and simplicity. Dr. Jabez True boarded in this family and kept a little office or shop, near to dwelling house,

No. 2, not figured in the plate.

No. 2. Captain Prince, wife and two children. He was a hatter by trade, from Boston, Massachusetts; a well educated man. Moved to Cincinnati, after the war.

No. 3. Moses Morse and wife. He owned four log houses standing side by side, and called "Morse's Row," which he rented to transient families. He was a painter of signs and various other callings, styling himself doctor. His tavern signs were all noted for having the device of a black horse on them, painted from a design cut in paste board. It was said that his road out, from New England to the Ohio River, could be traced all the way, by the tavern signs he had painted, paying all his traveling expenses by his skill in painting. These emblems of the publican's calling, the law required, much more strictly than at present, should be suspended at every inn side, as well as in well painted, fair letters over the retailer's door; as may be seen by examining the long obsolete territorial law, regulating taverns and retail stores.

No. 4. Peter Niswonger (Nighswonger), wife, and two or three children. Married Jane Kerr, the sister of Hamilton. He was of German descent, and born in Frederick County, Virginia. During the Revolutionary War himself and John, an older brother, came over the mountains, and lived in Wheeling, following the occupation of hunting. Peter was a stout built man, over six feet high, very muscular, and erect in his movements. Dark skin and hair, with coal black eyes; high cheek bones, with an immense roman nose knocked a little to one side, by some unlucky blow received in his amusements at fisticuffs, at which every hunter and backwoodsman was expected to be proficient. He was coarse and rough in his address, but possessed a kind heart. The costume worn by the rangers, to which class Peter belonged, was similar to that of the Indians, as being better adapted to a woodsman's life. To this he usually added the painting of the face, to make the resemblance more striking, when out on a tour of duty. His courage was of that cool, deliberate kind that never fails in the hour of peril. While he was living at Wheeling, the Indians made their last attack on that place, in great force. During the midst of the siege a large palisade gave way, and greatly elated the Indians, as it afforded an opening by which they could enter, or fire through it at their enemies within. Peter volunteered to go out and set it up, while those on the inside secured it with a chain. This service he performed, amidst a shower of bullets from the Indians, without a single wound, and returned through the sally gate to the admiration of the savages, and with the plaudits of his companions. After the war he settled at "Old Town Bottom," a little below Buffington's Island. As the game became scarce he moved further west on to the frontiers, where he could pursue his favorite vocation of hunting, unmolested by neighbors. His house stood on the west side of the street, near the Muskingum, but his range of duty lay on the Fort Harmer side, where he was employed as a spy, usually in company with John Warth.

No. 5. William Skinner and J. McKinley kept a retail store in this building during the war. After its close Mr. Skinner moved over to the Fort Harmer side.

No. 6. R. J. Meigs, jr., wife and one child. Charles Green and himself were in company in a store of goods, kept in a part of this building.

No. 7. Hon. Dudley Woodbridge, wife, and children. This building was a small blockhouse, a portion of which is still standing, enclosed in a frame dwelling house, now owned by J. Preston.

No. 8. A two story frame building, built by Judge Woodbridge, and occupied for a retail store by him for several years during and after the war. Muskingum Street was then the "cheap side," or "merchant's row," of Marietta, where all the business was done. Time, and the alteration of circumstances, make many changes in the affairs of men, as well as in the streets of a city.

No. 9. Captain Josiah Munroe, wife and two children, adults. He was a talented and useful man; and appointed the first postmaster in Marietta, in 1794.

No. 10. Captain William Mills, wife and one child. He was an officer in the United States service; died soon after the close of the war. His widow was well known to the inhabitants as a most excellent and pious woman; and subsequently the wife of Dr. True.

No. 13. Captain Jonathan Haskell commanded a company of United States troops, for the defense of the settlements, and made this house his head quarters. He was one of the Belpre associates, and lived there on his farm a number of years after the war.

No. 14. Hamilton Kerr. This should have been a small blockhouse. His mother lived with him after the death of his father, and a younger brother. He was one of the most active and useful of the spies. A biographical sketch will be given of him in the sequel.

No. 15. Colonel Ebenezer Sproat, wife and daughter. Commodore Abraham Whipple, wife and son, lived with him in the same house. The Colonel's wife was a daughter of Commodore Whipple. Soon after the peace he built the house where Captain D. Green now lives, and occupied it at the time of his death, in 1805. A biography of both these hardy pioneers will be given. The house stood on the ground now covered by Lewis's Hotel.

No. 16. Joseph Buell, wife and two children, with Levi Munsell and wife. This was the first frame building in the Northwest Territory, and in it Buell and Munsell kept a tavern and boarding-house. The corner of Holden's block of stores covers the ground occupied by this building. These two men had been sergeants in Colonel Harmer's regiment, and were greatly attached to each other. It was one of the earliest public houses kept in Marietta. Stephen Pearce kept a house of entertainment in Campus Martius, in the year 1792, but this was opened in 1790.

No. 17. William Stacey, son of Colonel Stacey, wife and two or three children. Settled in Rainbow, or Union Township, on the Muskingum, after the war.

No. 18. Joseph Stacey, son of Colonel Stacey, wife and two or three children. Also a resident of Union.

No. 19. James Patterson, wife and children. A celebrated fisherman, and supported his family chiefly by this employment.

No. 20. Nathaniel Patterson, wife and children. He died with the small pox.

No. 21. Captain Abel Matthews, from Hartford County, Connecticut, wife and six children. He was the father of John and Philo. John acted as drummer to the garrison. Settled in Rainbow or Union.

No. 22. Thomas Stanley, wife and three or four children, from Farmington, Connecticut. Served several years in the Continental Army, and was a Constable of Marietta, and Sergeant of the Ohio Company troops during the Indian war; subsequently built mills on Duck Creek. He was a public spirited, useful man, and one of the first settlers in Fearing Township.

No. 23. Eleazar Curtis, wife, and a number of children. He was from Massachusetts, and settled in Newbury, at the lower end of Belpre Township. Several of his sons live in that vicinity, and are prominent and valuable citizens.

No. 24. A range of log cabins, built for the use of the Ohio Company's laborers, and afterwards appropriated as barracks for the soldiers and the occupancy of emigrant families. They stood near the edge of the bank, opposite to Loomis's and Johnson's stores. Simeon Tuttle and family lived in blockhouse, No. 1.

All these tenements have long since passed away, like the people who dwelt within them, and their places are supplied with substantial brick buildings. It is, nevertheless, pleasant to look upon the likeness of what has been before our own times, and to dwell upon the remembrance of our hardy ancestors, who struggled long and manfully with famine, poverty, and the red men of the forest, to provide a home, not only for themselves, but for their children.

This little spot was the germ from whence has sprung the great state of Ohio, with its millions of inhabitants, and shall not its remembrance be preserved?

The inhabitants of this garrison suffered a good deal with sickness from small pox and scarlet fever. One of their most annoying and continual troubles was the difficulty they had in procuring meal and flour after they had raised the grain at the hazard of their lives. Their meal was made in hand mills, two only of which were owned in the garrison—one by Colonel Stacey, the other by Hamilton Kerr. There was a large, old coffee mill that once belonged to a ship of war, owned by Captain Mathews, the hopper of which would hold a peck of corn. This was in great demand. The finest of the meal was separated with a sieve, for bread, and the coarser boiled up with a piece of venison or bear meat, like hominy, making a rich and nourishing diet, well suited to the tastes and stomachs of the hungry pioneers. Licenses for taverns and retailing merchandise were given out by Colonel Meigs, who was the Commissioner for this purpose. The applicant had first to get a recommendation from the Judges of the Court of Quarter Sessions, and pay fifteen dollars for the license to the use of the county, and one dollar to the Commissioner.

The materials from which the sketch of the garrison and ancient town was drafted were procured from five individuals, who lived there during the war, three of whom are now living. Four of these persons made separate plans of the situation of the buildings, and wrote down the names of the families who occupied them. The compiler, from these several drafts, which were strikingly uniform in detail, was himself familiar with the early appearance of the town, log cabins and blockhouses. From these data, the present view of "the garrison at the point" has been made, and is doubtless as correct as the circumstances would permit.

Schools

Notwithstanding the poverty and privations of the inhabitants of the garrison, schools were kept up for the instruction of their children, in reading, writing, and arithmetic, nearly all the time of the war. The funds were partly provided by the Ohio Company, and the balance furnished from their own lank pockets. The teachers of these schools could not employ their time profitably in any other business, as there was nothing to do, and served for low wages. Jonathan Baldwin, from Massachusetts, liberally educated, kept nearly two years in the blockhouse on the Muskingum, and settled in Waterford. Mr. Curtis, single man, and brother of Eleazar Curtis, taught in a cooper's shop. Pie afterwards settled in Charleston, Virginia. Dr. Jabez True kept, also, in the blockhouse; so that there was no lack of effort in this important matter, on the part of the people of Marietta. In Campus Martius, a school was kept in the north-west blockhouse, in the winter of 1789, by Major Anselm Tupper, and every winter after that by several different teachers, among whom was Benjamin Slocomb, a well educated, but rather dissipated man, of Quaker parentage.

Doings of the Ohio Company in 1793

At a meeting of the directors of the company, who were the trustees of the donation tract, in May, 1793, the boundaries of the one hundred thousand acres were defined as follows, viz: *"south, on a tract of seven hundred and fifty thousand acres of land mentioned in the first section of said act; east, on the seventh range townships mentioned in the said first section; west, on a tract of two hundred and fourteen thousand two hundred and eighty-five acres of land mentioned in the second section of said act; and north, on a certain line surveyed by Israel Ludlow, as the northern boundary line of one million five hundred thousand acres of land, mentioned in the fourth section of the said act."*

In making their grants to individuals the trustees were guided by these rules. The grantee must be a male not under eighteen years of age, and at the time an actual settler residing at some of the stations of defense, or settlement, within the aforesaid three tracts of land, granted for the benefit of the Ohio Company associates. The present settlers within those tracts were to be first provided with lots. All contracts heretofore made with persons to settle on any part of the one hundred thousand acres to be carried into effect, as far as may be in the power of the trustees. This referred to the settlements at Waterford, Wolf Creek Mills, and Duck Creek, which were within the boundaries of the donation land; and as these lands were given by the United States partly to assist the Ohio Company in fulfilling their contracts with settlers, heretofore made at their own expense, it was decided that the donation lots at Belpre, sixty-eight in number, must be covered by a fifth division, or one hundred acre lot, drawn in the company lands, before the occupier could receive a lot in the donation tract, otherwise they would have two donation lots instead of one. As a large proportion of these men were proprietors in the company, the arrangement was easily made. General R. Putnam was appointed the superintendent for surveying and deeding the above lands, for which service he was allowed to charge five dollars, to be paid by the person receiving the deed. By the 17th of July, nine allotments had been surveyed in those portions of the tract most contiguous to the Muskingum River and Wolf Creek Mills, as settlements for associations of individuals, from ten to thirty-two in number, amounting to one hundred and seventy lots, or seventeen thousand acres; leaving only sixteen then in the colony, un-provided for. These drew lots soon after. The names of all these men are recorded in the journal of the company, showing as a historical fact that in July, 1793, there were only one hundred and eighty-six males, able to bear arms, within the three settlements of Marietta, Belpre, and Waterford.

The winter of 1793 was, in general, mild, especially the month of January; on the 30th of which there fell a snow of eighteen inches in depth, which exceeded that of any other since the settlement. The 1st of March following, the river Ohio was two feet higher than ever known before, overflowing all the low grounds, and the streets in the "garrison at the point."

In August the inhabitants suffered much from an epidemic scarlet fever that carried off quite a number of persons, chiefly children. The small pox also made its appearance early in the same month, breaking out among the soldiers of Captain Haskell's command. The Court of Quarter Session met on the 7th of August, and ordered the infected persons to be removed to a cabin near Mixer's Spring. On the 9th they had a special session, at the request of the inhabitants, and with the consent of the Captain, directed the sick to be removed to Devoll's Island. Several of the inhabitants took the disease, and some died. Since that year the small pox has not prevailed in Marietta.

An Indian killed on the south side of the Ohio

This event, although not transacted in the territory of the Ohio Company, is intimately connected with its history, and is related by John Wiser, who was well acquainted with the party, and received the narrative from his own mouth. In the autumn of the year 1793, Isaac Williams, who lived opposite to the mouth of the Muskingum, had been sick, but was now recovering. Feeling a returning appetite, he thought if he could get some venison (a favorite meat with the backwoodsmen), he should recover much more rapidly. Bird Lockhart, with his wife and eight children, together with several other families, lived in his garrison, and was a celebrated hunter, as well as a man of undaunted courage. Mr. Williams applied to him to go out into the woods and kill a deer. Bird readily consented, although in the midst of the Indian war, and very hazardous.

Taking his old horse, which was afflicted with the pole evil, and of so poor and homely an appearance that there was no danger of the Indians stealing him, he went out on to the heads of Worthington's Run, a small branch that falls into Hew's River, about six miles distant from the garrison. He soon killed two fine deer, dressed the meat, and packed it on to the old horse. Late in the afternoon he started on his return home. As he was winding along on the top of a ridge which divides the waters that fall into the Ohio from those of Worthington, in a curve of the old Indian path, made by the head of a hollow, as the sinuosities on the sides of the ridges, worn by the small branches, are called, he suddenly and quite unexpectedly met two Indian warriors in the trace, only a few rods before him. The Indians were as much surprised as himself. Both parties instantly sprang behind trees. One of his foes, in his haste, took a tree too small to cover him, so that the side of his hip presented a fair mark to the keen eye of Lockhart, who instantly fired and shot him through the hips, entirely disabling him. The other Indian, who was behind a larger tree, and considerably further off, seeing that Bird's rifle was now empty, rushed up to shoot him. As he approached, Lockhart was in the act of drawing out his ramrod from his rifle, after hastily pushing down a ball on to the powder, poured without measure from the horn. The rifles of the old hunters were generally of a large bore, and constructed so as to prime themselves. The Indian seeing this ran back to the tree he had left. Here they stood for a long time, watching each other until near the approach of night, both being too cautious and wary to uncover any part of his body from behind the tree of sufficient size for an effective shot.

Lockhart began to feel a little uneasy, as he saw the sun declining, lest he should keep close under cover until dark, and steal off undiscovered, and he should lose the chance of a shot at him. Being of a shrewd turn of mind and fruitful in expedients, he took his old low crowned beaver hat, and placing it on his wiping stick, slowly pushed it round the side of the tree; imitating as closely as he could the motions of a human head looking cautiously from behind the trunk, to get sight of the enemy. The Indian instantly caught a glimpse of the hat, and fired. Bird still further to deceive him, let the hat fall to the ground, which completed the delusion; as he instantly rushed forward with a yell to secure the scalp of his fallen foe. Lockhart suffered him to approach within a few yards of him, when he stepped out from behind his covert and deliberately shot him through the body. Both his enemies were now *"hors de combat;"* but deeming it imprudent to approach the wounded Indian, who had crawled further away, but still had his loaded rifle, he took a circuit round in search of his horse. But he had wandered out of sight; and as it was now nearly dark he returned to the garrison without him. The story of his day's adventures was soon related. The next morning a party went out conducted by Lockhart, where they found the Indian dead whom he last shot, but the wounded one was missing. The old horse was found by the same party on Carpenter's Run, about six miles above Marietta, near the Ohio River. It was supposed that the wounded Indian had contrived to catch the horse, as it was very gentle, and rode to this place. Here he either crossed the river, aided by some other Indians who belonged to the war party, or hid himself in the rocks. No trace of him could be found, and the men returned with the scalp of only one Indian.

During this year General Wayne, was busily engaged in collecting troops, magazines of provisions and erecting forts, preparatory to invading the Indian country. These movements occupied the attention of the western tribes, and in some measure checked the frequency and number of their war parties into the settlements of the Ohio Company, so that they were not much molested, but pursued their agricultural improvements, and were for the first time enabled to procure more grain than they needed for their own consumption. In the autumn of this year, two or three boats were loaded with corn, grown at Belpre and Waterford, and sold to the army contractors, at forty cents a bushel, and taken to Fort Washington. This market was of great service to the poor settlers, as it enabled them to purchase clothing and other articles, for the comfort of their families, which for the last three years many of them could not do. The distribution of the donation lots brought quite a number of young men into the country, and some new clearings were made during the winter months, as the Indians seldom left their villages for war at that season of the year. There was, therefore, less danger in the winter, and the settlers went abroad and visited each other much more frequently than in the summer.

Robert Warth killed

On the 10th of May, 1794, Robert Warth, who lived in Fort Harmer, was engaged at work, chopping on a log, to make rails for a fence in a new clearing, about three hundred yards from the garrison, and near the spot where Judge Fearing built his dwelling house. Two Indians had secreted themselves behind some brush, near the outer edge of the field, in the margin of the woods, and had probably seen him at work from the hill side. He had been chopping but a short time, when they rose up from their ambush, and shot him through the body. B. J. Gilman was only a few rods from him, but nearer to the river, overseeing the work. The Indians did not see him until both had fired at Warth; otherwise they might have shot him. They now gave chase to Gilman, trying to cut off his retreat to the fort, but being swift of foot escaped. John Warth, one of the spies, and brother to Robert, hearing the firing, rushed out of the fort with his rifle, as the Indians were ascending the steep side of the hill that overlooks the garrison, swinging the bloody scalp, and uttering their cries of victory. He sprang on to a log, which gave him a better view of them, and fired. The distance was more than two hundred yards, and yet it is supposed he hit one of them, as they ceased their shouts, while one was seen to falter, and with difficulty ascended the hill. A few years after, the bones of an Indian were found walled up in a small grotto, under a rock, about two miles from this place, near the path by which they retreated, which there was good reason to think were those of the wounded Indian. Mr. Warth was the last victim to savage hatred near Marietta.

Packet mail boats

Since the establishment of military posts on the Ohio River, by Congress, no regular intercourse was kept up with them by the government. Mail routes could not be conducted beyond Pittsburgh. All communications of importance were made through expresses, either on land through the wilderness, by way of Virginia and Kentucky, or by transient boats on the Ohio River. As this mode was slow, uncertain, and expensive, Colonel Timothy Pickering, the postmaster general, deemed it advisable to establish a more regular and certain mode, by which to communicate with General Wayne, and the army on the western frontier. The first mail route across the Alleghany Mountains was ordered by Congress, in September, 1786, from Alexandria, in Virginia, to Pittsburgh, by way of Leesburgh, Winchester, Fort Cumberland and Bedford; also from Philadelphia to the town of Bedford, and thence to Pittsburgh. On the 20th of May, 1788, Congress resolved that the Postmaster General be directed to employ posts, for the regular transport of the mail, between the city of Philadelphia and the town of Pittsburgh, by the way of Lancaster, York, Carlisle, Chambersburg, and

Bedford, and that the mail be dispatched once in each fortnight, from the post offices, respectively. (Journal of Congress.)

In April, 1794, with the aid and advise of Colonel O'Hara, army contractor, and Major Isaac Craig of Pittsburgh, a plan was devised of transporting the mail in light, strong boats, on the Ohio River; and put into operation early in the following June. These boats were about twenty-four feet in length, built after the model of a whale boat, and steered with a rudder. They were manned by five boatmen, viz. a coxswain and four oarsmen. The men were all armed, and their pieces kept dry in snug boxes alongside their seats. The whole could be covered with a tarpaulin in wet weather, which each boat carried for that purpose. For cooking and sleeping, they generally landed on the beach at the head of an island, where they would be less exposed to a surprise, or attack by the Indians. In ascending, as well as in descending, the boat was kept nearly in the middle of the river. The distance traveled against the current averaged about thirty miles a day, and double that downstream.

There were four relays between Wheeling and Cincinnati. The mail was carried by land from Pittsburgh to Wheeling The stations where the boats met and exchanged their mails, were Marietta, Gallipolis and Limestone, the distance between which was accomplished in seven days, both up and down; thus requiring about twelve days from Cincinnati to Wheeling, and half that time from Wheeling to Cincinnati. The transport by land required only one day, and two post riders, who exchanged their mails at Washington, Pennsylvania.

Postmasters were appointed at each of these towns, so that the citizens could have the advantage of the establishment, as well as the military. The Postmaster at Marietta was Captain Josiah Munro, an old officer in the continental line, during the war.

This mode of carrying the mail was kept up until 1798. After the treaty with the Indians in 1795, the mail was landed at Graham's Station, a few miles above Limestone, and transported on horseback to Cincinnati. So cautious were the conductors of these boats generally, that only one attack was made on them by the Indians. This happened in November, 1794, to a boat commanded by Captain Dugan; but at that time under the care of another man, employed for that trip. The packet was ascending the Ohio, and happened to have several passengers on board, as they sometimes did, and had reached within a few miles of the mouth of the Scioto, on the Indian shore. The man at the helm saw, as he thought, a deer in the bushes, and heard it rustling among the leaves. With the intention of killing it the boat had approached within a few rods of the land and the man in the bow had risen up with his gun to fire, when they received a whole volley, from a party of Indians who lay in ambush, and had made these signs to entice them to the shore.

One man was killed, and another desperately wounded. Several of "the row locks" were shot off, and their oars for the time rendered useless. The Indians rushed down the bank and into the water, endeavoring to get hold of the boat and drag it to the shore. The steersman, however, turned the bow into the current, and one or two oars soon forced her into the stream, beyond the reach of their shot. One of the hands, who had been a drummer in St. Clair's army, and had probably witnessed the appalling effect of the Indian yell, became so alarmed that he jumped into the river, as the boat was turning from the shore. A stout Indian dashed into the water and swam after him, with his drawn knife in his teeth. Wilber's pantaloons, being thick and heavy, impeded his motions so much in swimming that the Indian gained rapidly on him. He made an attempt to pull them off, and got one leg free, but sank under the water while doing it.

He was now worse off than before, as they dragged behind and nearly paralyzed all his efforts. The Indian was within a few yards of him, and escape seemed hopeless; when making another desperate effort he succeeded in freeing himself from the encumbrance. In accomplishing this last struggle he again sank entirely beneath the surface, and came up greatly exhausted, with the Indian within striking distance of him. As his enemy slackened his exertions, to draw the knife from his teeth and give the fatal stab, Wilbur having his legs now free, and quickened by the sight of the gleaming blade, upraised in the hand of the Indian, threw all his remaining strength into one convulsive effort, and forced himself beyond the reach of the descending knife, which plunged harmless into the water, within a few inches of his body. Before his enemy could repeat the blow he was several feet ahead of him, and nearly in the middle of the river. The Indian now gave up the pursuit, and retreated to the shore.

Nearly exhausted by fear and fatigue, and chilled with the coldness of the water, Wilbur reached the opposite bank with great difficulty. In the meantime the boatmen, thinking him drowned or killed, pushed downstream, and did not land until they came to the station, about thirty miles below. Wilbur however made himself a raft, and descended the river to Graham's in safety. By this disaster the line of communication was interrupted for a trip or two, but was soon after resumed, and not broken again, except by the ice in winter, when the boats were laid up for a few weeks, until the system was abandoned in the year 1798, for the more feasible one by land.

Doings of the Ohio Company

In January, 1795, a party of surveyors was sent out with a guard of fifteen men, on account of the war, not yet closed, to run the line between the fourteenth and fifteenth ranges. They proceeded up the Hockhocking in canoes, which shows that it was an open winter. At this time the two townships reserved for the benefit of a university were reconnoitered. In November, at a meeting of the agents and proprietors, it was decided that the number of shares actually paid for amounted to eight hundred and seventeen. In December, on a petition from the French emigrants at Gallipolis, to purchase the lands on which their town was located, it was resolved that they should have it at one dollar and twenty-five cents an acre, which sum was far below its value, and was a generous act in the company.

In December, the two townships of land appropriated for the benefit of a university, were selected by the agents as the best in the purchase, and were numbers eight and nine, in the fourteenth range. They now constitute the township of Athens and the township of Alexander, in Athens County.

In January, 1796, the company made a further appropriation of one hundred and forty-seven dollars, to Rev. D. Story, for services as a religious teacher, so that he was in their pay from 1789 to 1796.

After the close of the Indian war, and peace was restored to the harassed settlements, few events of an interesting character transpired. The inhabitants who had been for five years confined to the walls of their garrisons, and only went abroad, with the fear of death from the lurking savage continually in their minds, now gladly went forth to their labors free of restraint. Each man took possession of his lands, and commenced clearing and cultivating his farm. Mills were erected, roads opened, and bridges built, as rapidly as the sparse population of the country would allow. Many new inhabitants moved into the country from the eastern and middle states, induced by the rich soil and temperate climate of the valley of the Ohio; while the Virginia and military lands of the United States called many more who had earned an interest in the bounty lands, by their services in the continental armies.

Nevertheless, it was not until the year 1798, that the whole Northwestern Territory contained five thousand free male inhabitants, the number required to entitle it to a territorial legislature, although it embraced the present states of Illinois, Indiana, Michigan and Ohio. Under the ordinance for the government of the territory, one representative was allowed to every five hundred male inhabitants. No man was eligible to this office who had not been a citizen of the United States three years, and a resident in the district, or else have resided in the district three years. He must also possess in his own right a fee simple of two hundred acres of land within it. An elector must have a freehold of fifty acres, and be a citizen and resident in the district two years, to entitle him to vote for a representative.

Washington County then embraced within its limits a territory that now constitutes many counties, among which are Athens, Gallia, Meigs, Morgan, Muskingum, Coshocton Belmont, Guernsey and Monroe; and was entitled to two representatives. By a proclamation of Governor St. Clair, this election took place on the third Monday in December, 1798, and was a memorable day in the annals of the territory as that in which the elective franchise was first exercised north-west of the river Ohio.

Colonel R. J. Meigs and Paul Fearing, Esq., were chosen by the inhabitants of Washington County as their representatives, for the term of two years. Soon after the election the Governor directed the representatives to meet at Cincinnati on the 22d day of January, 1799, for the purpose of nominating ten persons, residents in the territory, and each possessed of a freehold of five hundred acres of land; from whom the president might select five, and commission them to act as a legislative council, for five years. This meeting, at an inclement season of the year, required no little labor and privation, on the part of the representatives to accomplish. The distance they had to travel, on horseback, was from two to four hundred miles, through a wilderness; carrying their provisions and blankets; camping in the woods at night, a part of the time; swimming their horses across the streams and getting along through the forest by the blazed trees, or the compass as they best could. There were no roads but bridle paths, or the old trails of the hunters. After leaving Belpre, the representatives from Marietta found no settlements until they reached the Scioto salt works, the present county seat of Jackson. The next habitation of man was at Chillicothe, where a town had been commenced two years before. From thence to Cincinnati there was no settlement, until they reached the waters of the Little Miami.

When the object of the assembly was accomplished, the governor prorogued the meeting, and directed them to assemble on the 16th of September following, and the members returned to their homes by the same laborious routes, to be again traveled over at a more temperate season of the year, and when the streams of water were at a lower stage.

The general assembly was composed of a Governor, Legislative Council, and House of Representatives. The first House of Representatives contained twenty members. Colonel Robert Oliver, from Washington County, was a member of the Council. All the acts passed by the House and Legislative Council were to be approved by the Governor before they became laws; and without his assent were nugatory.

The Governor vetoed a number of the bills passed at this session, which greatly offended the republican spirit of the house, and was doubtless the cause of the very limited powers delegated to the Governors of Ohio, under the constitution of the state, which was formed soon after. The political parties of Federalist and Republican were then unknown, and did not enter into the elections of the territory until the year 1800, or about the period of the reign of Thomas Jefferson. During this session of the legislature, a delegate was elected to represent the territory in Congress. The choice fell on W. H. Harrison, Esq., afterwards Governor of Indiana, and President of the United States. The delegate had the liberty of debating on any question, but not the right to vote.

In the year 1800 a census of the United States was taken, and the territory was found to contain forty-two thousand inhabitants. On a petition of the people, Congress, on the 30th of April, 1802, granted them the liberty of forming a constitution, and becoming a member of the confederacy. The law provided that every twelve hundred inhabitants should have one representative in the convention for forming a constitution. The election took place on the second Tuesday of October, and Washington County was entitled to four delegates, who met in convention at Chillicothe the 1st of

November, 1802. The delegates from this county were Rufus Putnam, Benjamin Ives Gilman, Ephraim Cutler and John McIntyre. After a session of twenty-nine days, they framed our present constitution, which was approved by Congress, but was never submitted to the voice of the people.

CHAPTER XVI.

In the winter following the landing of the first pioneer corps at Marietta, the directors of the Ohio Company sent out exploring parties to examine their purchase, which was as yet a *"terra incognita."* The main object of these committees was to select suitable places for the formation of their first settlements. Among the earliest and most desirable locations reported, was a tract on the right bank of the Ohio River, commencing a short distance above the mouth of the Little Kanawha, and extending down the Ohio four or five miles, terminating at the narrows, two miles above the Little Hockhocking. About a mile below the outlet of the latter stream, the river again bent to the south, inclosing a rich alluvion, extending two or three miles in length and a mile in width, where was formed another settlement, called Newbury, or the lower settlement; but included within the boundaries of Belpre. The main body of the new colony tract was divided into two portions, and known as the "upper and middle" settlements.

The lands on the river were of the richest quality; rising as they receded from the Ohio on to an elevated plain, thirty or forty feet higher than the low bottoms and extending back to the base of the hills. This plain was in some places more than half a mile in width, forming with the bottoms alluvious of nearly a mile in extent. The soil on the plain was in some places a fertile, loamy sand; in others inclined to gravel, but everywhere covered with a rich growth of forest trees, and producing fine crops of small grain.

About a mile below the Little Kanawha, this plain came into the river, presenting a lofty mural front of eighty or a hundred feet above the surface of the water. This precipitous bank is continued for half a mile, and on its brow, and for some distance back, is clothed with evergreens, being chiefly different varieties of the cedar. That portion of the plain is known by the name of "The Bluff," and is located near the head of Blennerhasset's Island, close by the landing and crossing place to the mansion erected a few years after by this celebrated man.

"The Bluff" divided the upper settlement from those below. The upper lay in a beautiful curve of the river, which formed nearly a semicircle, the periphery of which was about a mile and a half, and rose gradually from the bank of the river on to the second bottom by a natural glacis, the grade and beauty of which no art of man could excel. From the lower end of "The Bluff," the plain gradually receded from the river, leaving a strip of rich bottom land, about three miles in length, and from a quarter to a third of a mile in width. This distance, like that portion above, was laid off into farms, about forty rods wide and extending back to the hills, which rose by a moderate slope, to an elevation of an hundred feet above the surface of the plain, and were clothed with oak and hickory, to their tops. This charming location was well named "Belle-prairie," or beautiful meadow, but is now generally written Belpre.

The settlement was composed of about forty associates, who formed themselves into a company, and drew their lots after they were surveyed and platted, in the winters of 1788-9. The larger portion of the individuals who formed this association had served as officers in the late war, and when the army was disbanded, retired with a brevet promotion. To a stranger it seemed very curious that every house he passed should be occupied by a commissioned officer. No settlement ever formed west of the mountains contained so many men of real merit, sound, practical sense, and refined manners. They had been in the school of Washington, and were nearly or quite all of them personally acquainted with that great and good man.

"In this little community were found those sterling qualities which should ever form the base of the social and civil edifice, and are best calculated to perpetuate and cherish our republican institutions. Some of them had been liberally educated, and all had received the advantages of the common New England schools in early life. They were habituated to industry and economy, and brought up under the influence of morality and religion. These men had been selected to lead their countrymen to battle and to defend their rights, not for their physical strength, as of old, but for their moral standing and superior intellect. In addition to these advantages they had also received a second education in the army of the revolution, where they heard the precepts of wisdom and witnessed the examples of bravery and fortitude; learning at the same time the necessity of subordination to law and good order, in promoting the happiness and prosperity of mankind." (MSS notes of Judge Barker.)

The Belpre associates had passed the winter in Marietta, and commenced moving on to their farms early in April, 1789; several families however did not occupy their lands until the following year. Log houses, generally of small dimensions, were built on or near the bank of the river, for the convenience of water and a more free circulation of air, into which their families were moved. Then commenced the cutting down and girdling the immense forest trees which covered the rich bottoms, and lifted their lofty heads toward the clouds. A fence of rails and timber was built on the backside of their fields, next the woods, to protect their crops from the cattle, but left open on the river bank. The paths between the neighboring houses ran through their fields, or on the outside of the fence in the margin of the woods. In several places springs of pure, cool water gushed out under the banks of the river, and ran in gentle rills to the Ohio, affording a rich treat to the fortunate neighbors in the heat of summer, when compared with the warm and often turbid water of the river, the beverage of most of the early settlers on the borders of the "Belle Riviere."

Captain Zebulon King killed by the Indians

Soon after the pioneers had commenced laboring on their lands, their ardor was for a while paralyzed, and their hopes of an undisturbed and quiet possession of their new homes greatly marred, by the murder of Captain King by the Indians. His land lay in the middle settlement, and while he was busily engaged in chopping, on the 1st day of May, he was shot and scalped by two Indians, it was thought at the time, who had escaped from confinement at Fort Harmer, where they had been detained since the outrage at Duncan's Falls, the summer previous. Captain King was from Rhode Island, where his family yet remained; he intending to move them out after he had prepared a house, and raised a crop for their support. He had been an officer in the United States army, and was a most excellent man. His loss was deeply felt and lamented by all his fellow pioneers.

Famine at Belpre

Owing to the great and laborious task each man had to perform in preparing and fencing his land for the reception of the seed, it was past the middle of June before all their corn was planted. Late as it was, if the sun could have penetrated the thick branches of the girdled trees, and thoroughly warmed the earth, pushing forward the growth of the corn as it does in an open sunny exposure, there might yet have been a tolerable crop; but while the tender ears were yet in the milk, a frost early in October nipped and destroyed the hopes and the labors of the husbandman, leaving him with a scanty allowance for the winter, and the prospect of great suffering before another crop could be raised; and although two or three hundred acres had been planted in the settlement, the amount fit for use was very small.

The calamity was general throughout the region west of the mountains, and was the more severely felt, as Indian corn was their only resource for bread. In the older settlements at head waters, there was a tolerable crop of wheat and on the old and early planted fields, the corn had ripened before the appearance of the frost, so that those who had money could purchase bread for their families. But few, however, of the new settlers had the means of doing this; their cash being spent on the journey out, and for provisions since their arrival. By the middle of February the scarcity of bread stuff began to be seriously felt. Many families had no other meal for their bread than that which was made from the moldy corn, and were sometimes destitute even of this for several days in succession. Such portions of the damaged grain as could be selected, hard enough for meal, sold for nine shillings, or a dollar and fifty cents a bushel; and when ground in the hand mill and made into bread, few stomachs were able to digest it, or even retain it for a few minutes; it produced sickness and vomiting. The late Charles Devoll, Esq., one of the early settlers, but then a small boy, used to relate with much feeling his gastronomic trials with this moldy meal, made into a dish, called "sap porridge," which, when composed of sound corn meal, and the fresh saccharine juice of the maple, afforded both a nourishing and a savory food.

The family had been without bread for two days, when his father returned from Marietta, just at evening, with a scanty supply of moldy corn. The hand mill was put into immediate operation, and the meal cooked into "sap porridge," as it was then the season of sugar making. The famished children swallowed eagerly the unsavory mess, which was almost as instantly rejected; reminding us of the deadly pottage of the children of the prophet, but lacking the healing power of an Elijah to render it salutary and nutritious. Disappointed of expected relief, the poor children went supperless to bed, to dream of savory food and plenteous meals, unrealized in their waking hours.

It was during this period of want that Isaac Williams, a plain hearted, honest backwoodsman, who had been brought up on the frontiers, and lived on the Virginia shore, opposite the mouth of the Muskingum, displayed his benevolent feelings for the suffering colonists. He had opened an extensive tract of corn land three years before, and being enabled to plant early, had raised, in 1789, a large crop of several hundred bushels of sound corn. With a liberality which should ever make his name dear to the descendants of the pioneers, and to all who admire generous deeds, he now in their most pressing necessity, distributed this corn among the inhabitants, at the low rate of three shillings, or fifty cents, a bushel, the common price in plenteous years; when at the same time he was offered and urged to take a dollar and a quarter, by speculators, for his whole crop; for man has ever been disposed to fatten on the distresses of his fellow man. Turning from them with a blunt but decided refusal, he not only parted with his corn at this moderate rate, but also prudently proportioned the number of bushels, according to the number of individuals in a family. An empty purse was no bar to his generosity or the wants of the needy applicant, but he was equally supplied with him who had money, and a credit given until a more favorable season should enable him to pay the debt. Such deeds are rare in a highly civilized community, and were more common in the early settlement of the country than since. The coarse hunting shirt, and rough bear skin cap, often enclosed a tender benevolent heart, and covered a wise, thoughtful head.

Hospitality was one of the cardinal virtues with the early settlers, and no people ever practiced it more heartily and constantly than the pioneers along the borders of the Ohio. The corn of this good man supplied their wants for a season, but was all expended long before the crop of 1790 was fit for use. Articles of food were found in the natural productions of the earth, which necessity alone could have discovered. A portion of the inhabitants only had salted any meat in the preceding autumn; there being but a few hogs or cattle in the country, except here and there a cow, or a yoke of oxen, brought on by the colonists from New England. Their animal food, therefore, was mainly procured from the woods, and consisted of venison, with now and then that of the bear. The wild animals were scarce in all this region of country; having been killed or driven away by the Indians in the preceding year.

The new settlers were but little skilled in hunting, and their venison was chiefly procured from the old border settlers at Bellville, a station distant twelve or fourteen miles below, on the Virginia shore; who had been brought up in the woods. A few of the more able families hired one of these men by the month to hunt for them during the spring and summer; but their success was small, barely supplying their daily wants.

In the spring the wild deer are very thin and poor, and their flesh of an inferior quality. The river afforded an abundant supply of fish; but it so happened that but a few of the inhabitants were skilled in the art of taking them. Salt was also so scarce and dear, being eight dollars a bushel, it could hardly be afforded to cure them, so that what was caught one day must not be kept longer than the next. Fortunate was the family that had been able to save a few pounds of salt pork or bacon to boil up with the native growth of esculent plants that began early in the spring to appear in the woods.

Of these, the nettle afforded the earliest supply, which in some places grew in large patches, and whose tender tops were palatable and nutritious. The young, juicy plants of celandine afforded also a nourishing and pleasant dish. It sprang up about the old logs and fences round the clearings, especially were brush had been burnt the year before, with astonishing luxuriance; and, being early in its growth, afforded a valuable article of food before the purslain was of sufficient size for boiling.

This latter vegetable, however, was their main dependence at a later period. Wherever the soil had been broken by the planters and exposed to the sunshine, a luxuriant crop of this nutritious plant sprang up from the virgin soil, where the seed had been scattered ages before, by the Creator of all things, and had lain dormant in the earth. In spots where not a single plant of purslain was seen while covered with the forest, and probably not a shoot had grown for ages, it now sprang up as if by magic. The rich, luxuriant soil produced an abundant supply of this nourishing vegetable. When boiled with a small piece of venison and a little salt, it furnished the principal food of the inhabitants for six or eight weeks, although many lived on it without any meat for many a day.

Toward the close of their sufferings, so great was the scarcity that, in one of the most respectable and intelligent families, which happened to be rather numerous, the smaller children were kept on one boiled potato a day, and finally were reduced to half a one. The head of the family had held the office of a Major in the army of the United States, and was one of the most worthy and excellent men in the colony. His children, with their descendants, now rank among the first for influence and wealth in the state of Ohio. The mother of these famished and half starved children did all she could for their comfort, and those around her. A young man, who owned a lot adjacent to her husband's, among her other multifarious engagements, she had consented to cook for, but ate his meals at his own cabin. The bread was made of poor, musty meal; and while it was baking she always sent the children away to play, and immediately locked it up in the young man's chest, lest they should see it, and cry for a piece of that which she had no right to give them. This young man was from Boston, and educated at Cambridge College. When a few kernels of corn were dropped in grinding in the hand mill, the children picked them up, like chickens, and ate them raw.

A few of the inhabitants had cows, for which the forest, in summer, afforded ample supplies of food. Their milk assisted greatly in the support of their owners, and especially their children. In the latter part of winter, the sap of the sugar tree, boiled down with meal, made a rich, nourishing food. This tree was so abundant, that great quantities of sugar could have been made to enlarge their scanty stores of food; but the want of kettles prevented their profiting from this prolific magazine, which the God of nature has stored up for his children. By the middle of July, the new corn was in the milk, and fit for roasting and boiling; this, with the squashes and beans, ended their fears of actual starvation. So urgent was their necessity, however, that they could not wait for the vegetables to attain their usual size, before they were deemed fit for eating, but the beans, as soon as the pods were set, and the grains of corn formed in the ears, were gathered and boiled up with a little salt and meal, if they had any, into a kind of vegetable soup, which was eaten with great relish by the half starved children and their parents. As the season was remarkably favorable, the sight of the rich crop of corn was hailed as a jubilee, not only by man, but by the domestic animals, some of which had suffered equally with their masters. Even the dogs fell upon the young and tender corn at night, and devoured it with eagerness. It was sometime before they could discover this depredator of their crops. By watching, they caught the dogs in the act of tearing down and eating the corn, and were compelled to tie them up at night, until it became too hard for them.

During the whole summer, a great scarcity of animal food was felt. In August, the family of one of the most enterprising and worthy men in that suffering community had been without any meat for several days. Having one of those long barreled fowling pieces, which he had been accustomed to use along the shores and inlets of Rhode Island, he walked out into the woods, with little hopes of success. Directly he came across a fawn, or half grown deer, and at the first fire brought it to the ground. While in the act of cutting its throat, and he felt sure that all this meat was his own, he said his heart and affections rose up in a glow of gratitude and thankfulness to the Almighty, such as he had never felt before, for this unexpected and striking interposition of His Providence, in this his time of need. This man had been several times in battle, and escaped without a wound; and yet no event in his previous life had awakened his gratitude like this. It was the first and only deer he ever killed. The meat served to supply their wants for several days.

The bountiful crops of the following autumn soon made amends for their long lent, of more than three times forty days continuance. The deer and turkeys that now came round their fields in numerous flocks, supplied them with the greatest abundance of animal food; causing them to forget the sufferings of the past, and lift their hearts in gratitude to that God, who had thus bountifully spread a table for them in the wilderness. Like the quails about the camp of the Israelites, the turkeys came up to their very doors in such multitudes, that none but the most skeptical could fail of seeing the hand of a kind Providence, driving them from their coverts in the forest so near their dwellings, that they could be killed or taken within their fields. They were so abundant, and so little accustomed the sight of man, that the boys killed many of them with clubs, and the aid of their dogs. This year terminated their trials and sufferings from the want of food. All the subsequent years were crowned with abundant crops, and their greatest troubles arose from the danger of being killed by the Indians, while cultivating their fields. But habit soon inured them to trials of this kind; and they went forth to their labors with the consciousness that they were better able to contend with and overcome the savages, than to strive against the allotments of Providence.

Two boys killed at Neil's Station

In August the settlement was alarmed by the killing of two boys by the Indians, at Neil's Station, a small stockade on the Little Kanawha, a mile from its mouth and in the immediate vicinity of Belpre. It was alarming as it manifested the hostility of the Indians, who might at any time fall upon and kill the inhabitants, when they least expected it, and for which they were not prepared, as they pretended to be at peace with the whites. The boys were twelve and fifteen years of age, and belonged to a German family that lived in a small cabin, about forty rods above Neil's blockhouse. They had been down to the station Saturday afternoon, and just at night, on their way home, went into the edge of the woods, on the outside of a cornfield, to look for the cows. The Indians were lying in ambush near the path, and killed them with their tomahawks, without firing a gun. Their bodies were not found until the next morning, but as they did not come home, their parents were fearful of their fate. That night the Indians attempted to set fire to the blockhouse by enclosing a brand of fire in dry poplar bark, and pushing it through a port hole. It was, however, discovered and extinguished, by a woman who lay, in bed near the port hole, before it communicated to the house. In the morning the alarm was given, and a party of armed men went out from Belpre, and assisted in burying the two boys. The Indians departed without doing any other damage.

Mill at Little Hockhocking

In the spring of the year 1790, the necessity of building a grist mill became so apparent, that some of the enterprising inhabitants, among them Griffin Green, Esq., and Robert Bradford, entered into the laborious and expensive undertaking. Their bread stuff thus far had been ground on the hand mill. Two mill wrights from Red stone, by the name of Baldwin and Applegate, who had assisted at the mill on Wolf Creek, were employed as architects. The Ohio Company made a donation of one hundred and sixty acres of land at the mill site, to encourage the work. The dam was erected and the timbers prepared for the mill, by the 1st of January following, when the Indian war broke out, and the work was suspended, and not again resumed until after its close. The spot chosen was on a southern bend of the stream, where it approaches within a mile and a half of the Ohio. A broad, low gap in the river hills, made it easy of access from the settlements. The check put to the work by the war was a sad disappointment to the inhabitants, who had again to labor at the hand mill, until the autumn of the following year, when the floating mill built by Captain Devoll relieved them of one of their most grievous burdens. At the close of the war, the work was completed, and the site has been occupied by a mill to this day.

CHAPTER XVII

Indian war

The suffering and distress attendant on a famine had no sooner disappeared, than they were assailed by a new calamity. The county court of quarter sessions met at Marietta on the first Monday in January. A considerable number of the most active men were called there to attend as jurors, witnesses, &c. As it was a laborious task to get there by water, in canoes, many of them went up on Saturday and Sunday, preceding. The court had barely opened on Monday, when word was brought of the sacking and slaughter at Big Bottom. It was immediately adjourned, and the men returned to their homes full of anxiety for the fate of their own families. Notice had been sent to the settlers at Belpre, from Wolf Creek Mills, at the same time it was sent to Marietta. The women and children suffered much from fear, expecting every hour that the Indians would attack them.

The inhabitants were scattered along on the river bank, living in their log cabins, without any preparation for defense, not expecting an Indian war, as a treaty had been made with them only two years before. Captain Jonathan Stone, at the upper settlement, had built a small blockhouse for his dwelling and into this the women and children were gathered on Monday night. On Tuesday there was a general muster of all the heads of families, to consult on what was best to be done. They decided on collecting them together, about thirty in number, at the middle settlement, where Colonel Cushing and Colonel Battelle had already built two large log houses, and erected a spacious, strong, and well arranged garrison, sufficient for the accommodation of all the inhabitants. The spot selected was on the bank of the river, about half a mile below "The Bluff," and nearly against the center of Backus's Island. A swamp about six rods back from the Ohio protected its rear, while the river defended the front. The upper and lower ends opened into a smooth, level bottom, suitable for a road by which to enter or depart from the garrison. The work was commenced the first week in January, and was prosecuted with the utmost energy, as their lives, apparently, depended on its completion.

As fast as the blockhouses were built, the families moved into them. They were thirteen in number, arranged in two rows, with a wide street between, as shown in the engraving. The basement story was in general twenty feet square, and the upper about twenty-two feet, thus projecting over the lower one, and forming a defense from which to protect the doors and windows below, in an attack. They were built of round logs a foot in diameter, and the interstices nicely chinked and pointed with mortar. The doors and window shutters were made of thick oak planks, or puncheons, and secured with stout bars of wood on the inside. The larger timbers were hauled with ox-teams, of which they had several yokes, while the lighter for the roofs, gates, &c, were dragged along on hand sleds, with ropes, by the men. The drawing was much facilitated by a few inches of snow, which covered the ground. The pickets were made of quartered oak timber, growing on the plain back of the garrison, formed from trees about a foot in diameter, fourteen feet in length, and set four feet deep in the ground, leaving them ten feet high, over which no enemy could mount without a ladder. The smooth side was set outward, and the palisades strengthened and kept in their places by stout ribbons, or wall pieces, pinned to them with inch treenails on the inside. The spaces between the houses were filled up with pickets, and occupied three or four times the width of the houses, forming a continuous wall, or enclosure, about eighty rods in length and six rods wide. The palisades on the river side filled the whole space, and projected over the edge of the bank, leaning on rails and posts set to support them. They were sloped in this manner for the admission of air during the heat of summer. Gates of stout timber were placed in the east and west ends of the .garrison, opening in the middle, ten feet wide, for the ingress and egress of teams, and to take in the cattle in an attack. A still wider gate opened near the center of the back wall, for hauling in wood, and all were secured with strong, heavy bars. Two or three smaller ones, called water gates, were placed on the river side, as all their water was procured from the Ohio. When there were signs of Indians discovered by the spies, the domestic animals were driven within the gates at night. At sunset all the avenues were closed.

Every house was filled with families and as new settlers arrived occasionally during the war, some houses contained three or four. The corner blockhouses, on the back side of the garrison, were provided with watch towers, running up eight feet above the roof, where a sentry was constantly kept. When the whole was completed, the inmates of the station called it "Farmer's Castle," a name very appropriate, as it was built and occupied by farmers. The directors of the Ohio Company, with their characteristic beneficence, paid the expense of erecting three of the blockhouses, and the money was distributed among the laborers. The view of the castle from the Ohio River was very picturesque and imposing; looking like a small fortified city amidst the surrounding wilderness. During the war, there were about seventy able bodied men mustered on the roll for military duty, and the police within assumed that of a regularly besieged fort, as in fact it was a great portion of the time, the Indians watching in small parties, more or less constantly, for a chance to kill or capture the inhabitants when they least expected it. At sunrise the roll was called by the orderly sergeant, and if any man had overslept in the morning, or neglected to answer to his name, the penalty was fixed at the cutting out the stump of a tree level with the ground, they being thickly scattered over the surface enclosed within the castle. This penalty was so rigidly exacted, that few stumps remained at the close of the war. A regular commander was appointed, with suitable subalterns.

Farmer's Castle
Belpre, Ohio
From a sketch by C.W. Elliott

Major Nathan Goodale was the first Captain, and held that post until he removed into his own garrison in 1793, when Colonel Cushing took the command. The flag staff stood a few yards west of the back gate, near the house of Colonel Cushing, on which floated the stars and stripes of the union. Near the flag staff, was a large, iron Howitz, or swivel gun, mounted on a platform incased in wood, hooped with iron bands and painted to resemble a six pounder. It was so adjusted as to revolve on a socket, and thus point to any part of the works. During the spring and summer months, when there was any probability of Indians being in the vicinity, it was fired regularly, morning and evening. It could be distinctly heard for several miles around, especially up and down the Ohio; the banks and hills adjacent, re-echoing the report in a wonderful manner. This practice no doubt kept the Indians in awe, and warned them not to approach a post whose inmates were habitually watchful, and so well prepared to defend themselves. Around this spot, it was customary for the loungers and newsmongers to assemble, to discuss the concerns of the castle, and tell the news of the day, while passing away the many idle hours that must necessarily fall to the lot of a community confined to such narrow limits. It was also the rallying point in case of an assault, and the spot where the muster roll was called morning and evening. The spies and rangers here made report of the discoveries to the Commandant; in short it was the "*place d' armes*" of Farmer's Castle.

In the upper room of every house was kept a large cask, or hogshead, constantly filled with water, to be used only in case of a fire, either from accident, or from an attack by the Indians. It was a part of the duty of the officer of the day to inspect every house, and see that the cask was well filled. Another duty was to prevent any stack of grain or fodder being placed so near the castle as to endanger the safety of the buildings, should the Indians set them on fire, or afford them a shelter in time of assault. They also inspected the gates, pickets, and houses, to see that all were in repair and well secured at night. They received dispatches from abroad, or sent out expresses to the other stations. Their authority was absolute, and the government strictly military.*

* Weeping Willow.—The largest willow in this part of the state now marks the site of Farmer's Castle. It was, planted when a small twig by E. Battelle, in the year 1793, at the northeast corner of the garrison, near his father's blockhouse. In the year 1844, it measured fourteen and a half feet in circumference, at ten or twelve feet from the ground, and still larger higher up, where the branches put forth. The top covers an area of sixty-five feet in diameter. It is a noble monument of by-gone days, and the father of willows in Ohio.

The greatest and principal danger to the settlers arose from their exposure to attack while engaged during the spring and summer months in working in their fields. The clearings of some of the inhabitants lay at the distance of three miles, while others were within rifle shot of the garrison. Those could only be visited in companies of fifteen or twenty men. Their exposure was not confined to their actual engagement in their fields, but chiefly in going to and returning from their labor. While at their work, sentries were constantly placed in the edge of the adjacent forest; and flanking parties examined the ground when marching through the woods, between the upper and lower settlements. It was a great labor to transport their crops when harvested so long a distance, although it was chiefly done by water carriage.

For these reasons, in the second year of the war, it was decided as best for them to divide into smaller communities. Accordingly, a strong, stockaded garrison was built, three miles above, called "Stone's Garrison," and one a mile below, called "Goodale's Garrison." To these several of the families removed whose lands lay adjacent, and continued to occupy them to the close of the war. Fresh emigrants, however, continually arrived, so that Farmer's Castle remained crowded with inhabitants.

The crops of the settlers were confined chiefly to Indian corn, beans, potatoes, turnips and pumpkins, with a little wheat and rye. They also raised hemp and flax, for domestic use. Until the erection of a "floating mill," in the fall of 1791, a noted era in the annals of Belpre, their meal was all ground in the primitive hand mill. But little wheat was raised until after the close of the war, when mills were built on the creeks. By the aid of a bolting machine, turned by hand in the garrison, the floating mill furnished the flour for many a noble loaf of bread, and the crusts of numerous pumpkin pies, the only fruit afforded for this use at that day.

The winter following the first occupation of Farmer's Castle was one of severe privation in the article of meat. Late in the fall of 1791, the fat hogs were all collected and slaughtered in company, and hung up in an outhouse near the garrison, to cool and dry through the night. During this period it accidentally took fire, and burnt up all their winter store of meat, to their great loss and disappointment. A number of other hogs were killed and destroyed by the Indians, which had been left at their out-lots and fattened in pens. These were visited by their owners once in three or four days, and fed from corn left in the field for that purpose.

Under these discouraging circumstances, the inhabitants contributed all the money they could gather, which was but a small sum, and dispatched two active young men, by land, to "Redstone," to purchase a supply of salt meat and a few barrels of flour. It was a hazardous journey, not only in danger from Indians, who, since St. Clair's defeat, were still more harassing to the inhabitants, but also from the inclemency of the season, it being the fore part of December. They, however, reached head waters unmolested, made their purchases, and were ready to descend the river, when it closed with ice.

In the mean time nothing was heard from the two messengers by the inhabitants at the castle, and the winter wore away in uncertainty as to their fate. Some thought they had decamped with the money, and others that they had been killed by the Indians, as the news of St. Clair's defeat reached them soon after their departure; while the more reflecting were firm in their confidence of the integrity of the young men, and attributed their silence to a want of opportunity to send them a letter, as the river was closed, and no regular mail was then established.

The last of February the ice broke up in the Ohio, with a flood of water that covered the banks, and inundated the ground on which the garrison was built. Early in March the young men arrived, with a small Kentucky boat, loaded with provisions, and entering the garrison by the upper gate, moored their ark at the door of the commandant, to the great joy and relief of the inhabitants.

After the disastrous events of the campaign of 1791, a small guard of United States troops was stationed at Belpre, usually consisting of a Corporal and five men. Their principal duty was to watch the garrison, while the inhabitants were abroad in their fields, or at any other employment. They also served in rotation with the inhabitants in standing sentry in the watch towers.

John L. Shaw, well known in Marietta for many years after the war as an eccentric character, of great wit and powers of mimicry, was Corporal of the Guard for a time, and a great favorite with the inmates of the castle. He was subsequently a sergeant in Captain Haskell's Company from Rochester, Mass. During Wayne's campaign, while stationed at "Fort Recovery," he had a narrow escape from the Indians. In October, 1793, contrary to orders, he ventured out into the forest near the fort, to gather hickory nuts, and had set his musket against a tree. While busily engaged, with his head near the ground, he heard a slight rustling of the leaves close to him. Rising suddenly from his stooping posture, he saw an Indian within a few yards, his tomahawk raised ready for a throw, while at the same time he called out in broken English, "prisoner, prisoner!" Shaw having no relish for captivity sprang to his gun, cocked it, and faced round, just as the Indian hurled his hatchet. It was aimed at his head, but by a rapid inclination of the body, it missed its destination, and lodged the whole width of the blade in the muscles of the loins. By the time he had gained an erect position, his enemy was within two steps of him with his scalping knife. Shaw now fired his gun with such effect as to kill him on the spot, and so near its muzzle as to set his calico hunting shirt on fire. Before he could reload, another Indian rushed upon him, and he was obliged to trust to his heels in flight. He ran in the direction of the fort, but a fresh Indian started up before him, and he was obliged to take to the woods. Being in the prime of life and a very active runner, he distanced all his pursuers, leaping logs and other obstructions, which the Indians had to climb over or go round. After fifteen or twenty minutes of hot pursuit, which the shrill yells of the Indians served to quicken, he reached within a short distance of the fort, and met a party of men coming out to his rescue. They had heard the shot, and at once divined the cause, as no firing was allowed near the fort, except at the enemy, or in self defense. Shaw's life was saved from the rifle of the savages, only by their desire of taking a prisoner, to learn the intentions of General Wayne.

Hostility of the Indians

The first actual demonstration of hostility, after the inhabitants had taken possession of their new garrison, was on the 12th of March, by some of the same party who had attacked the settlement at Waterford, and killed Captain Rogers at Marietta. The settlers who had evacuated their farms, of necessity left a part of their cattle and fodder on the premises; while those near the castle were visited daily to feed and milk their cows. On this morning Waldo Putnam, a son of Colonel Israel Putnam, and grandson of the old veteran General, in company with Nathaniel Little, visited the possession of the former, half a mile below, to milk and feed the cows. While Waldo was in the posture of milking, Little, who kept guard, discovered an Indian in the act of leveling his gun at him. He instantly cried out "Indians, Indians!" Just as the gun cracked, Waldo sprang to one side, and the ball struck the ground under the cow where he was sitting. They instantly ran for the garrison, when three Indians sprang out from the edge of the woods and joined in the pursuit, firing their rifles at the fugitives as they ran, but happily without effect. They were soon within a short distance of the garrison, when a party of men rushed out to their rescue, and the Indians retreated, after killing several of the cattle, and among them a yoke of oxen belonging to Captain Benjamin Miles, which were noted for their size, being fifteen hands high and large in proportion.

In the subsequent year, while Messrs. Putnam and Little were at the same place, very early in the morning, a small dog that was a few rods in advance gave notice of danger by barking violently at some hidden object which his manner led them to suspect must be an Indian. Thus warned they began slowly to retreat and look carefully for their enemy. The Indians, three or four in number, watching them from their covert behind a brush fence, now jumped from their hiding place and gave chase. The two white men quickened their speed, and crossed a deep gully which lay in their path on a log, barely in time to prevent the Indians from cutting off their retreat. They had examined the ground, and expected to take them prisoners or kill them at this place. Seeing them past the defile they now commenced firing at them, but missed their object. In the ardour of pursuit, they rushed up to within a short distance of the castle, when Harlow Bull, a fierce little warrior, who had just risen from bed, and was only partly dressed, heard the firing, and rushed out at the gate with his rifle and discharged it at the Indians, at the same time returning their war whoop with a yell nearly as terrific as their own. Several of the soldiers soon after appeared in the field, when the Indians retreated to the forest, greatly disappointed in their expected victims. No pursuit was made by the garrison, as their object was not so much to kill the Indians, as to defend themselves.

After the fugitives were safe within the walls, considerable alarm was for a time felt for Major Bradford, who had gone out with them, but fell a good way behind his company, on account of a lame foot, from a recent wound. He had nearly reached the gully, or defile, when the Indians begun the pursuit, and knowing he could not keep pace with the others, he jumped down the bank of the river near which he was hobbling along, before he was seen by the Indians; and keeping under cover of its shelter, he reached the garrison unnoticed, and came in at one of the water gates. For a few minutes his family was fully persuaded that he was killed, as his companions could give no account of him.

Death of Benoni Hurlburt by the Indians

On the 28th of September, 1791, Joshua Fleehart and Benoni Hurlburt, who had both been brought up on the frontiers, and accustomed from boyhood to a hunter's life, left the garrison in a canoe to hunt and visit their traps near the mouth of the little Hockhocking, distant about three miles below. Fleehart was a celebrated hunter and trapper. Like many other backwoodsmen he preferred following the chase for a living to that of cultivating the earth. Numbers of them depended on the woods for their clothing as well as their food, being in this respect very much like the savages. Hurlbut's family, from the oldest down to the youngest, were clothed in dressed deer skins. They had hunted lately a good deal together, and supplied the garrison with fresh meat. On their way down, as they passed the narrows above the mouth of the creek, the two hunters were strongly induced to land and shoot some turkeys which they heard gobbling on the side of the hill, a few rods from the river. It was a common practice with the Indians, when in the vicinity of the whites, to imitate the notes of this bird, to call out some of the unwary settlers within reach of their rifles. After listening a few moments, the nice, discriminating ear of Fleehart in such sounds satisfied him that they were made by Indians. Hurlburt did not believe it; but was finally induced not to land, lest it might be so.

They proceeded on, and entered the mouth of the creek, where his companion landed and traveled along in the edge of the woods in search of game, while Fleehart paddled the canoe further up the stream. As they had seen no more signs of Indians, they concluded that the gobbling this time was done by the turkeys themselves. In a short time after Hurlburt left the canoe, the report of a rifle was heard, which Fleehart at once knew was not that of his companion, and concluded was the shot of an Indian. He landed the canoe on the opposite shore, and running up the bank secreted himself in a favorable spot to fire on the Indians should they approach to examine the creek for the canoe. He directly heard a, little dog that belonged to his companion in fierce contest with the Indians, trying to defend the body of his master; but they soon silenced him with a stroke of the tomahawk. After watching more than an hour, so near that he could hear the Indians converse, and the groans of the dying man, but out of his sight and the reach of his rifle, the Indians being too cautious to approach where they expected danger, he entered his canoe and returned to the garrison, which he reached a little after dark, and reported the fate of his companion.

The subsequent events render it probable, that the Indians had seen them on their way down, and failing to induce them to land by imitating the call of the turkey, through the caution of Fleehart, had watched their future course, and running across the point of land between the Ohio and the Hockhocking, were ready to fire upon Hurlburt as he walked leisurely along looking for game. He had often been warned of the danger attending his trapping excursions by the cautious old soldiers of the garrison; but having been acquainted with Indian warfare, he did not look upon them with the dread of a New England man, but always said *"he was not afraid of any Indian."*

The next morning a party of men, conducted by Fleehart, went down by water, and found him dead and scalped on the ground where he fell, with the body of the faithful dog by his side. They brought him up to the castle, where he was buried.

Mr. Hurlburt was over sixty years old, and had moved into the country from Pennsylvania, in the fall of 1788 and lived for a time in Marietta. He served as hunter to a party of Ohio Company surveyors in 1789, and was esteemed as an honest, worthy man. He was the first man killed in Belpre after the war broke out.

CHAPTER XVIII.

Transactions at Belpre

The death of Mr. Hurlburt was a source of additional terror and dread to the elderly females in the garrison, whose fears of the Indians kept them in constant alarm, lest their own husbands or sons should fall a prey to the rifle or tomahawk of the savages. They had but little quiet except in the winter, during which period the Indians rarely made inroads, or lay watching about the garrisons. But as soon as the spring began to open, and the wild geese were seen in flocks steering their course to the north, and the frogs heard piping in the swamp, they might invariably be expected lurking in the vicinity. So constantly was this the case, that the elder females and mothers, with the more timid part of the community, never greeted this season of the year with the hilarity and welcome so common in all parts of the world, and so desirable as releasing us from the gloom and storms of winter. They preferred that season to any other, as they then felt that their children and themselves were in a manner safe from the attack of their dreaded foe. They, therefore, regretted its departure, and viewed the budding of the trees and the opening of the wild flowers with saddened feelings, as the harbingers of evil, listening to the song of the blue bird and the martin with cheerless hearts, as preludes to the war cry of the savage.

Much of our comfort and happiness depends on association; and though surrounded with all that the heart may crave, or our tastes desire, yet the constant dread of some expected evil will destroy all peace of mind, and turn what otherwise might be joy into sorrow. The barking of the watch dogs at night was another source of terror, as it was associated with the thought that some savage foe was lurking in the vicinity. The more timid females, when thus awakened in the night, would rise upon the elbow and listen with anxious care for the sound of the war whoop, or the report of the rifle of the watchful sentry; and when they again fell into a disturbed slumber, the nervous excitement led them to dream of some murderous deed, or appalling danger. Several amusing incidents are related of the alarms in the garrison from the screams of persons when asleep, and dreaming that they were attacked by Indians. Amid the peace and quiet of our happy times, we can hardly realize the mental suffering of that distressing period.

Mutual Insurance Society

Soon after the commencement of the war, the inhabitants who owned cattle and hogs formed themselves into a society for the mutual insurance of each other's stock, against the depredation of the Indians; and also for carrying on their agricultural labors. Each one was accountable for any loss, in proportion to the amount he owned. For this purpose the animals were appraised at their cash value, and recorded in a book by the secretary. Quite a number of cattle and hogs were killed or driven away by the savages during the war, the value of which was directly made up to the owners by the company. Horses, they did not attempt to keep, during the war, as they were sure to be stolen, and were a means of inviting the Indians into the settlement. It was a wise and salutary arrangement, and found to be very useful in equalizing the burdens and losses of a community who had located themselves in the wilderness, and had to encounter not only the toil and privations of reclaiming their new lands from the forest, but also to contend with one of the most subtle, revengeful, and wily enemies the world ever produced.

The leading men in Belpre had been acquainted during their service in the army, at a time which tried men's souls, and they felt a degree of kindness and interest in each other's welfare not to be found in any other community. Their mutual dangers and sufferings bound them still closer together in the bonds of friendship. There was also an amount of intelligence and good sense, rarely found in so small a number, as will be more distinctly shown in the biographical sketches attached to this work.

Floating mill

Early in the summer of 1791, the settlers being disappointed in completing the mill commenced on the little Hockhocking, by the Indian war, concluded to build what might be called a "floating mill." This could be anchored out in the river, and be safe from destruction by Indians. The labor of grinding corn on a hand mill, for a community of more than one hundred and fifty persons, was a task only known to those who have tried it. Griffin Greene, Esq., one of the Ohio Company directors, and also an associate in

Farmer's Castle, had traveled in France and Holland three or four years before, and in the latter country had seen a mill erected on boats and the machinery moved by the current. He mentioned the fact to Captain Jonathan Devoll, an ingenious mechanic, of ardent temperament, and resolute to accomplish anything that would benefit his fellow men; and although Mr. Green had not inspected the foreign mill so as to give any definite description, yet the bare suggestion of such a fact was sufficient for Captain Devoll, whose mechanical turn of mind immediately devised the machinery required to put it in operation. A company was formed and the stock divided into twelve shares, of which Captain Devoll took one third, and Mr. Green about a fourth; the rest was divided among five other persons. When finished it cost fifty-one pounds eight shillings, Massachusetts currency, according to the old bill of expenditures now in the family. The mill was erected on two boats; one of them five, the other ten feet wide and forty-five feet long. The smaller one was made of the trunk of a large hollow sycamore tree, and the larger, of timber and plank, like a flat boat. They were placed eight feet apart, and fastened firmly together by beams, running across the boats. The smaller boat on the outside supported one end of the shaft of the water wheel, and the larger boat the other, in which was placed the mill stones and running gear, covered with a tight frame building or mill house, for the protection of the grain and meal, and the comfort of the miller. The space between the boats was covered with planks, forming a deck, fore and aft of the water wheel. It was turned by the natural current of the water, and was put into motion, or "cheeked", by pulling up or pushing down a set of boards, similar to a gate, in front of the wheel. It could grind from twenty-five to fifty bushels of grain in twenty-four hours, according to the strength of the current. The larger boat was fastened by a chain cable to an anchor made of timbers and filled with stones, and the smaller one by a grape vine to the same anchor. The mill was placed in a rapid portion of the Ohio, about the middle of Backus's Island, a few rods from the shore, and in sight of the castle. The current here was strong, and the position safe from Indians. With the aid of a bolting cloth in the garrison, turned by hand, very good flour was made, when they had any wheat. The day of its completion was a kind of jubilee to the inmates of the castle, as it relieved them from the slavish labor of the hand mill, which literally fulfilled the prediction to Adam, *"in the sweat of thy brow shalt thou eat thy bread."* The floating mill was a great relief to the settlers, and was visited by all the settlers on both sides of the Ohio, for the distance of twenty miles, in their canoes, the only mode of transportation at a period when there were neither roads or bridges in the country.

This settlement was begun at the same time with that at Belpre, considered a part of it, and called "the Lower Settlement." The location was six miles below "Farmer's Castle," and was commenced by about fourteen associates. On the breaking out of hostilities, the 2d of January, 1791, they left their new clearings and joined the garrison at Belpre. Finding it out of their power to cultivate their lands at so great a distance, early in the spring of 1792, the men returned and built two blockhouses, with a few cabins, and enclosed the whole with a stockade, on the bank of the river, opposite to a spot called "Newbury Bar," and moved back their effects, It now contained four or five families, and eight single men; in all, about twenty souls.

A man by the name of Brown, from head waters, with his wife and four children, had recently joined the settlement, and commenced clearing a piece of land, about eighty rods from the garrison. On Sunday, the 15th of March, it being a mild and pleasant day, his wife went out to see him set some young fruit trees they had brought with them. Not apprehending any danger from the Indians so near the garrison, she took along with her the children, carrying a sucking infant in her arms, and leading another child of two years old by the hand; while Persis Dunham, a girl of fourteen years, the daughter of widow Dunham, and a great favorite with the settlers, for her pleasant disposition, kind, conciliating manners, and beautiful person, led another child, and the fourth loitered some distance behind them. When they arrived within a short space of Mr. Brown, two Indians sprang out from their concealment; one of whom seized Mrs. Brown by the arm, and sunk his tomahawk in her head. As she fell, he aimed a blow at the infant, which cut a large gash in the side of the forehead, and nearly severed one ear. He next dashed his hatchet into the head of the child she was leading, and with his knife tore off their scalps. The other Indian fell upon Persis and the remaining child, sinking his tomahawk into their heads, and tearing off their scalps with the remorseless fury of a demon.

The men in the garrison, hearing their screams, rushed out to their rescue; but only saved the little fellow who loitered behind, and commenced firing at the Indians. Brown, whom they had not discovered before, now came in sight, but, being without arms, could render no assistance. The Indians immediately gave chase to him, but he escaped and reached the garrison. As the men were not familiar with Indian warfare, no effective pursuit was made; whereas, had there been several backwoodsmen among them, they would doubtless have been followed and killed.

When the bodies of the slain were removed to the garrison, the poor little infant was found in a state of insensibility, lying by the side of its dead mother. It finally revived, and was nursed with great tenderness by the females of "Farmer's Castle," where the child was soon after brought, whose deepest sympathies were awakened by its motherless condition, pallid features, and ghastly wound, which had nearly deprived it of all its blood. By great care it was again restored to health, and the father, with his two remaining children, returned to his relations. The 1st of April the settlement at Newbury was again evacuated, and not repossessed until the close of the war.

Scarlet Fever

In the summer of 1792, in addition to their other calamities, the inhabitants of Farmer's Castle were assailed with scarlet fever and putrid sore throat. It commenced without any known cause or exposure to contagion. The disease was sudden and violent in its attack and very fatal; some of the children dying in twenty four hours. It was of a very putrid type, and the seat of the disease confined chiefly to the fauces and throat, many having no scarlet efflorescence on the skin. It continued for several weeks, and overwhelmed this little isolated community with consternation and grief. Medicine seemed to have little or no effect in arresting the progress, or checking the fatal termination of the disease. It gradually subsided, after carrying off ten or fifteen children. Like many other epidemics it was most fatal in the first few days of its appearance. It was confined to Belpre, while Marietta and the other settlements escaped its ravages. In the summer and autumn the inhabitants were more or less affected with intermittent fevers of a mild type, to the production of which, no doubt, the swamp back of the garrison afforded a large share of the malaria. Bilious Fever also, occasionally attacked the new settlers, but the disease was seldom fatal, and gave way to simple remedies.

Schools

No people ever paid more attention to the education of their children, than the descendants of the puritans. One of the first things done by the settlers at Belpre, after they had erected their own log dwellings, was to make provision for teaching their children the rudiments of learning, reading, writing and arithmetic. Bathsheba Rouse, the daughter of John Rouse, one of the emigrants from near New Bedford, Massachusetts, was employed in the summer of 1789, to teach the small children, and for several subsequent summers, she taught a school in Farmer's Castle. She is believed to be the first female who ever kept a school within the present bounds of Ohio.

During the winter months, a male teacher was employed for the larger boys and young women. Daniel Mayo was the first teacher in Farmer's Castle. He came from Boston, a young man, in the family of Colonel Battelle, in the fall of the year 1788, and was a graduate of Cambridge University. The school was kept in a large room of Colonel Battelle's blockhouse. He was a teacher for several winters, and during the summer worked at clearing and cultivating his lot of land. He married a daughter of Colonel Israel Putnam, and after the war, settled at Newport, Kentucky, where his descendants now live. Jonathan Baldwin, another educated man, also kept school a part of the time during their confinement in garrison. These schools had no public funds as at this day to aid them, but were supported from the hard earnings of the honest pioneers.

Religious exercises

The larger portion of the time during the war, religious service was kept up on the Sabbath, in "Farmer's Castle," by Colonel E. Battelle. The people assembled at the large lower room in his blockhouse, which was provided with seats. Notice was given of the time when the exercises began, by his son Ebenezer, than a lad of fifteen or sixteen years old, and a drummer to the garrison, marching the length of the castle, up and down, beating the drum. The inmates understood the call as readily from the "tattoo," as from the sound of a bell; and they generally attended very regularly. The meeting was opened with prayer, sometimes read from the church service, and sometimes delivered extempore, followed by singing, at which all the New Englanders were more or less proficient. A sermon was then read from the writings of some standard divine, and the meeting closed with singing and prayer. There was usually but one service a day. Occasionally, during the war, the Rev. Daniel Story visited them and preached on the Sabbath; but these calls were rare, owing to the danger of intercourse between the settlements from the Indians. After the war his attendance was more regular, about once a month; on the other three Sabbaths, religious services were still kept up by Colonel

Battelle at a house erected on "The Bluff," which accommodated both the upper and middle settlements, until the time of their being able to build other and more convenient places of worship. This holy day was generally observed and honored by the inhabitants; but not with that strictness common in New England. Very few of the leading men at that day were members of any church; yet all supported religion, morality, and good order.

A list of the families which lived in "Farmer's Castle"
at Belpre, in the year 1792.

By looking at the sketch of the garrison, the reader will see a number attached to each blockhouse, and thus recognize the domicile of every family.

Farmer's Castle
Belpre, Ohio
From a sketch by C.W. Elliott

No. 1. Colonel Ebenezer Battelle, wife, and four children, viz: Cornelius, Ebenezer, Thomas and Louisa. Cornelius and Thomas, soon after the close of the war, went to the West, Indies, where a rich uncle put them into lucrative employments. Thomas married a daughter of Governor Livingston, of New York, and Cornelius the daughter of a rich planter. Louisa remained single and resided in Boston, the birth place of her mother. Ebenezer settled on a farm in Newport, in this county, and has a numerous family of children, noted for their intelligence and respectability.

No. 2. Captain William James, wife, and ten children, from New England, viz: Susan, Anna, Esther, Hannah, Abigail and Polly; William, John, Thomas and Simeon. William was killed by the Indians at the sacking of Big Bottom. The others all married and settled in the vicinity, either in Ohio or Virginia.

Also, Isaac Barker, wife, and eight children, from near New Bedford, Massachusetts. Michael, Isaac, Joseph, William, and Timothy; Anna, Rhoda, and Nancy. All of whom subsequently married and raised families, in Athens County, where Mr. Barker settled after the war.

Also, Daniel Cogswell, wife, and five children. John, Abigail, Peleg, Job, and Daniel. He was noticed for his eccentricity and love of fun. Settled after the war, below Little Hockhocking, where the children now live.

No. 3. Captain Jonathan Stone, wife, and three children, from Massachusetts, viz: Benjamin Franklin, Samuel, and Rufus Putnam — two others born after the war. He lived in the upper room, while the lower was used for a work shop. Benjamin Franklin settled in Belpre, where the children now live; Samuel in Licking county, and Rufus Putnam near McConnellsville, on a farm, where his children now reside.

No. 4. Colonel Nathaniel Cushing, wife and six children, from Boston, Massachusetts, viz: Nathaniel, Henry, Varnum, Thomas, Sally and Elizabeth. These all married and settled in Ohio. Three other daughters were born after the war.

Also, Captain Jonathan Devoll, wife, and six children, lived in the upper room of the same building, from Howland's ferry, Rhode Island, viz: Henry, Charles, Barker, Francis, Sally and Nancy, with a nephew, Christopher Devoll, whom he adopted when a child. He was the son of Silas Devoll, captain of marines on board the ship Alfred, under Commodore Abraham Whipple. He was taken prisoner, and died in the prison ship, at New York. Christopher acted as a spy for some months near the close of the war. After the peace, he returned to Rhode Island, and followed the sea.

No. 5, contained three families, viz: Isaac Pierce, wife, and three children, Samuel, Joseph, and Phebe. Joseph settled in Dayton, Ohio, and held some of the most responsible stations; Samuel became a sailor; Phebe married and settled also in Dayton. Nathaniel Little, wife, and one child; he settled in Newport, where some of the children now live. Joseph Barker, wife, and one child; Joseph, born in Belpre; after the war he settled on a farm, six miles up the Muskingum. He held some of the highest offices in the county; raised a numerous family of children, who rank among the most useful and intelligent citizens in the country.

No. 6. Major Nathan Goodale, wife, and seven children, Betsy, Cynthia, Sally, Susan, Henrietta, Timothy, and Lincoln. Henrietta died of the small pox; Timothy was a young man, and served a part of the time as a ranger. He died soon after the war. The daughters all married and settled in Ohio. Lincoln studied medicine, but afterwards entered into trade and settled in Columbus, where he became distinguished for his wealth, many amiable qualities, and especially his affectionate kindness to his more dependent relatives.

No. 7, in the south-west corner of the garrison, contained three families, viz: A. W. Putnam, wife, and one child. William Pitt, born in the garrison; he married the daughter of Daniel Loring, Esq. Also, D. Loring, wife, and seven children, Israel, Rice, and Jesse, Luba, Bathsheba, Charlotte, and Polly; Israel was a young man, and after the war settled near Gibson's Fort, Miss., where he became very wealthy in lands; Rice and Jesse settled in Belpre, on farms; Rice held the office of Associate Judge of the Court of Common Pleas, and Jesse was Sheriff of the county several years. The daughters all married and settled in Ohio, where their descendants now live. Major Oliver Rice lived in the family of Mr. Loring. Captain Benjamin Miles, wife, and five children, lived in the same blockhouse, from Rutland, Mass., viz: Benjamin Buckminster and Hubbard, twin brothers, William, Tappan, and Polly. Benjamin Buckminster settled in Athens, and followed merchandise, Tappan became a preacher of the gospel; Hubbard settled in Illinois; and William and Polly lived in Belpre, all married, with numerous descendants.

No. 8, contained Griffin Green, Esq., wife, and four children, from Rhode Island; Richard, Philip, Griffin, and Susan, all married and settled in Ohio, but the younger son. Phebe Green, a niece, lived with them, and married Captain Jonathan Haskell, of the army, and settled in Belpre, on a farm. Their descendants live in this county.

No. 9, contained two families, viz: John Rouse, wife, and eight children, from Rochester, Mass.; Michael, Bathsheba, Cynthia, Betsy, Ruth, Stephen, Robert, and Barker. The latter were twins. Robert died of the scarlet fever. These children married and settled in this county; Cynthia to the Honorable Paul Fearing, and Betsy to Colonel Levi Barber. These men were highly respected, and held some of the most honorable posts, both of them having been members of congress.. Their descendants are among the most respectable citizens of the state. Also, Major Robert Bradford, wife, and three or four children, from Plymouth, Mass. Several of these children died of scarlet fever; others were born after the war and now live in Ohio.

No. 10. Captain John Levins, wife, and six children, from Killingly, Connecticut, viz: Joseph, a young man, and John, a boy of ten years, Nancy, Fanny, Esther, and Matilda. Nancy married to Jonathan Plummer; Betsy, to Dr. Mathews, of Putnam, Ohio; Esther, to Mr. Sanford, of Alexandria, D. C.; Fanny, to Joseph Lincoln, while in garrison—he was for many years a merchant in Marietta, and an excellent man—and Matilda to John White. Also, Captain William Dana, wife, and eight children, from Watertown, Mass.; Luther and William were young men, Edmond, Stephen, John, Charles, and Augustus, Betsy, Mary and Fanny; Augustus and Fanny were born in the garrison; all these married and settled in Washington County, some in Belpre, and some in Newport, which was a colony from Belpre. Charles and John settled in Mississippi.

Between No. 10 and No. 11, there was a long, low building, called the Barrack, in which a small detachment of United States troops was quartered.

In No. 11, Mrs. Dunham, the widow of Daniel Dunham, who died in 1791, with one son and two daughters. Simeon Wright married one of the girls, and lived with her. She was the mother of Persis, killed by the Indians. Also, Captain Israel Stone, wife, and ten children, from Rutland, Massachusetts, viz: Sardine, a young man, Israel, Jasper, Augustus, B. Franklin, and Columbus; Betsy married to T. Guthrie, of Newbury; Matilda to Stephen Smith, of Rainbow; Lydia to Ezra Hoit (Hoyt), mouth of Big Hockhocking; Polly to John Dodge, of Waterford; and Harriet, born in the castle, to James Noles of Newbury. The sons and their descendants settled and live in Washington County.

In No. 12, lived Benjamin Patterson, wife, and six children; three of the rangers, or spies, who were single men, boarded with him, viz: John Shepherd, George Kerr and Mathew Kerr. This man, Patterson, served as a spy three years for the settlements at Belpre, and then moved down the river. He came from Wyoming, in Pennsylvania.

"At the period of the controversy between the states of Pennsylvania and Connecticut, relative to their conflicting claims to land on the Susquehanna River, Congress appointed Timothy Pickering, of Salem, Massachusetts, a man of Spartan integrity, to go upon the ground and, with others, try to adjust the difficulty. While there, this same B. Patterson, with two other men, took Mr. Pickering from his bed at night, and conveyed him three or four miles into the woods, and bound him fast to a white oak sapling, and left him there to die of starvation. After two or three days, Patterson's conscience so worried him that he relented, and, unknown to his companions, he went and unbound him, setting him at liberty. For this outrage he left Wyoming, and fled to the state of New York; and from thence, after a time, to Marietta. It was not uncommon for such persons to visit the new settlements, but finding their characters after a time following on after them, they proceeded further down the river." (MSS. notes of Judge Barker.)

Benoni Hurlburt, wife, and four children, lived in the same house at the time of his death. His family settled in Amestown, Athens County, where his descendants now live.

No. 13. Colonel Alexander Oliver, wife, and eleven children, from the west part of Massachusetts, viz: Launcelot, a young man, Alexander, John and David. They settled in Ohio. Two of Alexander's sons are now preachers of the gospel in the Methodist church. David studied medicine, and settled in the western part of Ohio. The daughters were named, and married, as follows, viz: Lucretia, to Levi Munsel, and lived several years in Marietta; his son, Leander, was the first man, born in Ohio, who held a seat in the legislature. Betsy, to Honorable Daniel Symmes, of Cincinnati; he was the first register in the United States land office at that place. Sally married to Major Austin, of the United States army, and settled in Cincinnati. Lucretia, to George Putnam, son of Colonel Israel Putnam; Mehala, to Calvin

Shepherd, son of Colonel Shepherd, of Marietta; Electa, to O. M. Spencer, of Cincinnati. He was cashier of the Miami Exporting Company Bank, and his son, R. O. Spencer, is said to be the first preacher in the Methodist Church who was born in Ohio. He is now an elder; Mary to Oliver Wing, of Adams, in this county. The descendants of Colonel Oliver rank with the most active, useful, and wealthy citizens of Ohio.

In No. 13, also lived Colonel Daniel Bent, wife, and four children, from Rutland, Massachusetts, viz: Nahum, Daniel, Dorcas, and one daughter married to Joel Oaks of Newbury. Dorcas married William Dana of Newport. Some of their descendants are living in this county, and some in Missouri. Silas Bent, Esq., the oldest son of the colonel, and wife, also lived there with two or three children. He was one of the judges of the court of common pleas, appointed by Governor St. Clair. After the purchase of Louisiana, he moved to St. Louis, and was employed in surveying the United States lands. One of his sons became the head of a fur trader's company, and established a fort high up on the Arkansas River. Elijah Pixly, wife, and two children, from Wyoming. He served a part of the time as drummer for the garrison, and was a celebrated maker of drams, using for this purpose a block of sassafras wood, which made a very light and neat article.

Several other families lived in Farmer's Castle for a short time and then proceeded down the river; but the above list contains nearly all the permanent and substantial heads of families who settled in Belpre in 1789 and 1790.

Joshua Fleehart, wife, and four children, lived in a small cabin east of blockhouse No. 3. He was a noted hunter, and supplied the garrison with fresh meat. Soon after the war closed, he moved nearer to the frontiers, where he could follow trapping and hunting to better advantage. One of his hunting adventures is related in the transactions of the year 1794.

A list of the unmarried men at Farmer's Castle

Jonathan Waldo, from Pomfret in Connecticut; Daniel Mayo from Boston, Massachusetts; Jonathan Baldwin, liberal education, from New England, kept a school in blockhouse No. 3; settled at Waterford. Cornelius Delano, from Massachusetts; acted as a spy two or three years, and married a daughter of Major Goodale. Joel Oaks, from Connecticut, acted as a spy.

James Caldwell, from Wheeling, Virginia, also acted as a spy. Wanton Casey, married Betsy Goodale, and returned after the war to Bristol, Rhode Island. Stephen Guthrie and Truman Guthrie settled in Newbury. Captain Ingersoll from Boston, to which place he returned at the close of the war, Ezra Philips, Stephen Smith, Howell Bull, from New England, an active intelligent man. After the war he settled in Natchez, Mississippi, and engaged in trade. Samuel Cushing, from New Bedford, Massachusetts, settled near Natchez and became a rich cotton planter. William and John Smith, brothers from Rhode Island. William settled on a farm below Marietta and was living in 1845. Jonas Davis, from New England, was killed by the Indians. Doctor Samuel Barnes, a physician, from Massachusetts, married a daughter of Major Goodale, and settled near Athens, where he died. His widow subsequently married to J. Kilburn of Worthington, and is still living.

Within the walls of Farmer's Castle, there were assembled about two hundred and twenty souls. Twenty-eight of these were heads of families. A number of those enumerated as children were males above sixteen years, and enrolled for military duty. Others were young women from sixteen to twenty years of age. Among the other inmates of the garrison the name of Christopher Putnam, or "Kitt," as he was familiarly called, must not be forgotten. He was a colored boy, of sixteen or eighteen years of age, who had been the personal or body servant of General Israel Putnam, during the latter years of his life, and after his death lived with his son, Colonel Israel Putnam. In the fall of 1789, Colonel Putnam came out to Marietta with his son, Aaron Waldo, and brought Kitt with him. In the autumn of 1790, the Colonel returned to Connecticut for his family. That winter the war broke out, and he did not move them on until 1795. Kitt remained at Belpre with Mr. Putnam, in the garrison, and was a great favorite with the boys. He was their chosen leader in all their athletic sports for his wonderful activity and much beloved for his kind and cheerful disposition. When abroad in the fields cultivating or planting their crops, he was one of their best hands, either for work or to stand as a sentry. On these occasions he sometimes took his station in the lower branches of a tree, where he could have a wider range of vision, and give early notice of the approach of danger.

Under the watchful vigilance of Kitt, all felt safe at their work. After he was twenty one years old and became a free man, he lived with Captain Devoll, on the Muskingum, and assisted in tending the floating mill, and clearing the land on the farm. At the election for delegates, under the territory, to form a constitution for Ohio, Kitt was a voter; and was probably the first and only black who ever exercised the elective franchise in Washington County, as after the adoption of that article, all colored men were disfranchised. He died about the year 1802, much lamented for his many personal good qualities and industrious habits.

Some readers may be led to ask of what use, or what profit, can there be in reciting the above long list of settlers? It may be answered, that to most inquiring minds, it will be a subject of deep interest to know the names and read a brief description of the persons who braved the dangers of the savages, and the privations of the wilderness; who first opened the forest of Ohio to the light of the sun; and led the way in the cultivation and civilization of the fair valleys of the Muskingum and Ohio, now peopled by more than a million of souls. In the absence of all notices of births, or the names of emigrants, in our township or county records, these names may be highly useful to the future biographer or historian, in tracing out the origin and pedigree of some worthy citizens, or the date of their ancestors' settlement in Ohio; and although the world is full of books, it is to be hoped that this one will not be the least interesting among them, especially to the people of the south-east portion of Ohio.

Of the spies or rangers

To the vigilance and courage of the men engaged in this service, may in part be attributed the fact, that so few losses were sustained by the inhabitants, during the Indian war, compared with that of most other border settlements. This species of troops were early employed by the Ohio Company, at the suggestion of General Rufus Putnam, who had been familiar with their use in the old French war, and subsequently taken into the service of the United States. The duty of the spies was to scour the country every day the distance of eight or ten miles around the garrisons, making a circuit of twenty five or thirty miles, and accomplishing their task generally by three or four o'clock in the afternoon. They left the garrison at day light, always two in company, traveling rapidly over the hills, and stopping to examine more carefully such places as it was probable the Indians would pass over, in making their approach to the settlements, guided in this respect by the direction of the ridges, or the water courses.

Their circuit in Belpre was over the hills on to the waters of the Little Hockhocking River, and up the easterly branches across to the Ohio, striking this stream a few miles above the entrance of the Little Kanawha, and thence by the deserted farms down to the garrison. The spies from Waterford made a traverse that intersected or joined their trail, forming a cordon, across which the enemy could rarely pass without their signs being discovered.

While they were abroad the inhabitants, at work in their fields or traveling between the stations, felt a degree of safety they could not have done, but for their confidence in the sagacity and faithfulness of the spies. They were generally men in the prime of life, of active, powerful frames, and tried courage. Their dress in summer was similar to that worn by the Indians. Their pay was five shillings, or eighty four cents, a day, as appears from the old pay rolls. They were amenable to the commanding officer of the station, but under the direct control of Colonel Sproat, who was employed by the United States. They had signs known to themselves, by which they recognized a ranger from an Indian, even when painted like one.

Their watchfulness, no doubt, saved numbers of the inhabitants from the rifle of the savage, while several of them lost their own lives in this hazardous employment. At certain seasons of the year, when their services were not constantly required in the woods, as during a spell of severe cold weather, they sometimes all met together from the different stations, and amused themselves for a few days, at one of the garrisons, especially at Christmas or new year, playing at foot-ball, wrestling, and running, in all of which they could display their activity and vast muscular powers to advantage. Shooting at a mark was another pastime in which they took great pleasure, and showed wonderful skill. The men who served at Belpre, but not all at one time, two or three being the proportion for one garrison, were Cornelius Delano, Joel Oaks, Benjamin Patterson, Joshua Fleehart, George Kerr, John Shepherd, and James Caldwell. The two first were New England men; the other five had been brought up on the frontiers.

Smallpox

In September, 1793, the small pox was introduced within Farmer's Castle, whose walls could not protect them from this insidious foe, by B. Patterson, one of the spies. He was at Marietta, where it prevailed, and thinking himself exposed to the contagion, was inoculated by Dr. Barnes, who was then there, and engaged him to inoculate the rest of his family.

Great was the consternation of the married females and children, when the news of the small pox being among them was made known. Their sufferings and losses from the Scarlatina were still fresh in their minds, and the dreaded name of small pox seemed like the final sealing of their calamities. Few if any of the inhabitants, except the old officers and soldiers of the army, had gone through with the disease. A meeting was directly called of the inhabitants, and it was voted, as there was now no chance of escaping it, cooped up as they were in the narrow walls of a garrison, to send to Marietta for Dr. True, to come down and inoculate them in their own dwellings. The doctor accepted of the invitation, and Farmer's Castle became one great hospital, containing beneath each roof more or less persons sick with this loathsome disease. The treatment of Doctor True was very successful, and out of nearly a hundred patients not one died. A few years after this period, that blessed prophylactic, vaccination, was discovered by Jenner and no one now *need to die* with smallpox. Of those under the care of Dr. Barnes, in Major Goodale's garrison, a colony which moved out of Farmer's Castle in the spring, two or three died; among them was a child of Patterson. The cause of its fatality was the failure of those first inoculated to take the disease, probably from deteriorated matter; and several took it the natural way, so that on the whole they got through with this pest very favorably.

Domestic manufactures

Many families who had been brought up on the frontiers, depended entirely on the skins of animals killed in the chase, for clothing. Whole households from the oldest to the youngest were clad in dressed deer skins. Some of them possessed great skill in making them soft and pliable, equal to the finest cloth. Before the introduction of sheep, buckskin pantaloons were in general use by all the farmers' boys. The New England settlers, with most of the frontier inhabitants, made cloth of various materials. For the first two or three years, hemp was raised in small quantities; water rotted, and manufactured into cloth by the industrious females of the garrison. Flax was also raised.

"In the spring of 1790, Captain Dana sowed a piece of flax, pulled it early in June, while it was in the blossom, water rotted it in a swamp near the river, had it dressed out and spun in the family, and wove into substantial cloth by his son William. It was made into shirts and trousers for the boys, and worn at the celebration of the 4th of July, in Belpre; showing an activity and dispatch which few at this day can equal."* (*MSS. notes of Judge Barker)

Nearly every family had their spinning-wheels and loom. With these the girls and young women used to congregate in companies of ten or fifteen, in the spacious rooms of the blockhouses, and cheer each other at their labors, with the song and sprightly conversation.

They used also to stir up their ambition with trials of skill, in spinning the largest number of skeins in a given period of time.

For the first few years cotton was raised in small quantities and manufactured into stockings, or cloth, with hemp or flax. The rich, virgin soil of the bottoms, and the long, warm summer of this climate, caused it to flourish and be nearly as productive as it now is in Tennessee. After a few years, the early frosts of autumn destroyed much of it before the floss was formed, and taught them that this was not the proper climate for cotton. Captain Devoll invented a machine with rollers which separated the seeds from the cotton in quite an admirable manner, but not quite equal to Whitney's celebrated gin. He also constructed a mill, with wooden rollers, worked by oxen, for crushing the green stalks of Indian corn, from the juice of which a rich syrup or molasses was made in considerable quantities. When carefully purified it answered well for the sweetening of puddings, pies, &c.

About the year 1800, Dr. Spencer, of Vienna, Wood county, Virginia, raised in his garden cotton, the stems of which were eight or ten feet high, and produced forty pounds of long, fine cotton in the seed on three square rods of ground. It was planted early in April, by a colored woman who had been familiar with its culture in the south. It must be recollected that cotton at this period was worth from forty to fifty cents a pound, and was just coming into cultivation as a staple of the southern states.

Rice, of the variety called "upland," was also raised in small quantities, during the early years of the settlements; showing that this climate could produce several articles now brought from abroad, should the necessities of the people ever require it.

Silk worms were raised by the females in General Putnam's family, and the cocoons reeled and spun into strong sewing thread as early as the year 1800. They were fed on the leaves of the white mulberry, raised from seeds brought from Connecticut. Some of the trees are yet standing.

Sheep were not introduced until after the war, in the year 1797, or '98; the first came from Pennsylvania. For more than twenty years, nearly all the cloth worn in the families of farmers, and many in town, for every day dresses, was made in the houses of the wearers, by their wives and daughters. Necessity, as well as economy, led to this domestic manufacture. Foreign cloth was too dear for common use, and only worn for nice dresses. This kind of employment conduced greatly to the health of the females, and such diseases as curved spine, dyspepsia, or consumption, were very rare, and almost unknown.

CHAPTER XIX.

Division of the inmates of Farmer's Castle

Early in the spring of 1793, the large community in Farmer's Castle found themselves so much straitened for room, and withal so inconvenient cultivating their lands at such a distance from their dwellings, that they concluded to divide their forces and erect two additional garrisons, to be occupied by the families whose lands lay in their vicinity. Accordingly one containing two blockhouses was built, half a mile below, enclosed with palisades, and called "Goodale's Garrison," and one on the bank of the Ohio, two miles above, called "Stone's Garrison," and the families moved into them that spring. The upper one contained four blockhouses, a school house, and several log cabins, accommodating about ten families, and the lower one six. Wayne's army was now beginning to assemble on the frontiers, and the sight of numerous boats, almost daily descending the river with provisions and detachments of troops, whose martial music enlivened the solitary banks of the Ohio, removed their apprehensions of a general attack from the Indians, so depressing after the defeat of General St. Clair.

Captivity of Major Goodale

On the 1st day of March, 1793, the colony met with the most serious loss it had yet felt from their Indian enemies, in the captivity and ultimate death of Major Goodale. On that day he was at work in a new clearing on his farm, distant about forty or fifty rods from the garrison, hauling rail timber with a yoke of oxen from the edge of the woods which bordered the new field. It lay back of the first bottom on the edge of the plain, in open view of the station. An Irishman, named John Magee, was at work grubbing or digging out the roots of the bushes and small saplings on the slope of the plain as it descends on to the bottom, but out of sight of Major Goodale. The Indians made so little noise in their assault, that John did not hear them. The first notice of the disaster was the view of the oxen seen from the garrison, standing quietly in the field with no one near them. After an hour or more, they were observed still in the same place, when suspicion arose that some disaster had happened to Mr. Goodale. One of the men was called, and sent up to learn what had happened.

John was still busy at his work, unconscious of any alarm. In the edge of the woods there was a thin layer of snow, on which he soon saw moccasin tracks. It was now evident that Indians had been there, and had taken him prisoner, as no blood was seen on the ground. They followed the trail some distance but soon lost it. The next day a party of rangers went out, but returned after a fruitless search. The river at this time was nearly at full bank, and less danger was apprehended on that account; it was also early in the season for Indians to approach the settlements. The uncertainty of his condition left room for the imagination to fancy everything horrible in his fate; more terrible to bear than the actual knowledge of his death. Great was the distress of Mrs. Goodale and the children, overwhelmed with this unexpected calamity. His loss threw a deep gloom over the whole community, as no man was more highly valued; neither was there any one whose councils and influence were equally prized by the settlement. He was in fact the life and soul of this isolated community, and left a vacancy that no other man could fill. *"His memory was for many years fresh and green in the hearts of his cotemporary pioneers, now all passed away, and is still cherished with respect and affection by their descendants."*

At the treaty of 1795, when the captives were given up by the Indians, some intelligence was obtained of nearly all the persons taken prisoners from this part of Ohio, but none of the fate of Major Goodale. About the year 1799, Colonel Forrest Meeker, since a citizen of Delaware county, and well acquainted with the family of Major Goodale, and the circumstances of this event, when at Detroit, on business, fell in company with three Indians, who related to him the particulars of their taking a man prisoner, at Belpre, in the spring of 1793. Their description of his personal appearance left no doubt on the mind of Colonel Meeker of its being Major Goodale.

They stated that a party of eight Indians were watching the settlement for mischief; and as they lay concealed on the side of the hill back of the plain, they heard a man driving or "talking to his oxen," as they expressed it. After carefully examining his movements, they saw him leave his work, and go to the garrison, in the middle of the day. Knowing that he would return soon, they secreted themselves in the edge of the woods, and while he was occupied with his work, sprang out and seized upon him before he was aware of their presence, or could make any defense, threatening him with death, if he made a noise or resisted. After securing him with thongs, they commenced a hasty retreat, intending to take him to Detroit, and get a large ransom. Somewhere on the Miami, or at Sandusky, he fell sick, and could not travel; and that he finally died of this sickness.

A Mrs. Whittaker, the wife of a man who had a store and traded with the Indians at Sandusky, has since related the same account. That the Indians left him at her house, where he died of a disease like a pleurisy, without having received any very ill usage from his captors, other than the means necessary to prevent his escape. This is probably a correct account of his fate; and although his death was a melancholy one, among strangers, and far away from the sympathy and care of his friends, yet it is a relief to know that he did not perish at the stake, or by the tomahawk of the savages.

Amusements in Farmer's Castle

During the long and tedious confinement of the inhabitants to their garrison, various were the modes sought out to make the time pass as happily as their circumstances would allow. The sports of the young men and boys consisted of games at ball, foot races, wrestling, and leaping, at all which the larger number was adept. Foot races were especially encouraged, that it might give them an advantage in their contests with the Indians. Those of a more refined character, in which both sexes could participate, consisted chiefly in dancing. Parties of young people from Campus Martius and Fort Harmer used to come down as often as four or five times a year, and join in their festivities. These visits were made by water, in a barge or large row boat, attended by a guard of soldiers from the fort. They brought musicians with them, who were attached to the military service. A player on the violin, from Gallipolis, named Vansan, one of the French emigrants, was celebrated for his musical talents, and always accompanied the young men from that place in their visits to Farmer's Castle, where they were very welcome visitors. It is true, they did not abound in nice cakes and rich wines; but they treated their guests with the best they had, while the hilarity and cheerful looks of the company made amends for all besides. The garrison at Belpre contained about twenty young females in the prime of life, with fine persons, agreeable manners, and cultivated minds. A dangerous recreation of the younger girls was, to steal out of the castle in the pleasant moonlight evenings of summer, and taking possession of a canoe, push it silently up the shore of the Ohio, for a mile or more; then paddle out into the middle of the river, and float gently down with the current. Some favorite singer then struck up a lively song, in which they all joined their voices, making sweet melody on the calm waters of the "Belle Riviere," greatly to the delight of the young men and guards on the watch towers, but much to the alarm of their mothers, who were always in fear of the Indians. But their young and cheerful hearts thought little of the danger, but much of the amusement on the water, and a brief escape from the confinement within the walls of the garrison.

Promenading up and down the smooth broad avenue between the rows of blockhouses, about eighty rods in extent, was also another favorite summer evening recreation for the young people, while the elder ones gathered in cheerful groups at each other's dwellings, to chat on their own affairs, or the news of the day, collected as it might be from the passing boats, or the rangers in their visits to the other garrisons. Newspapers they had few or none of, until some years after the war, the first printed in Marietta being in 1802, with the exception of a chance one sent out from a friend east of the mountains, by some moving family. After a mail route was established in 1794, they were more common. Early in autumn, parties of the young folks visited the island, on which several families resided, for the purpose of gathering grapes, papaws, nuts, &c. On the heads of the islands, at that day, there grew a very fine, rich, red grape, said to have been scattered there from seeds left by the early French voyagers; it is, however, probable they were a native variety, fitted to grow in a sandy soil. The ground beneath the lofty trees was but little encumbered with bushes, and afforded beautiful walks, where there was no danger from the lurking savages, whose swarthy visages were mingled more or less with the thoughts of their most cheerful hours.

The 4th of July was regularly celebrated in a bowery within the walls of the garrison, where the old officers and soldiers of the revolution again recounted the trials and hardships of that eventful period, over a flowing bowl of whisky punch, while the report of their little noisy Howitz awoke the echoes among the neighboring hills, at the announcement of each patriotic toast. A celebration of this glorious day without gun powder or punch would at that time have been called a burlesque.

Perpetual motion

This desideratum in mechanics, so long the study and perplexity of many ingenious minds, has long since been abandoned as untenable by the true philosophers of science. Nevertheless, it still continues to have its advocates, and sincere believers in its practicability. During the early period of the confinement of the settlers to their garrison, Griffin Green, Esq., a man of great ingenuity and inventive powers, undertook to build a machine which should possess the principle of perpetual motion. He supposed it might be applied to the propelling of boats on the western rivers, and to the turning of mills. It consisted of a large wheel, with projecting arms; along the side of each was a groove or bog, containing a leaden ball of one or two pounds weight. As the wheel rotated on its axis, the balls rolled out to the extremity of the descending arms, while on the opposite side, as they rose, the balls descended to the foot of the arms, thus lessening the weight on the ascending side, and increasing it on the descending. When put in motion, it revolved on its axis very beautifully, and continued to move for some time; and could all the friction have been avoided, and the resistance of the atmosphere, it might have been applied to some useful purpose; but with these two impediments it after awhile ceased to move, and consequently was very reluctantly abandoned.

The inventor, however, had this to console him that it approached as near to perpetual motion as it was in the power of man to create. The machinery was constructed by Captain Devoll, and was greatly admired for the perfection and beauty of its workmanship. It was several months in building, and served as a fruitful source of conversation for the wise and knowing ones of the garrison.

First wheat in Ohio

Captain Truman Guthrie, from Connecticut, sowed the first wheat ever committed to the earth in Ohio. He came to Marietta late in the fall of 1788, and brought with him a small parcel of wheat. Soon after his arrival, a piece of land of a few square rods, near Campus Martius, was enclosed with a brush fence, sowed with wheat, and covered with the hoe. It produced a fair crop, and proved that the soil and climate of the new purchase were congenial to its nature. Very little wheat was raised until after the close of the war.

Adventure of Joshua Fleehart with the Indians,
in the winter of 1793-4.

This man was born on the frontiers of Pennsylvania, and from his boyhood had been brought up in the woods, knowing as little of letters as the red man of the forest, whom he greatly resembled in habits and instincts. His frame was of the largest size, over six feet in height, with stout, muscular limbs. His face was broad, with high cheek bones; eyes small, deep set, and shaded with thick, bushy brows. He had three brothers, equally gigantic with himself, and two sisters, full six feet in height. Among all the backwoodsmen, he was most noted for his tact in following the trail of an Indian, or a wild beast, through the pathless forest. By long practice and patient observation, aided by a natural intuition, he had arrived at a degree of skill in this hunter's art that seemed almost superhuman. His dress was very similar to that of the Indians, with moccasins and leather leggins. The rifle he carried was of the largest caliber and, like himself, unusually long, and so heavy that few men could hold it steadily at arm's length. In his powerful grasp this gave it great steadiness, and enabled him to strike a small object at a hundred yards distance, with wonderful accuracy. At the breaking out of the war, he was living, with a wife and four children, on the island, since called Blennerhasset's.

Being favorably known as an expert hunter, he was invited to come and live at Farmer's Castle, and supply them with meat from the woods. He accordingly came over, and lived in a small cabin, preferring it to the larger blockhouses. In the most dangerous times, he would hunt fearlessly in the adjacent forest and if there was an alarm given while he was inside the garrison, that Indians had been seen near, or were expected to attack it, he would take his trusty rifle and sally out into the woods to watch their motions and get a chance to kill some of them; saying that he could do more service there, and felt more free and courageous when behind a tree, fighting the Indians in their own way, than when confined to the shelter of a blockhouse. He was also a thorough adept in the art of trapping, knowing, as if by instinct, the haunts of the beaver, and familiar with its habits, as well as with all the baits and essences most likely to lure it within the jaws of his traps.

Having become tired of the sameness of garrison life, and panting for that freedom among the woods and hills to which he had always been accustomed, late in the fall of 1793, he took his canoe, rifle, traps, and blanket, with no one to accompany him, leaving even his faithful dog in the garrison with his family. As he was going into a dangerous neighborhood, he was fearful lest the voice of his dog might betray him. With a daring and intrepidity which few men possess, he pushed his canoe up the Scioto River a distance of fifteen or twenty miles, into the Indian country, amidst their best hunting grounds for the bear and the beaver, where no white man had dared to venture. These two were the main object of his pursuit, and the hills of Brush Creek were said to abound in bear, and the small streams that fell into the Scioto were well suited to the haunts of the beaver.

The spot chosen for his winter's residence was within twenty-five or thirty miles of the Indian town of Chillicothe, but as they seldom go out far to hunt in the winter, he had little to fear from their interruption. For ten or twelve weeks he trapped and hunted in this solitary region unmolested; luxuriating on the roasted tails of the beaver, and drinking the oil of the bear, an article of diet which is considered by the children of the forest as giving health to the body, with strength and activity to the limbs. His success had equalled his most sanguine expectations, and the winter passed away so quietly and so pleasantly, that he was hardly aware of its progress. About the middle of February, he began to make up the peltry he had captured into packages, and to load his canoe with the proceeds of his winter's hunt, which for safety had been secreted in the willows, a few miles below the little bark hut in which he had lived. The day before that which he had fixed on for his departure, as he was returning to his camp, just at evening, Fleehart's acute ear caught the report of a rifle in the direction of the Indian towns, but at so remote a distance, that none but a backwoodsman could have distinguished the sound. This hastened his preparations for decamping. Nevertheless he slept quietly, but rose the following morning before the dawn; cooked and ate his last meal in the little hut to which he had become quite attached.

The sun had just risen, while he was sitting on the trunk of a fallen tree, examining the priming and lock of his gun, casually casting a look up the river bank, he saw an Indian slowly approaching with his eyes intently fixed on the ground, carefully inspecting the tracks of his moccasins, left in the soft earth as he returned to his hut the evening before. He instantly cocked his gun, stepped behind a tree, and waited until the Indian came within the sure range of his shot. He then fired, and the Indian fell. Rushing from his cover on his prostrate foe, he was about to apply the scalping knife; but seeing the shining silver broaches, and broad bands on his arms, he fell to cutting them loose, and tucking them into the bosom of his hunting shirt. While busily occupied in securing the spoils, the sharp crack of a rifle and the passage of the ball through the bullet pouch at his side, caused him to look up, when he saw three Indians within a hundred yards of him. They being too numerous for him to encounter, he seized his rifle and took to flight. The other two, as he ran, fired at him without effect. The chase was continued for several miles by two of the Indians, who were the swiftest runners. He often stopped and "treed," hoping to get a shot and kill or disable one of them, and then overcome the other at his leisure. His pursuers also "treed" and by flanking to the right and left, forced him to uncover or stand the chance of a shot.

He finally concluded to leave the level grounds, on which the contest had thus far been held, and take to the high hills which lie back of the bottoms. His strong, muscular limbs here gave him the advantage, as he could ascend the steep hill sides more rapidly than his pursuers. The Indians, seeing they could not overtake him, as a last effort stopped and fired. One of their balls cut away the handle of his hunting knife, jerking it so violently against his side, that for a moment he thought he was wounded. He immediately returned the fire, and, with a yell of vexation, they gave up the chase.

Fleehart made a circuit among the hills and just at dark came in to the river, near where the canoe lay hid. Springing lightly on board, he paddled downstream. Being greatly fatigued with the efforts of the day, he lay down in the canoe, and when he awoke in the morning was just entering the Ohio River. Crossing over to the southern shore, he, in a few days, pushed his canoe up to Farmer's Castle, without further adventure, where he showed the rich packages of peltry, as the proceeds of his winter's hunt, and displayed the brilliant silver ornaments, as trophies of his victory, to the envy and admiration of his less venturous companions. It was no uncommon occurrence for the western hunters to spend months all alone in the woods, although they generally preferred one or two comrades.

Scarcity and value of salt in Farmer's Castle,
with the first visit of the whites to the Scioto salines

Among the other privations and trials of the early settlers in the Ohio Company's lands, was the dearness and scarcity of marine salt. From 1788 to some years after the close of the war, their salt was all brought over the mountains on pack horses, at an expense to the consumer of from six to ten dollars a bushel. The salt was of the course, Isle of May variety, of an excellent quality, and measured instead of weighed as it now is. A bushel of this salt weighs about eighty pounds, while one of our present bushels weighs only fifty pounds. It was as late as the year 1806, when the change took place in the mode of vending this article, after salt was made in considerable quantities at the new salines on the Big Kanawha.

Its great scarcity was a serious drawback on the prosperity of the country, and a source of annoyance to the people. The domestic animals suffered from its want, as well as man; and when ranging in the woods, visited the clay banks, that sometimes contained saline particles, licking and gnawing them into large holes. The deer licks, so common at that day, were seldom anything more than holes made in the clay by wild animals, and filled with water, sometimes of a brackish quality. Nearly all the salines since worked were first pointed out to man by the deer and buffaloes. This was the fact at Salt Creek and at Kanawha. It was hoped that as the country was opened and cultivated, salt springs would be found sufficient for the wants of the inhabitants; but it was a dark and doubtful feature in the future prosperity of the country.

In the autumn of the year 1794, Griffin Greene, Esq., whose fertile mind was always full of projects for the benefit of the country, had heard from the report of some white man, who had been a prisoner with the Indians, that while he was with them, they had made salt from a spring on a tributary branch of the Scioto River, afterwards known as Salt Creek. He described the spot as somewhere near the present location of the town of Jackson; and although it was in the midst of the Indian war, and in the vicinity of their towns, so great was the anxiety to ascertain its truth, that a company was formed to visit and search out the spring.

Mr. Green associated with him in the enterprise Major Robert Bradford and Joel Oaks; he paying one half the expenses and his two partners the other. A large pirogue was provided, with provisions for twelve men for ten or twelve days, the period supposed necessary to accomplish the journey. They hired some of the most experienced woodsmen and hunters from Bellville, as guides and guards. Among them was Peter Anderson, Joshua Dewey, and John Coleman, all noted for their bravery, and knowledge of the woods.

They left Farmer's Castle in the fall of the year, at a time when the water in the Ohio was quite high; accompanied with the good wishes of their neighbors for their success, but damped with many fears and evil forebodings from the dangers that attended the enterprise. The Indians had, for many years, kept with jealous care the knowledge of the locality from the whites, viewing the spring as a valuable gift from the Great Spirit to the red men, and with the game and fish, as perquisites to which the pale faces had no right. It was not known that any white man had ever been at the salines, except when visited by some prisoner, in company with the Indians, and who even then did not let him actually see the spot, but only the salt made by them at the time of the visit.

At the mouth of Leading Creek the adventurers landed their boat, secreting it among the trees and bushes as well as they could. This point is about forty miles from Jackson, and probably about thirty miles from the heads of the south branch of Salt Creek; but of the actual distance they were ignorant, only knowing that it lay some distance beyond the west boundary line of the Ohio Company lands. After several days travel, and making examinations, they fell upon a stream which led in the right direction, and following it down, soon met with paths leading, as they supposed, to the spring. They soon discovered where fires had recently been made, and searching carefully in the bed of the creek, found a hole which had been scooped out by the Indians in the sand rock, and filled with brackish water. A small brass kettle which they had with them for cooking, when filled with the water and boiled away, made about a table-spoonful of salt.

Although the water was weak, yet it proved that they had discovered the long talked of and desirable fountain, whose waters afforded the precious article of salt. It was like the discovery of the philosopher's stone to the alchemist, for every ounce of it could be turned into gold. After spending one night and part of a day at the place, they commenced their homeward journey, well pleased with the success of their search. They dare not stay longer and make a larger quantity, lest some straggling Indian should discover them, and give notice to the village at Chillicothe, distant about twenty-five miles. They were too numerous to fear any small hunting party.

Their return to the mouth of Leading Creek was accomplished in a much shorter period than in going out. The night after they left Salt Creek, while all were buried in sleep by their camp fire, they were awakened by a terrific scream. All sprang to their feet, seized their arms, and extinguished the fire, expecting every moment to hear the shot and the shouts of the savages. After listening a minute or two and no enemy appearing, they began to inquire into the cause of the alarm, and found that one of the parties had been seized with the cramp in his sleep, and made this terrible outcry. They were rejoiced that it was from no worse a cause, and lay down quietly until morning. When they reached the mouth of Leading Creek, the water had fallen ten or twelve feet, and had left the pirogue high and dry on the land. It required half an hour or more to launch the boat and get under way.

By the time they had reached the middle of the Ohio, proposing to cross over and go up on the Virginia shore, a party of Indians appeared on the bank, at the spot they had just left, in hot pursuit. Fortunately they were out of reach of their shot. The adventurers felt very thankful for their providential escape, for had their pursuers reached the river a few minutes sooner, while all hands were engaged in getting the boat into the water, they would in all probability have fallen a sacrifice to the Indians. At the treaty two years after, an Indian who was with the pursuing party told Colonel Lewis, of Kanawha, that the whites had been discovered while at the creek boiling the salt, by two Indians who were then on a hunt, and had seen the smoke of their fire. They were too weak to attack so large a party and hastened back to their town for assistance. Twenty Indians immediately went in pursuit, but greatly to their disappointment, did not overtake them until they had left the shore and were out of danger. They reached the garrison unmolested, and relieved the fears of their families and friends as to their safety, it having been in fact a very dangerous enterprise.

So desirable a discovery was considered to be very valuable, and Esq. Green, in a visit he made to Philadelphia soon after, sold the right of his discovery, for the benefit of himself and partners, to John Nicholson, a merchant of that city, for fifteen hundred dollars, who was to come into possession of the spring, by purchasing the land on which it was situated, as soon as it was surveyed by the United States and offered for sale. But so very valuable were these lands considered, that they were never offered for sale, but were ceded, with other salt springs, to the state of Ohio, when it became a member of the confederacy in 1802, as one of its most precious acquisitions, and under an express stipulation that the state should never sell them, or lease them for more than ten years at any one time. Small quantities of salt were made here as early as 1797, by individuals on their own account, gradually increasing in quantity until they came under the control of the state. The greatest quantity was made in the years 1806 and 1808, when there were twelve or fourteen furnaces in operation, averaging from fifty to sixty bushels a week, or about twenty thousand bushels a year. The price at this period was from two and a half to three dollars a bushel and the larger portion of the middle counties in the state were supplied from these salines; the salt being transported on pack horses. The northern and eastern portions received their salt from the Onondaga works, in New York. Some estimate may be formed of the immense labor required, when it is stated that the brine was so weak as to require from five to seven hundred gallons of water to make a bushel of salt. The manufacture of this article has ceased at these salines for more than twenty years, and the land has been sold by the state to individuals for farming purposes.

Progress of the settlement at Belpre

After the division of the settlers into smaller communities, their farming operations were carried on with much less trouble and labor, and also to a larger extent. Familiarity with danger had removed a part of its dread, and new lands were cleared in addition to those opened before the war, so that some of the stronger-handed began to have produce for sale, especially Indian corn, which was now in demand as an article of forage, for the numerous teams of oxen and pack horses employed in the transport of provisions and munitions of war for the army assembled at the frontiers.

The threatened invasion of their country occupied the thoughts and attention of the Indians more than usual, and their war parties did not harass the settlements on the Ohio as frequently as in past years. A regular system of defense, and constant watchfulness, was kept up by the whites, under the direction of the old veterans who were at the head of the settlements. They had no horses for them to steal, and the savage who receives no pay from his tribe for military services, always aims to make his attack where he can get some plunder as well as scalps; being equally avaricious with the white man. In addition to the constant care required for the sustenance and defense of their families, provision was also made for their future comfort. Nurseries of apples and peaches were planted, from seeds obtained east of the mountains, or at head waters; and scions of the finest apples to be found in New England, were sent out by Israel Putnam during the war, and engrafted ready for the use of the inhabitants as soon as it should close, which they hoped would be before long, as the army under General Wayne was sufficient to defeat any body of warriors the Indians could assemble. In the course of the summer of the year 1794, their hopes were realized, and the savages so entirely routed, that further fears of their hostility ceased to alarm them.

Murder of John Armstrong's family

Among the Indian depredations of this year, may be reckoned the massacre and captivity of this family. Mr. Armstrong was a native of Pennsylvania, and had moved to Ohio, from head waters, in the autumn of 1793 and passed the winter with his family at the Upper Settlement, in the blockhouse of Isaac Barker, a little above the head of Blennerhasset's Island. Himself and Peter Mixner, another frontier man, were interested in a small floating mill, which was moored in the rapid water at the head of the island, on the Virginia shore. It being inconvenient crossing the river so often, they concluded to build each of them a log cabin, a short distance above the mill, and move their families over. It was thought by many of the inhabitants to be a hazardous movement, on account of danger from the Indians. But the vicinity of the garrison on the Ohio side, and a stout blockhouse on the island, half a mile below, they thought would deter the Indians from an attack on them. Mrs. Armstrong was much opposed to the arrangement, and went over with her eight children with great reluctance. She had an awful dread of the Indians, since the murder of her father and mother by them, a year or two before, in Mifflin County, Pennsylvania.

For some reason, now unknown, Mixner built himself another cabin, about a hundred yards above, in the midst of the trees, and moved his family into it, leaving the first unoccupied, only a few days before the attack, which was ultimately the means of saving their lives.

There was very little ground yet cleared round the house, but he had enclosed a small piece and brought over a sow and pigs, which were confined in a pen near the house. On the night of the 24th of April, toward morning, he was awakened by the barking of his faithful watch dog. An old she bear, a night or two before, had attempted to carry off his pigs, and he now thought she had again returned.

Without putting on his clothes, he seized his rifle, unbarred the door, and rushed out to the aid of his dog, which was barking violently at some object which he could not distinctly see. As he approached nearer, he caught the glimpse of three or four Indians, whose presence had aroused the ire of his dog. He instantly fired at them and halloed, "Indians! Indians!" He retreated into the house, fastened the door, and went up into the loft, where three of the larger children slept; while the two smaller ones, with the infant, lodged below, with himself and wife. By the time he had reached the loft, the Indians, with the aid of a heavy rail and their tomahawks, had burst open the door and taken possession of the house. Finding he could make no effectual resistance for the defense of his family, he pushed apart the loose shingling of the roof, jumped down to the ground, and, unseen by the Indians, retreated to the mill, where two of his oldest boys, who aided in tending it, were sleeping. When the savages entered the house, Mrs. Armstrong, with the infant in her arms, attempted to escape, by getting out at the top of the low, unfinished chimney, which was made of logs; but her foot slipped and she fell back again, breaking her leg in the fall. The Indians then tomahawked and scalped her, with the two younger children. On visiting the loft, they found Jeremiah, about eight years old; John, ten; and Elizabeth, of fourteen years. These they did not kill, but took as prisoners.

In the meantime, Mixner, hearing the gun and the noise at Armstrong's cabin, came out to learn the cause. Listening carefully, in the stillness of the night, he heard the Indians in busy conversation. Calling up his wife, who was incredulous as to the cause, he bade her hearken to the voices, which he could hear distinctly, but could not understand. Mrs. Mixner, who had been a prisoner with the Wyandots, and understood their language, learnt that they were seeking and inquiring of each other for the family that lived in the other cabin, but was now empty. He lost no time in hurrying his family into his canoe, and paddled out into the middle of the river, letting the boat float slowly and silently by the cabin of his neighbor. Hearing the low moaning and stifled sobs of Elizabeth, at the murder of her mother and the children, he hailed, and asked, "What was the matter, and what had happened." One of the Indians, who spoke English, bid her say, "that nothing had happened," or he would kill her. In the bitterness of her anguish she was obliged to comply, and answered as she was directed. Having landed his family on the island, Mixner gave the alarm about the same time that Armstrong did.

Early in the morning a party of men went over from the island and from Stone's garrison, but the Indians were beyond their reach. They brought the dead bodies across the river and buried them. The faithful dog was found in the house, with his lower jaw nearly severed from a stroke of the tomahawk in his attack on the Indians. That day a party of twenty men, from the island and from Farmer's Castle, went in pursuit of the Wyandots, whom they afterwards ascertained were about twenty in number. They had been out on a marauding excursion in the vicinity of Clarksburgh, Virginia, and, discovering these two new cabins built since any of them were last here, concluded to attack them. The pursuing party of whites found by their trail where they had raised their sunken canoes, and crossed the Ohio, to the Big Hockhocking, up which they pushed their boats several miles, when they left them, and traveled by land.

By the prints of the children's feet in the mud, they ascertained that the prisoners were yet alive; and, lest they would kill them if they were overtaken by the whites, they gave up the pursuit, and returned downstream, and across the Ohio, in the bark canoes left by the Indians.

On their arrival at the Wyandot towns, the children were adopted into different families. Jeremiah, the youngest, whose life was saved by the kind offices of a young warrior of the party, was taken by the celebrated chief, Crane, who is represented to have been a kind hearted, humane man, and used him well. A portion of the time, during his captivity, was spent where the town of Columbus now stands, which was claimed by the Wyandots, and who had a large field of corn in the prairie near Franklinton. Elizabeth, after several removes, married a man by the name of Dolson and settled near Malden, in Upper Canada. John and Jerry were given up after the close of the war. The latter for several years kept a tavern in Columbus, and is well known, not only to the citizens of that place, but to many of the inhabitants of Ohio, who have been members of the legislature. He is still living, and resides at Havana, in Licking County, Ohio.

Jonas Davis killed by the Indians

The last of February, 1795, about ten months after the massacre of Armstrong's family, Jonas Davis, a young man from Massachusetts, and an inmate of Stone's Garrison, at the upper settlement, had been to Marietta, by land, and on his return, at the mouth of Crooked Creek, three miles above the garrison, discovered an old skiff, or small boat, that had been thrown on shore among some drift wood, by the high water. Nails being scarce and dear at that time, he concluded to go up the next morning, with some tools, pull it to pieces and get out the nails. While busily occupied with the old skiff, a war party, consisting of two Indians and a negro who had been adopted into their tribe, happened to be in that vicinity looking for an opportunity to kill or plunder the whites, heard him at work, and creeping up carefully to the edge of the bank, shot him, without his being aware of their approach; as was afterwards ascertained from one of the party, at the treaty of Greenville, in August following, where many things were disclosed in relation to their depredations on the settlements, that could only be learned from the Indians themselves. He was scalped, stripped of his clothing, his tools taken away, and his dead body left by the side of the skiff. As he did not return that night, fears were entertained of his fate, and the next morning a party of armed men went up, under the guidance of one of the rangers, where they found Davis as above related. He was brought down to the garrison and buried.

His death was the more distressing as he was shortly to have been married to a daughter of Isaac Barker, one of the inhabitants of the garrison, and his wedding suit already prepared. Had he followed the rules of the station, which strictly forbade any one going out alone beyond gunshot of the blockhouses, he would have escaped this untimely fate. The victory over the Indians by Wayne, and their general quiet demeanor since, no doubt induced him to think there was little or no danger. But as no treaty was yet concluded with the Indians, strict discipline was kept up in all the garrisons until after that period, and no trust placed in their forbearance; for although greatly humbled, yet their hatred of the whites was not lessened by their defeat.

The day after the death of Davis, a party of four young men, headed by John James, one of the most active and resolute of the borderers, proceeded down the Ohio, in a canoe, in pursuit of the murderers of Davis. The rangers at Gallipolis had ascertained that a party of Indians was hunting on the head of Symmes's Creek, and from the direction pursued by the war party in their retreat, they were led to think they belonged to that band. With all diligence they hastened on to the mouth of the Big Kanawha, in expectation of being joined there by volunteers from the garrison; but none turned out, declining to do so on account of the armistice made with the Indians after their defeat by General Wayne. Proceeding on to Gallipolis, and making known the object of their pursuit, four men volunteered their aid and joined them. From this place they hastened onward to Raccoon Creek, and ranged up that stream one day, without making any discovery of the Indians. Here one of their men fell sick and turned back, while another had to accompany him, leaving only six to continue the pursuit.

The following day they reached the heads of Symmes's Creek, where is a large pond, about a mile long and a quarter of a mile wide, a famous place for trapping beaver. They soon fell upon signs of the Indians, and on a bush by the edge of the pond found an Indian's cap, made of beaver skin, which he had left to mark the spot where his trap was set. Mr. James took this into his own keeping.

As it was near sunset, the party secreted themselves behind a large fallen tree, waiting for night, when they intended to attack the Indians in their camp, make one fire, and rush on with their tomahawks, not thinking the hunting party could number more than eight or ten men, but they subsequently found they amounted to near forty, divided into two camps, one on each side of the pond. They had lain concealed but a short time, when an Indian, who had been out hunting came in sight, and was closely examining the trail made by the whites, knowing it was that of strangers. When he came within forty or fifty yards, one of the party, Joseph Miller, fired, and the Indian fell. As Mr. James rushed up with his tomahawk, he raised the war cry, and was instantly answered by his comrades from their camp, distant not more than two or three hundred yards, for they directly came rushing up in force, before James could accomplish his purpose, and, with his party, was obliged rapidly to retreat, as the Indians far outnumbered them. Seeing the whites likely to escape, they set their dogs on the trail, who came yelping and barking at their heels, like hounds in pursuit of a fox.

Fortunately it soon came on so dark that their enemies could not see their trail, and followed only by the barking of the dogs. For a day or two preceding, it had rained heavily, and when they reached the east fork of the creek, it was too high for fording. They hastily made a raft of dry logs, but it became entangled in the bushes, in the creek bottom, which was all overflowed, so that they had to abandon it. Their escape this way being cut off, they were forced to return to the ridge, between the two branches, and travel up until they could cross by fording. A little before morning they halted, and rested themselves until daylight, the dogs for some time having ceased to pursue them, or by barking give notice of their position. Soon after his they found a fordable place in the creek, and crossed over. Here they lay, an hour or two, waiting for the Indians, expecting them to pursue the trail with daylight, and intending to fire upon them when in the water; but they did not come, having probably crossed higher up the stream. When they reached Raccoon Creek, that was also full, and had to be crossed on a raft. The party reached Gallipolis the next day at evening, much wearied with their toilsome and exciting journey.

Colonel Robert Safford of Gallipolis, then acting as a ranger went out the next morning and found the trail of the Indians pursuing the whites to within a short distance of the town. The pond on Symmes's Creek is distant about one hundred miles from Belpre, and shows this to have been one of the most hazardous, daring, and long continued pursuits, after a depredating band of Indians, which occurred during the war; reflecting great credit on the spirited men who conducted it. It was the last warfare with the savages from this part of the territory.

In the spring of 1796, following the treaty of peace at Greenville, the inhabitants were released from their five years imprisonment in garrison, and issuing forth began to spread themselves up and down in the land. Many fresh emigrants also arrived and strengthened their numbers. In a few years large farms were cleared and buildings erected; roads were opened and bridges built over many of the small streams so that wheel carriages could be partially used. Large orchards were planted out, of the finest engrafted varieties of fruit, by the inhabitants of Belpre, who for many years in advance of other parts of the country, sent boat loads of fruit to the settlements on the Mississippi River.

For a number of years, while the Connecticut men were preparing the "Western Reserve" for the immense dairies that now enrich them, the people of Belpre furnished more cheese for the downriver trade than any other district west of the mountains, and was at that period as famous for its cheese as the "Reserve" is now.

Since that time the farmers have turned their attention to other branches of agriculture, more profitable to them, especially the growth of fruit. For many years, sixteen cents a pound was the price paid for cheese, sold to the trading boats at their dairy doors.

The farmers in this settlement, for quite a long time, stood at the head of all others in the southeast quarter of Ohio, for intelligence, neatness of agriculture, and comfortable dwelling houses; and even at this day of wealth and improvement in all the older portions of the state, would not fall much in the back ground.

In the stormy period of political strife, which attended and followed the elevation of Jefferson to the presidency of the United States, they remained firm to the principles of Washington; and as he had been their model in the camp, they remained true to his precepts at the ballot box.

Note. — For many facts in the history of Belpre, the writer is indebted to E. Battelle, Esq., and Captain Charles Devoll.

P. S. There were killed by the Indians, within the bounds of the Ohio Company settlements, and on the shore of the Ohio opposite, no less than thirty-eight persons, and ten were taken prisoners; while it is not certainly known that the whites killed more than four Indians.

CHAPTER XX.

History of the settlements at Waterford and Wolf Creek Mills

In the winter of 1789, an association was formed by the residents in Campus Martius at Marietta, to form a settlement about twenty miles up the Muskingum River, on lands donated by the Ohio Company to actual settlers. It was called the "second association," that at Belpre being the first. It consisted of thirty-nine members; a part of whom were to settle at Wolf Creek, about a mile from the mouth, for the purpose of erecting mills. The main body of the donated lands lie on the east side of the Muskingum; and the portion of it bordering on the river was divided into lots of ten or fifteen acres each, for the purpose of making the settlement more compact, and the inhabitants near to each other for mutual assistance and defense in times of danger from the Indians; while the other portion of the hundred acres was located at a greater distance. These lots commenced where the town of Beverly now stands, and extended down the river about two miles.

On the west side of the Muskingum the settlers laid out a village in a bend of Wolf Creek at the mouth, so nearly surrounded by water, as to be called "The Peninsula." It was arranged after the plan of some of the New England villages, each lot containing five acres, bordering on a street six rods wide, located on the fertile alluvions of these streams. They were subject to the rules prescribed by the donating committee, as to the manner of settlement, building blockhouses, keeping an able bodied, well armed man on each lot, called "manning the lot," as before noticed in the transactions of the Ohio Company. At least twenty of the associates were bound to be on their lots by the 1st day of September, 1789, and the balance by the same day in 1790. Two blockhouses were to be built by the 20th of July; one on the east side of the river, and one at the mill seat near the forks of Wolf Creek. The first one was built by the time specified, but the other was not. During the Indian war a blockhouse was built at "The Peninsula," for the safety of the

377

men while at work on that side of the river, and occupied by Major Dean Tyler, and some others.

On the 20th of April, 1789, the members of the new colony left Campus Martius, and embarking with their families and household goods in a large pirogue and several canoes, landed that evening at Tuttle's Run, near where Judge Gilbert Devoll afterwards lived, and took possession of their woodland homes. The number of men who came up at this time was nineteen, and several more joined them during the summer. In a few days, by aiding each other, every family was in possession of a small but comfortable log cabin; and by the middle of May, each man had cleared and fenced a half acre or more of ground about his house, for a garden. When this was accomplished they began preparing land for a crop of corn. About sixty or eighty rods back from the river bank, the alluvions rose gradually on to an extensive plain, or second bottom, which was nearly a mile in length, and from one third to half a mile in width, and might contain one hundred and fifty or two hundred acres. The soil was a sandy loam, covered with a coat of black, vegetable mold, several inches in depth. This spot had probably, at a remote period, been cultivated by the Indians, as many such places are found at various points on the Muskingum, covered with a growth of saplings, while the adjacent lands are coated with forest trees. The autumnal fires of the Indians, followed up regularly for a long series of years, had prevented their growth into trees, which had doubtless at some remote time covered it as well as the neighboring hills.

The plain was now clothed with a thick coat of bushes, shrub oaks, and briers, from six to eight feet high, while here and there among them lay the prostrate trunks of decaying trees. An ample supply of leaves covered the surface of the earth, as it had providentially escaped the last year's autumnal burning. Selecting a fair, windy day, early in May, fire was applied in several places on the windward side of the plain. The leaves and rotten wood soon ignited, and with a rushing sound like that of distant thunder, the destroying element in a few hours swept this growth of saplings from the earth, thus accomplishing the work of twenty men for a whole month. By this summary process the plain was cleared as if by magic, and made ready for the seed of the planter. With joyful hearts the colonists entered directly on the labor of planting, and found they had nothing to do but cut away a few of the larger saplings, the fire having entirely devoured all the smaller ones. They did not attempt to plow the land, as it was yet full of roots, but with their hoes dug holes in the soft mold to receive the seed corn, potatoes, and pumpkins. The season was favorable, and all their crops grew with such rapidity, and ripened so rapidly, that they escaped the destructive frost which early in October greatly injured or destroyed the corn in the other settlements, especially at Belpre.

The Waterford settlers were indebted to the fortunate circumstance of finding this plain ready cleared to their use, for their escape from the pinching famine, which so sorely beset the other colonists in the following year. It afforded two advantages highly conducive to this favorable result. In the first place it enabled them to plant their crop considerably earlier than those who had to clear away the forest, or even to girdle the trees. In the second place the soil having long been exposed to the sun and winds, possessed the qualities of an old cultivated field, which is well known to ripen its productions, and especially Indian corn, two or three weeks earlier than lands just reclaimed from the forest. Their field was also clear of the shade of deadened trees, which retards the ripening of grain. Under these favorable circumstances they raised the first year from eighty to one hundred acres, yielding about thirty bushels of sound corn to the acre.

On the 3d day of May the inhabitants were called together by a letter from General Putnam, notifying them of the murder of Captain King, at Belpre, by the Indians. They immediately organized themselves into a military company, choosing William Gray, Captain, David Wilson, Sergeant, and Andrew Webster, Corporal. They also voted that a blockhouse should be erected, near the center of the settlement, under the direction of Colonel Robert Oliver. It was ready by the 2d day of July, as their next meeting for business was held in it. The new settlement was called Plainfield by the inhabitants for one or two years, but changed to Waterford by the Court of Quarter Sessions, in December, 1790. (" MSS. record of association.")

Wolf Creek Mills.

Simultaneously with the settlement at Plainfield, a company of three men, viz: Colonel Robert Oliver, Major Haffield White, and Captain John Dodge, with a number of laborers, commenced operations for the erection of a mill on Wolf Creek, about a mile from the mouth. At the spot chosen for the location, the bed and banks of the creek are cut out of the solid limestone rock, by the wear of water in the course of ages, to the depth of ten or twelve feet, and thirty yards in width.

Wolf Creek Mills 1789
From a sketch by C. W. Elliott

There is also at this spot a rapid of several feet fall, forming a very eligible site for a mill. The cedars and other evergreens, which overhang the rocky borders of the creek, add greatly to its picturesque beauty. Three comfortable log cabins were soon erected for the convenience of their families and workmen, which with the mills are shown in the annexed drawing. By great industry and perseverance the dam and mills were built in the course of that year, and by March following the grist mill, as well as the saw mill, was in operation. The mill stones were procured from Laurel hill, in the vicinity of Brownsville, which affords a hard conglomerate rock, very suitable for grinding Indian corn and rye, but not of a proper texture for the manufacture of flour. These stones are in use at this day. The iron crank for the saw mill was manufactured at New Haven, Connecticut, and said to have been transported across the mountains to Sumrill's ferry on the back of a pack horse; and from thence by water to the mills. When put in operation they fully answered the expectations of the builders. From tradition we learn that the grist mill, with a good head of water, could grind a bushel of corn into fine meal in four minutes. In the summer of 1790, it furnished a large portion of the meal for Marietta, besides those in the vicinity. Early in the following year the Indian war commenced, and the settlement at the mills, called

"Millsburgh," was broken up, and the mill company removed their families to Marietta. During the war, parties composed of twenty or thirty men, sometimes went up by water with their grain, a part of them marching by land, in sight of the boats, as guards. While the load was grinding, sentries were placed in the adjacent forest to protect the workmen from the attack of Indians. It is a curious fact that the mills stood unmolested, during the four years of the war, although signs of the savages were often seen in and around them. They probably considered them a good decoy to entice their enemies within their reach, and afford them an opportunity of waylaying and destroying them. In the daily scouts of the rangers, they sometimes passed by the mills, and once to their surprise found the grist mill in operation. As no one visited this spot but the spies, they at once knew it was done by the Indians. After the war closed, the mills were repaired and put again into use. They were the first ever built within the bounds of the state of Ohio. A few acres of land were cleared and fenced around the cabins at the mills, but large fields were not opened as at Plainfield, their chief attention being given to the erection and completion of these structures. During the summer regular progress was made in clearing and opening their lands.

In July the Rev. Daniel Story visited the settlement, and preached one Sabbath at Millsburgh, where the inhabitants from the east side of the Muskingum also attended. There being no house large enough for the congregation, the services were performed in the open air, under a beech tree. This was the first sermon preached in Waterford. Mr. Story several times repeated the visit during this and the following year, and even during the war occasionally preached in the garrison, so that although in the depths of the wilderness, and surrounded by hostile savages, they were not wholly deprived of a preached gospel.

John Gardner taken by the Indians

Soon after the colonists commenced their settlement on the east side of the river, a portion of the members of the association began to clear their lots in the village on "The Peninsula," west of the Muskingum. One of this number was John Gardner, a young man from Marblehead, in Massachusetts. He had been bred a sailor. When the Ohio Company sent out their first detachment of pioneers, he enlisted in their service, and was one of those who landed at the mouth of the Muskingum the preceding April.

Jarvis Cutler, a young man from the same state, and son of Dr. Cutler, was also one of the associates, and one of the pioneer party. He had joined company with Gardner, and they agreed to assist each other in clearing their lands. One day the last of September, Mr. Cutler left him busily engaged at his work, and went to Marietta to purchase a supply of salt and other necessaries which they needed. Soon after his departure, Gardner being a little weary with his work, sat down on the trunk of a large tree which he had just felled, near the spot where Bowen's store now stands. While sitting here, with his rifle by his side, busily engaged counting some balls which he had poured from his bullet pouch into his hand, four Indians and a white man paraded themselves before him, within thirty feet of the log, without his hearing their approach.

The white man beckoned, and told him, in broken English, to come to him. Returning the balls to their place, and taking his gun in his hand (as it was a time of peace, and several parties of friendly Delawares were hunting in the vicinity), he without hesitation approached the party. As he came up, the white man took his gun, saying he wanted to look at it, and handed it to one of the Indians, who passed it to the next, and so on to the last, who was without a rifle, and kept it. Another Indian pulled off his hat, while a third threw a cord over his neck, and two of them took him by the hands and led him into the woods, bidding him to make no noise.

On their way to their camp, they passed near to the mills then building on Wolf Creek, and from the top of the ridge along which the path led could distinctly see the people at their work, but were screened themselves from observation by a thick growth of hazel bushes. After marching in silence two or three miles up the creek, they reached the Indian camp, where they had two or three horses, of their own, and a number of bells which they had stolen from the settlers' cows. Among the horses Gardner saw one which he knew, a small mare, belonging to Judge Devoll. This one the Indians called "a squaw horse," not knowing the English word for a female. The Indians now mounted their horses and rode by turns, not having enough for all; but made Gardner walk, secured by a rope, held by him whose turn it was to go on foot. Their course was nearly southwest, leading over on to the waters of Federal Creek. At night they encamped without kindling a fire, giving the prisoner a small piece of jerked meat for supper, as they had but little for themselves. Before they laid down to sleep, a stout sapling was bent down and fastened to the ground, on which they made him lie, with his hands bound behind him with leather thongs, while another cord fastened him to the trunk. They then tied the cow bells to the branches, so that their noise would awake them if he attempted to escape, and lay down themselves near him.

Being much fatigued with the long march and excitement of the day, he made no attempt to escape that night, but lay quietly on his rough bed.

In the morning a fire was kindled, and after smoking their pipes and eating a little jerked meat, they proceeded on their march. During the day he was questioned as to his ability in building cabins. He answered that he was master of that art; and, to encourage him, they promised, if he would stay quietly with them after they arrived at their village, he should have a young squaw, and be made a good Shawnee. In the course of the day, during a short halt, they cut off a part of his hair and painted his face, after the Indian fashion.

The second day they encamped before night and two of the Indians went out to hunt meat for supper. While they were gone, Gardner was directed to gather wood and kindle a fire. They soon returned with the carcasses of a deer and a bear. Their flesh was roasted, and their prisoner received a plentiful meal, the first he had eaten since he had been with them. At night he was secured in the same way as before. Towards morning it became cloudy, and there fell a moderate rain. He now made up his mind to escape, if possible, having no relish for an Indian wife. The rain moistened the dry leather thongs with which he was bound, and rendered them more pliable. By continued and cautious efforts, for several hours, he finally succeeded in getting loose and slipping gradually from the prostrate sapling without waking the Indians. By the glimmering light of the fire he stepped gently to the sleeping Indian who had possession of his rifle, and by whose side it lay. This he seized as his rightful property, but was obliged to leave his powder horn and bullet pouch, as the Indian had the belt to which they were attached round his body. Without any delay, he sallied out into the woods in the direction of home, and walked all the remainder of the night. At day light he took an easterly course, and traveled rapidly all day without stopping, except to drink from the small branches which he crossed. At night, not thinking it safe to kindle a fire, he crept into a hollow log, closing the opening with brush and leaves. This kept him more warm than in the open air, and protected him from wolves. In the course of the second day of his escape, he fell upon the west branch of Wolf Creek, and by following down the stream came to a spot which he recognized as having once seen before, when out hunting; this gave him fresh spirits, which had began to flag a little, from the exhaustion of hunger and his lonely condition. Having no ammunition he could kill nothing for food, although the woods abounded in game. A little before night he reached the mills, and was heartily greeted by his friends, who were aware of his mysterious disappearance and thought the Indians must have taken him away. In the mean time Jarvis Cutler had made his trip to Marietta, and returned to the mills, wholly unconscious of the romantic adventure of his companion. The meeting was very gratifying to them both; and the next morning with renewed spirits they returned to the scene of their woodland labors, where they had parted four days before.

1790

The year 1790 was passed without any untoward event and the clearings of the settlers kept gradually extending. A number of new families were added to the settlements, and nearly every lot had its occupant, so that there were about forty able bodied men in the two stations of Millsburgh and Plainfield. The woods abounded with wild game, and the turkeys and deer came into their enclosures, so that any good marksman could kill them without going forty rods from his door.

Quite a large number of friendly Indians, belonging to the Delaware and Ottawa tribes, spent the summer on the waters of Wolf Creek, and other streams within a few miles of the settlers, and often visited them for the purposes of trade, exchanging their meat for Indian corn and vegetables. They seemed in no way hostile or offended at their taking possession of the country, as it had been given up to the United States by treaty, with the full consent of their leading men. As the winter approached they began to draw further away from the settlements, and retired towards their towns. The campaign of General Harmer into the country of the Shawnee had greatly offended that warlike tribe, as well as the rest of the Indians. For this reason the directors of the Ohio Company were apprehensive of danger, and began in the fall of this year to make preparation for defense. A company of rangers was enrolled and put under the charge of Colonel Sproat. A part of these were enlisted at Plainfield; and in December eight or ten of them, by turns, daily scouted the woods back of the settlement to give notice of the approach of hostile bands. No serious danger, however, was apprehended, but motives of prudence caused them to take this step. Had they been really fearful of the outbreak which soon after followed, more precautions would have been taken in the erection of garrisons and blockhouses for the protection of the inhabitants.

Hostility of the Indians
Attack on Big Bottom

In pursuance of the resolution of the Ohio Company, to grant donation lands to actual settlers, several new stations were commenced in 1790, as inhabitants came into the country. A company, or association, composed of thirty-six men, in the autumn of this year, began a settlement at Big Bottom. It lies on the Muskingum River, about thirty miles above the mouth, and is so named from its size, being four or five miles in length, and containing more fine land than any other below Duncan's Falls. On the first or low bottom, a few rods from the left bank of the river, they erected a blockhouse of the largest size. A short distance from the garrison, the land rises several feet on to a second bottom, which stretches out into a plain of half a mile in width, to the base of the hills. A few yards above the blockhouse, a small drain put down from the plain into the river, forming a shallow ravine. A small opening had been cleared about the building, on the river side, surrounded by the adjacent forest. The associates were chiefly young, unmarried men, but little acquainted with Indian warfare or military rules.

"Those most familiar with the Indians, had little doubt of their hostility, and strongly opposed the settlers going out that fall, and advised them to remain until spring, by which time the question of war or peace, would probably be decided." "But the young men were impatient of delay, and confident in their own ability to protect themselves. They went; put up a blockhouse, which might accommodate the whole of them on an emergency. It was built of large, beech logs, rather open, and not well filled in between them. This job was left for a rainy day, or some more convenient time. They had also neglected to enclose their house with palisades, and ceasing to complete the work, the general interest was lost in that of the convenience of each individual. Another error was the neglect of any regular system of defense, and the omission of setting sentries. Their guns were lying in different corners of the house, without order. About twenty men usually slept in the building, a part of whom were absent at the time of attack. At one end of the house was a large, open fireplace, and when the day closed, all came

in, and built a large fire and commenced cooking and eating their supplies."
(MSS. of Colonel Barker.)

The weather, for some time previous to the attack, had been quite cold, and the Muskingum River frozen over since the 22d of December, so as to be passable on the ice. On Sunday, the 2d day of January, 1791, it thawed a little, with the ground partially covered with snow. In the depth of winter, it was not customary for the Indians to go out on war parties, and the early borderers had formerly thought themselves safe from their depredations during the winter months. About twenty rods above the blockhouse and a little back from the river, two men, Francis and Isaac Choate, members of the association, had erected a cabin, and commenced clearing their lots. Thomas Shaw, a hired laborer, and James Batten, another of the company, lived with them. About the same distance below the garrison, was an old clearing, and a small cabin, made several years before, under the laws of Virginia, which two men, Asa and Eleazar Bullard, had fitted up, and now occupied. The Indian war path, from Sandusky to the mouth of the Muskingum, passed along on the opposite ridge, in sight of the river.

The Indians, who had been hunting and loitering about the settlements during the summer, were well acquainted with the approaches to the white settlements, and with the manner in which they lived, each family in their own cabin, not apprehensive of danger. With the knowledge of these circumstances, they planned and fitted out a war party for the destruction of the Waterford settlement. It is supposed they were not aware of there being a station at Big Bottom, until they came in sight of it from the high ground on the west side of the river, in the afternoon of the 2d of January. From the ridge they had a view of all that part of the bottom, and could see how the men were occupied, and the defenseless condition of the blockhouse. After completing their reconnaissance and holding a council as to the mode of attack, they crossed the river on the ice a little above, and divided their warriors into two divisions; the larger one to assault the blockhouse, and the smaller one to make prisoners of the men in the upper cabin without alarming those below. The plan was skillfully arranged and promptly executed.

Cautiously approaching the cabin they found the inmates at supper; a portion of them entered the door, while others stood without, and spoke to the men in a friendly manner. Suspecting no harm they offered them food, of which they partook. The Indians seeing some leather thongs in a corner of the room took the whites by the arms, making signs that they were prisoners

386

and bound them. Finding it useless to resist against superior numbers, they submitted to their fate.

While this was transacting at Choate's cabin, the other party had reached the blockhouse unobserved; even the dogs gave no notice of their approach by barking, as they usually do, the reason of which probably was that they were also within by the fire, instead of being on the watch for their masters' safety.

The door was thrown open by a large, resolute Indian, who stepped in and stood by its side to keep it unclosed, while his comrades without shot down the white men around the fire. Zebulon Throop, from Massachusetts, who had just returned from the mills with a bag of meal, was frying meat, and fell dead into the fire; several others fell at this discharge. The Indians now rushed in and killed all that were left with the tomahawk. No effectual resistance seems to have been offered, so sudden and unexpected was the attack, by any of the men, but a stout, resolute, backwoods Virginia woman, the wife of Isaac Meeks, who was employed as their hunter, seized an axe and made a blow at the head of the Indian who opened the door; a slight turn of the head saved his skull, and the axe passed down through his cheek into the shoulder, leaving a huge gash that severed nearly half his face. She was instantly killed with the tomahawk of one of the other Indians, before she could repeat the blow. This was the only injury received by the savages, as the men were all killed before they had time to seize their arms, which were standing in the corners of the room. While the slaughter was going on, John Stacey, a young man in the prime of life, the son of Colonel William Stacey, sprang up the ladder into the upper story and from thence on to the roof of the house, hoping to escape that way, while his brother Philip, a lad of sixteen years, secreted himself under some bedding in one corner of the room. The Indians on the outside watching that none escaped, soon discovered John on the roof and shot him, while he was in the act of begging them "for God's sake to spare his life, as he was the only one left." His appeal to the Indians was heard by the two Ballards, who alarmed by the firing at the blockhouse had run out of their cabin to learn the cause. Discovering the Indians around the house, they sprung back to the hut, seized their rifles and put out into the woods, in a direction to be hid by the cabin from the sight of the Indians. They had barely escaped when they heard their door burst open by the savages. They did not pursue them, although they knew they had just fled, as there was a brisk fire in the chimney, and their food for supper smoking hot on the table.

After the slaughter was over, and the scalps secured, one of the most important acts in the warfare of the American Indians, they proceeded to collect the plunder. In removing the bedding, the lad Philip Stacey was discovered. Their tomahawks were instantly raised for his destruction, when he threw himself at the feet of one of their leading warriors, begging him to protect him. The savage either took compassion on his youth, or else his revenge being satisfied with the slaughter already made, interposed his authority and saved his life. After removing everything they thought valuable, they tore up the floor, piled it over the dead bodies, and set it on fire, thinking to consume the blockhouse with the carcasses of their enemies. The structure being made of green beech logs, would not readily burn, and the fire only destroyed the floors and roof, leaving the walls still standing.

A curious fact, showing the prejudices of the Indians, is related by William Smith, who was one of the associates, but providentially absent at the time of the attack. He was at the place the second day after, and says, the Indians carried out the meal, beans, &c., which they found in the house before setting it on fire, and laid them in small heaps by the stumps of trees, a few paces distant. They probably thought it sacrilege to destroy food, or that it would give offense to the Great Spirit to do so, for which he would in some way punish them. No people were ever more influenced in their actions by auguries and omens, than the savages of North America.

There were twelve persons killed in this attack, viz: John Stacey, Ezra Putnam, son of Major Putnam, of Marietta; John Camp, and Zebulon Throop, from Massachusetts; Jonathan Farewell, and James Couch, New Hampshire; William James, Connecticut; John Clark, Rhode Island; Isaac Meeks, wife, and two children, from Virginia. These men were well armed, and no doubt could have defended themselves against the Indians, had they taken proper precautions. But they had no veteran Revolutionary officers with them to plan and direct their operations, as they had at all the other stations. If they had picketed their house and kept a regular guard, the Indians probably would not have ventured an attack; but seeing the naked blockhouse, they were encouraged to attempt its capture. Colonel Stacey, an old soldier, familiar with Indian warfare in Cherry Valley, where he formerly lived, visited the post on the Saturday previous, and seeing its insecure condition, gave them a strict charge to keep a regular guard, and prepare immediately strong bars to the door, to be shut every night at sunset. They, however, apprehending no danger, did not profit by his advice.

The two Ballards after effecting their escape traveled rapidly down the river about four miles to Samuel Mitchell's hunting camp. Captain Rogers, a soldier of the Revolution, a fine hunter, and afterwards a ranger for the garrison at Marietta, was living with him and a Mohican Indian, from Connecticut, by the name of Dick Layton. Mitchell was absent at the mills; Rogers and Dick were lying wrapped up in their blankets sleeping by the fire. They were awakened and made acquainted with the cause of their untimely visit, and the probable fate of the people at the blockhouse. Seizing their weapons without delay, they crossed the river on the ice, and shaped their course through the woods for Wolf Creek Mills, distant about six miles, and reached there by ten o'clock that evening.

On announcing the news of the attack on Big Bottom, and the probable approach of the Indians to the mills; great was the consternation and alarm of the helpless women and children. Several additional families had joined this station since the year 1789, but a number of the leading men were absent to attend the court of quarter sessions, which was to set at Marietta on Monday. This rendered their condition still more desperate, in case of an attack, which they had every reason to expect before daylight in the morning. The gloom of night greatly added to their distress, and gave energy to their fears. Under the direction of Captain Rogers, who had been familiar with similar events, the inhabitants, amounting to about thirty souls, principally women and children, were all collected into the largest and strongest cabin, which belonged to Colonel Oliver, and is the one standing nearest to the mills, in the drawing.

The people at Millsburgh had neglected to erect a blockhouse, as they were instructed to do, and now felt the need of one. Into this cabin they brought a few of their most valuable goods, with all the tubs, kettles and pails they could muster, which Captain Rogers directed to be filled with water from the creek, for the purpose of extinguishing fire, should the Indians attempt to burn the house, which was one of their most common modes of attack. The door was strongly barred, and windows made fast; the men, seven in number, were posted in the loft, who by removing a few chunks between the logs, with here and there a shingle from the roof, soon made port holes from which to fire upon the enemy. Like a prudent soldier, their leader posted one man as a sentry on the outside of the house, under cover of a fence, to give timely notice of their approach. It was a long and weary night, never to be forgotten by the mothers and children, who occupied the room below, and thought they should be first sacrificed if the Indians entered the house. Just before daylight the sentinel gave notice of their approach. Several were obscurely seen, through the gloom of night, near the saw mill, and their movements distinctly heard as they stepped on some loose boards. Their tracks were also seen the next morning in some patches of snow. Finding the people awake, and on the lookout for an attack, they did nothing more than reconnoiter the place, and made their retreat at day dawn, to the great relief of the inhabitants.

Samuel Mitchell was dispatched early in the night to give the alarm to the people at Waterford, and two runners were sent to Marietta. Nothing could better demonstrate the courage and humanity of Captain Rogers, than his conduct in this affair, thus to weaken his own means of defense by parting with some of his most active and brave men to notify the sleeping settlers of their danger, when he had every reason to expect an attack from an overwhelming force in a few hours. Mitchell on his way to the river called at the cabin of Harry Maxon, near the mouth of the creek. He was gone to Marietta, but his wife, and Major Tyler, who lived with him, crossed over with Mitchell on the ice, to awaken and notify the people of the danger that awaited them. They first called at the dwelling of the widow Convers, whose husband had died of smallpox the year before; it stood near the center of the present town of Beverly. She was the mother of eight children; the two oldest were sons; James, a young man, and Daniel, a lad of fifteen, who was shortly after taken by the Indians. In one hour from the time the alarm was given by Mitchell, these two young fellows had visited every cabin in the settlement, extending for two miles up and down the river. With all the haste the emergency required, and with as little noise as possible, the inhabitants assembled in their only blockhouse, which was quite small, and stood near the lower part of the donation lots.

The terror of the women and children, hurried out of their beds at midnight, was not much less than that of those at the mills; but it so happened they had a larger number of old soldiers among them, as but few were absent at the court. The blockhouse was about fifteen feet square, and sheltered that night twelve heads of families, with their wives and children, amounting in all to sixty-seven souls, no alarm took place that gloomy night, save the noise of the watch dogs, which were left out of doors to give notice by their barking of the approach of the savages. Early in the morning, scouts of the most active men were sent out to reconnoiter and search for signs of the enemy. None however were seen. In the course of the day they visited their deserted houses for food, which they had no time to take with them in the hurry of the preceding night. The escape of the two Ballards was a merciful and providential event for the settlers of Waterford. If these men had been killed, or captured, the Indians would that night have fallen on the unsuspecting inhabitants in their sleep, who were far less able to resist than the people at Big Bottom, nearly all of them living detached in their log cabins. It is morally certain this would have been their fate, as the Indians fitted out the war party with the express object of destroying these two settlements, and had said that before the leaves again covered the trees, they would not leave a smoke of the white man on this side of the Ohio River.

The next day, or the 4th of January, Captain Rogers led a party of men over to Big Bottom. It was a melancholy sight to the poor borderers, as they knew not how soon the same fate might befall themselves. The action of the fire, although it did not entirely consume, had so blackened and disfigured the dead bodies, that few of them could be recognized. That of William James was known by his great size, being six feet and four inches in height, and stoutly made. As the earth was frozen on the outside, a hole was dug within the walls of the house, and the bodies consigned to one grave. No further attempt was made at a settlement here, until after the peace. Big Bottom now forms a quiet and beautiful agricultural district, in the township of Windsor, Morgan County.

The party of warriors from the mills having joined their companions early in the day, preparation was made for their homeward march. They knew from the escape of the men from the deserted cabin, and their observations at the mills, that the settlement below was aware of their vicinity and that further attempts at that time would be useless.

The Indians engaged in this massacre were Delaware and Wyandot, and from the best information subsequently collected from the prisoners, were about twenty-five in number. Before departing, they left a war club in a conspicuous place, which is their mode of letting their enemies know that war is begun and is equivalent to a written declaration among civilized powers. As it was quite uncertain, whether the wounded Indian would live or die, lots were cast on the prisoners for one to be sacrificed as an offering to his spirit, and to fulfill their law of revenge. The lot fell on Isaac Choate. He was directly stripped of his own comfortable dress and habited in that of the wounded Indian, all clotted and soaked with blood, and loaded with a part of the plunder; while his own clothing was put on his disabled enemy. As he was now a devoted victim, he was not suffered to travel in company with the others, but placed under the charge of two warriors who kept him a considerable distance in the rear, but generally in sight of the main body.

By careful attention to their wounded comrade (no civilized people being more kind than the Indians to their disabled fellows), he finally recovered, and Choate's life was spared. Had he died, his fatal doom was inevitable. As soon as the distance and the short days of winter would permit, the party reached the British post at the rapids of the Maumee River; soon after which Colonel McKee, the Indian agent, redeemed Francis Choate from his captors.

It is said he was induced to this kind act from motives of humanity, and on account of his being a member of the brotherhood of Free Masons. In a few days he was sent to Detroit, and, embarking in a sloop, went down the lake to Niagara; and from thence through the state of New York to his home in Leicester, Massachusetts.

His brother, Isaac, was taken to Detroit by the Indians at the same time, and falling in with a citizen of that place who traded with them, persuaded him to advance the ransom demanded; promising to remain there and work at his trade, as a cooper, until he could repay the money. By his diligence and activity, in a few months, he earned the sum required, repaid the debt, and returned down the lake to his home in the same way.

Thomas Shaw was kept by the Indians at the rapids for some months, when he was redeemed by the noted Colonel Brandt, without any expectation of its being refunded to him again. He soon after went to Detroit and worked for a French farmer, near that place. Colonel Brandt met with him at that place, and, finding him an expert axeman and familiar with clearing land, persuaded him to go down and live with a brother-in-law, a physician, living on a farm, a few miles out from the fort, at Niagara.

Young Philip Stacey died of sickness, at the rapids.

James Patten, a middle aged man, was adopted into an Indian family, and retained until the peace of 1795.

CHAPTER XXI.

The next day after the attack at Big Bottom, the settlers at the mills and at Waterford held a council to decide on what was the best course to pursue in the present emergency. They were not able to retain and defend both stations. It was finally decided to build a strong garrison on the east side of the river, and to evacuate the settlement at the mills. Several of the leading men at this place moved to Marietta, while others joined the station at Waterford.

The spot chosen for the location of the fort was in a bend of the river, about half a mile below the present town of Beverly. The land near it is fertile, and extends back, nearly half a mile, to the base of the hills. On the opposite shore, it rises abruptly into a high hill, or ridge, which, with artillery, would command the ground on which the fort stood. But as their enemies had no guns larger than rifles, no danger was apprehended from this source. The only disadvantage would be the facility it gave their enemies for inspecting the interior of the garrison from its lofty summit, at least two hundred feet above the river, and learning the movements of the whites. The form of the fort was triangular, which is rather uncommon in military defenses.

But as they were in a hurry and it saved them one line of curtains, while the blockhouses at the angles defended the sides just as well as in any other form, it was adopted.

The base of the triangle rested on the river, distant only a few paces from the bank, and was about two hundred feet in length. One of the other sides was somewhat longer, so that the work was not a regular triangle. At each corner, was a two story blockhouse, twenty feet square below, and a foot or two more above. The two longer sides were filled in with dwelling houses, some of which were two stories high, and others of a less height, while a considerable portion were built barrack fashion, with only one roof, pitched inward, so that the rain from it fell within the garrison. The spaces not occupied by buildings were filled in with stout pickets. Broad, substantial gates, near the northern blockhouse, led out through the palisades into the highway and fields, while a smaller one in the curtain on the bank, called the water gate, afforded an opening to the river.

Fort Frye
Waterford 1792
From a sketch by C. W. Elliott

A line of palisades, twelve feet high, at the distance of thirty feet, enclosed the whole, and descended to the river. The space covered by the fort contained about three fourths of an acre. Near the center of the interior, they dug a well, lest in a siege the Indians might cut them off from the river. A blacksmith's shop was also built in this area. Their wood for fuel was kept on the outside, between the pickets and the walls of the fort. By diligent and assiduous labor, aided by ten or twelve men sent up by the Ohio Company, the buildings were erected, and pickets set by the last of February, but the gates were not hung until early in March.

The accompanying drawing, made from the recollection of Colonel Convers, who lived there and assisted in building it, is probably a pretty correct representation of "Fort Frye," as it was called by the inhabitants.

The following is a list of the heads of families, and single men, who lived here during the war:

Captain William Gray, wife, and two children, Commander of the Garrison;

Major Phinehas Coburn, wife, and three sons, young men, Phineas, Nicholas, and Asa.

Judge Gilbert Devoll, wife, and two sons, young men, Gideon, and Jonathan — one daughter; also,

Wanton Devoll, wife, and one child;

Allen Devoll, wife, and three or four children;

Andrew Storer, wife, and five children;

Widow of B. Convert, and eight children, James a young man, and Daniel a lad of fifteen years;

George Wilson, wife, and two children;

Jeremiah Wilson, two sons, and two daughters;

Benjamin Shaw, wife, and three children;

Nathan Kinney, and wife;

Joshua Sprague, wife, and two children;

Major John White, and wife; William Sprague, wife and two children;

Noah Fearing, wife, and several children;

Andrew Webster, and son;

Harry Maxen, and wife;

Daniel Davis, wife, and two sons, young men, William, and Daniel, jr.;

David Wilson, wife, and one child;

Benjamin Beadle, and wife.

Single men — William McCullock, Neal McGuffey, Andrew McClure, William Newel, these four served as rangers, for the garrison; Samuel Cushing, William Lunt, Jabez Barlow, Nathaniel Hinkly; Doctor Thomas Farley, was a Physician and practiced medicine; Doctor Nathan McIntosh, was Surgeon's Mate, appointed by the Ohio Company for the soldiers, and afterwards accepted and paid among the troops in the service of the United States. The spring after the war began, eight or ten soldiers were sent up from Fort Harmer, and continued through its course, to assist in defense of the settlement.

Attack of the Indians on the garrison

Toward the last of February, following the massacre at Big Bottom, the Delawares and Wyandots, at Sandusky, planned another war party, to strike a blow at the settlements of Duck Creek and Waterford, as they had failed to do so in January, on account of the notice given to the inhabitants, by the escape of the Ballards.

It so happened that a civilized Indian, named John Miller, a descendant of King Philip's tribe, who had come out with General Varnum, as a servant, from Rhode Island, in 1788, was there at the time. He had spent the summer of 1790, in Waterford, and being an expert hunter, supplied the settlers with wild meat from the woods. In the fall of that year, young George White Eyes, a son of the Delaware Chief of that name, passed through Marietta, on his way home to his tribe, he having been educated at Dartmouth College, by the United States, as a token of respect for his father, who was always a friend to the whites.

As he passed up the Muskingum River he met with John, and hired him at a certain price per month, to go with him to Sandusky, and hunt for him on the route. The time having expired, for which he had engaged with White Eyes, he felt desirous of returning to his old friends at Waterford. He therefore joined the young men in their war dances, as is their custom before going on the war path, and gained their consent to go with them, with considerable reluctance on their part, as they were jealous of his attachment to the whites.

Early in March the party arrived at the foot of Duncan's Falls, on the Muskingum River, about forty miles above Waterford. As they approached the vicinity of their enemies, their jealousy of John increased, and one old warrior, in their council, proposed putting him to death, alleging as a reason, that he had been visited with ominous dreams the last night, by which he was assured that John would betray them by giving notice to the whites of their designs. He however protested his innocence of any such intention, and his great regard for the Indians. As it happens in most questions, the warriors were divided in their opinion of John's integrity, and finally concluded not to kill him. To strengthen the favor of his friends, and induce them to leave him at the camp, he purposely cut his foot with a hatchet, while preparing wood for the fire, so badly that he could not travel.

Before leaving him on the morning of their departure, the jealous old warrior insisted that he should be tied and secured in the camp so that he could not escape. His arms were fastened, but so loosely that he could easily get his hands to his mouth, and then tied to a stout sapling by the camp fire. A little dry venison was left for food, with a large portion of their camp equipage, and a considerable quantity of powder and lead.

As soon as John thought them at a proper distance, he commenced the trial of freeing himself from confinement, but so securely had they bound him that it was nearly sun-set before it was accomplished. Deeply intent on giving notice to his Waterford friends, and highly indignant at the treatment of the Indians, he immediately set to work with his hatchet to cut grape vines and fasten together some logs and dry wood into a raft. Before leaving the camp he threw a large portion of their ammunition into the river, putting however a good share on to the raft, for his own use, and as presents to his friends at Waterford; to whom nothing was more acceptable than the nice glazed rifle powder procured by the Indians from the English traders at Detroit.

It was nearly dark when his preparations were completed. He immediately put out into the stream, which happened to be almost full bank, from the late rains, for the garrison at Waterford, well knowing that the lives of the people at that place might depend on his reaching there before the Indians.

The settlers had treated him with uniform kindness, and his whole life had been passed in the society of white men, so that his attachment to them was much greater than to his own color. The current was so strong that it wafted his light craft at a rapid rate, and he passed the camp of the Indians, at the mouth of Bald Eagle Creek, just as day was breaking in the east. With fear and trembling he saw their camp fire on the bank of the river, and started at the crack of their rifles as they shot at the turkeys on their roosts on the tall trees of the bottom, a few rods from the river. John lay close and quiet on the raft, not daring to move either hand or foot to accelerate his progress from this dangerous neighborhood. By good fortune he passed without being discovered, or if seen in the dim twilight of the morning, the raft was taken for one of those clumps of drift wood so often found floating on the river after a rise of the water. As soon as he was out of sight of the camp fire, he plied his paddle with such diligence, that he landed his flotilla, about nine o'clock, a little above the garrison.

He had to approach the post with caution, lest he should be mistaken for a hostile Indian and fired at by the sentry. As soon as he could be heard, he hailed and announced his name. He was told to approach and on the guard being called, was admitted within the fort. John soon made known the cause of his visit to Captain Gray, the Commandant. A council of the officers and older men was assembled, who carefully questioned him as to his knowledge of the approach and intentions of the Indians. After relating all he knew of their designs, and his escape, as above related, he requested the loan of a canoe to take him to Marietta, saying he intended to return with all speed to Rhode Island, for if they caught him, they would roast him with a slow fire. They gave him a canoe, and a letter to the directors of the Ohio Company, who rewarded him for his fidelity. He soon after returned to his old home, and never again visited Ohio.

Various were the opinions of the council of war at Fort Frye, as to the motives of John in bringing the intelligence. Some thought he was in league with the Indians and sent in as a spy to view the condition of the garrison, and then make his escape to their enemies. They, however, concluded to act as if the notice was the truth, and proceeded with all haste to finish and strengthen their defenses, doubling their guards at night, and keeping a vigilant watch. The large gates were not yet made, nor all their outworks completed. In two days they had it all finished, and just at evening hung their strong outer gates, secured with heavy wooden bars. That night was passed more quietly, as they now felt comparatively safe.

As the Indians had not yet appeared, nor any signs of them been seen by the rangers, their suspicions of John's false alarm began again to revive, and many to think and say there were no Indians near them. It seems that the reason of this delay was occasioned by their changing the time of attack. After leaving John, they concluded to destroy the settlement at Duck Creek first, and then come over to Waterford, not being aware of the evacuation of that station immediately after the affair at Big Bottom. On reaching the forks of the creek, they were not a little vexed to find the houses vacant, and the cattle all driven away. Full of ire at the disappointment, they turned away on their trail, and hastened over to Muskingum. They reached the vicinity of the garrison on the evening of the second day after John's arrival, wholly unconscious of his escape or that the whites had any knowledge of their approach.

Early the following morning, which was the 11th day of March, they posted their warriors along the margin of the plain, while four or five went below to the deserted houses and fodder stack, expecting their enemies out to feed their cattle or to milk their cows. Wilbur Sprague, a young man, had gone out very early, before it was light, to milk a cow, which was kept at their deserted cabin, eighty or one hundred rods below. He had finished his task, and commenced his return to the fort, before the Indians saw him. They immediately fired at him, and rushed on in pursuit. One of their balls took effect in the hip, and nearly disabled him. He, however, ran to within a few rods of the gate, and fell down under cover of a large stump of a tree, which protected him from further injury. His brothers, Jonathan and Nehemiah, rushed out and brought him in, amid a shower of bullets from the Indians. They escaped unharmed, although several shots struck the gate, and others threw up the mud and earth around them.

When the firing commenced, McCullock and McGuffy, the two spies, were at their breakfast, preparing to go out on their daily range. They instantly hurried out, to learn the cause. It seems that several of the flanking party of Indians, who fired at Sprague, were dressed with hats and match coats, like those worn by the soldiers of the garrison, which they had procured from the English traders, and used as a decoy. McCullock, seeing these men, thought they were a party of whites, from Marietta, and ran up near to them, with the intention of assisting them to enter the fort, and escape from the Indians on the edge of the plain who had commenced firing at the garrison. When he had approached within fifty or sixty yards, one of them called out, in broken English, *"Come on, my good fellow, we'll protect you;"* while another, behind a tree, raised his rifle to fire at him. At this instant, Wanton Devoll, who stood looking out from a loop hole, in the upper story of the blockhouse next the river, screamed at the top of his voice, *"Look out, that man is going to shoot you!"* As the gun cracked, he sprang to one side, and the ball passed through the body of his faithful dog who had run out with his master, and was a few paces behind him. Perceiving his mistake, he turned and ran from his deceitful foes for the garrison, not in a straight course, but in a zigzag manner, jumping from side to side, as is often the manner of the Indians, when endeavoring to avoid the aim of their enemies. A number of shots were fired at him by the other Indians, but he escaped unharmed. Samuel and William Sprague, brothers of Wilbur, thinking there were no Indians near, had just left the fort in a canoe for Marietta, and had proceeded down about a quarter of a mile, when the firing commenced.

Hearing the shots, and the yells of the Indians, the truth of John's statement flashed across their minds; they instantly put about, and by keeping close under the edge of the bank, escaped detection, and entered the water gate unobserved. The Indians finding themselves so manfully opposed, a constant fire being kept up at them from the garrison, whenever they appeared in sight, ceased any further attempts at its capture, and commenced shooting the cattle of the settlers, which they found at the vacant clearings. They killed not less than twenty-five or thirty head, and drove away two yoke of oxen and several cows to Sandusky, some of which were seen at that place, by Daniel Convers, about six weeks after. When they had completed their mischief, they retired beyond the reach of gunshot on to the edge of the plain, in fair sight of the garrison.

Judge Devoll had in his possession a long barreled, large bored, old ducking gun. Seeing a group of savages in the border of the clearing, making obscene gestures and defying the whites, he elevated his gun from one of the upper loop holes and fired into the midst of them, aiming at one who was more noisy than the rest, pointed out to him by his daughter, who stood by his side during the whole attack, and often showed him the best chances for a shot. The group directly scattered; and one of them went limping from the ground, shot through the hip, as was ascertained after the peace. They soon left the vicinity of the fort, but continued for several days to lurk about and harass the other settlements, killing Captain Rodgers at Marietta, and firing at Waldo Putnam at Belpre.

During the attack on the garrison, Jabez Barlow, (a simple hearted, misanthropic old bachelor, one of the Waterford associates, and brother of Joel Barlow, the poet.) lived about a mile below, in a small cabin by himself, having refused to move into the garrison, alleging as a reason, that he had never harmed the Indians and they would not injure him. During the first few months of the settlement, he lived in the upright trunk of a large, hollow, sycamore tree. Being of a religious turn of mind, and somewhat of an enthusiast, he fully believed that the word of God, contained in his Bible, would protect him from all harm. He had just risen from bed, and hearing the continued firing, he started to go up to the garrison. When he reached about half way, the firing ceased, and thinking they had been shooting at a mark, he retraced his steps. As he approached within a few rods of his clearing, he saw the back of an Indian standing in the door way of his little cabin, inspecting the interior. Greatly alarmed at this unexpected sight, he instantly dropped down on to the earth, amidst the dead weeds and bushes which surrounded him, and sheltered him from view. The Indians, after plundering the house of such articles as pleased them, breaking up his pot and kettle, and tearing a number of leaves from the large Bible which lay on the table, and scattering them over the floor, departed without suspecting the vicinity of the owner. Fearing that the dreaded Indians were still near him, Barlow continued in his present concealment without stirring until night. In the evening there came on a heavy rain, which made it very dark. He now started for the garrison, following the little blind path as well as he could, and fancying every dusky object an Indian, he reached the gate of the fort about eight o'clock. Here he hailed the guard, who inquired very strictly his name, at that time of night, and, fearing an ambush from the savages, whether he had any Indians with him. After some parley he was admitted. Finding the Delawares paid no respect to his Bible; he deserted the little cabin and lived in the fort until after the close of the war, when he returned to his former home in New Hampshire.

The greatest injury suffered by the settlers from this attack was the loss of their cattle, which could not be replaced but at a great expense. No lives were lost, and only one of their number was wounded, who recovered after a long and painful illness. The kind hand of Providence, setting the councils of the Indians at naught, and overruling their plans for the good of the whites, may be clearly traced in all these transactions. The escape of John Miller to give notice of their approach, and the changing of their minds on the way, going first to Duck Creek, gave the settlers time to complete their defenses, and be ready to repel the attack of their foes. Without these interpositions it is more than probable many lives would have been lost, and perhaps the garrison destroyed. The Indian war party was composed of about thirty Indians.

Captivity of Daniel Convers

After the defeat and disappointment of the Indians in their attack on the garrison, no other attempt was made to harass the settlements until the last of April following. The small domestic lots near the garrison had been planted, and the inhabitants had commenced work in the large field on the plan. In the forenoon of the 29th of April, the men with their usual guard had been out to work in this enclosure; at noon it began to rain and they did not go out again. Some of the young men were in want of a new drum for the use of the garrison, and as they could not work that afternoon, concluded to go and cut a tree suitable for making the hoop, or body of the instrument. While talking over the matter some of the older and more cautious men advised them not to do so, as it was reported that an Indian had been seen that morning on the other side of the river. They, however, did not credit the report, and thought there was no danger. Accordingly, Jonathan Sprague, Nehemiah Sprague, and Daniel Davis, being well armed, went out, accompanied by Daniel Convers, then a lad in his sixteenth year who was unarmed, and went with them by way of amusement. Between the fort and the field was a patch of forest yet un-cleared, in which they soon selected a suitable tree about forty or fifty yards from the edge of the field. Jonathan Sprague was the axeman, and as he pulled off his coat to begin work, handed his gun and powder horn to young Convers, who stood by his side. Nehemiah was posted a few yards distant as a kind of guard, while Davis was within a step or two, looking at the work.

Jonathan had made but a few strokes into the side of the tree, when nine Indians rose up from behind some brush that lay near the edge of the field, distant not more than forty yards, and fired. So sudden and unexpected was the discharge that the report of their guns and the sight of the Indians fell at the same instant on the astonished woodsmen. The splinters, from the bushes and bark of the tree, flew thick around them, but not one was killed, or even wounded; a ball passed through Jonathan's shirt and waistcoat, barely grazing the skin, without drawing blood. He instantly snatched his gun from the hands of his companion, and in despair called out *"What shall we do!"* Daniel Convers, who was constitutionally brave, and not easily alarmed, boldly answered, *"Why, tree and fire,"* knowing that the guns of the Indians were now empty, and there was no immediate danger.

But his men, without any attempt at resistance, all ran as fast as they could for the fort. They were young soldiers, and not much accustomed to Indian warfare and besides the number of the Indians was three times their own. Daniel having no arms, two of the Indians chased and took him prisoner, while the others having their loaded guns to protect them, were not pursued. Had they treed and fired, they would probably have killed one or two Indians, or at least beat them off until aid came from the fort and so all have escaped.

A short time before this affair, there had been a bounty offered of fifty dollars for Indian scalps. Young Convers, whose head was full of the prospect of getting a bounty, afterwards said that between the time of the volley from the Indians and the retreat of his own party, when they might have returned the fire with the prospect of killing some of them, the thoughts of the bounty were constantly in his mind and only dissipated by their seizing him and making him a prisoner; a proof that he was not overcome with fear at this sudden attack. The Indians had secreted themselves in this position on the margin of the field while the men were gone to their dinners, with the expectation of their returning in the afternoon.

The captors of young Convers seized him by the hands and hurried him down to the river, where they had two or three bark canoes, and crossed over, landing at the mouth of Wolf Creek fearing an attack from the men in the garrison. Having no further use for their frail boats, they punched holes with the paddles in the bottoms, and sank them. The war party was composed of Chippewas and Wyandots. With all haste they went to the place where their baggage was secreted in an old hollow tree a little above the mouth of the creek, and began their journey homeward, scattering off singly through the woods so as to leave as little trail as possible, and coming together again after a few miles.

They traveled that afternoon north-westerly until they struck the old Indian path from Sandusky to Fort Harmer, which was a plain, beaten track, used by the Indians for several years past when going with peltry to trade at Marietta. The evening was rainy and night very dark, but as they wished to get as far as possible from the whites, fearing they might be pursued, they did not stop until quite late. With this long and rapid march, Daniel became so tired and sleepy that he could not keep his eyes open and nodded as he went; when, finally, they made a halt. From their great and habitual caution, no fire was kindled. Before laying down they tied a long leather thong round their captive's wrists, and stretching out the ends of it on the ground, two Indians lay down on each side of him, passing it under their bodies so as to awaken them if he attempted to escape. The Indians did not sleep much, but lay chattering and talking nearly all night. At daylight they recommenced their journey. An old Ottawa Indian who was painted black, as a token that he killed all, and took no prisoners, while those painted in other colors, make prisoners if they choose, complained that he was sick, and gave his pack to Daniel to carry.

It was very heavy, and beyond his strength to sustain for any long distance. After traveling about three miles, they stopped at a little run to drink, when he threw it to the ground, exclaiming "*me sick too.*" He knew the Indian would resent it and expected every moment a blow from his tomahawk, but he was so wearied with the load, and vexed at his captivity, that he cared but little for the consequences. Contrary to his calculation the Ottawa picked up the pack without speaking, while the Indian, who claimed him as his property by the right of capture, instantly patted him on the back, exclaiming "*ho yee,*" in token of his approval of the act and admiration of his spirit. The second day at evening, having reached the head waters of Jonathan's Creek, or Moxahala, a distance of forty or fifty miles, and out of danger of pursuit, they halted before night, kindled a fire, and killed a deer for supper. Here they gathered a parcel of wild onions, and cooked with the venison in their kettles, which, as they had no salt, made a tolerable seasoning. That night they cut his hair in the Indian fashion, leaving a long lock on the top of the head, called "the scalp lock," which was braided into a cue. They also painted one of his eye lids red.

In the course of the third day they came to a historical or hieroglyphic tree, on which was painted, in a rude manner, a war party, describing their number and the direction in which they were going. The warriors now figured on the same tree their own number and indicating the capture of one prisoner. It is their custom when marching in single file to place the prisoner behind the leader, and he is further indicated by being figured without arms. In this case, to show that their prisoner was a boy, he was made of less size than the armed warriors. This was a spot well known to the Indians, and where another war path came in. Here the two Ottawa men left them, as the path led to their village. Before going they shook hands very kindly with the other Indians, not forgetting the little prisoner, who received as hearty a shake as any of them. From this place they went on as rapidly as they could, without any delay, to Upper Sandusky.

In the first cabin they entered, were seen several scalps, suspended on a pole, a disheartening and melancholy sight for the prisoner. In it was a crabbed old Indian who, after shaking hands quite cordially with the warriors, saluted Daniel with a hearty cuff on the side of his head, by way of savage welcome. With the accustomed hospitality, he fed his guests on hominy, and when they left him, accompanied them some distance down the Sandusky River. In the course of that afternoon, they met a white man and negro, both on horseback. The white man was an Indian trader and said but little to the prisoner, while the negro came up very kindly and shook him by the hand; inquiring with apparent interest whether any of his friends had been killed, and where he was taken prisoner. That night they encamped in the woods, and had nothing for supper among eight persons but one wood chuck, or ground hog. Here the Indians gave him a small blanket and a pair of moccasins, he being very thinly clad and barefoot at the time of his capture, and so continued all the journey out.

The next morning the party came to an Indian hut, where they made a halt. The owner was absent, but soon came in, with a bridle in one hand, and a hickory stick in the other. After shaking hands with his countrymen, he turned round, and by way of salutation gave their prisoner two or three severe blows with his hickory. Daniel gave him a scrutinizing look in return, and mentally resolved, that if he ever had an opportunity hereafter, he would be fully revenged on him. At this place they procured some food, and traveled on down the river until they came to a vacant hut, where they passed the night. Here he saw a cow that belonged to his mother and was driven away by the Indians at the time of their attack in March. She directly knew her old friend Daniel, came up to him, and looked as if she felt sorry for his unhappy condition. The oxen and other cattle were at Lower Sandusky.

As a proof that there is some kind feeling in savages, that day, as they approached a village on a prairie, two Indian boys came up, and taking him by each hand, ran with him past the town, and then stopped. This was evidently done to screen him from the sight of those in the village, who have a cruel custom of making all the prisoners who pass through their towns run the gauntlet. On the tenth day of his captivity, or the 9th of May, the party arrived at Lower Sandusky, where there was a large Indian village. Here they crossed the Sandusky River in a canoe. As soon as they had landed an Indian came up, took Daniel by the hand, and bid him go with him. He hesitated for a moment, when one of the warriors motioned him to go. He ran with him up the river bank about twenty rods and stopped, appearing very friendly, and no doubt took this course to keep him out of the sight of the other Indians belonging to the town. While waiting there for his party to join him, a large Indian came to him who was drunk, and struck him over the eye, knocking him down. The eye instantly swelled so that he could not see with it. As he repeated the blow, an elderly Indian who was much smaller ran up to his rescue, and seizing the drunken one by the hair, jerked him to the ground and beat him severely. He then in a very kind manner took young Convers by the hand, calling him, in broken English, his friend. At the same time two squaws came up and expressed their pity for the poor young prisoner.

They went away, but directly returned, bringing some hominy and meat for him to eat; thus showing that the female heart in the savage, as well as in the civilized races, is readily moved at the sight of distress, and ever open to compassion and kindness. The party to which he belonged encamped near this spot; and during the night some of the warriors who had been present at the attack on the garrison at Waterford, and driven away the cattle, hearing from their countrymen the result of their foray at the same place, and the ill treatment of their prisoner by the drunken, Indian, came into the camp, and passed the night to protect him from any further abuse.

The next day they moved with their captive down the Sandusky, to the head of the bay, and stopped a short time at Mr. Whitaker's, an Indian trader. He had a white wife who, like himself, was taken prisoner in childhood, from western Virginia, and adopted into the tribe. The trader made them a present of a loaf of maple sugar which they divided, giving Daniel a share. In the season of sugar making, it is often used by the Indians as food. Whitaker said but little to the prisoner, lest he should excite the jealousy of the warriors. Just below the trading house they crossed the head of the bay, landing at a place where there was a large camp of Indians. Among them was an old man who had lost his nose. He took quite a fancy to the white prisoner, and wanted him to sing. That evening they went to the house of a Frenchman, named La Ponce, who was a baker, and gave them some nice flour bread, the first good food he had eaten for eleven days. Here they passed the night. The following day he arrived at the mouth of Portage River, which was the 11th of May, and was delivered over to his new master, who had bargained for him the day after he was taken prisoner, but was not transferred until he could pay the purchase money, or articles to be received in exchange. Captives belong to the warrior who first lays his hand upon them; at that moment it is optional with him, either to kill or to take alive; if he chooses the latter they belong to him to dispose of for his own benefit. This, among savage races, has been a custom from the earliest times, and is doubtless the origin of slavery.

The price paid for young Convers, was a horse and several strings of wampum, the Indian substitute for money. The prisoner was fortunate in this exchange as his new master and mistress were both very kind hearted people. His condition was not that of a slave but rather an adoption into the family, as a son. The Indian's wife, whom he was directed to call mother, was a model of all that is excellent in woman; being patient, kind hearted, humane, and considerate to the wants and comfort of all around her, and especially so to their newly adopted son. To sum up her excellences in a brief sentence of the captive's own language, *"As good a woman as ever lived!"*

How few among the more civilized race of whites would ever imitate the Christian charities, of this untaught daughter of nature! Who among us would adopt an Indian captive into our household and treat him with all the kindness and affection bestowed upon our own children? Yet this was not uncommon among the savages of North America, and is a redeeming trait among their many cruel customs.

It is to be regretted that the Indian names of these good people are forgotten, for it would be a pleasure to know and preserve them. They were members of the Chippewa tribe. The family was composed of the Indian, his wife, a son about the same age as his adopted brother, and two daughters who were younger. All their worldly wealth consisted of three horses, a canoe, two or three brass kettles, tomahawks, guns, knives, and traps, with a few blankets. Their house, or wigwam, was a movable one; made of flag matting, wound spirally round poles stuck into the earth in a circle, and tied together at the top in the shape of a cove, making quite a picturesque appearance, when grouped together in a village. It is a common mode of constructing their dwellings along the low shores of the bays and marshy grounds, where the flag grows in great abundance. They are easily taken down and rebuilt; or moved from place to place in their canoes. His Indian father gave him as good a dress as he could afford, composed of a calico shirt, leggins, and moccasins. He cut his hair short, and by way of ornament put a jewel in his nose.

From the mouth of the Portage River the family went over to Maumee Bay, spending their time in hunting, fishing and trapping, in which Daniel assisted with cheerfulness, and being naturally of a lively disposition, soon gained the good will of the Indians. The Chippewas are a far less thrifty people than the Delawares and many of the other tribes; seldom raising any corn or vegetables, but depending on fishing and hunting for food. This is probably in part owing to their location along the lake shores, and about the mouths of the streams, being less favorable to cultivation than higher and more inland situations. Four or five weeks were spent on the borders of the bay, passing up and down from the mouth to the rapids. While they were at this place, his Indian mother was attacked with a severe and dangerous illness, so that they all thought she must die. After his father, who was a doctor, had exhausted all his simple remedies in vain, he as a last resource appealed to the Great Spirit, in behalf of his sick wife.

Among them the dog is considered a sacred animal and never used for food. One day a squaw, who had probably been consulted on the occasion, came into the lodge with a young dog or pup, concealed under her blanket. She stood and looked a few minutes at the sick woman without speaking, dropped it on the ground and went out. The Indian doctor, or priest, took it up and killed it as an offering to the deity, probably sprinkling some of the blood on the sick. He then, with his adopted son, took the dead dog into the canoe and crossed the bay, where it is about three miles wide, to the Indian burying ground, and interred it. Not a word was spoken during the whole ceremony; yet doubtless many sincere but simple prayers were, offered up from the heart to Him who has compassion on the red man as well as the white, in the day of his calamity. The sacrifice "offered in faith," was accepted; and the sick woman soon after was restored to health.

While they were at the head of the rapids, young Convers saw Colonel McKee, who had a trading house at that place, and who informed him of the freedom of the two Choates, taken prisoners at the massacre of Big Bottom. The fore part of July they left the bay and went up a little above Detroit, apparently to attend a council of Indians, who had assembled to the number of nearly a hundred. For some weeks before this time Daniel had been quite ill with the fever and ague, brought on him from his exposures to the sickly, damp air of the bay shore, and the change in his diet, from the nourishing food of the settlers at Waterford, to the meager fare of the Indians, composed of fresh fish and the flesh of muskrats, without any salt or farinaceous matter, as they raised no corn. His Indian father and mother did all they could with their simple remedies to cure him, but without much benefit.

While at this new camp, he one day strolled along the shore of the river, a little above the town, and fell in company with a white man, unloading hay from a raft, who, learning his captive condition, told him of an Indian trader, named James Van Sheicke Riley, who lived at Saginaw Bay, but was then in Detroit, to purchase goods; and if he could find any means of acquainting him with his situation, he would aid him in regaining his liberty.

On the night of the 14th of July, the Indians were to have a grand dance. Just as the drums were beating the evening roll call, and the flag was lowered in the fort of Detroit, he strolled away from the encampment, and passing through a field of rye, which partly concealed him, succeeded in reaching the house of a Frenchman, who could talk some English. On making known to him his condition and wishes, he kindly concealed him in his chamber, until notice could be sent to Mr. Riley, which he did by his son. He came to him soon after dark, and arranged the plan for his rescue.

While they were in the loft of the Frenchman's house, several Indians came into the room below, in search of the fugitive. The owner of the house stoutly denied having seen any such person as they described. Young Convers now expressed his fears, in a low whisper, that there was no chance of escape; but Riley, who was a stout, athletic man, with an oath, bid him not to fear, for he could whip a dozen Indians, and had often done so in their drunken frolics.

After a while they departed, and the trader went away, saying that at daylight he would send a young, active Frenchman, with a horse, and have him taken into the fort. The night passed quietly, and at early dawn a man on horseback appeared at the door, behind whom he mounted, and making a rapid circuit round the land-side of the fort, came up to the gate just as the guard were throwing it open. His conductor took him to another Frenchman, who concealed him that day in his barn. A lad, the son of his protector, who could speak English, French, and some of the Indian tongues, came and spent the day with him; bringing him food, and cheering him with his lively prattle. In the course of the day, his friend Riley made known the escape and hiding place of the young American captive, to Major Smith, the Commander of the fort (then a British post), who that evening sent his own son, about the age of Daniel, to conduct him to the garrison hospital, where his declining health could be restored and would also afford a safe retreat from the Indians, whose perseverance in search of the runaway, for two or three weeks, was unceasing. But all their inquiries were fruitless, as no one betrayed him, or gave the least hint where he was. As they could hear nothing of him, his Indian father and mother thought he was killed, as they would not believe he would run away from them, and sincerely lamented his loss.

Mr. Riley, who so generously aided in planning his rescue, sometime after returned to the state of New York, and was for several years a postmaster in Schenectady. Young Smith was very assiduous and devoted to the welfare of his Yankee friend, whose pale face and hollow cheeks won deeply on his sympathy. He furnished him with a suit of his own clothes, in place of the Indian dress which he still wore, and brought him wine and other nice things from his father's table. Invigorated by this generous diet, and aided by the attention of the English surgeon, in about four weeks, the health of his protégé was fully restored, when his sparkling eyes and lively conversation fully repaid him for all his trouble. While secreted in the hospital, Thomas Shaw, one of the prisoners taken at Big Bottom, called to see him. It was near the middle of August, when one of the few vessels, which at that day navigated Lake Erie, was about to sail for Niagara. In this vessel Major Smith procured for him, and paid the expense of, a passage down, at the same time charging the captain to treat him kindly, and giving him a letter to the commander at Fort Erie, with instructions to send young Convers on, from post to post, until he reached the United States. Shaw went down with him, in the same schooner, to Niagara, where they arrived in about a week.

Here he stayed four weeks, waiting for a passage, boarding in the mean time with a Mr. Seacorn, who kept a tavern, and urged him to stay all winter and go to school, but the commander of the post advised him to go on. From this station he was sent to Cattarque, on the Canada shore of Lake Ontario, since called Kingston, and from there on to Montreal, and St. Johns. The British officers at all the posts uniformly treated him with kindness. At St. Johns, they were at dinner, when the sergeant of the guard handed them his letter of passport. They directly invited him in and seated him at the table; giving him a glass of wine, accompanied with kind words and smiling faces It was a season of festivity, when the generous cheer had softened their hearts. An order was drawn on the commissary for stores to take him through the wilderness to Castleton, in Vermont. Fortunately a party of horse dealers, who had been with a drove to St. Johns, were now ready to return to Vermont, and he went on with them. From Castleton he traveled to his relations in Killingly, Connecticut, but did not get back to Marietta until February, 1794.

Amid the bloodshed and gloom that darken the atrocities of the Indians, and for many years kept the pioneers in a constant state of watchfulness and fear, there now and then appears a bright spot like a star in the opening clouds of a dreary night. The humanity displayed by the British officers, among whom our prisoners were thrown in the war of 1791, as well as in the preceding hostilities in Kentucky, as testified by Boone, Kenton, and others, deserves our notice and highest commendation. Colonel Convers testifies to the uniform humanity with which he was treated, and the utmost deference paid to his condition and wants at every post which he visited. Their reception of him was not only humane, but kind, and gentlemanly. Such conduct from the subjects of a nation whom we had so long been in the habit of considering our enemies, cannot be too highly applauded, and should never be forgotten.

CHAPTER XXII.

Strength of the garrison. — Watchfulness of the settlers. — Hamilton Kerr. — Spies at Waterford. — 1793. — Adventure of Judge Devoll. — Abundance of wild game. — Schools.—Religious worship.— 1794. — Increase of the settlement. — Amusements.—Abel Sherman killed. — Condition of the settlement.—1795. — Sherman Waterman killed. — Settlers leave their garrisons. — Salt springs. — Value of salt. — Company formed to manufacture salt. — Description of the works.—Two of the salt makers lost in the woods. — Sufferings by cold and hunger. — Great change in the condition of the country.

The Indians, after their failure in the attack on the garrison in 1791, made no other serious attempts to break up the settlements as they had threatened to do. They probably discovered that they were inadequate to any successful assault on a well garrisoned post, with blockhouses and pickets, without the aid of artillery, and this they could not command. They therefore ceased to send out large war parties against the whites but continued to harass them by small bands of four or five warriors, who killed their cattle, and otherwise annoyed them, by constantly keeping them on the watch, when abroad at their work in the field. Their attention was also called off by inroads which were made into their own territories by bands of white men from Kentucky, after the defeat of the army under General St. Clair. This victory gave them great confidence in their own powers, and for a time threatened to overwhelm the frontier settlements. But the gradual assembling of another army and the posts erected near their own frontiers, served in some measure to check their incursions, and damp their hopes of finally driving their enemies south of the Ohio.

It is truly wonderful, how small were the number of lives lost by the Waterford settlement, placed as they were on the extreme frontier, and at a distance of twenty miles from any assistance. War parties often passed by them on their way to western Virginia, and frequently without disturbing them. They had no ancient grudge against the colonists of the Ohio Company to revenge, as they had against the Virginians; the former having uniformly treated them with kindness, before the breaking out of the war. They sent no expeditions into the Indian country to destroy their villages and crops, but remained peaceably at home attending to the cultivation of their lands, and when the Indians came about them, seldom pursued them. They felt no ill will toward the savages, and only armed to keep possession of their farms, and defend themselves against their attacks. It was with them a war of defense, and one which would never have taken place, but for the cruel and unjust treatment of them by the lawless hunters and borderers, of the frontiers of Virginia, and Kentucky. When war parties came round the settlements, they generally found the inhabitants on their guard. If in the fields at work, they always saw two or more sentries placed in the edge of the woods, watching for their approach, while the guns of the laborers, fifteen or twenty in number, were placed under the care of a sentinel, in a spot where they could seize them in a moment. In going to, and returning from their labor, flank guards marched on each side, to give notice of any ambuscade. A guard was kept day and night in the watch tower of the fort, who from his lofty post had a wide range over the district around. The spies or rangers daily traversed the woods for eight or ten miles distance, and immediately returned to give notice if they discovered any signs of Indians, within the circuit of their range, Over foes who were so habitually and constantly watchful, it was difficult for the savages to gain an advantage; and they seldom made an attack where the chances of success are doubtful. At night they sometimes approached the burning log heaps, in the adjacent clearings, and were dimly seen by the sentinel flitting around or past the flames. On these occasions they now and then snatched a burning brand from the heap within the range of rifle shot from the garrison, for the purpose of kindling a fire for themselves, at a more safe distance in the woods.

On one of these occasions when William Sprague was sentry, he saw and fired at an Indian, who dropped the brand and ran. The moccasin tracks of the two Indians who visited Marietta so often, one with a remarkably large and the other with a small foot, were several times seen in the plowed fields at Waterford. It is a very singular fact, that during the period of the war, no conflict took place between the white rangers and the Indian scouts, although they were daily abroad in the woods, and must often have been near each other. Hamilton Kerr one day, as he was ranging the forest a few miles east of Marietta, came unexpectedly upon an Indian at the distance of about eighty yards. He was a fine, tall fellow, who stood leaning on his rifle, with his back towards him, apparently in deep contemplation. Kerr instantly stopped, and as he raised his rifle to his face, cocked it. The click of the lock warned the Indian of his danger; his practiced ear knew that sound from every other. Without even turning his head, he dashed off like a stricken deer behind the trees, and was seen no more.

The rangers at Waterford for the first year were Neal McGuffy and William McCullock. In subsequent years, William Newel, Andrew McClure, and John White, acted in this capacity.

McGuffy was an eastern man and a soldier. He was a Lieutenant in the army of the United States during the Revolutionary War; a very brave man, and distinguished for his heroism at the Battle of Germantown; possessed great coolness and intrepidity in times of danger, and was of essential service to the Waterford settlement during the period of hostilities, He died at that place some years after the peace.

William McCullock was brought up on the frontiers of Virginia, near Wheeling, and from his youth acquainted with Indian warfare. He came to Waterford about the time the war began, and was employed as a ranger. After the peace he married a daughter of Isaac Zane, whose mother was an Indian. She was said to be a superior woman for intelligence and beauty. He settled at Mad River, on lands given him by Mr. Zane, who owned a large tract presented him by the tribe into which he was adopted. At the time of the late war, he joined the American troops as a volunteer, and was killed at the battle of Brownstown, greatly lamented by the army.

Narrow escape of Judge Devoll and son

Mr. Devoll and his son, Gilbert, jr., were both celebrated as expert fishermen, especially in that branch of the art called "spearing," or "gigging." It was practiced in a light canoe, with one man in the stern as steersman, while the sportsman stood in the bow with a slender pole, made of tough ash wood, sixteen feet in length, to one end of which was attached an iron with three prongs, like a trident, six or eight inches in length, the points armed with sharp barbs. This simple instrument an active man would throw to the distance of thirty or forty feet, and pierce a fish at every cast. It required much practice of the eye to judge of the right direction in which to make the throw, as the angle of refraction of the rays of light, reflected from the fish in the water, was very different from that of an object in the air. It also required great muscular strength and quickness of action to give the spear sufficient projectile motion. In the hand of an experienced fisherman it was an instrument of sure and fatal destruction to the finny race. At the period of the arrival of the colonists on the shores of the Ohio and Muskingum Rivers, their waters abounded in fish, to an extent and number that one of the present day would hardly credit.

The banks of these streams, in the vicinity of the settlers, had for a long period been destitute of any permanent inhabitants, and were only visited occasionally by the surrounding savages, who had their villages on the heads and branches of the tributary streams. Under this immunity, the fishes had increased at an astonishing rate. This store, which would seem to have been providentially accumulating for the use of the new settlers, afforded no inconsiderable portion of the animal food used by the inhabitants of Waterford, during the dark period of the Indian war. In the spring months, while the waters were turbid, great numbers were taken with the hook, on what were called "trot lines." In the summer and autumn, when the water was clear, the favorite mode was by spearing, and so plentiful were the fish, that in passing from Waterford to Marietta in a canoe, Allen Devoll and David Wilson have oftentimes taken from four to six hundred pounds. They were also taken in this way during winter, through a hole cut in the ice, where the water was deep.

In one of his fishing excursions in the summer of 1793, Gilbert Devoll, with his son, Wanton, had proceeded up the river about four miles to the mouth of Olive Green Creek, up the still waters at the outlet of which he was slowly pushing, by using the unarmed end of the spear as a setting pole, looking carefully ahead for fish, when he was suddenly startled by the snort of a horse, apparently only a few rods from the bank. In a moment after, it was answered by another. Knowing that there were no horses belonging to the garrison, he at once concluded they were Indian horses. Motioning to his son to keep quiet, he silently backed the canoe out of the mouth of the creek into the river.

The thick foliage of the overhanging branches of the sycamores, which lined the banks of all the streams, protected them from the view of any one, unless placed near the edge of the bank. With his sight fixed on the shore, expecting every moment to see the swarthy visages and flashing eyes of the savages, with their rifles peering from the covert of the trees, he rapidly, but quietly, gained the opposite side of the Muskingum undiscovered, and hastening homeward to the garrison, gave notice of his alarm. The next morning an armed party, headed by the rangers, visited the spot, and found the ashes and embers of a recent fire, where a band of Indians had encamped, within a few rods of the creek. The horses no doubt discovered their proximity by the acuteness of their smell, being able to distinguish between that of white men and Indians. The horses of whites have often been known to give notice of the vicinity of Indians in the same manner. The conclusion of the rangers was that the Indians were either asleep, or out watching the garrison, at the time the horses gave the alarm, or they would hardly have failed to search for the cause. By such slender chances, or rather providential occurrences, the early pioneers often escaped with their lives, during the period of Indian hostilities.

Schools, religious worship, etc.

During the larger portion of the time, especially in the winter, schools were supported and kept up, for the instruction of children. Joseph Frye and Dean Tyler were liberally educated men, and were employed at different times as teachers. The lower stories of the blockhouses afforded suitable rooms; that in the north-east angle was chiefly devoted to public uses, and a sentry constantly posted in its lofty watch tower. Religious worship was kept up generally on the Sabbath, under the guidance of Major Dean Tyler, who read a sermon from the works of some of the old standard divines, accompanied with singing and prayer. A large portion of the inhabitants attended these services, and especially when the Rev. Mr. Story came up from Marietta, which he occasionally did, during the whole period of the war. These pastoral visits were made by water, attended by an armed guard, with two or three men as scouts on the shore, to give notice of any hidden foe in the woods. They were always made in safety, and must have been highly appreciated by the inhabitants, or they would not have undergone the labor and hazard of the voyage. A reverential respect was paid to the Sabbath by nearly all the inhabitants, which may be attributed to their early habits, being generally descendants of the puritans, and also to the wholesome laws of Governor St. Clair, who paid special and early attention to this subject, as well as to the suppression of profanity and immorality among the citizens under his charge. He truly acted the part of a father, as well as governor, of the infant colonies; and his name and character ought to be far more highly esteemed and known, than they now are by the people of Ohio.

In the course of the year quite a number of inhabitants were added to the garrison, being called in by the notice published and sent abroad into the neighboring states of there being one hundred thousand acres of land to be given away to actual settlers. The assembling of the army by General Wayne on the frontiers, occupied the attention of the Indians, and the colonists were not so often molested. They had also become more familiar with war, after a training of three years, and began to have more confidence in themselves, and less dread of their enemies. From the accession of so many additional families, the room within the garrison began to be straitened, and the inhabitants thought it best to send out a small colony, and erect defenses on the Muskingum, at the mouth of Olive Green Creek, four miles above Fort Frye. In the spring of this year a blockhouse was erected, with three or four cabins, and the whole enclosed with pickets. This station sheltered about thirty souls, and the names of the families were as follows, viz:

George Ewing, wife, and seven children; among them was Thomas Ewing, then about four years old, and since distinguished as one of our most eminent public men.

Ezekiel Hoit, wife, and family of children;

Abel Sherman and wife, two sons, young men;

Ezra Sherman, and wife, also a son of Abel;

Aaron Belong, wife and son, two daughters.

Mathew Gallant, wife, and several children. Mathew was quite celebrated among the pioneers for his eccentricities and hardy exploits, some of which are related in the second volume of the American Pioneer.

Amusements of the early settlers

Games at ball of various kinds, with foot races, were their favorite sports, especially when celebrating the anniversary of the 7th of April, which was strictly kept for many years by all the inhabitants. At these games both old and young zealously engaged. Dancing was another diversion much practiced by the youth, and encouraged by the elders, as affording a healthy exercise in which the females could also bear a part. No distinctions of family, or office, were then made; all were on a level, and all exposed to the same dangers and privations, rendering them mutually dependent on each other, for aid and assistance. They were united in bonds of friendship like one great family, bound and held together in a common brotherhood by the perils which surrounded them. In after years, when each household lived separate in their own domicile, they looked back on these days with satisfaction and pleasure, as a period in their lives when the best affections of the heart were called forth and practiced towards each other. On festive occasions, such as Christmas and New Year, they were so unfortunate as not to be possessed of a single violin in the garrison; while a few years later, nearly every keel boat and barge on the western rivers carried one or more fiddles, and every night the men amused themselves with a hornpipe on the deck of the boat, or by the campfire. This practice was no doubt introduced by the French boatmen from Kaskaskia and St. Louis, who were always fond of the dance, and the music of the viol. A pretty good substitute was, however, found on these joyous occasions, in the voice of an elderly man, who had been a sailor in his youth, and was familiarly known, to the inmates of the garrison, by the name of Uncle Sam Mitchell, or more briefly, "Uncle Sam." He was fond of a dram, and with the aid of the enlivening beverage, would keep up a strain of fine vocal music the whole night. When toward daylight he became a little drowsy, a kind word and another glass set all right again. He oftener tired out the dancers, than they him. The older married men amused themselves with a game at whist, and passed the time very agreeably on these evenings, over a bowl of hot whisky punch and a plentiful supper, at which the good wives sometimes joined, although they usually preferred their tea to any other enlivening drink. By the aid of such homely and simple pastimes, the five years confinement within the walls of the garrison passed cheerfully and rapidly away.

Abel Sherman killed by the Indians

Early in June, 1794, a small war party, of three Indians, visited the Waterford settlement, for the purpose of plunder and scalps. One of their common modes of waylaying the inhabitants was to take possession of the cows, which during the summer ranged in the woods, and found an abundant supply of food in the luxuriant growth of pea vine and buffalo clover that grew spontaneously in the forests. In this instance, they kept the cows of the settlers at Olive Green, back in the hills, for one or two days, knowing that their owners would not fail to come out in search of them, and they could capture or kill them without danger to themselves. Among the cows was one belonging to Abel Sherman, a stout, resolute old man, of nearly sixty years. Against the advice of the other settlers, he determined to go out alone in search of the missing animals. With his gun on his shoulder, he wandered down along the margin of the river about four miles, to the garrison, at Waterford, thinking that perhaps they might have fallen in company with the cattle of that settlement, and come in there; or that some of the rangers might have seen them in their daily rounds. When he reached that post, he could gain no tidings of them. It was now near the close of the day, and his friends urged him to stay all night with them, as it was more than probable the Indians were watching the path, and were the cause of the absence of the cows. The resolute old man would not listen to their advice, but insisted on going home that evening. He had approached within a quarter of a mile of the station, when he found, near the mouth of a run, since called "Sherman's Run," a nice patch of May apples, fully ripe. The sight of the fruit tempted him to stop, and gather a quantity for the women and children. He had nearly filled the bosom of his hunting shirt, when rising up from his stooping posture, he saw an Indian within a few paces of him. Instantly springing to his gun that stood against a tree, he raised it to his shoulder, and fired at his enemy, in nearly the same instant that the Indian did at him. Sherman fell dead with a ball through his heart, while his own shot broke his adversary's arm, near the shoulder.

The report of the two discharges was distinctly heard at the little garrison, and his eldest son, Ezra, a stout, athletic man, and a fine woodsman, instantly said that one of those shots was from his father's gun, a large musket. He seized his arms, and rushed out in search of him, although strongly opposed by the men in the garrison, who were aware of the danger, knowing that the Indians never ventured into the settlements alone. Fearless of consequences, in a few minutes he was on the ground where his father fell, and found him already dead, and his scalp taken off. The Indians had immediately fled, knowing, or fearing that pursuit would be made from the garrison. Some of these particulars were ascertained after the peace, from an Indian who was present at the time, and came in to trade with the whites. He said the Indians had determined not to fire on a single man, but to make him a prisoner; or else to wait until more than one came out after the cows; but their discovery by Sherman, and his prompt action, led them to kill him in their own defense. The next day a party of men from the fort at Waterford went up and buried him near the mouth of the run where he fell.

Flourishing condition of the settlement

Although constantly in danger from their savage foes, these hardy pioneers of the forest not only maintained their ground, and supported their families, but they annually enlarged their borders, clearing new fields and increasing the amount of their crop. So that in the autumn of the year 1794 they loaded two boats with corn, amounting to two thousand bushels, or more, over and above their own wants. The corn was purchased by the army contractor for the troops at Fort Washington, or Cincinnati. The price was forty cents a bushel, and was a great relief to their necessities, as the wardrobes of many families had become quite scanty, from their inability to renew them. Sheep had not yet been introduced into the country, and all their home spun garments were made from flax and hemp, or the skins of the deer, which, when nicely dressed, afforded warm and comfortable jackets and pantaloons for the men and boys. They were much worn for many years in the early settlement of the country. The woods furnished an abundance of venison and turkeys, more than equaling in numbers the domestic animals of the present day. On the rich soil of the alluvions, corn grew with astonishing luxuriance, and afforded not only bread, but a surplus for fattening hogs; so that they soon added nice pork and bacon to their other luxuries. The great crops of acorns and beech nuts, in some seasons, fattened their hogs without any corn. They lacked for nothing really essential to civilized life, but salt. This article was enormously dear, not less than eight and sometimes ten dollars a bushel, so that the health and comfort of both man and beast often suffered for the want of it.

1795
Sherman Waterman killed by the Indians

In the spring of the year 1795, some young men, who had drawn donation lots on the south branch of Wolf Creek, about three miles from the Waterford garrison, concluded to clear their lands in company. Their names were William Ford, William Hart, Jacob Proctor, John Waterman, and Sherman Waterman. A small blockhouse was built on John's land, and they commenced the labor of cutting down the heavy timber that covered the creek bottom. Although after the defeat of the Indians by General Wayne in

August preceding, little danger was apprehended from them, yet as peace was not finally concluded, they as a matter of precaution thought it prudent to work in company, and so day by day alternately labored on each other's lots.

On the 15th of June, the fore part of the day was wet, with heavy showers of rain at intervals, so as to discourage them from their common work of chopping, and they concluded to spend the forenoon in a little enclosure near the house which was occupied as a garden. During a hard shower they retreated into the house. Sherman Waterman, wanting some fresh bark to put in the bottom of his sleeping birth, had gone down to the creek, a few rods distant, to procure it. In a few minutes the report of a rifle was heard. Each man seized his gun, and stepped to a port hole to discover the enemy. Directly Waterman came running towards them, and fell down exhausted from loss of blood, within a few yards of the house. He had been shot through the region of the liver, while busy at his work, and they continued to fire several shots at him after he fell, but dared not pursue him for fear of his companions in the blockhouse. While he thus lay exposed to the rifles of the Indians, begging his friends to assist him, William Hart and one other man rushed out amid the shot of the enemy and brought him into the house, unharmed themselves. The guns of the men soon caused them to retreat; when William Hart volunteered to go and carry notice of the disaster to the fort at Waterford.

A party of men, led by McGuffy, soon came up and took the wounded man in a bark canoe, down the creek to Tyler's blockhouse, where he died that night. On examining the vicinity for signs, or a trail of the Indians, they found, near a deep ravine that the white men were in the daily habit of crossing on a log, as they went out to their work, the spot where the Indians had lain in ambush that night. Not far from the end of the log was discovered a blanket and several silver brooches, which they had left as a decoy, to attract the attention of the whites, and while in a cluster and off their guard examining the articles, which doubtless some of them would notice and pick up, fire upon them, with the probability of killing them all. This device was often practiced, and with fatal effect, on a party of men under Captain Ogle in the narrows below Wheeling. But the rain of that morning providentially prevented this tragic catastrophe, and none but Waterman came within the reach of their rifles. He was the last man killed by the Indians in Washington

County. The old blockhouse was still standing in 1845, while those who built it are all in their graves.

Salt springs

At the conclusion of the Indian war, and the consummation of peace in 1795, the inhabitants sullied out of their garrisons, as the children of Noah did from the ark, and took possession of the earth, from which they had so long been hindered by their savage foe. Many of their privations and difficulties now ceased, while others remained in full force; among the latter was the enormous cost of culinary salt, which still remained at eight dollars a bushel, and greatly checked that free use of it, so necessary to the comfort and health of the inhabitants. It had been rumored, in the first settlement of the country, that salt springs existed on a stream since called Salt Creek that falls into the Muskingum River at Duncan's Falls; and a party had been sent up from Marietta, during the war, at great hazard from the Indians, to search for it. They however were unsuccessful, not having the time necessary for a thorough exploration. White men, taken prisoners by the Indians, had seen them make salt at these springs, and had noted their locality, so that from their description a skillful woodsman could find them. Feeling seriously the difficulties under which they labored, the inhabitants had a meeting and sent an exploring party of their best hunters to search for them. The attempt was successful. After their return, in the summer of 1796, a company was formed of fifty share holders, at one dollar and fifty cents each, making a capital of seventy-five dollars, with which to purchase castings and erect a furnace, for the manufacture of salt. Twenty-four kettles were bought at Pittsburgh and transported by water to the foot of Duncan's Falls, and thence carried on pack horses about seven miles to the salt licks. A well was dug near the edge of the creek, fifteen feet deep, down to the rock which formed the bed of the stream, through the crevices in which the salt water came to the surface. The trunk of a hollow sycamore tree, three feet in diameter, was settled into the well and bedded in the rock below, so as to exclude the fresh water. A furnace was built of two ranges, containing twelve kettles in each; a shed erected over the works, with a small cabin for the workmen to live in. The water from the well was raised by a sweep and pole. The company was divided into ten classes of five men each, who in rotation worked for two weeks at a time. The works were kept in operation night and day, the men standing regular watches. By the aid of a yoke of oxen, and one man to chop and haul wood, they could make about one hundred pounds of salt in twenty-four hours, it requiring about eight hundred gallons of water for fifty pounds. When the value of the labor and the cost of the outlay are estimated, the price of the salt was at least three dollars a bushel. It was also of a dark color, and inferior quality, much impregnated with bitter water, or muriate of lime. The greatest advantage to the company was, that the salt was procured by their own labor instead of their money, which was very scarce and difficult to get. Thus was the first salt made in the valley of the Muskingum. The saline was distant forty miles by land from Waterford, and during the winter, the provisions used at the works were packed out on horseback, and the salt came to the settlement in the same way, thus enhancing the expense and labor of procuring it, so that the actual cost could not have been less than four dollars a bushel. A part of the year the intercourse was by water to Duncan's falls, and thence by land. The company was kept up for three or four years, when the springs fell into other hands, and finally became the property of the state, and were leased out at a fixed rent.

Sufferings of two of the early salt makers

Two of the men engaged in salt making, were Judah Ford and Captain William Davis. They had gone up to the works the last of November; soon after which the weather set in very cold, and the men whose tour of duty followed theirs did not come to relieve them as was expected. They therefore remained until the 22d of December, when their stock of food was all exhausted, except a little venison bought from a hunting camp of Indians near them and it was absolutely necessary that provision should be brought up from Waterford, or the works abandoned. Three men were left to continue the labor, and the two above named started that day for home. Their road led through the woods without any trace, or marked trees, as this was the first season of salt making, and the intercourse thus far conducted by water. A year or two later a road was marked out by the United States and the mail carried on horseback from Marietta to Zanesville, passing directly by the salt works. Their outfit for the journey consisted of one small blanket, a single charge of gun powder, a flint, and an old jack knife, with a piece of tow string cut from a bag for tinder, and about two pounds of venison.

Not being familiar with the woods, they hired a hunter who was at the works to pilot them on to the head of Meigs Creek; but it began to snow when they had gone about three miles, and he left them on a ridge which he said would take them to that creek. It continued to snow nearly all day and fell about four inches deep. By the middle of the afternoon, they came to the end of the ridge, and descended down on to the low ground between the forks of a creek, which they supposed, was Meigs Creek. Just before night the weather cleared and became very cold. They spread their blanket on the snow and began the operation of kindling a fire. The snow rendered it difficult to procure wood that would burn, and kept them busy all night collecting fuel to keep up the fire. It was intensely cold. The beech trees froze so hard as to crack and snap like pistols, a proof of the extreme severity of the frost. They comforted themselves with the thought of the warm bed they should sleep in the next night; not once suspecting that the stream on which they encamped was not Meigs Creek. In the morning they left their uncomfortable bivouac by early daylight. The weather was still colder than at night, and was ascertained by a thermometer at Marietta to have been fifteen or twenty degrees below zero.

They started off at a brisk pace, to keep themselves from freezing, and as the sun shone that forenoon, they discovered that the stream run east, instead of south-west, as they knew Meigs Creek did. Thinking perhaps it might soon change the direction, they continued on downstream, until it run nearly north-west, and the body of water was larger than Meigs Creek at the mouth. This confirmed them in the belief that it was Wills Creek, a large tributary of the Muskingum, which enters that river high up, many miles above any settlements. Just before sun down, the)' stopped and kindled a fire, against a dead beech tree, and having gathered wood for the night, they set up some large chunks to break the force of the wind against their heads and backs. They now examined their feet, which had been freezing for several hours, and found the heels, toes, and sides severely frozen and very painful. After eating the small morsel of venison that remained, they began to discuss the probable result of their condition. They had no axe to prepare wood for the fire, and only a single priming of powder left to kindle one again, nor any gun to kill game. They were forty miles from Waterford when they started, and must now be, after two days rapid traveling, nearly double that distance. They were both thinly clad for winter, and had no blanket to cover them at night, the one they had being spread under them to protect them from the snow. The debilitating effects of the cold, with the want of food and sleep, had greatly enfeebled them; but they were men of sound sense and great resolution, two valuable qualities in cases of difficulty and danger. After a cold and windy night, they hailed the approach of day with gladness, although it brought no relief to their sufferings; the blessed light of the sun being as welcome to the woods-lost landsman after a gloomy night, as it is to the ship wrecked seaman. The result of their deliberation was, to retrace their steps if they could, to the salt works. Their feet, when they attempted to stand on them, refused to perform their office, but after going a mile or two became so benumbed with the cold, that they did not feel any pain or soreness. Life or death now depended on their own exertions, and redoubling their efforts, they reached their first night's encampment a little before sunset. Having no food, they concluded, as the moon was near its full, to continue their journey as far as they could. While in the low ground their former tracks in the snow served as a clue to lead them from the labyrinth, but when they ascended on to the ridge, the wind and the snow, which fell after they passed along, had obliterated this guide.

While ascending the hill their strength failed, so that they found they could not go much farther, and concluded to stop, and kindle a fire. An old dry top of a fallen chestnut tree, about half way up, offered them a favorable spot. They halted, spread their blanket on the snow, produced the flint and old knife, with a piece of the tow string, and the last little parcel of powder. Davis, whose hands had been wrapped in the blanket all day, took the flint and knife, but so benumbed were his fingers, that at every stroke one or the other would drop from his grasp. It was a trying moment, as their lives depended on the success of their efforts, for without a fire they must certainly freeze to death. At length the life giving spark was elicited, the powder flashed, the tow string caught the blaze, and after a good deal of blowing a fire was kindled, with the dry pieces collected from the decayed tree. After another long and tedious night, watching their fire and the progress of the moon, which to them seemed to stand still, as in the time of Joshua, the dawn of another morning appeared.

Their feet having been frozen and thawed two or three times, were now much swollen and excessively painful. After a number of efforts to stand upon them, they at length succeeded in reaching the top of the ridge, and their feet losing all feeling, from the effects of the cold, they put forward at their usual pace. Without any distinct knowledge of their position, they supposed they were about twelve miles from the salt works. In coming out, three days before, they knew they had not crossed any water course after the guide left them. The ridge was very devious in its direction, and they sometimes found themselves wandering off from it down some point or spur, and had to retrace their steps back again, causing them to travel two or three miles to gain one ahead.

About the middle of the day they strayed again from the ridge into a deep hollow, and being tired of going back, concluded to see the result. They soon came on to a small branch, and as they had heretofore gone down stream, now thought they would go up. In about half a mile it conducted them back on to the ridge again. Davis led the way as well as he could, and Ford followed, stepping in the tracks his companion made in the snow. They had been on the ridge but a short time, when the former stepped on the leg and foot of a deer, which was covered with the snow, bringing it to the surface. Ford instantly caught sight of it and asked him to stop. On examining, they recognized it as the one they had seen three days before, lying on the ground, just as the snow was beginning to fall, left there by some hunter. From this simple talisman they knew that they were near the spot where their guide had left them.

Mr. Ford says, in his manuscript notes of the affair, *"Had it not been for this interposition of Providence in our behalf, causing us to go out of the way and following up this very run and guiding our feet to this little sign, which lay concealed at least four inches under the snow, we might have wandered through the woods until night overtook us"!* But by this providential interference, and the help of some slight marks made by the hunters, they struck Salt Creek about two miles above the works and followed it down, reaching the station at four o'clock in the afternoon, the fourth day of their wandering.

Great was the surprise of their friends at their appearance, who, knowing the severity of the cold and their destitution for food, were much alarmed for their lives. On examining their condition they found that the water from the blisters had frozen their stockings to their feet, so that they were separated with great difficulty. Poultices of slippery elm bark were applied in the best manner their means would afford. It was fifteen days before they could be removed, when some pack horses came up with provisions, and they rode home. Mr. Ford lost a portion of the bones from three toes, and the upper part of one ear. Davis was deprived of one great toe, and all the others much mutilated. The former of these men who was then nineteen years old, and the latter some years more, both lived to see salt so abundant as to sell for twenty-five cents a bushel.

The foregoing narrative describes only one of the many trials which attended our forefathers in the settlement of the wilderness in the valley of the Muskingum. Numbers of these men were spared to see this region, which they found a dense forest, filled with savages and wild beasts, covered and dotted with towns and villages. Streams which no larger craft than the light canoe of the Indian had navigated since the creation, are now traversed by steamboats, whose noisy engines waken the sleeping echoes of the hills, and cause the shores to tremble with the strokes of their wheels. The lights of science and of art have removed the long reign of darkness, and the simple aborigines of the forest have been supplanted by civilization and the cultivation of the white man; and although we may deplore their misfortunes and pity their calamities in their removal from the land of their fathers, yet who shall say that the hand of God hath not directed it and his will ordained it as productive of the greatest good to the human race, and to the glory of His great name?

P. S. The principal facts in the history of Waterford were furnished by the following persons, who were actors in these scenes: Phineas and Nicholas Coburn, Deacon Wilson, Allen Devoll, Mrs. Story, Colonel Convers, and Mrs. McClure, the daughter of Judge Devoll. Dr. G. Bowen also afforded valuable aid in collecting facts.

CHAPTER XXIII.

The face of the country, for many miles back from the Ohio, and along the principal streams, is broken and hilly. The hills are not placed in regular ranges, like those which form the chains of mountains, in the heads of the Monongahela River, and in various other places, but are without order, and would seem to have been formed by the wasting away of the rocky strata on which they are based, by running water, and the action of the elements. They vary in height from one hundred and fifty to four hundred feet, sinking in many places near the heads of streams, to low undulations. The bottom lands along the borders of the rivers are not very low, and only overflowed in high floods. Extensive marshes, or ponds, are unknown in this part of the state. The lands are generally dry, and the larger portion of them will in a few years be under cultivation. At the period of the first settlement in 1788, one dense, continuous forest covered the whole region, entirely unbroken by the hand of civilization, except a small tract under the walls of Fort Harmer. The uplands presented a most enchanting appearance to the eye of the hunter or traveler. No brushwood then marred the fair beauty of the forest; but the view was extended from hill to hill amid the tall shafts of various species of trees without obstruction; while the mingled branches above afforded no unapt resemblance to the interior of the dome of an immense temple.

The yearly autumnal fires of the Indians, during a long period of time, had destroyed all the shrubs and under growth of woody plants, affording the finest hunting grounds; and in their place had sprung up the buffalo clover, and the wild pea vine, with various other indigenous plants and grapes, supplying the most luxuriant and unbounded pastures to the herds of deer and buffalo, which tenanted the thousand hills on the borders of the Ohio. The wild turkey, in countless flocks, roamed at large amid these beautiful forests, feasting on the acorns, chestnuts, and fruit of the beech, which the bountiful hand of the Creator had furnished in quantities adequate to the wants of all his creatures. The rivers were filled with delicious fish, in such abundance, that at certain seasons of the year the smaller tributaries might be said to have been "alive with them," and in the language of an old and early settler, *"The*

431

hook could hardly be dropped into the water without falling on the back of a fish." How abundantly had the Father of all provided for his children! and nothing but that love of war and bloodshed, which was so assiduously cultivated by the Indian, combined with the natural depravity of the human heart, could have prevented the aboriginal owners of this beautiful country from having been among the most happy of mankind.

On the uplands, the principal growth of forest trees consisted of the various species of oak, poplar, hickory, and chestnut. In some districts were found extensive woods of yellow pine and in tracts remote from the older settlements it is yet found in abundance. On the bottoms, or alluvions, and on the north sides of rich hills, the beech, sugar maple, ash, and elm, were the prevailing growth; while the sycamore lined the borders of the rivers, where its roots could be refreshed by the running water. Along these streams the red man pushed his light canoe, rejoicing in the wild freedom of the forest, and happily unconscious of the approaching fate which threatened his race, and was soon to banish all but his name from the face of the earth.

Along the borders of the Ohio River the climate is supposed to be more mild, than in the same parallel east of the Alleghany Mountains. This difference may in part be occasioned by the prevalence of southerly and south-westerly winds, and from there being no very high lands between us and the Gulf of Mexico, to reduce their temperature. The soil also, being of an argillaceous and loamy quality, radiates less rapidly the free caloric, than a rocky, or gravely, surface of country. The annual temperature at the mouth of the Muskingum, in latitude thirty-eight degrees, and twenty-five minutes, is found to be about fifty-three degrees of Fahrenheit. The temperature of the water in wells corresponds with the thermometer. The climate is very variable; and subject to sudden and great changes. These extremes are of short duration, very cold or very hot weather continuing for a few days only. The mercury has been known to rise to ninety-nine degrees in summer, and sink twenty-two degrees below zero in winter; making a range of one hundred and twenty-one degrees. On Tuesday the 3d of February, 1818, snow fell to the depth of twenty six inches, and lay on the ground for nearly three weeks. On the 9th of that month, the mercury in the morning was at twenty degrees below zero. On the 10th it sunk to twenty-two, but by the 12th the weather was quite mild. On these two cold mornings, a thick vapor, like steam from boiling water, rose from the Ohio River, and soon congealing, fell in large flakes of snow, all over the adjacent bottoms, affording the novel spectacle of a shower of snow from a clear and cloudless sky. All the peach trees, except in some sheltered spot, were killed down to the surface of the snow, and many shrubs and trees of the forest perished from the effects of this uncommon degree of cold. In winter the mercury does not often fall below zero, and seldom so low as to destroy the embryo buds of fruit trees.

In December, 1796, about Christmas, there was an excessive cold spell of weather. The rivers were frozen over to the depth of nine inches, soon after which there fell two feet of snow. In February, 1799, the cold was nearly as severe, and the snow quite deep. As the country becomes more cleared of its forests, there is no doubt it will be subject to greater extremes of heat and cold, with sudden transitions of temperature, than it was when covered with trees. Had we an ocean on the west and north-west, with no intermediate ranges of mountains, it is probable that cultivation would ameliorate our winters, as it has done in Europe. But the Rocky Mountains, and elevated prairie country on the west, will ever render it liable to be visited with dry, cold, westerly winds, during the winter and spring months, similar to those of China, blowing over the ranges of the Caucasus and elevated plains of Northern Tartary.

Another serious difficulty we have reason to fear will follow, as the effect of cutting away the forest, and that is excessive droughts in summer. The regularity and frequency of the summer rains will in a manner cease, and the principal falls will be in the spring and autumn; this has been the fact in other countries remote from the ocean, from the same cause, and must be so here; more especially in a flat country removed from mountain ranges, which act as conductors in drawing water from the clouds. Our rivers and creeks already feel the effects of cultivation, and afford a less uniform and steady flow of water in the summer months, than they formerly did.

At the first settlement of Marietta, a small creek which passes through the southern half of the town, called "The Tiber," rose from springs within two miles of the city. During the few first years, it was a steady stream all the year, and the early settlers thought would be permanent, and when collected in a reservoir, furnish them with water by means of an aqueduct. But of late years the bed of the stream is often dry in the month of May. The springs which supplied it, while sheltered by the forest, were perennial; but as soon as the trees were cut away, letting in the sun and air, they failed.

From an average of twenty-seven years, twenty-two of which were noted by us, it is found there are twenty-seven days in the year on which the thermometer rises to eighty degrees, and above; and the same number in which it sinks to thirty, and below. This distribution, however, varies greatly in different years, as will be seen in the following table, embracing a period of twenty-seven years. It also exhibits the amount of rain and melted snow, the mean temperature of each year, with the highest and lowest grades of heat, and the mean of the summer and winter months. It is deficient in portions of the years 1823 and 1824. Joseph Wood, Esq., late Register of the United States land office at Marietta, furnished the data up to the year 1823. Although this table occupies but a small space, yet in it there are embodied the results of not less than thirty-three thousand observations on the temperature and rains. Those on the winds and barometer, amounting to nearly as many more, are not here exhibited:

A condensed Meteorological Table, kept at Marietta, Ohio, from the year 1818 to 1846.

Year.	No. 1	No. 2	No. 3	No. 4	No. 5	No. 6	No. 7	No. 8
1818	—	51	——	74.00	—22	99	——	50.92
1819	54	68	38.22	74.33	13—	90	55.62	36.30
1820	58	51	35.50	73.70	— 0	90	53.68	39.71
1821	82	50	32.78	73.80	—20	90	53.14	43.32
1822	66	54	31.19	75.90	— 2	86	54.87	43.38
1823	—	—	29.10	——	— 7	—	——	*40.00
1824	—	64	——	75.80	14—	94	——	—
1825	52	96	36.32	——	— 6	94	——	—
1826	68	111	32.25	72.51	— 1	95	54.00	41.60
1827	55	98	33.30	76.67	— 2	95	54.92	41.48
1828	55	84	42.97	72.06	10—	94	55.22	49.50
1829	87	81	32.88	71.49	2—	92	52.38	39.52
1830	61	91	36.57	72.88	— 5	94	54.93	37.26
1831	99	72	30.75	71.44	—10	90	51.00	53.54
1832	78	70	29.30	69.31	— 9	92	52.42	48.33
1833	76	85	36.00	68.37	6	95	54.56	40.37
1834	75	100	35.83	72.42	— 0	95	52.40	34.66
1835	82	57	31.95	68.90	—15	89	50.65	42.46
1836	107	81	29.84	71.55	—18	88	50.03	36.09
1837	107	63	31.13	69.25	4	89	51.57	43.75
1838	78	102	30.42	74.23	—10	96	50.62	35.48
1839	84	75	34.11	69.88	— 4	92	52.54	33.27
1840	85	73	33.27	70.78	— 4	90	52.35	39.08
1841	73	89	35.33	67.45	— 4	94	52.83	42.07
1842	67	56	36.66	67.28	5	90	52.18	42.80
1843	102	89	32.33	71.15	— 0	92	50.77	41.76
1844	78	84	34.21	70.97	— 0	90	53.25	36.64
1845	88	79	36.60	71.16	— 2	92	52.75	33.90
1846	52	91	29.91	71.05	3—	92	53.64	46.27

* 1823, was an uncommonly wet year, and as only eight months are noted, it is probable the amount of rain was at least fifty inches.

Column No. 1, indicates the number of days in each year on which the mercury fell to and below thirty degrees. No. 2, the number of days on which it rose to and above eighty degrees. No. 3, the mean temperature of the winter months, No. 4, the mean of the summer months, No. 5, the greatest degree of cold, No. 6, the greatest of heat, No. 7, the mean temperature of the year, No. 8, the amount of rain and melted snow in inches and hundredths; the mean amount of which for twenty-six years is forty-one inches; while the mean for the last seven years is only thirty-eight inches, showing a falling off of three inches in the annual amount. Whether this may be all attributed to the cutting away of the forests, or to some other cause, is yet uncertain, until the country is still further opened and future observations made. The warmest part of the day in summer is between three and four o'clock, P. M.; the coolest just before sunrise. February is usually the coldest month, although our winters vary much in this respect; it sometimes being December and then again January. In the former month we have the greatest depressions of temperature, probably from there being in that month the greatest falls of snow. In common winters the snow is only a few inches deep, and lies on the ground but a short time. The greatest snow storms are usually accompanied with wind from the north-west. In cold and dry winters the rivers are obstructed and sometimes closed with ice, but if the winter is wet they remain open, and sometimes entirely free of ice.

From the 1st of April to the last of May, in the early settlement of Ohio, the weather was usually mild and fine, so that the planting of Indian corn was finished by the 7th of April, that day being for many years a holiday, in commemoration of the landing of the forefathers at Marietta; but of late years the spring months are changed, so that we have severe frost in May. This was remarkably the fact in May, 1834, when there were hard frosts every morning from the 13th to the 18th of the month. It had been quite an early spring, all the forest trees were in full leaf by the latter part of April, and the peach in bloom on the 8th of that month. To show the variations of the seasons and the capricious habits of the climate, the blossoming of the peach tree may be noticed in different years. In 1791, this tree was in bloom at Waterford, sixteen miles north of Marietta, the last of February. In 1806, at Belpre, ten miles south on the 25th of February, and in 1808 on the 28th of that month. In 1837, it bloomed on the 28th of April, and the apple on the 5th of May, a difference of sixty-two days. In 1843, it was retarded to the 25th of April, and the apple to the 5th of May. The most usual period of late years is about the middle of April, while formerly it seldom was later than March.

When the Ohio Company settlers first landed at the mouth of the Muskingum, on the 7th of April, 1788, the grass, pea vines, and other herbage, were a foot high on the bottoms and hill sides, so that their cattle and horses found an abundant supply of food. Untimely frosts did, however, visit the country, at a very early period, but more rarely than of late years. On the morning of the 16th of June, 1774, it is stated by Henry Jolly, Esq., formerly an associate judge of this county, that there was a frost in the country about Washington, Pa., where he then lived, which cut down the corn, and killed the leaves on the forest trees, but it sprang up again so as to make a crop. It was the year of Dunmore's Indian war. The country in the Ohio Company's purchase is at a much lower level, and probably did not feel the effects of this frost. On the 5th day of May, in the year 1803, there was a fall of snow at Marietta, and over the western country, four inches deep, followed by hard frosts on two or three nights. All the fruit was killed, apples at the time being of the size of ounce bullets, so that the trees must have bloomed early in April. This event was the more remarkable from its great extent, embracing all the middle and eastern states from Ohio to Massachusetts, where we then lived, and well remember the curious appearance of the apple trees in full bloom and covered with snow. It may be noted as a general rule, that very early springs are more liable to late frosts, than those which are more backward.

While the earth was defended from the rays of the summer sun, and protected from the cold blasts of winter by an impenetrable covering of fallen leaves, and a thick growth of forest trees, there can be no doubt of the winters being milder, and the summers more temperate, than at present.

It was especially noticed in the summer nights, which were so cool as to render a blanket both a pleasant and desirable covering to the sleeper. On the alluvions the earth, when protected by the forest from the influence of cold winds, and covered with a thick coat of fallen leaves, never froze; while in an adjacent cleared field it froze to the depth of several inches. The warm vapor constantly rising from the earth, served to temper the atmosphere and render it milder than at present. There was also, more or less uniformly, back of the bottoms, strips of wet land, called slashes, or swamps, which kept open during the winter, and discharged a steady supply of vapor of the same temperature of the earth, thus aiding in keeping up the warmth of the surrounding atmosphere. It is true there were some very cold winters and deep snows, but they were not so changeable as now; nevertheless it yet remains certain, that the winters are much more uniform, while a country is covered with the forest, and not subject to such sudden changes of temperature as they are in an open region. In New England, since the forests were cut away, they have much less snow than they had one hundred years ago.

The summers are as much changed as the winters; fifty years since, they were more humid, and there was more generally that condition of the atmosphere which we call *sultry,* and now experience in warm weather after a heavy rain. This constant humidity of the air was occasioned by the regular evaporation of moisture from the leaves of the trees, shrubs, and plants that clothed the face of the earth, and shut out the drying influence of the sun and air.

The same causes kept the surface constantly moist, and afforded a regular supply of water to the springs, during the summer as well as the winter, protecting the tender roots of the grasses and other plants from the cold, caused them to vegetate early in the spring, and bring forth a plentiful supply of herbage for the wild animals of the forest, and the domestic cattle of the new settler.

In October, and fore part of November, the weather is usually serene and delightful, rivaling in the mellow and balmy state of the atmosphere, that of Greece, or Italy. It is in fact the most poetic season of the year. The various hues imparted to the forests by the advance of autumn, which daily changes and deepens their rich and gorgeous tints, when seen through the light mists of our "Indian summer," gives a charming and romantic view to the landscape, which few portions of the world can equal and none surpass.

The mean heat of July is found to be greater than that of any other month, but in August the mercury for a few days is usually higher than in July. The hottest days were sometimes followed by cool nights, more so than of late years. The morning is comparatively cool in the hottest season of the year, probably owing to the humidity of the atmosphere absorbing the free caloric and descending in dews and fogs; the latter being confined to the vicinity of water courses. The great abundance of forest trees is doubtless one cause of the greater humidity of the climate in this region of country, than in the same parallel east of the mountains. The quantity of rain which annually falls there, varies from twenty-four to thirty-six inches, while here on an average of twenty-six years, the mean amount is forty-one inches, varying from thirty-four to fifty-four inches. The humidity of the air, and long continued heat of summer, acts on the human frame much like a tropical climate, causing languor and a general debility, during the heat of summer, and lessening the muscular power both of man and beast.

The condition of the atmosphere also lessens its density, indicated by the settling of the mercurial column in the barometer. As to the general range of this instrument, it is not known to sink any lower, at the same elevation above tidewater, in the valley of the Ohio, than it does on the east side of the Alleghany range, although this has been formerly intimated. At an elevation of six hundred feet above tide water, its mean annual height at Marietta is twenty-nine inches and fifty hundredths, rising in clear cold weather, with the wind from the north-west, to thirty inches, and in great changes sinking to twenty-eight and a half inches. The greatest range is during the winter months and the least in summer, often standing for several days in succession without varying the fiftieth part of an inch. In winter the fluctuations are daily, and sometimes almost hourly, independent of the diurnal ebbing and flowing of the atmosphere. The seasons vary very considerably as to the distribution and quantity of rain, some being more wet, and others extremely dry, but seldom so much so, in either extreme, as to destroy the crops entirely. The years 1805, 1838, and 1845, were noted for excessive drought—especially 1845, when nearly all the crops of grass and grain were destroyed in the northern counties of the state.

The larger portion of the rain falls in moderate showers, though we sometimes have heavy rains, especially at or near the summer solstice. This was the case in the year 1837, and again in 1844. Hail storms are more common in May and June, than at any other time. They are of rare occurrence, and much less destructive to crops than in more mountainous countries. Those terrible electric phenomena called "tornadoes," seldom visit this portion of Ohio. For the last thirty-five years, not one has traversed this county, and from the rarity of those unerring marks left in their train for many years after, in the wide furrow of up turned forest trees, it is probable they were never very frequent in this part of the state.

The prevailing winds are from the south, south-west, and west; but also blowing many days in the winter from the north, and north-west. There are few winds from the east. The course of the winds regulates the temperature of the year, and the amount of rain. Westerly and northerly winds bring cold and drought, while the southerly and southeasterly, bring warmth and rain. A full demonstration of this axiom was seen in the spring of the year 1845, so notable for the cold drying winds from the west, and the excessive drought, which prevailed until the middle of June. By noticing the course of the winds in different years, we arrive at the cause of the variations in temperature. This is more especially true of the spring and winter months, westerly and northerly winds being invariably accompanied with cold backward and dry springs; while early ones are ever attended by southerly breezes, and plenteous showers of rain. The westerly and north-westerly winds traverse elevated and dry regions of country, deficient both in caloric and moisture, the two main principles in the support of vegetable life; while southerly breezes come charged with humidity and warmth from the valley of the lower Mississippi, bringing in their train the charms of Flora, and the rich bounties of Ceres. With the early vernal zephyrs of the south, the northerly migrations of the feathered race commence, along the westerly base of the Cumberland ranges of mountains, and up the valleys of the easterly tributaries of the Mississippi and Ohio Rivers. Sometimes their journeys are begun too early, as in the years 1816, 1834, and 1845, when thousands of birds whose food is furnished by insects, perished by the sudden transition of temperature, from the warmth of summer to the frosts of winter. It has been observed that our most healthy seasons are accompanied with northerly winds after rain, and that in the more sickly, they blow from the south, but in great epidemics, it is probable the winds have little or no influence on the source of disease. Sudden changes from heat to cold, in August and September, often produce sickness, when earlier in the season, before the body is debilitated by the heat of summer; the transition is borne without apparent harm.

Wild animals

Before the landing of the Ohio Company, wild game was very abundant in the vicinity of Marietta, deer and turkeys, with occasionally elk and buffalo. In the winter of 1792, Hamilton Kerr and Peter Niswonger killed six or seven buffaloes on Duck Creek, near a place called the "Cedar Narrows," in the present township of Fearing. They were fat, and of the first quality of meat. Judge Gilman, a nice connoisseur, thought them better than any beef he had ever eaten. Their food, altogether of the wild grapes, no doubt flavored and enriched their flesh. In the fall of the year 1790, after the famine, beech mast abounded in the forest on the bottom lands, which brought in the turkeys in such countless numbers, that the inhabitants were obliged to gather their corn before it was fully ripe to save it from their ravages; and to cover their stacks of grain with brush. One man killed forty in a day with his rifle. They were caught in pens, killed with clubs and dogs by the boys, until a turkey would not sell for six cents, the people being cloyed, like the Israelites with quails. They were very fat; and full grown ones weighed from sixteen to thirty pounds.

"In the winter of 1792-3, Kerr and Niswonger went from Marietta to the oak flats, ten miles west of the Muskingum, in the morning, and killed that day forty-five deer, and hung them up; came home at evening, and the next day went out with horses from Fort Harmer, and brought them all in.

"The migration of the grey squirrel is a very curious phenomenon, and not easily accounted for. In the autumn of certain years, they become itinerant, traveling simultaneously in millions from the north to the south; destroying whole fields of corn in a few days, if not immediately gathered, and eating everything in their way, like the locusts of Africa, while traveling forward without stopping long in any place; swimming large rivers; and perhaps before winter, return again by the same route toward the north." As the country has become more cleared of the forest, their numbers have greatly diminished. "Bears and panthers were common in the hills, but not Bo abundant as in many other portions of the country, neither were they so numerous or daring as the wolf and wild cat. They were all fond of hogs and pigs, but the two former were more shy, and did not repeat their visits with the pertinacity of the wolf, to the sheep fold and pen of the farmer."

"As an evidence of their strength, a panther killed a hog, belonging to Isaac Barker of Belpre, in the winter of 1794, or 1795, and carried him through the snow, nine inches deep, a considerable distance, without leaving any trail of the hog, and buried him by the side of a log. He was pursued in the morning, and killed on the hills two or three miles distant. Wolves were the most annoying and destructive; sometimes pursuing men who were unarmed, and forcing them to take shelter in a tree, to avoid their attack. The early settlers, to preserve their hogs, were obliged to build pens so high that the wolves could not jump or climb over them; or if in a low pen, covered with logs too heavy for them to remove. Large gangs of hogs in the woods could defend themselves by placing the young and feeble ones in the center of a ring, formed by the old and stronger animals. If a wolf came within their reach, they all fell upon him, and tore him in pieces with their tusks and teeth." (Colonel Barker's MSS. notes.)

The wolf, for thirty years, was a great hindrance to the raising of sheep, and for a long period the state paid a bounty of four dollars on their scalps. Neighboring farmers often associated, and bid an additional bounty of ten or fifteen dollars, so as to make it an object of profit for certain of the old hunters, to employ their whole time and skill in trapping this ferocious and villainous animal. At this period the race is nearly extinct, in the Ohio Company's lands, and sheep range at large, unmolested, except by dogs, now their worst enemy. The beaver disappeared, in a great measure, from this part of the country, with their friends and admirers, the Indians—at least few remained after they left here. The last seen on the Muskingum, was near Captain Devoirs Mill, about the year 1805, and was trapped by Isaac Williams.

Natural productions of the rivers

While the banks of the streams were covered with trees, they were plentifully stored with fish. This was especially so, when the Ohio was first occupied by the whites. There was then a great abundance of insects and food suited to their nature, and fewer enemies to destroy them. The white man had but just begun to disturb the finny tribes in these quiet waters, while the red man had for a long time nearly deserted their shores. Ignorant of the devices of man to ensnare them, they were easily taken by the single hook, the "trot line," or the spear.

"The black cat and the pike were the largest among the aquatic races. The yellow cat, white perch, salmon, spotted perch, sturgeon, and buffalo, were all fine fish, weighing from five to fifty pounds. A black cat was caught by James Patterson, a professed fisherman, in 1790, which weighed ninety-six pounds. He anchored his canoe at the mouth of the Muskingum, just at dark, threw out his lines, and wrapping himself in his blanket, lay down in the boat for a nap of sleep. This fish got fast to one of his hooks, and had strength to drag the canoe and light stone anchor from the edge of the shoal into deep water, and then float down to near the head of the island, where he found himself on awaking. These fish, when fat, make fine eating, especially if lightly salted and dried."

"The pike is the king of fish in the western rivers. Judge Gilbert Devoll took a pike in the Muskingum: which weighed nearly one hundred pounds, on the 2d of July, 1788. He was a tall man, but when the fish was suspended on the pole of the spear, from his shoulder, its tail dragged on the ground, so that it was about six feet in length. This enormous fish was served up on the 4th of July, at a public dinner. It was taken in the following manner:

"The Ohio Company's boat, the May Flower, was lying in the mouth of the Muskingum, and was used as a kind of store boat, and especially for dressing fish. A large pike was seen to come daily and feed on the offal, which was thrown over. He was rather shy at first, but soon became more familiar with the people on board. Preparing themselves with a light canoe, and proper fish spears, Judge Devoll and his son started the fish up the Muskingum, pursuing him by the wake made in the water, for nearly a mile, intending to tire him out. Seeing him to flag a little in the chase, they run above, and turned him down stream, plying all their strength to the paddle and pole, they followed him so rapidly that his strength was exhausted, and coming along side pierced him with their spears, and dragged him into the canoe.

"The most of the fish were taken on the trot line; a half barrel or more being often caught in a night. The Indians had a mode of taking large pike, which is still practiced by fishermen on the Ohio. A fish, weighing a pound or more, was fastened to a strong hook and line, by forcing it through the length of the body to near the tail. This was thrown out thirty or forty yards into the river, near the mouth of a creek, where pike lie in wait watching for prey, and then drawn rapidly into shore, so as to make the bait jump along on the surface, imitating a fish pursued by another. The pike, if in sight, instantly seized upon the fish, and was sure to be hooked." (Judge Barker's MSS. notes.)

To the early settlers on the borders of the Ohio and Muskingum, the fish of these waters furnished no small part of their animal food, especially in the spring and autumn. In the former period they were taken on hooks, but in September and October, when the water was low and clear, they were taken by torch light with the fish spear, or gig. A large torch of pine splinters was set up in the bow of the canoe to attract the attention of the fish, and give light to the sportsmen. A man in the stern guided the canoe, with a paddle, giving it a gentle motion, as the spearman directed. A skillful man would often load a canoe in a few hours. The fish seem to be amazed at the flame of the torch, and seldom try to escape, while by daylight they fly from their pursuers.

For the following valuable documents, contained in the appendix, the author is indebted to the Hon. Wilkins Updike, of Kingston, Rhode Island, who, a number of years since, when the pamphlets of General Varnum's oration, and the address of Governor St. Clair, were out of print, and only a solitary copy or two could be found in the land, took the precaution of preserving in manuscript these valuable memorials of early events at Marietta. From this he kindly furnished a transcript, in the spring of 1846, which is now copied in these printed sheets.

Since then a printed copy has been found among the papers of Griffin Greene, Esq., deceased, and is probably the only one in the State of Ohio. It is now in the library of the Cincinnati Historical Society.

AN ORATION,

DELIVERED AT MARIETTA, JULY 4, 1788, BY THE

HON. JAMES M. VARNUM, ESQ.,

ONE OF THE JUDGES OF THE WESTERN TERRITORY;

THE SPEECH OF HIS EXCELLENCY,

ARTHUR ST. CLAIR, ESQ.,

UPON THE PROCLAMATION OF THE COMMISSION APPOINTING
HIM GOVERNOR OF SAID TERRITORY, AND THE PROCEED-
INGS OF THE INHABITANTS OF THE CITY OF MARIETTA.

NEWPORT, R. I. PRINTED BY PETER EDES: 1788.

James Mitchell Varnum

The fourth of July, in the year of our Lord, one thousand seven hundred and eighty-eight, was celebrated, for the first time, at the city of Marietta, in the territory of the United States, northwest of the river Ohio. The day was announced by a federal salute at Fort Harmer, erected on the opposite bank of the Muskingum. The flag of the United States was hoisted in the forts, and the bastions and curtains decorated with standards.

At half past twelve, General Harmer, with the ladies, officers, and other gentlemen of the garrison, arrived at the city, upon the point formed by the confluence of the two rivers, where were assembled the gentlemen of the Ohio company, and the other people who composed the settlement.

In consequence of previous arrangements, at the particular request of the gentlemen concerned, an oration was delivered by the Hon. James Mitchell Varnum, Esq., one of the Judges of said territory. The following is an exact copy:

THE ORATION

This anniversary, my friends, is sacred to the independence of the United States. Every heart must exult; every citizen must feel himself exalted upon the happy occasion.

The memorable Fourth of July will ever be celebrated with gratitude to the Supreme Being, for that revolution which caused tyranny and oppression to feed upon their own disappointment, and which crowned the exertions of patriotism with the noblest rewards of virtue.

How execrable the system which grasped at the possession of our dearest rights, and how happy the sons of freedom in being rescued from the vilest servitude.

Recollection, thou faithful monitor of past barbarities, retire behind the curtain of oblivion, nor continue to open our wounds afresh. May the piercing groans of a dying father—the melting tears of a tender mother—the carnage of heroic brothers—the torturing shrieks of virgin innocence, and the agonizing pangs of sanctified connections, no more embrace the hallowed shrines of vengeance, nor interrupt the joys of men and angels!

If the praises of all the citizens of the United States have ascended, in annual commemorations, to the most perfect altar, meeting the approbation of Heaven, how elevated should our feelings be who celebrate, not only the common advantages of independence, but who, for the first time, recognize our own particular felicity in being placed upon this happy spot!

The fertility of the soil—the temperature and salubrity of the air—beautifully diversified prospects—innumerable streams, through a variety of channels communicating with the ocean, and the opening prospect of a prodigious trade and commerce, are among the advantages which welcome the admiring stranger.

> Sweet is the breath of early morn, her rising sweet
> With charm of earliest birds; pleasant the sun,
> When first, on this delightful land, he spreads
> His orient beams on herb, tree, fruit, and flower,
> Glist'ning with dew; fertile the fragant earth,
> After mild showers, and sweet the coming on
> Of grateful evening mild; the silent nights,
> With this her solemn bird, and this fair moon,
> And these the gems of heaven, her starry train."

Unfortunately for the United States, their progress to victory and independence was so rapid, as not to admit of a correspondent change in the nature of their governments.

The high station which, after a conflict of eight years, ranked them among the nations of the earth, created objects of the first magnitude. Prejudices too deeply imbibed, and riveted by the force of pre-existing opinion, and local habits, the offspring of unequal advances in civil society, were to be conquered and removed; the mechanic arts and liberal sciences to be promoted; trade and commerce to be directed in their proper objects, through channels entirely contrariant to colonial systems; new sources of revenue were to be opened, in the management whereof, experience as well as power were wanting; the variety of connections arising from their relative situations, laid the foundation for an almost entire change in criminal jurisprudence; the acquisition of immense tracts of territory, not within the limits of any particular state, and the boundless claims of some of the states or counties, not their own, were attended with innumerable difficulties, and threatened the most serious consequences. In short, the articles of confederation, founded upon the union of the states, were so totally defective in the executive powers of government, that's change in the fundamental principles became absolutely necessary, and but for those friendships which have formed and preserved an union sacred to honor, patriotism, and virtue, and, but for that superior wisdom which formed the new plan of a federal government, now rapid in its progress to adoption, the confederation itself, before this day, would have been dissolved! Then, indeed, might we have *"hung our harps upon the willows, for we could not have sung in a strange land."* Then we might have lamented, but could not have avoided the horrors of a civil war. Promiscuous carnage would have deluged the country in blood, until some daring chief, more fortunate than his adversary, would have riveted the chains of perpetual bondage!

But now anticipating the approaching greatness of this country, nourished and protected under the auspices of a nation, forming and to be cemented by the strongest and the best of ties; the active, the generous, the brave, the oppressed defenders of their country will here find a safe, an honorable asylum, and may recline upon the pleasure of their own reflections.

Every class of citizens will be equally protected by the laws; and the labor of the industrious will find the reward of peace, plenty, and virtuous contentment.

Until the new constitution shall so far have operated as to require the possession of Niagara and Detroit, we may possibly meet with some disturbances from the natives; but it is our duty, as well as interest, to conduct toward them with humanity and kindness. We must, at the same time, be upon our guard, and by no means suffer the progress of our settlement to be checked by too great a degree of confidence.

Were the paths of life entirely strewed with flowers, we should become too much attached to this world, to wish ever to exchange it for a more exalted condition. Difficulties we must expect to encounter in our infant state; but most of the distresses common to new countries we shall never experience, if we make use of the means in our power to promote our own happiness.

Many of our associates are distinguished for wealth, education, and virtue, and others, for the most part, are reputable, industrious, well informed planters, farmers, tradesmen, and mechanics.

We have made provision, among our first institutions, for scholastic and liberal education; and, conscious that our being as well as prosperity depend upon the Supreme will, we have not neglected the great principles and institutions of religion.

The United States have granted to us, in common with the whole territory, a most excellent constitution for a temporary government; they have provided for its regular administration, and placed at its head a gentleman of the first character, both for the many amiable virtues of his private life, and for the eminent talents, and unshaken fidelity with which he has sustained the most important appointment. We mutually lament that the absence of his Excellency will not permit us, upon this joyous occasion, to make those grateful assurances of sincere attachments, which bind us to him by the noblest motives that can animate an enlightened people. May he soon arrive. Thou gentle flowing Ohio, whose surface, as conscious of thy unequaled majesty, reflecteth no images but the grandeur of the impending heaven, bear him, oh, bear him safely to this anxious spot! And thou beautifully transparent Muskingum, swell at the moment of his approach, and reflect no objects but of pleasure and delight!

We are happy, my fair auditors, in expressing our admiring attachments to those elevated sentiments which inspired you with the heroic resolution of attempting the rude passage of nature's seeming barrier, to explore, in the rugged conditions of the field, the paradise of America. Gentle zephyrs, and fanning breezes, wafting through the air ambrosial odors, receive you here Hope no longer flutters upon the wings of uncertainty. Your present satisfaction, increasing by the fairest prospects, will terminate in the completion of all your wishes.

Amiable in yourselves, amiable in your tender connections, you will soon add to the felicity of others, who, emulous of following your bright example, and having formed their manners upon the elegance of simplicity, and the refinements of virtue, will be happy in living with you in the bosom of friendship.

To the secretary of war, whose exalted talents and long experience have enabled him to form the most perfect arrangements; we are greatly indebted for the aid of a corps high in the splendor of military discipline. We have received from the commanding general, and from all his officers, every mark of hospitality, friendship, and politeness. Our acknowledgments, therefore, are the more unreserved, as they flow from the most unequivocal feelings. Our friends — our country's friends—we embrace you as a band of brothers, connected by the most sacred ties! In the name of all who have fought, who have bled, who have died in the cause of freedom! In the name of all surviving patriots and heroes! In the name of a Washington! We declare that, in the honorable character of soldiers, you revere the sacred rights of citizens! Live then in this happy assemblage of superior minds! Whenever you may be called to the field of Mars, may you be crowned with unfading laurels! We know you fear not death — but, living or dying, may you receive the plaudits of grateful millions!

Mankind, my friends, have deviated from the rectitude of their original formation; they have been sullied and dishonored by the control of ungovernable passions; *"but rejoice, ye shining worlds on high,"* mankind are now upon the ascending scale; they are regaining, in rapid progression, their station in the rank of beings. Reason and philosophy are gradually resuming their empire in the human mind; and when these shall have become the sole directing motives, the restraints of law will cease to degrade us with humiliating distinctions, and the assaults of passion will be subdued by the gentler sway of virtuous affection.

Religion and government commenced in those parts of the globe where yonder glorious luminary first arose in effulgent majesty. They have followed after him in his brilliant course — nor will they cease until they shall have accomplished, in this western world, the consummation of all things.

Religion inspires us with the certain hope of eternal beatitude, and that it shall begin upon the earth, by an unreserved destitution to the common center of existence. With what rapture and ecstasy, therefore, may we look forward to that all important period when the universal classes of mankind shall be satisfied! When this new Jerusalem shall form an august temple, unfolding its celestial gates to every corner of the globe — when millions shall fly to it *"as doves to their windows,"* elevating their hopes upon the broad spreading wings of millennial happiness! Then shall the dark shades of evil be erased from the moral picture, and the universal system appears in all its splendor! Time itself, the area and the grave of imperfection, shall be engulfed in the bosom of eternity, and one blaze of glory pervade the universe.

General Varnum died at Marietta, January 10th, 1789, of consumption, six months after these events

ORDER OF THE CELEBRATION
JULY 4, 1788, AT MARIETTA

At two o'clock the ladies and gentlemen were conducted to a spacious bower, where they partook of .an entertainment, prepared for the occasion. After dinner the following toasts were drank:

1. The United States.
2. The Congress.
3. His most Christian Majesty.
4. The United Netherlands.
5. The Friendly Powers throughout the world.
6. The new Federal Constitution.
7. His Excellency General Washington and the Society of Cincinnati.
8. His Excellency Governor St. Clair, and the Western Territory.*
*A Federal salute at the garrison.
9. The memory of those who have nobly fallen in defense of American freedom.
10. Patriots and Heroes.
11. Captain Pipe, chief of the Delawares, and a happy treaty with the natives.
12. Agriculture and Commerce, Arts and Sciences.
13. The amiable partners of our delicate pleasures.
14. The glorious Fourth of July.

The greatest order, propriety, and harmony prevailed through the day, which was closed by a beautiful illumination of Fort Harmer.

Upon the 15th day of July his Excellency, the Governor, accompanied by Major Doughty of the artillery, arrived in the twelve-oared barge, completely manned. He was received at the garrison by General Harmer, with military honors, and every kind of polite attention, due to a character so eminently distinguished. The officers and men under the general's command appeared, if possible, more brilliant than usual. The anxious expectations of all the citizens were greatly satisfied, and a universal joy enlivened every countenance.

Upon the 18th following, in consequence of previous notice, his Excellency, attended by the Judges Parsons and Varnum, and Mr. Secretary Sargent, made his public entry at the bower, in the city of Marietta, where he was received by General Putnam, and all the citizens, with the most sincere and unreserved congratulation.

His Excellency was seated, and after a short interval of profound silence, arose and addressed himself to the assembly in a concise but dignified speech.

He was pleased to inform them that his happiness was extreme in meeting them upon so important an occasion; that he brought with him a most excellent constitution for the government of the whole territory, and to which he claimed their attention.

The ordinance of Congress of the 13th of July, A. D., 1787, for the government of the territory of the United States northwest of the river Ohio, was read by the Secretary. The commission of his Excellency, the commission of the Judges present, and the commission of the Secretary were also read, and the whole proclaimed; when his Excellency again arose, and made the following address:

ST. CLAIR'S ADDRESS

From the ordinance for the establishment of civil government in this quarter, that hath been just now read, you have a proof, gentlemen, of the attention of Congress to the welfare of the citizens of the United States, how remote so ever their situation may be.

A good government, well administered, is the first of blessings to a people. Everything desirable in life is thereby secured to them; and from the operation of wholesome and equal laws, the passions of men are restrained within due bounds; their actions receive a proper direction; the virtues are cultivated and the beautiful fabric of civilized life is reared and brought to perfection.

The executive part of the administration of this government hath been entrusted to me, and I am truly sensible of the importance of the trust, and how much depends upon the due execution of it. To you, gentlemen, over whom it is to be immediately exercised; to your posterity; perhaps to the whole community of America. Would to God I were more equal to the discharge of it! But my best endeavors shall not be wanting to fulfill the desire and the expectation of Congress, that you may find yourselves happy under it; which is the surest way for me, at once to meet their approbation, and to render it honorable to myself. Nor when I reflect upon the characters of the men under whose immediate influence and example this particular settlement, which will probably give a tone to all that may succeed it, will be formed, have I much reason to fear a disappointment. Men who duly weigh the importance to society of a strict attention to the duties of religion and morality; in whose bosom the love of liberty and of order is a master passion; who respect the rights of mankind, and have sacrificed much to support them, and who are no strangers to the decencies and to the elegancies of polished life.

I esteem it also a singular happiness to you, and to me, that the gentlemen appointed to the judicial department are of such distinguished characters, and so well known to you. On the one side the respect which is duo to their station is secured, while it will be yielded with the most perfect good will on the other. The authority of the magistrates will be so mixed with and tempered by the benignity of their dispositions, that you have reason to expect much satisfaction from it.

You will observe, gentlemen, that the system which hath been formed for this country, and is now to take effect, is temporary only; suited to your infant situation, and to continue no longer than that state of infancy shall last. During that period the judges, with my assistance, are to select from the code of the mother states, such laws as may be thought proper for you. This is a very important part of our duty, and will be attended to with the greatest care.

But Congress hath not entrusted this great business wholly to our freedom or discretion. And here again you have a fresh proof of their paternal attention. We are bound to report to them all laws that shall be introduced. They have reserved to themselves the power of annulling them, so that if any law, not proper in itself, or not suited to your circumstances, should be imposed, it will be immediately repealed; but with all the care and attention to your interest and happiness that can be taken; you have many difficulties to struggle with. The subduing a new country, notwithstanding its natural advantages is, alone, an arduous task; a task, however, that patience and perseverance will surmount. And these virtues, so necessary in every situation, but peculiarly so in yours, you must resolve to exercise.

Neither is the reducing a country from a state of nature to a state of cultivation so irksome, as from a slight or superficial view may appear. Even very sensible pleasures attend it. The gradual progress of improvement fills the mind with delectable ideas. Vast forests converted into arable fields, and cities rising in places which were lately the habitations of wild beasts, give a pleasure something like that attendant on creation; if we can form an idea of it. The imagination is ravished, and a taste communicated of the joy of God to see "a happy world."

The advantages, however, are not merely imaginary. Situated as you are, in the most temperate climate; favored with the most fertile soil; surrounded by the noblest and most beautiful rivers; every portion of labor will meet its due reward. But you have upon your frontier numbers of savages, and too often, hostile nations. Against them it is necessary that you should be guarded. And the measures that may be thought proper for that end, though they may a little interrupt your usual pursuits, I am certain, will be cheerfully submitted to. One mode, however, I will venture at this time to recommend, which as it is in every point of view, the easiest and most eligible, so, I am persuaded, it will be attended with much success. Endeavor to cultivate a good understanding with the natives, without much familiarity. Treat them upon all occasions with kindness, and the strictest regard to justice. Run not into their customs and habits, which is but too frequent with those who settle near them; but endeavor to induce them to adopt yours. Prevent by every means that dreadful reproach, perhaps too justly brought by them against all the white people they have yet been acquainted with, that professing the most holy and benevolent religion, they are uninfluenced by its dictates, and regardless of its precepts. Such a conduct will produce on their part the utmost confidence. They will soon become sensible of the superior advantages of a state of civilization. They will gradually lose their present manners, and a way may be opened for introducing amongst them the Gospel of Peace, and you be the happy instruments in the hand of Providence in bringing forward that time which will surely arrive, *"when all the nations of the earth shall become the kingdom of Jesus Christ"*

The present situation of the territory calls for attention, in various places; and will necessarily induce a frequent absence, both of the judges and myself, from this delightful spot; but at all times and places, as it is my indispensable duty, so it is very much my desire, to do everything within the compass of my power, for the peace, good order, and perfect establishment of the settlement; and as I look for not only a cheerful acquiescence in and submission to necessary measures, but a cordial co-operation, so I flatter myself my well meant endeavors will be accepted in the spirit in which they are rendered, and thus our satisfaction will be mutual and complete.

ANSWER TO THE GOVERNOR

During the address of his Excellency a profound veneration for the elevated station and exalted benevolence of the speaker; the magnitude of the subject; the high importance of the occasion; the immense consequences resulting; the glory, the grandeur of a new world unfolding; heaven and earth approving; called forth all the manly emotions of the human heart! At the close, peals of applause rent the surrounding air, while joyful echo reverberated the sound. Every citizen felt to the extent of humanity, and affection herself impressed upon the mind, in characters never to be obliterated; long live our governor!

Tho day following an answer was presented, in the name of all the people, to his Excellency, of which the following substantially contains what respected him, personally.

May *it please your Excellency:*

The people of this settlement, to whom you have been pleased to make known the constitution, your own commission, those of the judges, and that of the secretary, beg leave to approach you with the warmest affection, and sincerest regard. If unreserved confidence in the talents, abilities, and paternal friendship of your Excellency, can add to our felicity; if an almost enthusiastic ardor impelled us to form this settlement; if our efforts can succeed only under a wise government, equally and impartially administered; and if bowing the knee to heaven in humble thankfulness, that your Excellency in particular hath been appointed to preside over it, can increase your satisfaction, then indeed are we mutually happy.

The constitution itself we consider as the result of a wise and most benevolent policy; and we look up with veneration to the fathers of their country, whose care and attention follow us wherever we go; but the constitution is now the more dear to us; as we behold your Excellency, removing all your doubts and fears of your safe arrival; and mildly paving the way to regularity, order and perpetual harmony. We can form some idea of the arduous task imposed upon the governor of so extensive a country as the western territory; but whatever dangers may intervene, whatever difficulties may oppose the progress of your noble and beneficent designs, we will, as far as in our power, share in the burdens, alleviate your cares, and upon all occasions render a full obedience to the government and the laws.

We are fully persuaded, with your Excellency, *"that all the nations of the earth will become the kingdom of Jesus Christ."* And we exult in the firm belief that the great purposes of Heaven, in perfecting human reason, and attracting all mankind to the standard of one divine control, will be accomplished in this new world. We are equally ravished with the thought that the great Governor of the Universe hath raised up your Excellency, as an instrument to open the way to this transcendently glorious event, and that in this life you will anticipate the joys of Paradise!

Great Sir: we pray that heaven may grant to you, both in your public character and private life, all the felicity that can meet your expectations, or warmest desires. May you long enjoy the tranquility of a mind influenced by the principles of rectitude only; May the cold hand of death never arrest you, until you shall have accomplished all the objects which a great and a good man can embrace; and then when life shall lose her charms; when nature shall begin to sink beneath the weight of mortality, and when the mind impatient to be free, shall burst the brittle shell which holds it here, may you rise triumphant on cherub's wings to enjoy your God in realms of endless felicity!

A CONTEMPORARY ACCOUNT OF SOME EVENTS

Upon the twentieth, divine service was performed by the Rev. Dr. Brick, before a numerous, well-informed and attentive assembly. The sermon was well adapted to the occasion, and the first ever delivered in the Protestant style to a congregation of civilized people in the territory. The portion of divine truth selected for this occasion is contained in the nineteenth chapter of Exodus, and in the sixth and seventh verses: *"Now therefore, if you will obey my voice indeed, and keep my covenant, then ye shall be a peculiar treasure unto me above all people; for all the earth is mine. And ye shall be unto me a kingdom of priests, and a holy nation."*

His Excellency was present during the service, and afterward expressed much satisfaction. He particularly remarked that the singing far exceeded anything of the kind he had ever heard. Indeed it was enchanting! The grave, the solemn, the tender, and the pathetic were so happily blended, as to produce a most perfect harmony, and to melt the soul in sympathetic effusion of gratitude and adoration to the great Author of our religion, and had listening angels tuned their harps, they would have paused for a moment at the melodious sound.

Upon the twenty-eighth a law was published, regulating the militia of the county of Washington. The people were divided into senior and junior classes, and the first guard that mounted under this system, for watching and marching, was honored with five Colonels, one Major, and one Captain, late of the army of the United States, in the ranks.

His Excellency hath erected all the tract of territory, lying between the Pennsylvania west line, and the Scioto River, and between the Ohio and the north line, comprehending the lands in which the Indian titles have been extinguished, into a county, by the name of Washington, and the Judges, with his Excellency, are assiduously employed in their respective stations, for completing it as soon as possible, an uniform administration of justice. It is expected they will proceed to Fort Vincent and Kaskaskia as soon as the treaty with the Indians shall be finished, upon the important concerns of government

From the first establishment of the Ohio Company in this place, which was in April last, the Indians have frequently visited the settlement, and ever discovered a very friendly disposition. And saving the capture of a few boats near Limestone, and the falls of the Ohio, their depredations since the last year have been trifling, and their murders few in number. They have murdered some individuals in the Kentucky settlements, and have stolen horses from the Virginians. But in most instances of the kind, they have professedly avenged some injury, which before they had sustained. There are, however, scattered settlements, interspersed among the nations and tribes, of renegade Indians, as well as clans of robbers and money makers, in some of the states. It is extremely difficult to detect and bring to condign punishment, either; but upon a fair view of the matter, it will appear less injury hath been sustained, on account of Indian barbarity, than could rationally have been expected, considering the cruel, perfidious, unjust, and barbarous manner in which in many instances they have been treated.

The principle of revenge seems to be a natural passion, and the most irreclaimable perhaps of any that is implanted in the human breast. In the rude state of nature, this passion must be the more outrageous, as the ideas of men are few and simple: and consequently, reflection upon any particular subject is the more in time, as the imagination is not busied about the variegated objects which present themselves in civil and much more so in polished society. It is, therefore, a matter of policy as well as humanity, to reclaim the natives, if practicable, from the savage state, and raise them at least, into a relish for pastoral life. In most instances wherein they have been kindly though not too familiarly treated, they have behaved peaceably, and seem to have acquired a degree of civilization. They have seldom or never been known to violate a professed friendship. The Ohio company, therefore, have it in their power to gratify their inclinations, by living peaceably with these, their distant neighbors; and of forming and extending the settlement upon the best principles that ever attended an emigration.

The accounts that have been transmitted to the eastern and the northern states for several months past, of robbing, scalping, and murder, if really credited, would almost deter the bold and courageous from adventuring into this delightful country. But it should be considered that facts are augmented in a geometrical proportion to the distances in which they are related.

One fact is certain, that from the first settlement to this moment, no one of the settlers hath died or been killed, nor hath there so much as a horse been stolen.

The people are in great health, high spirits, and extremely happy; and they want nothing to complete their felicity, but their tender companions, whom they have left beyond the mountains, to participate with them in the rising glories of the western world.

AN ORATION,

DELIVERED AT MARIETTA, APRIL 7, 1789,

IN COMMEMORATION OF THE COMMENCEMENT OF THE SETTLEMENT FORMED BY THE

OHIO COMPANY:

BY SOLOMON DROWN, ESQ., M. D.

WORCESTER, MASS., PRINTED BY ISAIAH THOMAS, 1789.

CORRESPONDENCE

At a meeting of the citizens of Marietta, April 7th, 1789, voted that Rufus Putnam, Griffin Greene, George Ingersoll, Winthrop Sargent, and Ebenezer Battelle, Esq., be a committee to wait on Dr. Drown, and thank him for his Oration delivered this day, and to request a copy for the press.

Ebenezer Battelle, *Clerk.*

Sir,

After our acknowledgments to the Governor of the Universe for the occasion of this anniversary festival, we, in the name of the citizens of Marietta, return you our most cordial and sincere thanks, for your pertinent, ingenious, and elegant Oration, delivered this day, and request a copy for the press.

Rufus Putnam
Griffin Greene

George Ingersoll
Winthrop Sargent
Ebenezer Battelle

Dr. Solomon Drown

Gentlemen,

Gratitude to a generous and candid audience, for their favorable reception of the Anniversary Oration, and the obliging manner in which yon have imparted their resolve, render it impossible for me to decline a compliance with their request.

With sentiments of the most cordial respect and esteem,
I am, gentlemen, your obedient servant,

Solomon Drown.

Gentlemen Of Committee.

AN ORATION
DELIVERED AT MARIETTA, APRIL 7, 1789.

The expectation of so polite and respectable an audience, excited by the novelty of the occasion on which we are assembled, that of celebrating the first anniversary of the settlement of a new and widely extended territory, cannot fail to be productive of diffident emotions in him who has the honor to address you. Feeling his inability to perform, in the manner he could wish, the task allotted him in this day's solemnization, he will, however, strive to re-assure himself from the consideration of the candor he has already experienced, and this last mark of your favorable opinion; an honor to be cherished in his memory with the most affectionate gratitude.

Permit me then most cordially to congratulate you on the auspicious anniversary of the 7th of April, 1788, a day ever to be remembered with annual festivity and joy; for then this virgin soil received you first; alluring from your native homes, by charms substantial and inestimable.

A wilderness of sweets; for Nature here
Wantoned as in her prime, and played at will,
Her virgin fancies, pouring forth more sweet.
Wild above a rule or art,—the gentle gales
Fanning their odoriferous wings dispense
Native perfumes, and whisper whence they stole
Those balmy spoils.

Hail glorious birth-day of this western region! On such a day, in the same beauteous season, ancient poets feigned the earth was first created.

" In this soft season let me dare to sing
The world was hatch'd by Heaven's Imperial King
In presence of all the year and holidays of spring;
Then did the new creation first appear;
Nor other was the tenor of the year;
When laughing Heaven did the great birth attend.
And eastern winds their wintry breath suspend.
Then sheep first saw the sun in open fields;
And savage beasts were sent to stock the wilds;
Nor could the tender new creation bear
The excessive heats or coldness of the year;
But chilled by winter or by summer fired
The middle temper of the spring regained
When warmth and moisture did at once abound,
And Heaven's indulgence brooded on the ground."

First, let us pay our grateful tribute of applause to that 6rm band, who, quitting their families and peaceful habitations, foregoing all the endearments of domestic life, in the midst of a severe winter, set out on the arduous enterprise of settling this far distant region. And here my inclination would lead me to paint their unexampled perseverance in that inclement season; their numerous toils and dangers in effecting the great business of unbarring a secluded wilderness, and rendering it the fit abode of man; did not the presence of their worthy leader* prevent me from indulging it.

* General R. Putnam.

But of these worthies who have most exerted themselves in promoting this settlement, one, alas! Is no more; one whose eloquence, like the music of Orpheus, attractive of the listening crowd, seemed designed to reconcile mankind to the closest bonds of society. Ah! What avail his manly virtues now! Slow through yon winding path his course was borne, and on the steep hill interred with funeral honors meet. What bosom refuses the tribute of a sigh, on the recollection of that melancholy scene, when, unusual spectacle, the fathers of the land, the chiefs of the aboriginal nations, in solemn train attended; while the mournful dirge was rendered doubly mournful mid the gloomy nodding grove. On that day even nature seemed to mourn. O Varnum! Varnum! Thy name shall not be forgotten, while gratitude and generosity continue to be the characteristics of those inhabiting the country, once thy care. Thy fair fame is deeply rooted in our fostering memories, and,

> Non imber edax, non Agnito impotens,
> Possit divinese. aut innumerabilis,
> Annorum series, et fuga temporum." *—Hor.
>> * The force of boisterous winds and moldering rain.
>> Year after year, an everlasting train,
>> Shall ne'er destroy the glory of his name.

The origin of most countries is lost in the clouds of fiction and romance; and as far up as you can trace their history, you will find they were generally founded in rapacity, usurpation, and blood. It was not but by means of wars, horrid wars! That the Israelites gained possession of their long sought promised Canaan; driving before them the nations who had occupied that charming country. Rome itself, imperial Rome, the mistress of the world, was founded by a lawless and wandering banditti, with Romulus at their head, who was continually embroiled with one or other of his neighbors, and war the only employment by which he and his companions expected either to aggrandize themselves, or even to subsist. Singular, then, and before unheard of, are the circumstances of your first establishment, in this extensive territory; without opposition, and without bloodshed. How striking the contrast between such a manner of conducting an important enterprise, and the barbarism of the so much extolled heroic ages! The kind and friendly treatment of the Indians by the first settlers, has conduced greatly to the favorable issue of the late treaty. Such humane conduct, so easy to practice, cannot fail to have great influence, even on savage minds. Nor less the unwearied attention and patient equanimity of his Excellency, Governor St. Clair, amid the attacks of a painful disorder, and the delays naturally arising from the discordant interests of unconnected tribes. And here let us commemorate the virtues of the unassuming and most benevolent Mr. John Heckewelder, Moravian missionary among the Delawares. Such is his ascendency over the minds of the Christianized Indians, that to his kind offices in striving to effectuate the above happy event, no small share of praise is to be ascribed. But to whom is this settlement more indebted than to the generous chieftain and other worthy officers of yonder fortress, distinguished by the name of Harmer. With what cheerfulness and cordiality have ye ever entered into every measure promotive of the company's interest. Important is the station ye fill in every respect, and not least in this, that you seem reserved to exhibit to mankind a specimen of that military splendor, which ornamented the arms of America, and would do honor to the troops of any potentate on earth.

The gentle influence of female suavity are ever readily acknowledged by all who make the least pretenses to civilization. Happy in this respect, if we see the least spark of ferocity kindling in our breast, from the wildness of our situation, we have only to turn our eyes on the amiable patterns of the milder virtues, to quench the savage principle, and restore us to humanity. Enough cannot be said in commendation of your fortitude and generous resolution, my fair auditors, who apparently made so great a sacrifice in quitting your native homes and endeared connections, to settle in this remote wilderness, while those connections, loath to part, were fondly urging every dissuasion from the enterprise, and conjuring up a thousand difficulties that would obstruct your progress, or meet you here. But your laudable perseverance and equanimity have surmounted them all, and instead of being surrounded with howlings of wild beasts, and horrid yells of savages, which ye were warned to expect, on the delightful banks of the Muskingum, ye are favored with the blandishments of polished social intercourse. Are we indeed in a wilderness? The contemplation of the scene before me would almost lead me to distrust my senses. No wonder the gentle Spenser feigned such mingled beauty and elegance, by virtue brightened, could *"make sunshine in the shady grove."*

It would take up too much time to detail minutely your progressions in thus far effecting an important settlement. The marks of industry observable on every hand since your arrival, particularly the buildings on Campus Martins (forming an elegant fortress), do you great honor, and lead the admiring stranger to entertain a very flattering opinion of your growing greatness.

> All is the gift of industry: whate'er
> Exalts, embellishes, and renders life
> Delightful. Pensive winter cheered by him,

Sits at the social fire, and haply heart
The excluded tempest idly rave .along;
His harden'd fingers deck the gaudy spring.
Without him summer were an arid waste;
Nor to the autumnal months could e'er transmit
The full, mature, immeasurable stores.

Thus fair is the first page of our history, and may no foul blot hereafter stain the important volume which time is unfolding in this western world. But may it prove worthy, fraught with worthy deeds, to be rescued from the final conflagration, by some bright cherub's favoring arm, and displayed to the view of approving spirits in the realms of bliss.

This country will afford noble opportunity for advancing knowledge of every kind. A communication with all nations will enable you to introduce the most useful and excellent scientific improvements, which are to be found in every kingdom and empire on earth. Effectual measures have been taken by congress for cultivating and diffusing literature among the people, in appropriating large tracts of land for the establishment of schools, and a university. The institution of a public library would be of great benefit to the community, not only by affording rational amusement, and meliorating the disposition, but by giving those who have not a liberal education an opportunity of gaining that knowledge which will qualify them for usefulness.

Let us not pretermit the inviting fields, which is opening in this country for her rising sons of science. The botanist and mineralogist may range here with increasing delight. The antiquary, too, will not be destitute of a subject for disquisition. Those ancient works, exciting the admiration of every beholder, are the effect of great labor, and must have been built by a far different people from the present natives. They are undoubtedly of much higher antiquity, than some have imagined. And he who could command the labor, or draw forth the resources, of his country for such purposes, must have been invested with powers that bear no comparison with that of modern Sachems. If they aught resembled the Natches in their customs and manners, those elevated squares must have been the bases of their temples. But for what purpose was that towering mound erected! Is it the mausoleum of some illustrious potentate, and the reputed offspring of yonder glorious luminary? Or was it the altar on which they sacrificed to the bright God of day! Virgil relates the pious deeds of the Trojans, who renewed the funeral obsequies of Polydorus, and raised a large mound of earth for the tomb. Does not this render probable the conjecture that those former inhabitants, descended from some nations retaining the same customs!

But that for which this country will ever be most estimable, is, that under the auspices of firmly established liberty, civil and religious, and the mild government of national laws, every circumstance invites to the practice of husbandry, that best occupation of mankind, which is the support of human life, and the source of all its true riches. Delightful region! Bordering on the majestic Ohio, the most beautiful river on earth watered also by other large and navigable streams; favored with an excellent climate and fertile soil, which well cultivated, is a rich treasure to every family that is wise enough to be contented with living nobly independent. It is in such charming retreats, at a distance from the tumultuous hurry of the world, that one relishes a thousand innocent delights, and which are repeated with a satisfaction ever new. In those extensive and delightsome bottoms, where are seen so many different species of animals and vegetables, there it is we have occasion to admire the beneficence of the Great Creator. There it is, that at the gentle purling of pure and living water, and enchanted with the concerts of birds, which fill the neighboring thickets, we may agreeably contemplate the wonders of nature, and examine them all at our leisure. It is amid such happy, rural scenes, fanned by gentle breezes, wafting fragrance o'er the blossomed vale, that health and rejuvenescency of soul are indulged to mortals—the choicest of the favors of heaven. Nature's amiable bard, transported with the pleasures of a country life exclaims:

"O knew he but his happiness — of men
The happiest he! Who far from public rage,
Deep in the vale with a choice few retired,
Drinks the pure pleasure of the rural life.
What though from utmost land and sea purvey'd
For him each rarer tributary life
Bleeds not, and insatiate table heaps
With luxury and death! What though his bowl
Flames not with earthy juice; nor sunk in beds
Oft of gay care, he tosses out the night,
Or melts the thoughtless hours in idle state?
What tho' he knows not those fantastic joys,

That still amuse the wanton, still deceive;
A face of pleasure but a heart of pain;
Their hollow moments undelighted all?
Sure peace is his, a solid life estranged
To disappointment and fallacious hope;
Rich in content, in nature's bounty rich,
In herbs and fruits: whatever greens the spring,
When heav'n descends in showers and bends the bough,
When summer reddens, and when autumn beams;
Or in the wintry globe whate'er lies
Conceal'd and fattens with the richest sap;
These are not wanting; nor the milky drove
Luxuriant spread o'er all the lowing vale;
Nor aught besides of prospect, grove or song.
Here too dwells simple truth: plain innocence,
Unsullied beauty; sound unbroken youth:
Health ever blooming, unambitious toil
Calm contemplation and poetic ease.
The rage of nations and the crush of states,
Move not the man who from the world escaped
In still retreats and flowering solitudes,
To nature's voice attends from month to month,
Admiring sees her, in her every shape;
Feels all her sweet emotions at his heart;
Takes what she liberal gives, nor thinks of more.
He when young spring protrudes the bursting gems,
Marks the first bud and sucks the healthful gale
Into his freshen'd soul; her genial hours
He full enjoys, and not a beauty blows,
And not an opening blossom breathes in vain —
The touch of kindred too, and love he feels;
The modest eye, whose beams on his alone
Ecstatic shine; the little strong embrace
Of prattling children twined around his neck.
And emulous to please him, calling forth
The fond parental soul; nor purpose gay,
Amusement, dance or song, he sternly scorns;
For happiness and true philosophy
Are of the social still and smiling kind.

This is the life which those who fret in guilt.
And guilty cities, never knew; the life
Led by primeval ages uncorrupt,
When angels dwelt, and God himself, with man!"

Agriculture is a no less honorable than profitable art, held in the highest esteem among the ancients, and equally valued by the enlightened moderns. The Greeks ascribed its invention to Ceres, and her son Triptolemus, but the Jews with more reason to Noah, who immediately after the flood, set about tilling the ground, and planting vineyards. Agriculture has been the delight of the greatest men. We are told that Cyrus, the younger, planted and cultivated his garden, in a great measure, with his own hands, and it is well known that the Romans took many of their best statesmen and generals from the plow. There is indeed something truly great in the employment; it gives a nobler air to several parts of nature, filling the earth with a variety of beautiful scenes, and has something in it like creation. Homer, Virgil, and Horace, those greatest geniuses of all antiquity — with how much rapture have they spoken on this universally admired art! Our own countryman, the illustrious Jefferson, declares: *"Those who labor in the earth, are the chosen people of God—if he has chosen a people, whose breasts he has made his peculiar deposit for substantial and genuine virtue. It is the focus in which he keeps alive that sacred fire, which otherwise might escape from the face of the earth. Corruption of morals in the mass of cultivators, is a phenomenon of which no age, nor nation, has furnished an example. It is the mark set on those who, not looking up to heaven, to their own soil and industry, as do the husbandmen for their subsistence, depend for it on the casualties and caprice of customers. I repeat it again, cultivators of the earth are the most and independent citizens."*

The Emperor of China, to encourage this most important and delightful of arts, goes forth annually attended by his principal officers, and holds the plow with his own hands—which ceremony, of first opening the ground in the spring, is performed with great solemnity.

An Emperor of Morocco, Mahomet II (if I mistake not), being engaged in a war, solicited aid of a neighboring prince, and promised in return to communicate to him the Philosopher's Stone, which this emperor was imputed to possess. On the restoration of peace, being reminded of the agreement, a plow was sent with this memorable message: *"This is the genuine Philosopher's Stone, which properly used will be productive of the truest riches."*

I mention these anecdotes that you may know in what high estimation agriculture has ever been held, and that nothing hereafter will induce you to relinquish the solid advantages resulting from cultivating the soil, for the flattering and too often deceitful prospects afforded by trade and commerce; but like Virgil's old Corycian, on your own well cultivated fields, in the placid enjoyment of the fruits of your labor, may you equal in contentment, the wealth of kings.

We hope you enjoyed this book. For more great stories from our past please visit the Historical Collection at our web site.

Badgley Publishing Company

WWW.BadgleyPublishingCompany.com

Made in the USA
Middletown, DE
10 September 2022

72967133R00261